Preface

What Is LFG?

LFG is a theory of grammar which has a powerful, flexible, and mathematically well-defined grammar formalism designed for typologically diverse languages. LFG has provided the framework for a substantial amount of descriptive and theoretical research on many languages, including those in Australia (Warlpiri and Wambaya), America (Navajo, Plains Cree, Greenlandic), Europe (Welsh, Irish, English, German, Dutch, West Flemish, Icelandic, Norwegian, Finnish, Russian, Serbian/Croatian), Africa (Chicheŵa, Ewe, Moroccan Arabic), South Asia (Malayalam, Hindi), and East Asia (Japanese) which are discussed and analyzed in the text and problem sets of this book.

How Is it Different?

LFG is closely attuned to the overt perceptible expressions of language, and to the abstract relational information that they directly express. LFG has a constraint-based, parallel correspondence architecture; it has no serial derivations (unlike transformational grammar); there are no "deep structures" or "initial structures." Abstract relations are locally distributed as partial information across words and overt fragments of structure, and may be monotonically synthesized in any order or in parallel. Being designed for a wide range of nonconfigurational and configurational language types, LFG departs radically from most other grammar formalisms in one striking way: it is noncompositional, allowing the "content" of a constituent to vary depending on its context.

These descriptions may sound mysterious to the newcomer, but LFG is simple. Field linguists doing primary research on languages have found it easy to use. And because LFG is mathematically well defined and simple, it is also easy to implement. It has been employed in many computational systems, ranging from state-of-the-art industrial wide-coverage grammars used for machine translation and processing to pedagogical systems implemented on personal computers.

LFG is being used as a representational basis in the new crop of data-driven approaches to language, including Optimality Theoretic syntax and probabilistic analysis of natural language. There is an International Lexical-Functional Grammar Association (ILFGA) and several websites for LFG resources:

http://www-lfg.stanford.edu/lfg/
http://clwww.essex.ac.uk/LFG/

What Is in this Book?

This book provides both an introduction to LFG and a synthesis of major theoretical developments in lexical-functional syntax since the mid to late 1980s. It can be used both as a textbook for students and as a reference text for researchers. Many references to current work are given, but the only background required is some familiarity with elementary formal constructs such as the definition of functions and relations, and an understanding of the basic syntactic concepts of constituent structure and X' theory (such as in the short paper by Bresnan 1977). The problem sets provide a hands-on way of learning to use the formalism, analytic concepts, and variety of linguistic ideas that can be expressed.

What Is Not in this Book?

Research in LFG is the cooperative effort of an international community of diverse researchers, of which the author of this book – though one of the original developers of the theory – is just one. The goal of presenting a coherent and accessible view of the major developments in lexical-functional syntax has inevitably led to some neglect of important topics and alternatives. The deliberate omissions are these. I have omitted coverage of Optimality Theoretic syntax based on LFG (sometimes called "OT-LFG"); references can be found in Bresnan (1997a, 1998a, 1998b) and Sells (forthcoming), but this area is growing very rapidly. I have also omitted any account of probabilistic analysis of language using LFG, such as Data-Oriented Parsing ("DOP-LFG"); see Bod and Kaplan (1998), Johnson et al. (1999), Bod (1999) for several different approaches. This book is devoted to lexical-functional *syntax* and makes no attempt to cover current research in semantics within the LFG framework. (See Dalrymple 1999 for one recent line of research in semantics for LFG.) The very new development of Constructive Morphology is also not covered. (See Nordlinger 1998b, Barron 1998, Sadler 1998b, Sells 1999a, Lee 1999a, 1999b, and Sharma 1999.) New developments in coordination and feature resolution also had to be omitted because of time and space constraints (Dalrymple and Kaplan 1997, 1998). The

Lexical-Functional Syntax

Blackwell Textbooks in Linguistics

Lexical-Functional Syntax

Joan Bresnan

First published 2001

2 4 6 8 10 9 7 5 3 1

Blackwell Publishers Inc.
350 Main Street
Malden, Massachusetts 02148
USA

Blackwell Publishers Ltd
108 Cowley Road
Oxford OX4 1JF
UK

Library of Congress Cataloging-in-Publication Data
Bresnan, Joan.
    Lexical-functional syntax / Joan Bresnan.
        p. cm. — (Blackwell textbooks in linguistics ; 16)
    Includes bibliographical references and index.
    ISBN 0-631-20973-5 (alk. paper) — ISBN 0-631-20974-3 (pbk.: alk. paper)
    1. Grammar, Comparative and general—Syntax. 2. Lexical-functional grammar. I. Title. II. Series.

P291 B726 2000
415—dc21   00-034323

British Library Cataloguing in Publication Data
A CIP catalogue record for this book is available from the British Library.

Typeset in 10/12pt Sabon
by Graphicraft Limited, Hong Kong
Printed in Great Britain by Biddles Ltd, Guildford, Surrey

This book is printed on acid-free paper.

Contents

Contents

history of the development of LFG and its relation to other theories is also omitted and awaits another author. Despite these omissions, the reader of this book will have no trouble following current research, which can be closely tracked from the website resources mentioned above.

How to Use this Book

In teaching LFG from this text, I do not attempt to teach all of the formalism developed in part II at once. Instead I break chapter 4 into three parts:

- sections 4.1–4.5, followed by problem set 1;
- sections 4.6–4.7, followed by problem set 2;
- sections 4.8–4.9 (read with chapter 7).

Acknowledgments

It is a pleasure to thank the friends and colleagues who gave me detailed comments on earlier drafts of individual chapters or even the entire manuscript of this work: Farrell Ackerman, Avery Andrews, Judith Berman, Chris Culy, Mary Dalrymple, Yehuda Falk, Paul Kroeger, Helge Lødrup, Elaine Malkin and Stella Markantonatou, Chris Manning, Michiko Nakano, Louisa Sadler, and Peter Sells. The original problem sets and solutions were first edited in 1987 by Kristin Hanson, with the assistance of Heinrich Beck, Nick Clements, Mary Dalrymple, Jeffrey Goldberg, Jonni Kanerva, Yo Matsumoto, James McCloskey, Mariko Saiki, Stephen Wechsler, Michael Wescoat, Annie Zaenen, and Draga Zec. Subsequent contributions were made by Rachel Nordlinger and Ida Toivonen, and Ash Asudeh converted the files to LaTeX. I owe special thanks to Ron Kaplan for answering questions about formal issues with his usual blend of generosity and rigor, and in providing through Xerox PARC some financial assistance in the research and preparation of the manuscript.

For the personal support which made it possible for me to finish writing this book, and for the inspiration of living with a finisher and a champion, I also thank Marianne.

Part I On the Architecture of
Universal Grammar

Introduction

The search for a universal design of grammar has long motivated research in linguistic theory. Language is both universal among humans and specific to us. Any child can acquire fluent mastery of any of the thousands of human languages, given sufficient exposure, but no animal has this capacity. These simple facts have suggested to many linguists that there must be a universal design of grammar, a common organizing structure of all languages that underlies their superficial variations in modes of expression. If this universal grammar is a biologically given form of knowledge, as many linguists assume today, then study of the invariants of the structure of human languages may tell us something fundamental about the human mind.

This rationalist, universalist conception of linguistics has a long intellectual tradition, appearing in the works of philosophers and grammarians of the past six centuries. In this century it has been revived by Noam Chomsky. Chomsky's great achievement is to couple the universalist conception of language from the tradition of philosophical grammar with a far more precise model of linguistic structure adapted from the mathematics of formal systems developed in this century. This powerful combination of ideas, called "generative grammar," has revolutionized linguistic theory. In the methodological paradigm of generative grammar, formal representations of linguistic structures are developed and empirically tested against native speakers' knowledge of their language. Universal grammar limits the space of formal structures.

Generative grammar holds that language cannot be adequately characterized solely in terms of a formal description of its overt constituents, or "surface structure." A more abstract representation is also needed to represent the implicit linguistic knowledge of speakers. Chomsky has conceived of this abstract representation as a "deep" or initial structure which undergoes sequential serial operations (transformations) to derive the overt perceptible form. It is to explain how these abstract formal structures are acquired by speakers that Chomsky developed his rationalist epistemology: human beings possess an innate faculty specialized for language which enables them to acquire complex human languages despite the poverty of stimulus in their learning environment.[1]

Towards the end of the twentieth century, new formal ideas began to achieve prominence in linguistic theory, making use of parallel rather than serial structures and computations, and comparative evaluation of multiple overt structures rather than serial derivation of individual overt structures. These ideas are embodied in a family of nonderivational, constraint-based linguistic theories and in approaches based on optimization (both statistical and discrete). These newer theories are compatible with different linguistic epistemologies drawing on structuralist and functional/typological ideas which have both predated and coexisted with generative grammar. One such theory is lexical-functional grammar (LFG) (Kaplan and Bresnan 1982), which is the topic of this book.

Part I of this book empirically and informally motivates the LFG architecture by looking at the core linguistic phenomena which inspired it: nonconfigurationality, movement paradoxes, and the lexicality of relation changes such as passivization. Part II shows how the intuitive ideas of part I can be formally modelled as flexible correspondence mappings between parallel structures (categorial structure and functional structure). Part III presents a theory and typology of structure–function correspondences, and several case studies of languages in which syntactic functions are created morphologically rather than by constituent structures. Part IV motivates functional structure by showing how invariances of language are captured on functional structures and outlines a theory of how functional structures are projected from argument structures.

Note

1   Chomsky's 'poverty of stimulus' argument for universal grammar has attracted criticism (e.g. Van Valin 1994, Pullum 1997). The most controversial aspect is not the conclusion that humans have innate biological capacities that support language – no one doubts that the phonological structure of language is supported by our innate articulatory and perceptual systems – but the assumption that these capacities are specialized for acquiring grammatical systems – and grammatical systems of the specific types advocated by Chomsky. It is also true that sophisticated theories of learning may permit inferences about nonoccurring data which enrich the informativeness of the stimulus (e.g. Tesar and Smolensky 1998, Boersma and Hayes 1999).

1   Nonconfigurationality

One fundamental problem for the design of universal grammar is the great variability in modes of expression of languages. Languages differ radically in the
ways in which they form similar ideas into words and phrases. The idea of two
small children chasing a dog is expressed in English by means of a *phrase structure* in which conceptual components of the whole – the two small children and
the dog being two such components – correspond to single phrases. Phrases are
groups of contiguous words which are units for substitutions, remain together as
units under stylistic permutations and paraphrases of a sentence, constrain the
pronunciation patterns of sentences, and are subject to ordering constraint relative to other words and word groups. The (simplified) phrase structure of an
English sentence is illustrated in (1):

(1)

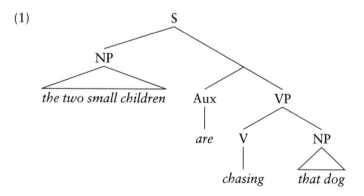

In this structure, *the two small children* and that *dog* are noun phrases (NPs), in
which the words cannot be separated, and there is also a verb phrase (VP). When
the phrases are freely broken up, the result is ungrammatical or different in
meaning:

(2)   a. *The two small are chasing that children dog.
      b. *The two small are dog chasing children that.
      c. *Chasing are the two small that dog children.
      d. *That are children chasing the two small dog.

The simple correspondence between conceptual units and phrases seems so natural to the English speaker as to appear a necessary feature of language itself – but it is not. Consider Warlpiri, a language of the people who have inhabited Australia since long before the colonization of that continent by English speakers.[1] Example (3) shows the phrase structure of a Warlpiri sentence expressing the same idea as the English sentence (1). But in Warlpiri, every permutation of the words in the sentence is possible, with the same meaning, so long as the auxiliary (Aux) tense marker occurs in the second position. In particular, the word orders of all of the bad English examples in (1) are good in Warlpiri.

(3) 'The two small children are chasing that dog'

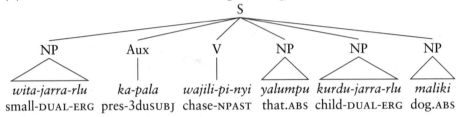

It is not true that Warlpiri lacks phrases altogether: syntactic analysis has shown that some phrases (NPs but not VPs) do optionally occur, and there is evidence for a somewhat more articulated clause structure including a focus position to the left of Aux.[2] But phrases are not essential to the expression of conceptual units. The coherence of a conceptual unit in Warlpiri is indicated by means of word *shapes* rather than word *groups*: noncontiguous words that form a conceptual unit must share the same formal endings – case and number morphology. Thus in (3) the word for 'small' shares the dual and ergative endings *-jarra* and *-rlu* with the word for 'child' which it modifies, and these endings differ from those of the words for 'dog' and 'that', which are null.

This difference between Warlpiri and English exemplifies a broad crosslinguistic generalization observed by many students of linguistic typology: across languages, there often appears to be an inverse relation between the amount of grammatical information expressed by words and the amount expressed by phrases. Languages rich in word structure (morphology) may make more or less use of fixed phrase structure forms (syntax). But languages poor in morphology overwhelmingly tend to have rigid, hierarchical phrase structures. The generalization is quite spectacular in some of the radically nonconfigurational languages of Australia, but there is evidence for it also in the other language types we will examine in part III. We can summarize this generalization with the slogan, "Morphology competes with syntax."

The idea that words and phrases are alternative means of expressing the same grammatical relations underlies the design of LFG, and distinguishes it from other formal syntactic frameworks. In addition, we cannot discount the effect of "configurational bias." Through historical accident, the resources of modern science and technology have been dominated by states whose national languages happen to be highly configurational. As a result, there has been a vast lack of knowledge of typological variation of language among the scientific establishment in computer science, logic, philosophy, and even among many theoretical linguists of a formal bent.

Although Warlpiri lacks English-style phrase structure, and English lacks Warlpiri-style case and agreement forms of words, there is evidence that they have a common organization at a deeper level than is apparent from their differing modes of expression. Similar conceptual units are expressed by the two languages – objects and their relations and motions, events and their participants, and human emotions, actions, and aims. And at an appropriate level of abstraction, similar grammatical constraints emerge.[3] For example, in English, a reflexive pronoun can be an object coreferring with the subject, but cannot be a subject coreferring with the object:

(4)   a.   *Lucy is hitting herself.*
      b.   **Herself is hitting Lucy.*

And the same is true in Warlpiri:

(5)   a.   *Napaljarri-rli   ka-nyanu paka-rni.*
           Napaljarri-ERG PRES-REFL hit-NONPAST
           'Napaljarri is hitting herself.'
      b.   **Napaljarri   ka-nyanu paka-rni.*
           Napaljarri. ABS PRES-REFL hit-NONPAST
           'Herself is hitting Napaljarri.'

This constraint holds in Warlpiri whether or not the subject is discontinuous. Indeed, this grammatical constraint on reflexive pronouns as subjects appears to be universal across languages. Apparent exceptions to this generalization have been found in some languages of the type called "ergative" (Kibrik 1985), but it has been argued that in some ergative languages the grammatical subject may correspond to the patient rather than the agent (Marantz 1984, Melc'uk 1988, Manning 1994). In such a language, *Lucy* in (4b) and not the reflexive pronoun would be the subject, and the universal generalization would stand.[4]

Thus while phrase structure does not universally correspond to conceptual structure, the more abstract grammatical functions it expresses – such as subject and object – do appear across languages. These grammatical functions represent classes of varying forms of expression that are equivalent under the correspondence mappings to argument structure (discussed below).

Here is the first choice point in the design of universal grammar: how to capture the abstraction of grammatical functions such as subject and object? The overwhelmingly predominant tendancy in modern linguistic theory – due to Chomsky – has been to define them as the familiar configurations of English phrase structure: the subject is an NP in configuration (6a), and the object is an NP in configuration (6b):

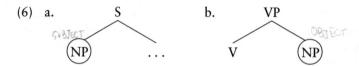

RELATIONAL DESIGN   V.S.   CONFIGURATIONAL DESIGN.

(6) a.   S   b.   VP

    SUBJECT   OBJECT

     (NP)   . . .   V   (NP)

For a language like Warlpiri, this choice amounts to the claim that it does have English-style phrase structure after all – not on the surface, where conditions on word order hold, but at an underlying level of representation at which the grammatical conditions on reflexive pronouns hold.[5] Let us refer to this as the *configurational design of universal grammar.* It is illustrated in (7)–(8):

X-BAR THEORY

(7) English:

S ⇒ S

NP · Aux · VP (V, NP)   ⇒   NP · Aux · VP (V, NP)

(8) Warlpiri:

S ⇒ S

NP · Aux · VP (V, NP)   ⇒   NP Aux V NP NP NP

Now it might be true that all languages do have an abstract level of grammatical structure which closely matches the surface organization of the grammars of English and other European languages. Perhaps it just happens that the biologically based universal design of grammar really does have the form of the language of the colonizers. But there is no evidence for this: for example, *none* of the properties of phrases that I mentioned – contiguity under permutation, grouping for pronunciation, ordering relative to other elements, and substitutability – supports the existence of a VP in Warlpiri, and what evidence there *is* for phrases in Warlpiri shows clearly that there is no VP in our original sense.[6] Moreover, there is evidence that the constraints on reflexive pronouns depend not directly upon phrase structure configurations, but on factors such as predication relations,

REJECTION OF THE CONFIGURATIONAL DESIGN OF UG

which are at best only partially reflected in phrase structure configurations.[7] Therefore the "deep" or underlying VP that must be postulated in (8) is devoid of the
original constituency properties of VPs.

Hence an alternative taken in the development of LFG is to choose a more
abstract representation of the grammatical functions subject and object, one which
is neutral between the differing modes of expression of languages. On this alternative, grammatical functions are *not* reducible to phrase structure configurations
as in (7). They are classes of differing formal expressions that are mapped into
argument structure in equivalent ways. Thus we have a differing picture of the
grammatical structures of English and Warlpiri:

(9) English:

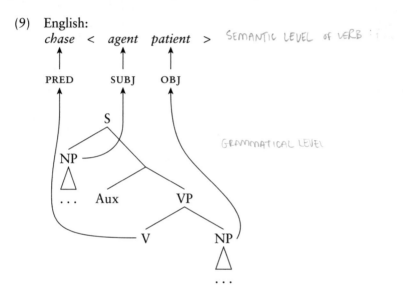

(10) Warlpiri:

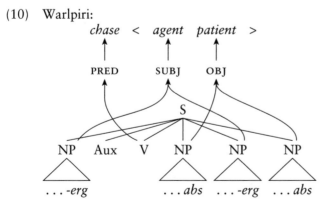

In this design, the grammatical functions subject and object are equivalence classes
which serve as the relators, or "links," between two formally different, parallel
structures: (i) the *argument structure*, which includes just those participants in
events and situations that are grammatically expressed, and (ii) the *expression*

structure, which consists of the modes of expression of the language. While phrase structure configurations distinguish the subject and object functions in English, the case inflections – "erg(ative)" and "abs(olutive)" – distinguish the same functions in Warlpiri. These functions differ overtly, as we have seen, but they show a similar system of correspondences to the argument structure. The system of functions that relates these two structures has been mathematically modelled by the *functional structures* of lexical-functional grammar (chapter 4). Let us refer to this as the *relational design of universal grammar*.

Does this choice of representations for grammatical functions make any difference, or are they just notational variants? In fact, there are interesting empirical consequences of the choice of design. The configurational design implies that specific elements of phrase structure – NPs, VPs, and their relations – appear not only in representing the modes of expression of English and similar European languages, but also in representing deeper aspects of grammatical organization: the abstract syntactic functions and the semantic predicate argument structures of all languages. The relational design, in contrast, implies that it is the distinctive structure of predicators and arguments and their grammatical functions that are relevant at the deeper levels. Let us now turn to evidence concerning the representation of predicate argument structure.

1.1   Predicate Argument Structure

It has been observed (Marantz 1984) that the representation of grammatical functions in terms of phrase structure categories such as NP and VP predicts asymmetries between these functions because of their asymmetric depth of embedding in the phrase structure representation:

(11)

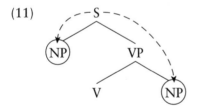

As we see in (11), the object forms a phrasal unit with the verb, while the subject forms a phrasal unit not with the verb, but with the verb phrase. And such asymmetries *do* show up. We have already seen the asymmetry between reflexives as subjects and objects in (4) and (5). Another example is the formation of idioms. With transitive verbs idioms are generally formed from a verb and its object, and not from a verb and its subject. For example, all of the examples in (12) have idiomatic interpretations, while those in (13) have only literal interpretations:

(12) idiomatic:
    a. *John blew his stack.*
    b. *Mary gave me a piece of her mind.*
    c. *Fred flipped his wig.*
    d. *Susan takes the cake.*

(13) nonidiomatic:
    a. *His stack blew John.*
    b. *A piece of Mary's mind gave me problems.*
    c. *Fred's wig flipped his friends.*
    d. *The cake takes Susan.*

There are exceptions: subject–verb idioms like *Your goose is cooked, The roof caved in on us*, and even (12b), where the idiomatic NP (*a piece of her mind*) is not the immediate object of the verb *give*. Such exceptions could be accounted for by hypothesizing that at the deepest level of structure, where semantic relations among predicates and arguments are represented, the NPs are indeed objects of their verbs, and that they are displaced from the object position in the derivation of the examples actually observed. Thus the fundamental idea is that semantic units of predicate argument structure correspond to deep phrase structure units.

But when we look more closely at the patterns of idioms and lexicalized expressions, a finer structure emerges (Kiparsky 1987, O'Grady 1998): it appears that there is a hierarchy among the semantic roles of arguments involved in the creation of idiomatic expressions. I give a simplified representation in (14):

(14) *agent > beneficiary > recipient > . . . > patient/theme > location*

Essentially, the agent is the participant in an event that causes or controls the action; the beneficiary is the participant who benefits from an action; the recipient is a participant who receives something, as in giving; the patient is the participant that undergoes the effect of the action; and the location can also be a participant in an action, event, or situation.

Verbs combine to form idioms most easily with arguments from the lower end of the hierarchy; as we ascend the hierarchy, idioms become increasingly rare. Thus there are idioms formed from a verb together with a phrase that replaces a literal locative argument:

(15) Verb + locative:
    a. *Mary put John to shame.*
    b. *Mary's innocent look took John in.*
    c. *This office has gone to the dogs!*

The verbs *put, take*, and *go* all take literal locative arguments, as in *Mary put her work to one side, She took the cat in through the window*, and *You shouldn't go to the dogs for advice*. And it is these arguments that can be replaced by constant expressions to form idiomatic combinations with the verbs, as in (15). Similarly, there are idioms formed from a verb together with a phrase that replaces a literal patient argument:

(16) Verb + patient:
     a. *John blew his stack.*
     b. *Mary gave me a piece of her mind.*
     c. *Fred flipped his wig.*
     d. *Susan handed me a can of worms.*

And there are idioms formed from a verb together with phrases that correspond to a patient and a locative:

(17) Verb + patient + locative:
     a. *Don't let the cat out of the bag.*
     b. *It's like carrying coals to Newcastle.*

But idioms based on a verb with the higher roles, beneficiary, recipient, or agent, are exceedingly rare and often even difficult to imagine.[8] The same hierarchy also accounts for the exceptional cases noted above, without recourse to the idea of movement of underlying NPs: in *The roof caved in* and *Your goose is cooked*, for example, the idiomatic subject is a patient-like argument of the verb, not an agent.

This pattern cannot be naturally explained in terms of the phrase structure groupings that are motivated by contiguity, substitutability, reorderings, and phonological phrasing: the conceptual unit expressed by the verbs and locative-replacing prepositional phrases in (15a, b), for example, is not a contiguous unit in the phrase structure of English, since verbs (in English) are in closest structural relation to their objects. Thus, the real generalization appears to be that arguments are semantically composed with their predicates in accordance with a hierarchy of semantic roles which reflects the lexical semantics of predicators.[9] Indeed, there is crosslinguistic evidence for the existence of such a hierarchy in the native languages of America, Africa, and Oceania. The hierarchy may well be universal.[10]

Even more striking evidence comes from a syntactically ergative language, where the patient of a transitive verb is the subject:[11]

(18) < *ag*   *pt*   >
        | |

     ... SUBJ

With respect to the thematic hierarchy of (14) the patient is the lowest argument of the argument structure; with respect to the phrase structure representation of (11) the subject NP lies outside of the VP, where it does not form a phrasal unit with the verb. Thus in such a language the predictions of the two designs of universal grammar diverge: idioms based on verb + patient should exist under the relational design of universal grammar, but should *not* exist under the configurational design.

Evidence from Dyirbal, a syntactically ergative language of Australia, supports the relational design.[12] In the following examples, a Dyirbal verb and noun stem are compounded to create an idiom; in each case the noun stem corresponds to the patient argument of the verb:

(19) **bana-l** < *ag* *pt* > COMPOUNDING v + N to form idioms
     'break'

                  buŋgu SUBJECT
                  'knee'
        buŋgu + bana-l 'bend over, fold'

In (19) the idiomatic expression for "bend over, fold" is created by combining the verb "break" with the noun stem for "knee," which corresponds to the argument that undergoes the action denoted by the verb. In English this argument would be an object of the verb, but in Dyirbal, it is the subject. The same is shown by example (20):

(20) **wuga-l** < *ag* *rec* *th* >
     'give'

                 mala SUBJECT
                'hand'
     mala + wuga-l 'give a hand to, help'

Here again the idiom is created by combining the verb 'give' with the nominal stem for 'hand', parallel to the English idiom "give a hand." The crucial point is that the 'hand' argument in Dyirbal is not the object of the verb, as it is in English, but the subject. The same is shown by (21), 'pull a smile':

(21) **yambu-l** < *ag* *pt* >
     'pull'

              miyey SUBJECT
             'smile'
    miyay + yambu-l 'make smile, laugh'

In each case, it is the hierarchy of roles in argument structure rather than the hierarchical position of arguments in the syntactic tree that constrains idiom formation.

What appeared at first to support the configurational design of universal grammar turns out to support the relational design. The predicate argument structure that represents the conceptual participants in events and situations has a distinctive structure of its own, which cannot be assimilated to the expression structures of English and other European language.[13]

because the idiomatic part is the subject, not object, as we might assume

1.2   Conclusion

In conclusion, an important source of empirical motivation for the relational design of universal grammar adopted by LFG is the existence of phrase structure nonconfigurationality. Although various degrees of nonconfigurationality occur across languages, as we will see in part III, the Australian languages are among the best exemplars of the phenomenon (Simpson 1991, Austin and Bresnan 1996, Nordlinger 1998b). This nonconfigurationality is possible because the same grammatical information can be specified by word *shapes* as by word *groups*; the functional structure of LFG characterizes this grammatical information in an abstract, neutral way, without configurational bias. Thus in "lexical-functional grammar" the term "lexical" refers to the fundamental fact that words, or lexical elements, are as important as syntactic elements in expressing grammatical information, and the term "functional" refers to the fact that this grammatical information is not identified with particular structural forms of expression, but is viewed as a system of abstract relators of expressions to eventualities.

Further Reading

For further readings which examine the evidence and issues of nonconfigurationality in more detail, Austin and Bresnan (1996) and Nordlinger (1998b) are recommended as particularly accessible.

Notes

1   See Dixon (1981) on the history and nature of Australian languages. Of the English colonization of Australia he writes, "I have chosen to write plainly, to talk of the white 'invasion' of Aboriginal Australian lands, avoiding euphemisms such as 'settlement', and not to gloss over murder – of people, tribes, and languages" (Dixon 1981: xiv). The Warlpiri grammatical phenomena discussed here come from Hale (1981) and Simpson (1983a, 1991).
2   See Austin and Bresnan (1996) for details.
3   The following illustration is from Simpson (1983a); see also Hale (1973).
4   There are some languages in which the most prominent argument structure role (sometimes called the "logical subject") plays the same role in binding as the grammatical subject (Kroeger 1993, Manning 1996). See part IV.
5   This hypothesis has taken several forms. One is that the underlying structure is a deep structure, which undergoes transformational "scrambling" rules to derive the modes of expression peculiar to Warlpiri (Hale 1973). But as Hale (1994) points out, the complete absence of movement rules elsewhere in Warlpiri renders this hypothesis unattractive. Another is that the underlying structure is a "lexical structure," which is not transformationally related to the surface forms, but represents the universal component of Warlpiri grammar in the phrasal forms of English (Hale 1983). This view has been criticized by Speas (1990) for adopting different theories of grammar for different language types, and has subsequently been abandoned by Hale (1994). A third and more recent form of the hypothesis based on work by Jelinek (1984) and

Baker (1991) assumes that overt NPs are not arguments but adjuncts to incorporated pronouns; see Austin and Bresnan (1996), Nordlinger (1998b), and Croft (1997) for criticism of the latter hypothesis.

6   The Aux in Warlpiri follows the first phrase of the sentence; the parts of a noun phrase can appear together in this position, but not the parts of a verb phrase. See Simpson (1991), Austin and Bresnan (1996), and Nordlinger (1998b) for more detailed discussion.

7   See part IV.

8   One involving an agent, verb, and patient together is *The cat's got your tongue*. Avery Andrews also points out idiomatic *The photography bug has bitten Fred* versus literal examples such as *The photography bug has eaten Fred* or *Folk dancing has bitten Fred*, and idiomatic *What's eating him?* versus literal *What's chewing on him?* or *That's eating him*. Manning (1996: 152) cites an attested example *The vultures are circling*.

9   Nunberg et al. (1994) suggest that idiom formation correlates with the animacy of arguments, and use this generalization to argue against the configurational approach of Marantz (1984) and others. O'Grady (1998) presents evidence favoring the thematic hierarchy over the animacy approach of Nunberg et al.

10 The evidence consists of the patterns of noun incorporation (Mithun 1984), and of the historical sequence in which pronouns become agreement markers (Givón 1976, 1984).

11 For a review of recent alternative analyses of ergativity and arguments in support of the present analysis of (syntactic) ergativity, see Manning (1994).

12 For information on the grammar of Dyirbal, see Dixon (1972). The examples of idioms in Dyirbal were provided by Bob Dixon with the assistance of Avery Andrews (personal communication).

13 There is a strong temptation in the configurational approach to postulate an initial phrase structure as a pure representation of the thematic hierarchy in terms of embedding within VPs. Though the same categorial labels and relations are used in the initial and derived phrase structures, completely different criteria are used to determine what is a "VP." Manning (1994) criticially discusses this approach in relation to ergative languages.

2 Movement Paradoxes

If typological considerations such as nonconfigurationality motivate a relational design of universal grammar, it is natural to ask how the evidence for syntactic transformations that we see in English and related languages can be accounted for within the same design of grammar. In these familiar languages, we see overt evidence that phrase structure constituents can be displaced from one position to another. The evidence takes the form of **extraction configurations**. An extraction configuration is illustrated by the set of sentences in (1):

(1) a.   We talked about *that problem* for days.
     b.   *That problem*, we talked about __ for days. → FRONTING
     c.   *We talked about for days.

In an extraction configuration, a displaced constituent is identified with a lexically empty position. Thus in (1b) the initial NP *that problem* appears to have been displaced from the usual position of a prepositional object, shown in (1a), to its sentence-initial position. The sign of displacement is the presence of a lexically empty position or gap in the clausal residue, which would be ill-formed on its own, as shown in (1c). An extraction configuration motivates the idea that the sentence-initial constituent in (1b) is moved from an underlying position where it is required:

(2) [*That problem*] we talked about __ for days.

Such extraction configurations seem to be direct evidence of the existence of syntactic transformations – structure-dependent operations that map underlying phrase structures representing grammatical relations onto the transformed structures that represent the surface forms of expression of language. If such movements are needed in English, it has been argued, then theoretical considerations of simplicity, universality, and the learnability in principle of language require them in all languages. This conclusion would support the configurational design of grammar.

In fact, we will see below that such movements arise in the LFG architecture from the interaction of general principles of structure–function correspondence, and can be explained without any loss of generality. Even more interestingly, it turns out that certain "movement paradoxes" favor this architecture over the movement transformations of the configurational design. We can conclude that the same theoretical considerations of simplicity, universality, and learnability in principle require the relational design of grammar for all languages.

A movement paradox is illustrated in (3). Note that there is a mismatch in category type between a seemingly moved phrase, the initial *that* complement in (3a), and the position it is supposed to be moved from, as illustrated in (3b). In (3) the moved phrase cannot appear in the position from which it is supposed to be moved, because it is of the wrong type of syntactic category for that position:

MOVEMENT PARADOX

(3) a. [*That he was* SICK]ₛ we talked about __ for DAYS.

b. *We talked about [*that he was sick*]ₛ for days.   ABOUT requires an NP

c.cf. We talked about [*the fact that he was sick*]ₙₚ for days.

The complex noun phrase in (3c) is fine as a complement to *about*. This preposition requires an NP complement, which is why (3b) is not grammatical (though it is perfectly interpretable).[1]

A related example of a movement paradox involves passivization of sentential complements. It is commonly assumed that the subject of a passive verb is moved from an underlying object position, as in (4):

(4) a. This theory captures *that fact*.

b. [*That fact*] is captured __ by this theory.

But with sentential complements this assumption breaks down with certain verbs for many speakers. The passive example (5a) is a grammatically well-formed sentence having a sentential subject, but the corresponding active (5b) is ill-formed for many speakers for whom the verb *capture* (like the preposition *about*) requires an NP object, as in (5c):

(5) a. [*That languages are learnable*]ₛ is captured __ by this theory.

b. *This theory captures [*that languages are learnable*]ₛ.   OK for me

c.cf. This theory captures [*the fact that languages are learnable*]ₙₚ.

How then could the sentential subject in (5a) have been moved from the object position in (5b)?

Another movement paradox occurs with VP preposing. In VP preposing, a topical VP complement to an auxiliary is shifted to the front of the sentence to emphasize the auxiliary, as in (6b). The specific verb form of the fronted phrase depends on the requirements of the auxiliary, as shown by the contrasts between (6a, b, c):

— TOPICAL VP COMPLEMENT TO AUXILIARY "WILL"

(6)   CONTEXT: I said I would meet you, . . .
  a.   . . . and [*meet you*] I WILL __!
  b. *. . . and [*met you*] I WILL __!
  c. *. . . and [*meeting you*] I WILL __!

The grammaticality or ungrammaticality of (6a)–(c) follows directly from that of the corresponding sources of movement shown in (7a)–(c), respectively:

(7)   a.   I will [*meet you*].
  b.   *I will [*met you*].
  c.   *I will [*meeting you*].

With the perfect auxiliary, however, there can be a mismatch between the fronted verb form (8a) and the *in situ* verb form (8b) (Andrews 1994: 218):

(8)   a.   She said she would meet me,
      and [*meet me*] she HAS __!   PARADOX
  b. *. . . and she HAS [*meet me*]!
  c.   . . . and she HAS [*met me*]!

How then could the VP in (8a) be moved from a postauxiliary position where it can never occur (8b)? The perfect auxiliary *have* in English requires that its complement verb be a past participle, as the contrast between (8b, c) illustrates. Paradoxically, then, an infinitive VP cannot in fact appear in the source position from which it is assumed to be moved. Nevertheless, it is quite natural in English for the infinitive form of the verb to appear in the fronted position, creating another movement paradox.

Subject auxiliary inversion provides still another kind of movement paradox. The contracted negative present tense auxiliary *be* in Standard English has a gap in its person–number paradigm, shown in (9):

EMPTY

E.g.
she said she'd go
And [go] she has
* she has [go].

(9)

	sg	pl
1		aren't
2	aren't	aren't
3	isn't	aren't

A form exists for every combination of person and number except for first person singular. Although nonstandard dialects have forms such as *ain't* or *amn't* which fill this gap, the Standard dialect does not make use of these forms:

(10) a.   I am not your friend.
  b.   *I ain't/amn't your friend.

Under subject–auxiliary inversion, many speakers of the Standard dialect find that it is natural to use the form *aren't* (Langendoen 1970, Hudson 1977, Dixon 1982, Gazdar et al. 1982, Kim and Sag 1996, Bresnan 1998a, b):

(11) a. Am I __ not your friend? (stilted or very formal)

b. Aren't I __ your friend?

If the inverted auxiliary in (11a) is derived by movement from an underlying postsubject position, where is it moved from? The form *aren't* cannot appear in the postverbal position:

(12) *I aren't your friend.

Movement paradoxes are problematic for two basic architectural assumptions of transformational theories: the representational assumption that the inner or underlying structure of language has the formal categorial properties of phrase structure (the configurational design of grammar), and the derivational assumption that the surface configurations of phrase structure categories are derived by transformational operations (movements) from basic syntactic representations of the same type.[2]

2.1   Theoretical Assumptions

The kind of category mismatches we see in the movement paradoxes are expected in the relational architecture of LFG, for the simple reason that the correspondence between structure and function is not perfect; there can be mismatches between the f-structure attributes of an element and the c-structure positions it can appear in. We will consider here just one example, in order to illustrate the principle. The diagram in (13) again informally depicts the architecture illustrated in (9) and (10) of chapter 1:

(13) Parallel structures (LFG):

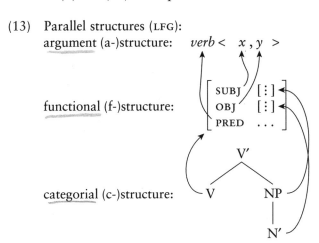

Each structure models a different dimension of grammatical substance: role, function, and category. Roles correspond to the grammatically expressible participants of eventualities (modelled by a-structure), syntactic functions belong to the abstract system of relators of roles to expressions (modelled by f-structure), and phrase structure categories belong to the overt structure of forms of expression (modelled by c-structure). The structures are associated by principles of functional correspondence (also called "linking" or "mapping" principles).

Let us take example (5a) by way of illustration.[3] The surface categorial structure can be depicted as in (14):

(14)

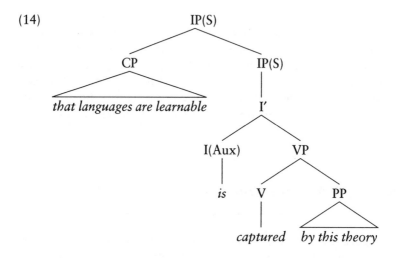

Observe that the *that*-complement is base-generated in topicalized position as a sentential complement (CP) adjoined to the sentence (IP) in the c-structure. The evidence for a subject-external position of the CP in English includes the observation that auxiliary inversion with the CP is not possible (Koster 1978):

(15)   a.   *That he'll be late* is quite likely.
       b.   *Is *that he'll be late* likely?
       c.   *How likely is *that he'll be late*?

General principles of structure–function correspondence for configurational structures (to be discussed in chapter 6) define the position of the adjoined CP as that of a topic (TOP) or focus (FOC) function, and tell us that the entire sentence corresponds to a single functional structure nucleus.[4] Because the CP is a non-nominal category, it cannot occupy the subject NP position as sister of I'. This follows from the constraint on structure–function association shown in (16) (Bresnan 1994a: ex. 88):

(16)   The canonical structural realization of subject and object functions is nominal.

⌐ CONSTRAINT ON STRUCTURE-FUNCTION ASSOCIATION

Although the CP cannot appear in the usual structural position of the subject, which is an NP position by (16), general principles of the theory nevertheless link the function of the topicalized phrase with the subject function in f-structure, as shown in (17). (The phrases in double quotation marks abbreviate the actual f-structure contents where they are not relevant to the discussion.) The first principle is simply that the subject is the default topic of its sentence, which we formalize (section 6.2.1) by optionally identifying SUBJ with TOP:[5]

(17)   Correspondences between c- and f-structures of (5a):

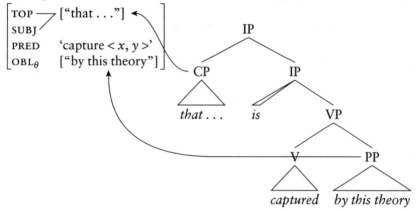

As we will see in chapter 4, the general principle of COMPLETENESS requires that the verbal a-structure requirements, including the demand for a subject, be met; so something must fill the SUBJ function in f-structure. COHERENCE requires that the grammaticalized discourse functions (TOP) and (FOC) be identified with a syntactic function such as SUBJ or OBJ; so the topicalized CP must fill some other function in the clause. UNIQUENESS prevents identifying the TOP with a syntactic function borne by a lexically filled constituent in c-structure, as we will see in chapter 4; so there must be an unfilled function – a gap – for the topic to fill. The gap is represented as the omission of the subject NP from its normal c-structure position as sister of I′. In this way the typical elements of an extraction configuration – namely, the identification of a displaced constituent with a lexically empty position – arise nonderivationally from general principles.

Finally, the passive relation follows not from NP-movement, but from principles of a-structure to f-structure correspondence provided by the lexical mapping theory. This part of the theory is discussed in subsequent chapters, but we can briefly illustrate the main point in (18). The passive a-structure is morpholexically associated with the passive participle of *capture*; it differs from the active in that the agent role (the *x* argument in our diagrams) is suppressed, and may be associated with an optional *by* phrase (OBL$_\theta$). The a-structure allows the patient role (the *y* argument) to be associated with either the SUBJ or the OBJ function, depending on context. It is the suppression of the agent which allows the theme role to correspond to the SUBJ function in this case:

(18)   Morpholexical correspondences between a- and f-structures of (5a):
       a-structure: *capture* < x   y   >

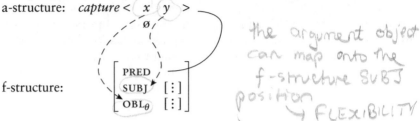

f-structure:

the argument object
can map onto the
f-structure SUBJ
position
      → FLEXIBILITY

Thus the reason that there can be a mismatch between the topicalized category CP and the object position of the verb *capture* is that the topicalized *that*-complement is flexibly mapped to its argument role by the correspondence theory. It is not linked to its argument role by a series of transformational movements from an underlying object position in phrase structure. And the reason for THIS is that the logical roles of phrases are not uniformly represented in phrase structure from. Role, function, and category are independent dimensions of linguistic substance. Within the constraints on their correspondences, mismatches are possible.

Why then is the active form (5b) *This theory captures that languages are learnable* ill-formed? The answer is simply that *capture* takes only objects as its complements and by (16) the canonical structural realization of objects is a nominal category, not a *that*-complement CP. When English verbs take *that*-complements, these complements are not objects, and the verbs are syntactically intransitive in this construction. The verb *care* is an example of the latter type:[6]

(19)   a.   I don't care *that languages are learnable.*
       b.   *I don't care *that.*
       c.   *That languages are learnable* isn't cared.

Observe that this architecture leads us to expect nonuniformities of syntactic categorization of parallel semantic categories across languages: if English sentential complement CPs can have the grammatical functions of subject and object in f-structure, as proposed here, and if subject and object are canonically realized as NPs in c-structure, as we have also hypothesized, then we should expect to find languages in which there are sentential complement NPs in c-structure. In fact, Bresnan (1995a) argues that Chicheŵa has nominal *kŭti* "that" complements, and there is evidence that this is true also for Dutch (Hoekstra 1984) and Spanish (Plann 1986, Luján 1994), to give just a few relevant instances.

In conclusion, we have seen in principle how both the typologically "exotic" property of nonconfigurationality and the category mismatches in extraction configurations found in English are comprehended by the same relational architecture of universal grammar. Chapters 4 and 5 present an explicit model of parallel structures and their correspondence mappings to make these linguistic ideas precise. The next chapter discusses our third motivation for the relational architecture, based on the lexicality of passivization and other changes in argument structure realization.

Further Reading and Discussion

Further readings which discuss the issue of category mismatches and imperfect correspondence between structure and function in a particularly accessible way are Bresnan (1995a, 1994a) on English, T. Mohanan (1994, 1995) and Butt (1995) on Hindi/Urdu, and Matsumoto (1996a) on Japanese.

Quite intricate argumentation is involved in evaluating the various movement approaches. For *that*-clause topicalization, analyses have been proposed involving (i) movement and deletion of an underlying resumptive pronoun (e.g. Koster 1978) or extraction of the topicalized complement, leaving "an invisible resumptive pronoun" which is in turn extracted (Postal 1994); (ii) movement of a null operator (Chomsky 1977); and (iii) movements that can change category type (Stowell 1981, Pesetsky 1982, Webelhuth 1992). For criticisms and alternative analyses to the approaches in (iii) see Bresnan (1991, 1994a, 1995a), Hoekstra (1984), Plann (1986), Luján (1994), and Neidle (1982a, 1988). For criticisms and alternatives to (ii) see Baltin (1982), Grimshaw (1993), Lasnik and Stowell (1991), Maling and Zaenen (1977), Müller and Sternefeld (1993). The problem with (i) is that in general, the kinds of phrases that can be topicalized do not coincide with the kinds of phrases that can bind resumptive pronouns. Quantifier phrases are one example discussed by Rizzi (1986), Rizzi and Roberts (1989: n. 1), Bresnan and Mchombo (1986: 279), Jelinek (1995), and Baker (1995), as illustrated by the Italian examples in (20):

(20)   a. **Nessuno, lo conosco in questa città.*
           Lit.: "Nobody, I know him in this city."
       b. NESSUNO, *conosco in questa città.*
           "Nobody do I know in this city."

There are other types of topicalized phrases which cannot bind resumptive definite pronouns (*pace* Postal 1994: 67–8), as we see in English:

(21)   a. An IDIOT he called me! Can you believe it?
       b. *An IDIOT he called me *it*! Can you believe it?

(22)   a. Last month I brought home a bold little kitten. ROSIE I named her.
       b. *ROSIE, I named her *it*.

It is true that a demonstrative pronoun can sometimes appear in these contexts: *Rosie – I named her that*, but it requires a very different phrasing from examples (21) and (22): there must be a pause between the initial NP and the sentence, each having its own intonational contour. In (21) and (22), in contrast, there is a single intonational contour for both the initial NP and the clause remnant, and the pitch on the NP is the prominence peak for the entire sentence. These facts suggest a different syntactic relation between the NP and the clause in the two cases. Thus the resumptive pronoun solution to the category mismatch problem with topicalized *that* clauses lacks independent motivation.

Notes

1   English differs in this respect from some other Germanic languages, such as Swedish. See Berman (1997) for a different analysis of similar facts in German within LFG. Note also that even in English, interrogative clauses are more nominal in character, appearing as prepositional complements: *We talked about whether you should be the one to go.* Also, in some dialects of English examples like (3b) do occur.

2   For some of these problems, various proposals have been made within the movement frameworks, but none of them is completely satisfactory and there is little agreement on the solutions. See Further Readings and Discussion for references. The movement paradoxes with VP preposing and auxiliary inversion have generally been ignored within the movement approaches. The former is analyzed by Andrews (1994) within LFG and the latter by Bresnan (1998a, b).

3   Grimshaw (1982b) sketches the essential outlines of the solution adopted here.

4   – corresponding to what Grimshaw (1991) calls an "extended projection."

5   The formal mechanism of functional identification of displaced constituents with other functions is discussed in chapters 4, 6, and 9.

6   Some verbs, like *believe*, share properties of both *capture* and *care*. Like *capture*, *believe* takes an object which alternates with a passive subject. But like *care*, *believe* allows a nonobject sentential complement. (See Grimshaw 1982b and Bresnan 1995a for further discussion of this analysis.)

3 Lexicality and Argument Structure

Briefly illustrated at the end of the previous chapter, the lexicality of passivization and other relation changing processes has been one of the fundamental motivations for the distinctive architecture of LFG from its beginnings (Bresnan 1978, 1980, 1982a, Mchombo 1978, Kaplan and Bresnan 1982). In this chapter we consider evidence for the lexicality of the passive.

3.1 Passive Relation Changes

Recall the configurational design of universal grammar from chapter 1. It implies that specific elements of phrase structure – NPs, VPs, and their relations – appear not only in representing the modes of expression of English and similar European languages, but also in representing more abstract aspects of grammatical organization: the predication relations and predicate argument structures of all languages. The relational design of universal grammar, in contrast, implies that grammatical functions are an appropriate abstraction for expressing predicate argument relations. LFG embodies the relational design of universal grammar.

In a generic transitive active clause, the agent (or actor) argument of the verb is expressed as the subject and the patient (or undergoer) argument as the object. In (1), for example, *the child* is the subject and *the cats* the object of the active verb *kisses*:

(1) The child kisses the cats at every opportunity.

In the passive voice, the mappings from semantic roles to grammatical functions differ, the undergoer now being expressed by the subject (with which the verb agrees in (2)) and the actor by an optional prepositional phrase. The core (subject or object) arguments of the passive verb have been reduced by one, rendering a transitive verb intransitive.

(2) The cats are kissed by the child at every opportunity.

In the configurational design of universal grammar, this remapping of roles to functions is effected in part by a syntactic movement of an NP from an under-lying transitive tree structure (3), where it receives the undergoer semantic role, to an external position as subject:

(3)

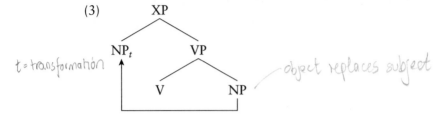

t = transformation

object replaces subject

In the relational design of universal grammar, in contrast, the remapping of predication relations can be characterized more abstractly as in (4):[1]

(4)

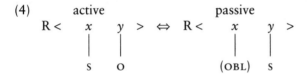

Here the active and passive verb forms share the same predicate argument structure (with roles indicated by variables x, y in (4)), and the roles are lexically associated with, or mapped to, alternative sets of grammatical functions, s (subject) and o (object). This characterization abstracts away from the language particular realizations of subject, object, and oblique (OBL) relations, which may be configurational or nonconfigurational.

In LFG, relation changes are thus lexical alternations in predicate–function mappings. How can such lexical alternations bring about syntactic movements? In LFG relation changes induce syntactic changes in forms of expression through general principles of completeness and coherence, which require that the functions required by each predicate match those instantiated in the c(ategorial)-structure (chapter 4). To see informally how lexical relation changes can induce syntactic changes, let us compare the passive in Malayalam (Dravidian language spoken in southern India) with that in English.[2]

Malayalam has both active and passive verb forms, which show the relation change given in (4). The passive verb form consists of a verb stem together with the suffix *-appet*. Both the active and passive verb stems undergo further inflection for tense. K. P. Mohanan (1982a) gives a variety of arguments that the Malayalam simple sentence has a nonconfigurational structure, lacking a VP, and that the noun phrases can occur in any order before the verb or, with marked intonation, after the verb. Malayalam uses case morphology to specify grammatical functions. For example, a nominative case-marked NP can be either a subject or an inanimate object; an accusative case-marked NP must be an animate object.

The principles of completeness and coherence ensure that the both active and passive verb forms occur with NPs of the required cases (in any order).

Compared to an active sentence, a passive sentence will show changes in transivity and the cases of the NPs satisfying the argument roles of the verb, but no changes in the possible structural positions of these NPs. This is illustrated in (5) and (6). The order of NPs in the Malayalam sentences of these illustrations is freely interchangeable: only the case marking of the NPs and the suffixation of -*appeṭ* to the verb mark the passive construction:

(5)

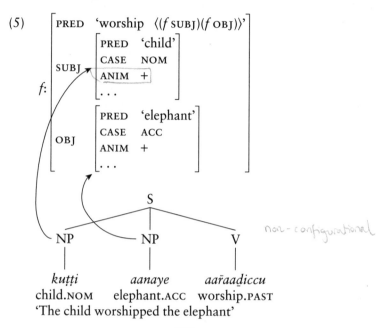

kuṭṭi	aanaye	aařaaḍiccu
child.NOM	elephant.ACC	worship.PAST

'The child worshipped the elephant'

(6)

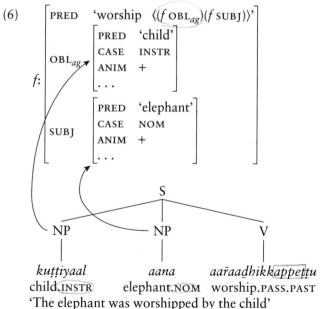

kuṭṭiyaal	aana	aařaadhikkappeṭṭu
child.INSTR	elephant.NOM	worship.PASS.PAST

'The elephant was worshipped by the child'

In <u>Malayalam</u>, then, the <u>syntactic</u> effects of the passive are found in case alternations rather than word order differences. There effects follow from the syntactic typology of the language (nonconfigurational dependent-marking – chapter 6) together with the universal principles of completeness and coherence. There is no syntactic derivation of the passive from the active.

As a second illustration of how the <u>syntax</u> of relation changes is induced from the lexical alternations by means of completeness and coherence, consider the passive in English. The passive verb form in English is the <u>past participle</u>. Only the active verb stem can be inflected for tense, since <u>participles are tenseless verb</u> forms. This morphological peculiarity entails that in tensed constructions, passivized verbs will occur only with tense-bearing verbs that can take participial complements, such as *get* (*John just got handed a can of worms*), *have* (*We had the agents sent phony passports*), *keep* (*She keeps her library painted a dark burgundy color*), or *be* (*John was handed a book*). The participle predictably appears without an auxiliary verb in tenseless constructions, such as relative adjuncts (*Anyone handed a can of worms should drop it*) or clausal adjuncts (*Handed a can of worms, John dropped it*).

The English simple sentence has a more hierarchical structure and rigid word order than that of Malayalam, and the grammatical functions are largely determined by the endocentric principles of chapter 6. In English the subject NP is usually preverbal, while the object NP is postverbal within the VP. The oblique functions of English are expressed by prepositional phrases, whose prepositions can be used analogously to case markers in certain instances. In particular, the preposition *by* carries a case feature associated with the OBL$_{ag}$ function.

Given the configurational typology and directionality parameters of English phrase structure, the same principles of completeness and coherence will induce rather different syntactic effects from the same lexical active–passive alternation that we saw in Malayalam. Compared with an active sentence, a passive sentence will show changes in the position of the NPs associated with the argument roles of the verb. In particular, the argument role which is associated with the object function in the active lexical form of the verb will be associated with the subject function in the passive lexical form of the verb. Since the object NP follows the verb, and the subject NP precedes the verb, the NP expressing this role will appear to shift positions from the active to the passive. In addition, in a tensed sentence, the passive participle must appear as the complement to another verb such as *be* that can carry the necessary tense feature.[3] These structural differences are illustrated in (7) and (8). (7) shows the c- and f-structures for an English active sentence corresponding to the Malayalam active example (5):

(7)

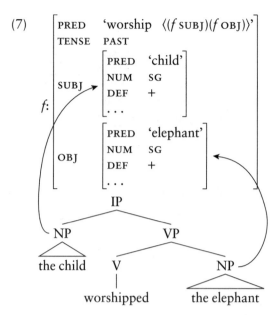

The careful reader may note that the English f-structure arguments differ from those of Malayalam in the attributes illustrated: the Malayalam arguments shown in (5) and (6) have CASE and ANIM features, for example. In general we will illustrate only those f-structure features which are both marked in the language and relevant to the point discussed in the text. (8) shows the c- and f-structures for an English passive sentence corresponding to the Malayalam passive example (6):

(8)

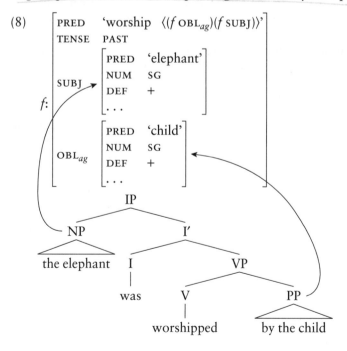

Thus, the apparent syntactic movement in English passivization is induced by the c-structure typology of English interacting with the principles of completeness and coherence. The lexical active–passive alternation preserves the syntactic patterns of structural form in English just as in Malayalam. There is no syntactic derivation of passives to change the grammatical functions of the arguments. The idea that passivization involves a syntactic transformation moving an NP (or DP) in a sentence from the object position to the subject position is (from the vantage of LFG) an illusion, an epiphenomenon of the lexical alternation.

3.2   The Lexicality of Relation Changes

In English there is evidence that passivization is a lexical relation change, not invoving syntactic transformations, in that it can feed lexical processes of derivational morphology (Bresnan 1978). The argument is quite straightforward.[4] We make the initial assumption – a standard assumption in morphology – that word formation processes such as derivation, compounding, and conversion are morpholexical and not synactic, and that the inputs to these processes are also morpholexical and not syntactic.[5] Then we observe that in many languages passivization, causativization, and other relation changing processes are inputs to lexical processes of derivational morphology such as nominalization, adjective formation, and compounding. It is not just the verb *forms* that are input to the lexical processes, but all of their attendant syntactic effects such as changes in transitivity. To maintain the syntactic derivation of passives or causatives by transformational movements, one must either duplicate these processes in the lexicon, an undesirable loss of generalization (as Bresnan 1982a argues), or else reconstruct lexical morphology in the syntax, contrary to our initial assumption.

3.2.1   Adjectives vs. verbs

First, English has distinct categories of adjective and verb, which display different morphological and syntactic properties. For example, adjectives but not verbs can be negated by *un-* prefixation (see (9a)). (There is a separate verbal prefix *un-* in *untie, unlock*, which reverses the action denoted by the base verb.) Adjectives but not verbs can be prenominal modifiers (see (9b)). Adjectives but not (transitive) verbs resist direct NP complements (9c). Adjectives but not verbs can head concessional relative phrases beginning with *however* (see (9d)).[6]

(9)   a.   *un-* prefixation: *happy/unhappy, clear/unclear,* **untouch,* *ungo
      b.   prenominal modifiers: A N vs. *V N
      c.   *[A NP]$_{AP}$ vs. [V NP]$_{VP}$: *supportive my daughter* vs. *support my daughter*
      d.   *however* AP vs. *however VP: *however supportive of her daughter she may have been* vs. **however supporting her daughter she may have been ...*

3.2.2 Participle–adjective conversion

Second, English has a general morphological process of participle–adjective conversion, which enables all types of verbal participles to be used as adjectives:

(10)   a.   *present participles*: a smiling child, a breathing woman, the boring story
       b.   *perfect participles*: a fallen leaf, an escaped convict, wilted lettuce
       c.   *passives*: a considered statement, the spared prisoners, an opened can

By the tests in (9), these converted participles are adjectives and not verbs. They appear prenominally, as in (10), and show other evidence of being adjectives:

(11)   *an unconsidered statement, however considered her statement may be been, unwilted lettuce, unbreathing*

See Bresnan (1982a) for discussion and analysis of more complex examples such as *rummaged around in.*

3.2.3 Passive participles convert to adjectives

Third, passive verb forms, being verbal participles, also undergo conversion to adjectives, as in (10c). As evidence for this conversion, the adjectival passives show the full range of passive participle morphology that we find with passive verbs:[7]

(12)

Verb	Participle	Adjectival Passive
sing	sung	an unsung hero
fight	fought	hard-fought battles
write	written	a well-written novel
give	given	a recently given talk
consider	considered	an unconsidered action
inhabit	inhabited	an uninhabited island
break	broken	my broken heart
split	split	split wood

If there were a separate morphological rule of "adjectival passivization" alongside of verbal passivization, these morphological parallels would be an unexplained accident. Further evidence comes from the fact that complex passives consisting of a passive verb and following preposition may also undergo conversion:

(13)   a.   After the tornado, the fields had a *marched through* look.
       b.   Each *unpaid for* item will be returned.
       c.   You can ignore any recently *gone over* accounts.

    d.   His was not a *well-looked on* profession.
    e.   They shared an *unspoken, unheard of* passion for chocolates.
    f.   Filled with candy wrappers and crumpled bills, her bag always had a *rummaged around in* appearance.

But exceptions to complex passivization are also exceptions to the adjectival passive:

(14)   a. *The twin is looked like by his brother.
        b. *a looked-like twin (cf. like-minded)

(15)   a. *No reason was left for.
        b. *the left-for reason (cf. each unpaid-for item)

Again, this fact would remain unexplained if there were a separate rule of adjectival passivization alongside verbal passivization.

3.2.4   *Differences between adjectival and verbal passives explained*

Certain differences between adjectival and verbal passives have a natural explanation on this theory. As noted above, English adjectives cannot take NP complements, but require a mediating preposition. (See (9c): *she is supportive her daughter, she is supportive of her daughter.*) Therefore, adjectival passives of ditransitive verbs are more restricted than verbal passives. When one of two NP objects is expressed as the passive subject of a verb, the other can remain as a complement of the verb, but as a bare NP it cannot be the complement of the converted adjective. Hence, when the NP complement is required by the passivized verb, the corresponding adjectival passive will be ill-formed. This observation explains the contrast between (16) and (17):[8]

(16)   a. A medal was recently given (to the winner.)
        b. The winner was recently given *(a medal).

(17)   a. a recently given medal
        b. *a recently given winner

Bresnan (1982a) originally attributed this contrast to the theme subject condition – the subject of predication of an adjective must be a theme – but in fact it already follows from the LFG principle of functional completeness discussed in the previous section and in chapter 4.

    Furthermore, when the passivized ditransitive verb does not require an NP complement, the adjectival passive is allowed:

(18) a. New skills were taught (to the children).
    b. The children were taught (new skills).
    c. The prisoners were spared (execution).

(19) a. untaught skills
    b. untaught children
    c. the spared prisoners

This generalization was observed by B. Levin and Rappaport (1986: 631) and dubbed the Sole Complement Constraint (SCC):[9]

(20) **The Sole Complement Constraint:**
    An argument that may stand as a sole NP complement to a verb can become the subject of predication of an adjectival passive.

The SCC already follows from Bresnan's (1982a) conversion analysis, without any extra condition.

    Finally, when the passivized verb requires a PP complement, the adjectival passive may be well-formed, but it cannot occur in prenominal position because of the generalization that nominals and the heads of their modifiers must be adjacent (Maling 1983): *a yellow book, *a yellow with age book, a book yellow with age*:[10]

(21) a. The pillows were being stuffed (with feathers).
    b. The feathers were being stuffed ??(into their pillows).

(22) a. stuffed pillows
    b.?? stuffed feathers
    c. feathers [still unstuffed into their pillows]$_{AP}$

A context in which the last example (22c) might be used naturally is the following: *I walked into the room looking for my sister, who works as a freelance pillow-stuffer. She was nowhere in sight, but there were pillows on the floor, half-stuffed pillows on the tabletop, and on a long counter I beheld heaps of feathers still unstuffed into their pillows.* The generalization underlying these facts (which is observed by Hoekstra 1984 and B. Levin and Rappaport 1986) also follows from the completeness principle of LFG: the absence of a required syntactic complement leads to a violation.

    Thus, there is no need to postulate a separate rule of adjectival passivization in addition to verb passivization to explain the above differences between adjectival and verbal passives: the differences as well as the similarities follow directly from the lexical morphological process of participle–adjective conversion together with general syntactic properties of adjectives and verbs in English. We need only assume that passivized verbs are available lexically to be converted.

3.2.5 Differences between adjectival and verbal passives unexplained

However, the present account is not sufficient. There are further differences between the verbal participles and converted adjectives that are not yet explained (Wasow 1977, Bresnan 1982a). First, verbal passives can be predicated of idiom chunks, but adjectival passives cannot:

(23) a. Advantage was not taken of my presence.
      b. *untaken advantage (cf. untaken seats)

Second, some verbs like *thank* have a verbal passive but no adjectival passive:

(24) a. We were thanked by our friends.
      b. *a thanked person

Third, intransitive verbs have past participles which undergo adjective conversion only in some cases:

(25) a. wilted lettuce   lettuce that has wilted
          elapsed time   time that has elapsed
          an escaped convict   a convict who has escaped
      b. *the run child   the child who has run
          *an exercised athlete   an athlete who has exercised
          *a flown pilot   a pilot who has flown
          *a recently left woman   a woman who has left recently

Nothing in the above account explains this.

   These further restrictions suggest that we must take into account the semantics of adjective conversion. It is clear that adjective conversion in general denotes a state derived from the semantics of the base verb. This seems to be true for all types of conversion, including the present participles (*a smiling woman*). In the case of the past participles, the early LFG attempt to characterize the semantics was the theme subject condition (Bresnan 1982a): the participles that do convert, as in (25a), have a theme subject, while those that do not, as in (25b), have an agent subject. This explanation is problematic in that it is not obviously applicable to examples like (19) *untaught children/skills*, where two distinct arguments must then be analyzed as themes (as B. Levin and Rappaport 1986 point out). However, there is a more adequate semantic account readily available. The state denoted by the adjective appears to be the result state of the eventuality denoted by the past participle (Langacker 1991: 202–3, Parsons 1990: 236, B. Levin and Rappaport 1989). Wilting involves an involuntary change of state, but even highly volitional eventualities such as having escaped can entail result states, such as freedom. Because the activity of running lacks an inherent result state, it is strange to say *a run child*. But when the goal is supplied to the activity, a result state is defined, and now conversion is possible (*a run-away child*). Similarly with other activities, such as exercising, flying, or travelling: when a goal or limit of some sort is supplied, a result state is defined and conversion is possible. Thus, the converted adjectives of the following past participles are all possible:

(26) a run-away slave   a slave who has run away
     an over-exercised athlete   an athlete who has exercised overly
     a flown-away bird   a bird that has flown away
     the widely-travelled correspondent the correspondent who has travelled
                                         widely

In contrast, the verb *leave* in (25b) is bad because the predicate focuses on the source of motion, not on the goal or result state (Adele Goldberg, personal communication). Verbal meanings having such an end-point or result state are often called "telic," and are identifiable by a variety of tests such as the ability to take bounding temporal adverbs (Vendler 1967, Dowty 1979). This generalization is reinforced by the contrast in (27), due to Adele Goldberg (personal communication):

(27) grown man vs. ??grown tree

Goldberg (ibid.) characterizes the contrast as follows: "The former refers to a culturally recognized end-point, namely adulthood, while the latter does not since there is no culturally recognized end state of treehood."

The same semantic generalization suggests that *a thanked person* will be ill-formed, because there is no salient result state defined by the process of thanking. Similarly, the complex predicates consisting of verb and noun combinations like *take advantage of* do not define a result state of the internal noun (e.g. *advantage*), which forms part of the idiom.

The hypothesis, then, is that English adjectival passives are just morphological conversions of lexically passivized verbs subject to the additional syntactic and semantic restrictions of adjectives. Not only may passive verbs be converted to adjectives, but so may other intransitive verb participles that meet the same conditions, as we see in (25), (26), and (27). The conversion analysis therefore has greater explanatory value than the earlier idea that there are distinct syntactic and adjectival rules of passivization in English (see Wasow 1977 for an early articulation of the dual passive analysis). The conclusion that passivization itself must be a lexical process has now been widely adopted in lexicalist constraint-based theories. (See Bresnan 1978 and Mchombo 1978 for early lexicalist statements of this argument.)

But there is an alternative way of capturing the generalizations across verbal and adjectival passives: suppose that both adjectival and verbal passives are derived by syntactic NP movement (B. Levin and Rappaport 1989). In particular, notice that the above examples of adjectives derived from nonpassive intransitive participles appear to involve **unaccusative** verbs.[11] Unaccusative verbs are analyzed by many researchers in the movement framework as being analogous to passive verbs, in that their surface subjects are derived by NP movement from an initial object position. The deverbal adjective might be morphologically formed by lexical processes, but its actual intransitivization would be accomplished by NP-movement in a way analogous to the syntactic passive, as illustrated in (28):

(28)

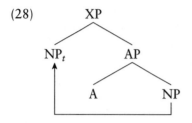

We thus have two alternative hypotheses, syntactic and lexical, for capturing the generalizations lost in postulating separate lexical and syntactic passive rules. If deverbal adjectival constructions require NP movement (as the syntactic hypothesis assumes), then it should be true that among intransitive verbs only those that permit NP movement can undergo adjective formation. But if deverbal adjectival constructions are lexically created by participle–adjective conversion (as the lexical hypothesis assumes), this restriction need not hold, as long as the formations meet the general requirements of adjectives. The following evidence favors the lexical hypothesis:

(29)   a well-prepared teacher   a teacher who has prepared well
       a confessed killer   a killer who has confessed
       a recanted Chomskyan   a Chomskyan who has recanted
       (un)declared juniors   juniors who have (not) declared [majors]
       a practiced liar   a liar who has practiced
       an unbuilt architect   an architect who has not built [buildings]

Verbs like *confess, recant,* and *declare* designate verbal actions that change one's moral, legal, or administrative status. These are strongly unergative verbs by tests proposed by B. Levin and Rappaport Hovav (1995):

(30)   *He confessed his way out of trouble, He recanted his way into acceptance by the functionalists, She declared her way from science into art.*

Build is another verb that results in a change of status (for an architect): *He built his way to fame.*[12]

Note finally that it is important not just that the adjectival passive's verbal base be telic (that is, have an end-point or result state), but that it predicate a result state of its *subject. Give up,* for example, is telic, to judge by the typical aspectual tests proposed by Vendler (1967) and Dowty (1979):

(31)   I gave up in a minute/??for an hour.

Yet the end-point state of giving up – being relinquished – is not predicated of the subject in (31); it applies only to what is given up, the unspecified object. Hence the adjectival passive of *given up* has only the passive reading (32b), not the perfect intransitive reading (32a):

(32) a. *given up students
      b. given up hopes for success

The semantic concept of result state thus suffices to explain some of the restrictions on adjectival passives that have been observed. But it is not a necessary condition: Ackerman and Goldberg (1996) show that there is a general pragmatic condition of informativeness at work as well. The following examples (from Adele Goldberg, personal communication) are adjectival passives based on atelic verbs, both activities (33) and states (34):

(33) long anticipated event
      much hoped for consequences
      much talked about idea
      strongly backed candidate

(34) much-loved doctor
      much-feared consequence
      communally owned property
      despised politician
      highly acclaimed actor
      well-known performer

Most of these examples require adverbial modification to be felicitous (cf. *??a talked about idea, ??a backed candidate, ??owned property*). The adverbial modification increases the informativeness of the attribute, and thus its acceptability. Pragmatic informativeness and the semantic result state condition are members of what may be a family of sufficient (but not necessary) conditions on the use of adjectives.

In sum, both present and past participles in English undergo conversion to adjectives. The past participles may be active or passive, "unaccusative" or "unergative," so long as they satisfy the complement restrictions on adjectives and the semantic/pragmatic conditions on adjectival states. There is no morphological rule of "adjectival passive" alongside a syntactic passive. There is only the verbal passive, a lexical relation change which may undergo the general lexical morphologial process of participle–adjective conversion. Participle–adjective conversion simply preserves the subject of predication of its verbal base.

Further Reading and Discussion

The same argument that Bresnan (1978) made from English evidence is made from Bantu evidence by Mchombo (1978) and Alsina (1990, 1999): passivization is a lexical relation change, not a syntactic transformation, and as such, it can feed lexical processes of derivational morphology – in this case, deverbal nom-inalizations. See also Alsina and Mchombo (1990), Alsina (1992), Bresnan and Mchombo (1995), and Mugane (1996).

If the general analysis given above is correct, then we can tell what must be involved in the relation change of passivization. It cannot involve the syntactic movement of an NP from an underlying transitive tree structure (3), where it receives an "internal" theta role, to an external position as subject, as assumed by B. Levin and Rappaport (1986). Because the adjectival passive is a lexical formation of derivational morphology, and not a transformational derivative of syntax, its internal role cannot be "externalized" by such a movement. B. Levin and Rappaport (1986: 654) propose that adjective conversion itself externalizes an internal role of the base verb. But this lexical process of adjectival externaliza-tion (or relation change) simply duplicates the effect of the syntactic externaliza-tion with passive verbs – precisely the analysis of adjectival passives that were originally shown to lose generalizations (Bresnan 1982a). To solve this problem, B. Levin and Rappaport (1986) propose that the externalization of the internal role required by adjectival passives can be derived from a single general fact about adjectives: that all adjectives must assign an external role. This is independently motivated by examples like (23) *untaken advantage.*

Now if all that is required is that an Adjective assign an external theta role, then the "unergative" verbal argument structures that deverbal adjectives may inherit should be fine (as in (29)). These verbal argument structures have an external role as their only role. But what then happens when an "unaccusative" or passive verbal argument structure is inherited by a deverbal adjective? By B. Levin and Rappaport's (1986) framework of assumptions, these verbs have only an internal role and no external role to assign. By hypothesis, these verbs pro-ject direct object NPs (or DPs) at a level of underlying syntactic structure prior to movement. If their internal arguments remain unexternalized inside the adjective, then the result will be ruled out by the general syntactic princples assumed by Levin and Rappaport (the theta-criterion, Projection Principle, Case theory). So if all that were required were that adjectives assign an external theta role, we might well expect that adjective conversion could apply *only* to unergative per-fect participles of verbs, and that adjectives based on passives and unaccusatives would be ungrammatical, contrary to fact.[13]

To solve this problem, we could propose that it is a general property of adject-ives not just that they assign an external role, but that they externalize an internal role – that is, that they are all unaccusative. This is obviously false for converted present participles. (The language of invective is rich with them: *a lying, cheating, thieving coward.*) But even if we restricted the externalization proposal to just the past participles (the passives and perfects), we still could not explain the unergative examples in (29).

Thus, the idea that argument structure projects or can be identified with an initial level of syntactic tree structure, to which argument-moving transformations apply, inevitably leads to losses of generalization. At that level, the subjects of unergatives and the underlying objects of passives and unaccusatives have nothing in common. Thus it is not the process of adjective conversion, but the base passive or unaccusative verb itself that must "externalize" its argument role, allowing it to be associated with the subject of predication. But this means that the relation change involved in passivization must itself be lexically available to processes of derivational morphology. It cannot be the result of syntactic movements on underlying tree structures.

Notes

1   In early LFG (Bresnan 1982c), passivization is regarded as a lexical redundancy rule; more currently, the theory of LMT (chapter 14) provides general principles from which these alternations follow. See Bresnan (1990) for arguments against the lexical rule approach.

2   The analysis of Malayalam presented here is based on K. P. Mohanan (1982a).

3   On the functional specifications of *be* relevant to this example, see chapter 6.

4   The following analysis is based on Bresnan (1982a) and B. Levin and Rappaport (1986). See these works and Ackerman and Goldberg (1996) for fuller references.

5   This assumption is a weak version of the lexicalist hypothesis, which is discussed further in chapter 6.

6   Maling (1983) gives a very useful critical discussion of the criteria for syntactically categorizing adjectives. She shows that some ostensibly syntactic criteria depend on semantics or syntactic functions, and that "transitive" adjectives having direct NP complements are extremely rare in modern English, but do occur as a vestige of historical changes.

7   A few adjectives like *drunken* reflect conversions of older participial forms not in current use.

8   The notation "*(...)" indicates that the parenthesized material cannot be omitted, while "(* ...)" means that the parenthesized material cannot be present.

9   Their formulation is "An argument that may stand as a sole NP complement to a verb can be externalized by APF [Adjectival Passive Formation]."

10   Again recall the interpretation of the parenthesis notation given in n. 8: "??(...)" means that the parenthesized material is ill-formed or very questionable when omitted.

11   Intransitive verbs are often classified into "unaccusative" or "unergative" depending on whether their subjects share properties of transitive objects or transitive subjects. In B. Levin and Rappaport's (1986) terms, "unaccusative" verbs have only an internal theta role to assign, while "unergative" verbs have only an external theta role to assign. The latter can be distinguished by their ability to occur in *the way* construction (e.g. *Fred danced his way into the kitchen*). See Bresnan and Zaenen (1990) and chapter 14 for analysis of this classification in LFG.

12   Caroline Heycock (personal communication) has suggested that *an unbuilt architect* might be used analogously to *an unplayed composer*, where the person is substituted metonymously for the works of the person. Certainly, *They never play that composer any more* involves this transfer, but the parallel *?They never built that architect* sounds somewhat odd. *That architect has never built (anything)* is easily interpreted as meaning that he has never had his designs built; this would be the hypothesized source of the perfect intransitive.

13 B. Levin and Rappaport (1986) actually rule out the possibility of grammatical examples like (29) by analyzing the adjectival perfect participles as being derived by the *passive* morpheme, which must suppress an external argument.

Part II Formally Modelling the Architecture

Introduction

Part I provided empirical motivation for the relational architecture of universal grammar incorporated in the design of LFG. This design hypothesizes formally distinct types of parallel structures flexibly related by correspondence mappings. In part II these intuitive ideas are made precise through the presentation of a mathematical model of the LFG architecture (Dalrymple et al. 1995).

All formal models require a certain simplicity to be both mathematically expressible and understandable, and for this reason they are inevitably crude and oversimplified ("idealized" is the term of choice) compared to the empirical reality they model. Nevertheless, a formal model offers to both the descriptive and the theoretical linguist the advantages of amplifying, extending, and clarifying the analytic imagination. The radically different formal architecture of LFG provides a true alternative perspective on syntactic theory and the nature of universal grammar.

Note, however, that the formal model of LFG is *not* a syntactic theory in the linguistic sense. Rather, it is an architecture for syntactic theory. Within this architecture, there is a wide range of possible syntactic theories and sub-theories, some of which closely resemble syntactic theories within alternative architectures, and others of which differ radically from familiar approaches. Specific (sub)theories to be discussed in subsequent chapters include extended X′ theory, the lexical mapping theory, pronominal binding and control theories, and a theory of agreement.

The reader who is not interested in the formal system may wish to skip over part II, but the theorist who wishes to gain a deeper understanding of the LFG architecture, and of the kinds of relations, analyses, and information flow expressible within it, is encouraged to study chapter 4 at least through section 4.7. (Sections 4.8 and 4.9 can be returned to when required, as the formal background for chapter 9.) At the end of this and other parts of this volume, the reader is directed to solve specific problem sets. These all presuppose knowledge of the formal model and the syntactic calculus.

4 A Formal Model of Syntactic Structure

In this chapter the original c-structure to f-structure correspondence of LFG is defined. Argument structure, which was subsequently integrated into the mathematical model, is reserved until chapter 14.

4.1 Design Principles

The formal model of LFG embodies three general design principles: variability, universality, and monotonicity.

4.1.1 Principle I: variability

The modes of expression of a language have a structure which we have called the "expression structure" or external structure. This is the structure that is organized for expression, its form determined by generalizations about the order, pronunciation, and form of words and their grouping into phrases of the language. The principle of variability states that external structures vary across languages. The formal model of external structure in LFG is the c-structure, "constituent structure" or "categorial structure." Sentences and phrases have constituent parts that can be ordered by precedence, dominance, and structural type; that is, they have c-structures. Fully inflected words are the terminal elements of the c-structures of sentences, and every word belongs to exactly one node (i.e., there is an injection from words to c-structure nodes). This restricted relation between c-structure and word structure, often referred to as lexical integrity, in fact gives rise to much of the variability of c-structures across languages, as we will see in part III.

A commonly used representation of c-structure is the context-free phrase structure tree, defined by context-free phrase structure rules augmented by regular expressions.[1] Examples are S → NP VP (for English) or S → C Aux C* (for Warlpiri), where "C" stands for any constituent type. This representation is mathematically and computationally well understood, and for these reasons has been incorporated within the simple formal model. More sophisticated and principled theories of c-structure based on extended X' theory, with its projections of both lexical (XP) and functional (FP) categories, have been adopted elsewhere in LFG (part III). From a formal point of view, however, these serve merely to restrict the class of possible c-structures. Hence nothing is lost for present purposes in presenting the formally simplest model.

4.1.2 Principle II: universality

The internal structure of a language is where the grammatical relations are represented, how syntactic functions are associated with semantic predicate argument relations. Syntactic functions are equivalence classes of forms of expression that behave alike under the mappings to argument structure. The internal structure is reflected in phenomena such as case government, pronominal binding, and agreement relations among the predicators and arguments of a sentence. The principle of universality states that **internal structures are largely invariant across languages**. The formal model of internal structure in LFG is the **f-structure**, "functional structure." The concepts of "subject" (SUBJ), "object" (OBJ), "predicator" (PRED), etc., appear at this level, because unlike NP, VP, V, etc., they abstract away from expression in terms of external order and category by taking as equivalent all those expressions that behave alike under the mappings to argument structure.

Note. In addition to the c-structure and f-structure, LFG postulates an a-structure, as discussed in previous chapters and in part IV below, and other dimensions of grammatical structure such as p-structure (prosodic structure)[2] and σ-structure (semantic structure).[3]

The external structure and the internal structure are different but parallel syntactic structures. It has been observed empirically that the units postulated for each structure do not in general converge. There are mismatches in category and configuration as discussed in previous chapters and the references cited there. For this reason we do not label these units within a common vocabulary such as NP, VP, V, etc. In LFG the internal structures are formalized as f-structures, which express universal grammatical relations in a theoretical vocabulary disjoint from that of external structures. The f-structure features of CASE, PERS, NUM, and the like are also disjoint from the expressions that mark these features (which are often morphological but may be syntactic, as in case clitics or number particles). Thus [CASE ACC] is an abstract feature quite distinct from an accusative case marker, and there need not be a one-to-one correspondence between the two, as discussed in Wierzbicka (1981).

4.1.3 Principle III: monotonicity

There is a very appealing idea that the internal structures of language should somehow be "transparent" in the external structures of language. This idea has been motivated by the *a priori* problem of language acquisition: how could children acquire human languages otherwise?

The most obvious conception of transparency is the idea that the internal and external structures must have the same form, which is embraced by the configurational design of universal grammar. Of course, this condition is not *necessary* to solve the problem of language acquisition, for any sufficiently predictable relation between the internal and external structures could provide just as plausible (or implausible) a solution. But it is this condition that has led (in the configurational design of universal grammar) to the attenuation of the classical properties of constituency (order, substitutability, relation to pronunciation) and to the concomitant adoption of increasingly abstract surface structures, which serve as a disambiguated representation of the meaningful internal grammatical relations. The semantically relevant information contained in the representations of internal structures is projected into the structural form of the representations of external structures.

The problem is that given principle II, this conception of transparency implies that the form of external structures is universal across languages, contradicting principle I. Constituent structure form is simply not the same in all languages; some make breathtakingly little use of it, compared to English. In LFG the correspondence mapping between internal and external structures does not preserve sameness of form. Instead it is designed to preserve inclusion relations between the information expressed by the external structure and the content of the internal structure. In a sense to be made precise in chapter 5, it has the mathematical property of **monotonicity**. As we will see, partial information about the abstract internal structure is locally distributed across the expression structure in such a way that the global internal structure can be inferred from the parts of the expression in any order. This property relies on the fact that the correspondence between c-structures and f-structures in LFG is a piecewise, monotonic function. This property is very simple to understand once the basic concept of f-structures and their formal relation to c-structures are developed.

4.2   The Definition of F-Structures

An example f-structure is given in (1). For the moment, we omit the internal structure of the PREDS:

(1)   *F-structure of* 'Lions live in the forest'

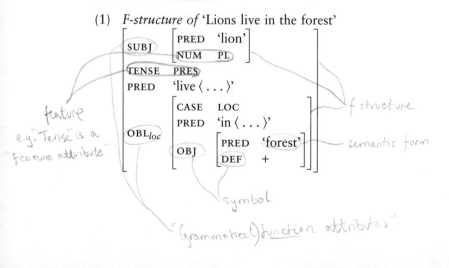

Mathematically, an f-structure is a finite set of pairs of attributes and values:

(2) $$\begin{bmatrix} attribute_1 & value_1 \\ attribute_2 & value_2 \\ \vdots & \vdots \\ attribute_n & value_n \end{bmatrix}$$ "attribute-value pairs"

Hence, the order of f-structure elements is not important, and the axioms of set identity apply. The elements are defined as follows:

- An attribute can be
  - a symbol, e.g. SUBJ, TENSE, NUM, PRED.
- A value can be
  - a symbol (e.g. PL), or
  - a semantic form (a complex symbol in single quotes – e.g. 'lion'), or
  - an f-structure (e.g. the value for SUBJ in (1)).

Note that symbols are simply strings of alphanumeric characters unbroken by spaces. The formal architecture allows for complete freedom of choice of symbols: instead of SUBJ and OBJ, for example, one might prefer SPEC and COMPL, or A, S, and O (for transitive subject, intransitive subject, and object, respectively). The choice of symbols and their relations is a substantive issue belonging not to the formal grammars, but to a particular linguistic theory of these grammars.

Linguistic terminology: A symbol-valued attribute–value pair is called a **feature**. An f-structure-valued attribute–value pair is called a **(grammatical) function**. In (1) we see that NUM, DEF, CASE, and TENSE are feature attributes, while SUBJ, OBJ, and OBL$_{loc}$ are (grammatical) function attributes. We can refer to an attribute whose value is a semantic form as a **semantic feature**.

Semantic features have a special property distinguishing them from other features: each instantiation or token of a semantic feature has a unique value. For example, two occurrences of the word *lions* in the same sentence will have different values of the PRED feature, call them 'lion$_i$' and 'lion$_j$'. (Ordinarily we suppress the unique indices of semantic forms in our illustrations.)

Thus, f-structures contain (grammatical) functions, and that suggests a reason for the name 'functional' structure. But there is another source for the name: an f-structure is a function in the mathematical sense. This follows from the uniqueness condition on f-structures:

(3) **Uniqueness Condition:**
    Every attribute has a unique value.

Note that different attributes may have the same value. Lines connecting two different attributes to the same value are often used to represent this identity graphically, as in diagram (17) in chapter 2. What the uniqueness condition rules out is a single attribute having nonidentical values:

(4)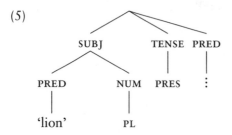

Because an f-structure is a <u>finite function</u>, we can enumerate its arguments and values in tabular form. The boxed graph representation we employ for f-structures reflects this table format. One might prefer a tree representation of f-structures, taking the values as daughters of the attributes:

(5)

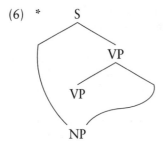

But trees have certain formal properties different from f-structures. For example, their branches are not supposed to join together. Every daughter node in a tree has a unique mother node:

(6) *   S

But trees have certain formal properties different from f-structures. For example, their branches are not supposed to join together. Every daughter node in a tree has a unique mother node:

In f-structures the same value may be shared by different attributes, a relation for which trees are not the natural representation.[4]

4.3   The Description of F-Structures

Viewing our example f-structure (1) as a function, we can fully describe it by specifying the value it associates with each argument (attribute):

(7) f_1 (SUBJ) $= f_2$ (function f_1, applied to SUBJ argument, has value f_2)
     f_1 (TENSE) = PRES
     f_1 (PRED) = 'live < . . . >'

f_1 (OBL$_{loc}$) = f_3
f_2 (NUM)   = PL
etc.

The notation for function application in LFG differs slightly from this, however. For standard mathematical $f(a) = v$, we write instead $(fa) = v$, moving the left parenthesis outside of the function:

(8) $(f_1$ SUBJ) = f_2
     $(f_1$ TENSE) = PRES
     $(f_1$ PRED) = 'live < . . . >'
     $(f_1$ OBL$_{loc}$) = f_3
     $(f_2$ NUM)   = PL
     etc.

Thus $(f_1$ SUBJ) = f_2 simply means that the function f_1, applied to the SUBJ argument, has the value f_2.[5]

In general, **for any f-structure f, (fa) = v if and only if the attribute–value pair <a v> is a member of f.** Since an f-structure is a finite set of attribute–value pairs, any f-structure can be completely described by a finite set of functional equations of this form, which is called a **functional description**. It is straightforward to reconstruct a functional structure from its functional description by forming the minimal set of attribute–value pairs that satisfy the functional description.

The language of functional descriptions is based on this underlying mathematical conception of f-structures as functions. For example, since the value of an attribute for a given function f_1 can be another function f_2, we can write (9b) for (9a):

(9) a. $(f_1$ SUBJ)   = f_2
         $(f_2$ NUM)   = PL
     b. $((f_1$ SUBJ) NUM) = PL   or $(f, SUBJ\ NUM) = PL$

For a chain of such function applications $(((f_1\ a_1)\ a_2)\ a_3) = v$, we write $(f_1\ a_1\ a_2\ a_3) = v$, omitting the parentheses.

Since in any functional equation $(f\ a) = v$, f must be a function, a a symbol, and v a symbol, semantic form, or f-structure, we can use function-valued descriptions in place of f, symbol-valued descriptions in place of a, and symbol-, semantic-form-, or f-structure-valued descriptions in place of v. Thus the following functional equations are all meaningful, and describe the f-structures given in (11a–c), respectively:[6]

(10) a. $(f_1$ SUBJ NUM) = SG
      b. $(f_1$ SUBJ)   = $(f_1$ XCOMP SUBJ)
      c. $(f_2$ (f_5 CASE)) = f_5, $(f_5$ CASE) = OBL$_{go}$

$(f\ a) = v$

f : function
a : symbol
v : symbol, semantic form, function

a. $(f_1\ SUBJ) = f_2$
$(f_2\ NUM) = SING$
etc

or $SUBJ\ [NUM\ SING]$

(11) a. $f_1:\begin{bmatrix} \text{SUBJ} & f_2:[\text{NUM} & \text{SG}] \end{bmatrix}$

   b. $f_1:\begin{bmatrix} \text{SUBJ} & f_2:[\text{NUM} & \text{SG}] \\ \text{XCOMP} & f_3:[\text{SUBJ} & [\ ]] \end{bmatrix}$

   c. $f_2:\begin{bmatrix} \text{OBL}_{go} & f_5:[\text{CASE} & \text{OBL}_{go}] \end{bmatrix}$

4.4 The Correspondence Between C- and F-Structures

The correspondence between a c-structure and f-structure for the sentence *Lions live in the forest* is illustrated in (12):

(12)

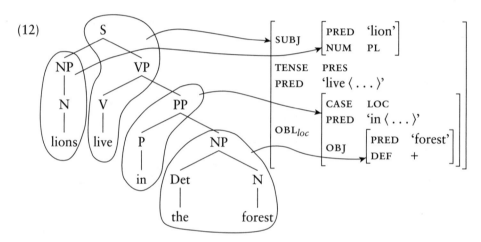

Observe that the correspondence between the nodes of the c-structure and the f-structure is many-to-one. Different c-structure nodes – for example, S, VP, and V – may correspond to the same f-structure. Observe also that the mapping is a piecewise correspondence, in that each node of the c-structure is mapped into an f-structure or subsidiary f-structure.

The mapping shown in (12) is definable by **local codescription of partial structures.** In other words, a description of each piece of the c-structure can be directly associated with a description of part of the f-structure, and conversely. Consider the top piece of the c-structure in (12), and the portions of f-structure corresponding to it, shown in (13):

(13)

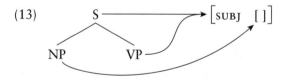

$\begin{bmatrix} \text{SUBJ} & [\ ] \end{bmatrix}$

Let us replace the mapping arrows connecting pieces of the two structures by indices:

(14)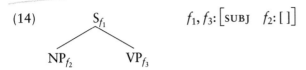

The local mother–daughter and sister relations of this partial tree structure can be described in familiar context-free phrase structure rule notation, which can be interpreted as tree admissibility conditions. Assuming that each node of that piece of c-structure corresponds to some initially undetermined f-structure, as in (15) –

$$(15) \quad S \ \rightarrow \ NP \quad VP$$
$$f_1 \qquad f_2 \quad f_3$$

– we can describe the effect of the mapping in (14) by means of the functional equations in (16):

$$(16) \quad S \ \rightarrow \qquad NP \qquad VP$$
$$f_1 \qquad\qquad f_2 \qquad\qquad f_3$$
$$(f_1 \ \text{SUBJ}) = f_2 \quad f_1 = f_3$$

(16) is a **codescription** of the partial c-structure and partial f-structure shown in (14).

Or consider the correspondence between the parts of the initial NP in (14):

$$(17) \quad NP \longrightarrow [\,]$$
$$| \qquad$$
$$N \qquad$$

Replacing the arrow with the indexed representation, we have (18):

$$(18) \quad NP_{f_2} \qquad f_2, f_4: [\,]$$
$$N_{f_4}$$

Again we can describe the relation of the partial f-structure to the partial c-structure by assuming the node-to-f-structure correspondences shown in (19) –

$$(19) \quad NP \ \rightarrow \ N$$
$$f_2 \qquad f_4$$

– and then specifying the f-structure by means of the functional equation in (20):

(20) NP → N
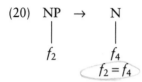

Again, what we have in (20) is a codescription of two partial structures.

Or again consider the top piece of the VP in the c-structure (12), which corresponds to the partial f-structure shown in (21):

(21)

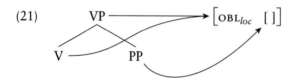

The indexed representation is (22):

(22) VP_{f_3} $f_3, f_5: \left[OBL_{loc} \quad f_6: [\ ] \right]$

V_{f_5} PP_{f_6}

Once again assuming the correspondence between the partial c-structure and the initially undetermined f-structures given in (23) –

(23) VP → V PP
      | | |
      f_3 f_5 f_6

– we can describe the mapping to the partial f-structure by means of the functional equations in (24):

(24) VP →   V   PP
      | | |
      f_3 f_5 f_6
             $f_3 = f_5$ $(f_3\ OBL_{loc}) = f_6$

Note on linguistic terminology. In each of the examples just given, two c-structure nodes, one of which dominates the other, are mapped into the same f-structure: this is true of V and VP in (21), N and NP in (17), and VP and S in (13). In this situation we speak of the dominated node as the **functional (f-structure) head** of the dominating node. The f-structure head is a category whose f-structure will be identified (and hence unified – see below) with that of its mother category. Functional heads are not always the same as structural heads: for example, two sister categories may be f-structure coheads, while only one of them is a c-structure head, as discussed in chapter 6 below.

Notice that phrase structure rules abstract away from the nodes of particular phrase structure trees to give general patterns for describing *any* tree. Thus, the rule S → NP VP refers to *any* node that is labelled S and asserts that such a node may dominate nodes labelled NP and VP, the former preceding the latter. But our functional descriptions so far are relative to particular f-structures. Thus, the f-structure names f_1, f_2, etc., that we used in our examples of codescriptions refer to particular f-structures associated with the nodes of a particular phrase structure tree. In order to use our codescriptions as general mapping rules for the language, however, we need to be able to refer to "whatever f-structure corresponds to this node" ('this node' being any node labelled by one of the symbols on the right-hand side of the c-structure rule) and "whatever f-structure corresponds to the mother of this node" ('the mother' being any node described by the left-hand side of the c-structure rule). The symbols ↓ and ↑ are used for just this purpose. So for the three examples of codescription given above, we can now write (25)–(27)[7,8] (Det is the category of "determiners" – definite and indefinite articles and demonstratives):

(25)

$$
\begin{array}{ccc}
 & \text{S} & \\
(\uparrow \text{SUBJ}) = \downarrow & & \uparrow = \downarrow \\
\text{NP} & & \text{VP}
\end{array}
$$

(26)

$$
\begin{array}{ccc}
 & \text{NP} & \\
\left(\begin{array}{c} \uparrow = \downarrow \\ \text{Det} \end{array} \right) & & \begin{array}{c} \uparrow = \downarrow \\ \text{N} \end{array}
\end{array}
$$

(27)

$$
\begin{array}{ccc}
 & \text{VP} & \\
\begin{array}{c} \uparrow = \downarrow \\ \text{V} \end{array} & & \left(\begin{array}{c} (\uparrow \text{OBL}_{loc}) = \downarrow \\ \text{PP} \end{array} \right)
\end{array}
$$
brackets indicate optionality

Representing the rules of codescription two-dimensionally, as in (25)–(27), gives an intuitive picture of their meaning, with the arrows positioned so as to point to the functionally related nodes. However, the constraints of typography have led to linear representations of the c-structure rules, with the functional schemata placed below the category symbols as in (28)–(30):

(28) S → NP VP
　　　　　　　($\uparrow$ SUBJ) = ↓ ↑ = ↓

(29) NP → $\begin{pmatrix} \text{Det} \\ \uparrow = \downarrow \end{pmatrix}$ $\begin{matrix} \text{N} \\ \uparrow = \downarrow \end{matrix}$

(30) VP → $\begin{matrix} \text{V} \\ \uparrow = \downarrow \end{matrix}$ $\left(\begin{matrix} \text{PP} \\ (\uparrow \text{OBL}_{loc}) = \downarrow \end{matrix} \right)$

Nevertheless, the meaning of these two types of representations is the same: they codescribe a partial c-structure and a partial f-structure. They are properly viewed as local constraints which hold in parallel of pairs of c- and f-structures. Functional equations written with $\uparrow$ and $\downarrow$ are called "functional schemata."

Recall now that fully inflected words are the leaves of the c-structure tree, in accordance with the integrity of the structural formation of words. However, words may carry the same types of functional information as phrases. A simple illustration of the fact that the words that constitute the leaves of c-structure trees carry functional descriptions of the same type as phrases is given in (31). Here the noun *lion* and its plural inflection *-s* each carry functional schemata as part of their lexical entries:[9]

(31) *lion* $(\uparrow \text{PRED}) = \text{'lion'}$
       -s $(\uparrow \text{NUM}) = \text{PL}$

The rules of English inflectional morphology combine this information when the inflected noun *lions* is formed. When the inflected noun is inserted in the c-structure, it gives rise to the correspondence shown in (32):[10]

(32) N $\longrightarrow$ $\begin{bmatrix} \text{NUM} & \text{PL} \\ \text{PRED} & \text{'lion}_4\text{'} \end{bmatrix}$
       |
      lions

We can see how this correspondence arises by means of the following indexed representation[11] –

(33) N_{f_4} *cf. earlier examples*
             |
            lions
         $(f_4 \text{ NUM}) = \text{PL}$
         $(f_4 \text{ PRED}) = \text{'lion}_4\text{'}$

– which describes the structural relations in (34):

(34) N_{f_4} $f_4\text{:}\begin{bmatrix} \text{NUM} & \text{PL} \\ \text{PRED} & \text{'lion}_4\text{'} \end{bmatrix}$
       |
      lions

Similarly, the verb *live* and its inflection *-s* both carry functional schemata in their lexical entries, as shown in (35). Note that the third personal singular morpheme *-s* is analyzed here as having an f-structure which is identified with the SUBJ value of the f-structure of its mother, the preterminal category V. The three equations given are equivalent to the pair of equations ($\uparrow$ SUBJ PERS) = 3 and ($\uparrow$ SUBJ NUM) = SG:

(35) *live* ($\uparrow$ PRED) = 'live $\langle \ldots \rangle$'
　　　-s　 ($\uparrow$ TENSE) = PRES
　　　　　 ($\uparrow$ SUBJ) = $\downarrow$
　　　　　　($\downarrow$ PERS) = 3
　　　　　　($\downarrow$ NUM) = SG

The rules of English inflectional morphology combine this information when the inflected verb is formed. When the inflected verb is inserted into the c-structure, these schemata generate a functional description as illustrated in (36):

(36)　　　　　　　 V_{f_5}
　　　　　　　　　 |

　　　　　　　 live s_{f_7}
　　　　 (f_5 PRED) = 'live $\langle \ldots \rangle_5$'
　　　　　(f_5 TENSE) = PRES
　　　　　　(f_5 SUBJ) = f_7
　　　　　　(f_7 PERS) = 3
　　　　　　(f_7 NUM) = SG

This functional description defines the structural relations shown in (37):

(37)　　 V_{f_5}　　　 f_5: $\begin{bmatrix} \text{SUBJ} & f_7: \begin{bmatrix} \text{NUM} & \text{SG} \\ \text{PERS} & 3 \end{bmatrix} \\ \text{TENSE} & \text{PRES} \\ \text{PRED} & \text{'live} \langle \ldots \rangle_5 \text{'} \end{bmatrix}$
　　　　　 |
　　　　 live s_{f_7}

And (37) is graphically represented as in (38):

(38)　　 V
　　　　 |
　　　 live (-s)

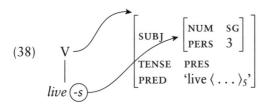

$\begin{bmatrix} \text{SUBJ} & \begin{bmatrix} \text{NUM} & \text{SG} \\ \text{PERS} & 3 \end{bmatrix} \\ \text{TENSE} & \text{PRES} \\ \text{PRED} & \text{'live} \langle \ldots \rangle_5 \text{'} \end{bmatrix}$

Observe that the graphic mapping arrows which link c-structures to f-structures depart from each c-structure element which bears a $\downarrow$ and arrive at the f-structure specified by that ↓. Thus there is no arrow pointing to the TENSE feature or value in (38), because, referring to (35), we see that the down arrows associated with the tense inflection designate the value of the SUBJ attribute alone.

We have now seen that the mapping between c-structures and f-structures is defined codescriptively by the grammar of the language. The grammar does not prescribe a particular computational process for deriving f-structures from c-structures (or the reverse). However, there is an algorithm for deriving an f-structure from a c-structure, given a set of c-structure rules and words, both annotated with functional schemata: the "solution algorithm."

4.5   The Solution Algorithm

Given a lexical-functional grammar and lexicon for a language ʟ, there is an algorithm for deriving the c-structure and f-structure of any sentence of ʟ.[12] The mapping of a string of words into a c-structure can be done via any of a class of familiar context-free phrase structure parsing algorithms.[13] (Ambiguous sentences may have multiple c- and f-structures.) We will therefore focus here on the derivation of the f-structure from a c-structure.

Let us take as our example the ill-formed sentence *Lions lives*, whose c-structure is given in (39):

(39)

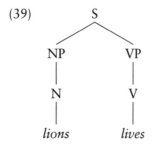

We assume as given the fragment of English grammar and lexicon shown in (40)–(44):

(40)   S   →   NP   VP
                ($\uparrow$ SUBJ) = ↓ $\uparrow$ = ↓

(41)   NP   → $\left(\begin{array}{c} \text{Det} \\ \uparrow = \downarrow \end{array} \right)$ $\begin{array}{c} \text{N} \\ \uparrow = \downarrow \end{array}$

(42)   VP   → $\begin{array}{c} \text{V} \\ \uparrow = \downarrow \end{array}$ $\left(\begin{array}{c} \text{PP} \\ (\uparrow \text{OBL}_{loc}) = \downarrow \end{array} \right)$

(43)   *lion*: N   (↑ PRED) = 'lion'
    -s: $infl_N$ (↑ NUM) = PL

(44)   *live*: V   (↑ PRED) = 'live ⟨ ... ⟩'
    -s: $infl_V$ (↑ TENSE) = PRES
            (↑ SUBJ) = ↓
              (↓ PERS) = 3
              (↓ NUM) = SG

Note that in (44) the indentation of the equations representing information carried by the verbal inflection has no formal significance; it is merely typographically set off to group related information visually. The use of the ↓ arrow here is formally well defined: the word itself (specifically the inflectional part of it) is mapped to an f-structure distinct from that of the mother node.

The method of solution proceeds in three steps: first, we **annotate** the c-structure METHOD tree with the appropriate functional schemata; second, we **instantiate** the schemata to generate a functional description; and third, we **solve** the simultaneous equations of the functional description by constructing the minimal f-structure that satisfies them.

Step 1 is illustrated by (45), an annotated c-structure tree for **Lions lives*:

(45)

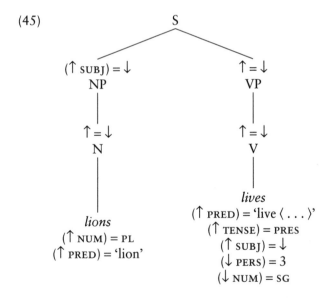

Note that both the lexical annotations and the c-structure rule annotations are added.

Step 2, instantiation, proceeds by first assigning a distinct index to the root node of the tree and to each node that bears an annotation containing ↓. Each index represents the unknown f-structure that corresponds to that c-structure node:

(46)

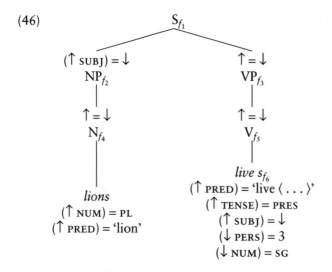

The second part of instantiation is to uniformly substitute the index of each node for every ↑ in the schemata of its daughter nodes and for every ↓ in the schemata of that node itself, as illustrated in (47):

(47)

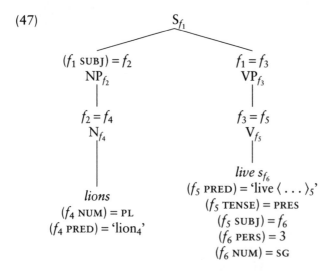

(Note that a unique index is provided to each semantic feature value whenever it is instantiated.) These instantiated functional equations are conjoined together into the functional description. Step 2 thus generates a functional description for the sentence.

Step 3 is to construct the minimal f-structure that satisfies the functional description generated by step 2. This is a straightforward process of hypothesizing an f-structure that makes each equation in the conjunction of all equations true, preserving functional uniqueness. It can be done in any order whatsoever, but for convenience we will proceed from the top of the tree down, and from left to right. From the NP node in (47), we know that $(f_1 \text{ SUBJ}) = f_2$; that is, f_1 has a SUBJ attribute whose value is f_2. Hence we construct the f-structure (48), and discard the equation we used to make it:

(48) f_1: [SUBJ f_2]

From the VP node in (47), we know that $f_1 = f_3$; that is, that f_1 is the same f-structure as f_3. We therefore add this information to (48), and discard the equation:

(49) f_1, f_3: [SUBJ f_2]

From the N node we next learn that $f_2 = f_4$; that is, that f_2 is one and the same as f_4, so we add this information, discarding the equation:

(50) f_1, f_3: [SUBJ f_2, f_4]

From the V node we have $f_3 = f_5$, so we add that information, following the same process:

(51) f_1, f_3, f_5: [SUBJ f_2, f_4]

Now from the leaves of the tree we gather much more information. From *lions* we have $(f_4 \text{ NUM}) = \text{PL}$ and $(f_4 \text{ PRED}) = \text{‘lion}_4\text{’}$, so we now know that f_4 is an f-structure with two attribute–value pairs, and we add this information as shown in (52), and discard the equations:

(52) f_1, f_3, f_5: $\left[\text{SUBJ} \quad f_2, f_4: \begin{bmatrix} \text{NUM} & \text{PL} \\ \text{PRED} & \text{‘lion}_4\text{’} \end{bmatrix} \right]$

Likewise, from *lives* we have $(f_5 \text{ PRED}) = \text{‘live} \langle \ldots \rangle_5\text{’}$, $(f_5 \text{ TENSE}) = \text{PRES}$, $(f_5 \text{ SUBJ}) = f_6$, $(f_6 \text{ PERS}) = 3$, and $(f_6 \text{ NUM}) = \text{SG}$. Adding the information from the first four equations, we have (53):

(53) f_1, f_3, f_5: $\begin{bmatrix} \text{SUBJ} & f_2, f_4, f_6: \begin{bmatrix} \text{PERS} & 3 \\ \text{NUM} & \text{PL} \\ \text{PRED} & \text{‘lion}_4\text{’} \end{bmatrix} \\ \text{TENSE} & \text{PRES} \\ \text{PRED} & \text{‘live} \langle \ldots \rangle_5\text{’} \end{bmatrix}$

But the last equation $(f_6 \text{ NUM}) = \text{SG}$ is inconsistent with what we already know about f_6 – namely, that it has a NUM attribute whose value is PL. Because every attribute must have a unique value, there is no f-structure solution to the functional description of (47). The sentence is ungrammatical. If instead we replaced *lives* with the present non-third person singular form *live*, the inconsistency would disappear, because the latter inflected form would carry the information that f_6 does not have the features of third person singular. (Negation and other boolean operations on functional schemata are taken up in the next section.)

Note that if there is one f-structure that satisfies an f-description, there are arbitrarily many other f-structures that satisfy the same description; such f-structures have additional attribute–value pairs that are not mentioned in the f-description, though they have in common all the pairs that do satisfy the f-description. Therefore, to determine a unique solution to a consistent f-description, we must take the minimal f-structure that satisfies the description, eliminating superfluous attribute–value pairs. It is important to observe that in Step 3 we have constructed the **minimal** f-structure that satisfies the f-description generated by Step 2.

Problems

The reader can now undertake problem set 1, which illustrates several linguistically interesting properties of the formal system as developed so far.

4.6   Defining versus Constraining Equations

The construction of an f-structure that satisfies a functional description has a 'make it so' character: whatever f-structure elements are identified by an equation are made to exist in the f-structure model. The equations of the functional description define the model, and so are called **defining equations**. However, it is often useful to identify some value of an attribute, without thereby making it exist.

Consider two types of verbal agreement morphology: one type requires the presence of a subject NP constituent having the specified agreement features; the other type is compatible with the presence or absence of a subject NP (as in "pro-drop" languages, chapter 8). In the pro-drop type, verbal agreement morphology may specify the properties of the subject by defining equations. The inflected verb itself thus creates the f-structure attribute–value pairs of the SUBJ, and any subject constituent NP that may be present must of course have consistent features, but need not be present to provide them. In the other type, verbal agreement morphology is not sufficient to definite the attributes of the subject; a subject NP constituent is necessary. For such purposes we might use **constraining equations** based on the constrained equality relation $=_c$. With the "pro-drop" morphology, $(\uparrow$ SUBJ NUM$) =$ SG defines the number assigned by a verb. With the non-pro-drop agreement morphology the constraint equation $(\uparrow$ SUBJ NUM$) =_c$ SG would require that there be a [NUM SG] feature in the f-structure; it does not create such a feature. Its effect is to require the presence of a subject constituent to provide the number feature.[14]

Constraining equations are interpreted as follows. When constraining equations are conjoined with defining equations, the solution algorithm simply sets aside all constraining equations until the minimal f-structure satisfying all of the defining equations has been constructed; at that point, the constraining equations are tested for truth. Thus defining equations apply before minimization, and constraining equations after minimization.

It is clear that the logic of functional descriptions can be extended to boolean combinations of equations involving disjunctions ($\vee$): the **disjunction** of two f-descriptions defines a set of alternative f-structures. Likewise, optionality parentheses around an equation define two alternative f-structures, one formed with the equation and the other formed without it. The solution algorithm applies to functional descriptions containing disjunctions in the following way. When a functional schema F consists of a disjunction of two schemata F_1 and F_2, then every other schema G conjoined with F is distributed over the disjuncts: $G \wedge (F_1 \vee F_2) = (G \wedge F_1) \vee (G \wedge F_2)$. Because disjunction has wide scope in this way, a functional description containing disjunctions is equivalent to a set of alternative functional descriptions containing only conjunctions. The solution algorithm finds the minimal f-structure that satisfies each of these alternative functional descriptions. When the alternatives contain constraining equations, the latter are applied to the minimal solution satisfying the defining equations in that particular alternative functional description. (Note that disjunction here is the normal inclusive disjunction: both disjuncts can be true of an ambiguous sentence.)

A boolean **negation** operator $\neg$ on equations can be defined via constraint equations. For example, $\neg(f \text{ TENSE}) = \text{PRES}$, also written $(f \text{ TENSE}) \neq \text{PRES}$, is a negative constraint equation, which is tested for truth after the minimal f-structure satisfying all of the defining equations has been constructed; it is true just if $(f \text{ TENSE}) =_c \text{PRES}$ is false.

The notation $(f\ a)$ is used as an **existential constraint,** meaning that f is constrained to have some value for the a attribute. The concept of existential constraint allows us to explain the meaning of the notation commonly used for the contents of semantic forms, illustrated in (54):

(54) $(\uparrow \text{ PRED}) = \text{'live } \langle (\uparrow \text{ SUBJ})(\uparrow \text{ OBL}_{loc}) \rangle \text{'}$

Both $(\uparrow \text{ SUBJ})$ and $(\uparrow \text{ OBL}_{loc})$ are interpreted as existential constraints required by the first and second arguments of 'live', respectively. All of the $\uparrow$s in schema (54) are uniformly instantiated together.

With these boolean operators on equations, it is possible to define **conditional equations,** which are useful in testing for the presence of a feature as a condition for functional specification. For example, Malayalam determines the functions of NPs on the basis of their case attributes, according to K. P. Mohanan (1982a). In Malayalam, a nominative case-marked NP can be either a subject or (if inanimate) an object; animate objects are accusative. A simple way of describing this kind of generalization is using the $\Rightarrow$ conditional, as in (55), where we use '[' and ']' to indicate the scope of the connective '&':

(55) a. ($\downarrow$ CASE) = NOM $\Rightarrow$ ($\uparrow$ SUBJ) = $\downarrow$
    b. [($\downarrow$ CASE) = ACC & ($\downarrow$ ANIM) = +] $\Rightarrow$ ($\uparrow$ OBJ) = $\downarrow$
    c. [($\downarrow$ CASE) = NOM & ($\downarrow$ ANIM) = –] $\Rightarrow$ ($\uparrow$ OBJ) = $\downarrow$

Intuitively, the conditional $A \Rightarrow B$ checks whether A is true of an f-structure, and if it is, then it defines B to hold of that f-structure. Thus (55c) checks whether <CASE NOM> and <ANIM –> are present in an f-structure $\downarrow$; if so, $\downarrow$ can be the value of the OBJ attribute.

    There is an interesting problem in the meaning of the conditional. If we interpret the $\Rightarrow$ simply as a standard conditional denoting material implication, then $A \Rightarrow B$ means $\neg A \lor B$. But this interpretation of (55a–c) does not have the effect we want: it can be satisfied if either disjunct is true; hence we can make B true regardless of whether A is true. In the case of (55a), an accusative NP could be defined by the equation as a subject! To solve this problem we define the conditional as follows:[15]

$$(56) \quad A \Rightarrow B \equiv_{df} \neg A \lor (A_c \land B)$$

According to this definition, $A \Rightarrow B$ says that either the constraint A does not apply or, in the minimal f-structure in which B holds as a defining equation, A must be true as a constraining equation.[16] The first disjunct allows an accusative object to satisfy (55a) vacuously. In this case the constraint (55a) is true but has no defining effect. The second disjunct requires the presence of nominative case in order for the equation to be able to define a subject: it says that in order for ($\uparrow$ SUBJ) = $\downarrow$ to have a defining effect, the constraint ($\downarrow$ CASE) $=_c$ NOM must be true. Under this definition, (55a) would exclude accusative subjects, because nominative case would be required of a subject by the conditional for it to define a subject.

    In problem set 3 and in chapters 6 and 9 we will illustrate the use of conditionals in modelling case licensing and the morphological licensing of grammatical functions, but recent developments in case theory in LFG (e.g. Nordlinger 1998b) suggest an alternative approach. We will not present the new theory here, but the reader of this chapter will be equipped to pursue this recent literature.

    We summarize the schemata which involve constraining equations in the following table:

(57) **Constraining Equations:**

$A =_c B$	positive
$\neg(A = B)$, $A \neq B$	negative
(fa)	existential
$A \Rightarrow B$	conditional (also defining)

The conditional $A \Rightarrow B$ contains B as a defining equation and the implicit constraining equations $\neg A$ and A_c, as explained in our discussion of (56).

4.7   Completeness and Coherence

Completeness and coherence are general well-formedness conditions on f-structures; these conditions are applied after the minimal f-structure has been constructed from the defining equations and any constraining equations have been satisfied. Completeness and coherence enforce an appropriate match-up, or linking, between the PRED feature and the surrounding syntactic functions of the f-structure. **Completeness** requires that every function designated by a PRED be present in the f-structure of that PRED.[17] Completeness also requires a further matching between PREDS and their f-structure functions: if a designator ($\uparrow$ GF) is associated with a semantic role by the PRED, the f-structure element satisfying the designator must itself contain a semantic feature [PRED v].[18] The class of functions that are designated by PRED elements is referred to as the **argument functions**.[19] As we will see in chapter 6, argument functions include (among others) SUBJ, OBJ, COMPL, but exclude ADJUNCT, FOC, and TOP. Violation of completeness is the source of the ill-formedness of the clausal residue of the extraction configuration of (1c) in chapter 2:

(58) *We talked about __ for days.

The PRED for (*talk*) *about* requires an OBJ. Even if we assume the presence of an empty category at the __ position to provide the prepositional object f-structure, that f-structure will lack the required semantic feature (a PRED value), and completeness will still not be satisfied.

Conversely, **coherence** requires that every argument function in an f-structure be designated by a PRED. Furthermore, any function that has a semantic feature must match up with a designator associated with a semantic role by its PRED. It is for this reason that (59) is ill-formed:

(59) *We talked *the man* about that problem for days.

The PRED of the intransitive verb *talk* has no OBJ designator. As a result, the NP *that problem* in object position in the VP of (59) cannot be matched to an appropriate function designator in the PRED. The f-structure of this example thus violates the coherence condition.

The **extended coherence condition** applies not just to argument functions, but to all syntactic functions, requiring that they be integrated appropriately into the f-structure (Zaenen 1985, Fassi Fehri 1984, Bresnan and Mchombo 1987). Argument functions are integrated into the f-structure when they are designated by a PRED as above. Nonargument functions are integrated if they bear an appropriate relation to a PRED. An ADJUNCT is integrated if its immediate f-structure contains a PRED. A TOP or FOC function is integrated whenever it is identified with, or anaphorically linked to, an integrated function. Examples were given in chapter 2 and are discussed in more detail in the next section.

Problems

The reader is now equipped to solve problem set 2.

4.8   Functional Uncertainty

Functional uncertainty is a means of extending functional descriptions to allow for variable chains of attributes that define possible paths through f-structures which may be unknown to us in advance (Kaplan and Zaenen 1989a, Kaplan and Maxwell 1988a). We have already seen that for a chain of function applications $(((f_1\ a_1)\ a_2)\ a_3) = v$, we write $(f_1\ a_1\ a_2\ a_3) = v$, omitting the parentheses. Here the string $a_1\ a_2\ a_3$ represents a fixed chain of attributes. Functional uncertainty extends functional descriptions to allow variable strings of attributes. Recall that for equations not involving functional uncertainty, we have the following fundamental relation between our descriptive constraint equation language and the f-structure objects of which they hold:[20]

(60) $(fa) = v$ holds if and only if f is an f-structure, a is an attribute and the pair $<a\ v> \in f$.

The standard constraint equation notation is extended in functional uncertainty from attributes a to strings x of attributes:

(61)   For strings x of attributes,
$(f\varepsilon) = f$, where ε is the empty string, and $(fax) = ((fa)x)$, where a is an attribute and x a possibly empty string of attributes.

In other words, an f-structure f as a mathematical function can be applied to any string x of attribute names by splitting off the first symbol a_1 of the string, taking the value of (fa_1) and applying it as a function to the substring of x left after splitting off a_1. When no more attributes are left in the string, the value of the whole chain of function applications is the value obtained by the last function application. Now functional uncertainty is defined as follows:

(62)   **Functional Uncertainty:**
For α any set of strings of attributes, $(f\alpha) = v$ holds if and only if for some x in the set of strings α, $(fx) = v$.

An equivalent definition (taken from Kaplan and Zaenen 1989a: equation (29)) is as follows:

(63) $(f\alpha)$ holds if and only if
$((fs)\ \mathrm{Suff}(s,\ \alpha)) = v$ for some symbol s,
where $\mathrm{Suff}(s,\ \alpha)$ is the set of suffix strings y such that $sy \in \alpha$.

Although we will not make use of this additional expressive power here, note that functional uncertainty is defined by Kaplan and Maxwell (1988a) for any strings that can be generated by regular expressions over attributes (that is, expressions involving the boolean operators and the Kleene *). When functional descriptions are extended by (63), both the problem of determining whether a functional description is true of a given f-structure and the problem of constructing a solution to a given functional description are decidable (Kaplan and Maxwell 1988a).

It is possible to impose various constraints on the variable strings x which limit the search space of f-structure paths. These off-path constraints play an important role in restricting the search space for an antecedent starting from an anaphor (Dalrymple 1993), and we will make use of them in chapters 10 and 11. We give here the formal definition (Ronald Kaplan, personal communication); see chapters 10 and 11 for illustrations and further discussion.

An **off-path constraint** ϕ is a combination of ordinary LFG schemata except that it can contain the metavariables $\leftarrow$ and $\rightarrow$ in addition to $\uparrow$ and $\downarrow$. Off-path constraints are paired with symbols in the regular languages of functional uncertainty. That is, the more primitive notion of functional uncertainty assigns an intepretation to expressions of the form $(f\alpha)$ where α denotes a regular language over attribute symbols. With off-path constraints, α denotes a regular language over attribute : constraint pairs. That is, each element of the alphabet is either an attribute symbol as before or a pair of the form $s : \phi$, where s is an attribute symbol and ϕ is an off-path constraint. (A symbol without a constraint can be interpreted as a pair $s : $ True.)

The $\leftarrow$ and $\rightarrow$ are instantiated with different values at each level of the f-structure that an uncertainty path runs through. Thus, the formal definition of off-path constraints must be provided by an extension to the basic recursive specification of ordinary uncertainty shown in (63). Here is the extended version (α ranging over symbol : constraint pairs):

(64) **Functional Uncertainty with Off-Path Constraints:**
      $(f\alpha)$ holds if and only if
      $((fs) \; \text{Suff}(s, \alpha)) = v \land \phi_{f/\leftarrow, (fs)/\rightarrow}$ for some pair $s : \phi$,
      where $\text{Suff}(s : \phi, \alpha)$ is the set of suffix strings y such that $s : \phi \; y \in \alpha$.

In this definition, $\phi_{f/\leftarrow, (fs)/\rightarrow}$ is the formula that results from substituting f for $\leftarrow$ and (fs) for $\rightarrow$ everywhere in ϕ.

We will make use of the notation called "inside-out functional uncertainty" (Halvorsen and Kaplan 1988, Dalrymple 1993). First we define 'inside-out' function application as in (65). This definition lets us look up one level to the next higher f-structure containing f' just as (fa) lets us look down one level to the next lower f-structure:

(65) **Inside-Out Function Application:**
      For any f-structure f' and attribute a, (af') designates the f-structure f such that $(fa) = f'$.

(66) **Inside-Out Functional Uncertainty:**
For any f-structure f', attribute a and string of attributes x, $(ef') = f'$ (e the empty string), and $(xaf') = (x(af'))$.
For α any set of strings of attributes, $(\alpha f) = v$ holds if and only if for some x in the set of strings α, $(xf) = v$.

With the addition of (66) we can now either start from a higher f-structure f and follow a path of attributes down to a lower f-structure f', or start from the lower f-structure f' and follow a path of attributes upward to the higher f-structure f. In the latter case, the notation (xf') designates the higher f-structure, call it f, for which there exists a path of attributes represented by x such that $(fx) = f'$.

Consider now the following inside-out functional uncertainty equation:

(67) $((xf')\text{TOP}) = f'$

By the definition in (66), (xf') designates some f-structure f_x such that $(f_xx) = f'$. Thus we can unpack (67) as in (68):

(68) $(f_xx) = f'$
$(f_x\text{TOP}) = f'$

This tells us, first, that there must be some f-structure f_x from which we can follow a path x of attributes leading us to the f-structure f', and, second, that the higher f-structure has a TOP attribute whose value is to be identified with the f-structure f'. Inspecting the structure (69), we can see that the outermost f-structure, f, has a TOP attribute, and that the string COMPL OBJ leads from this f-structure to f':

(69)
$$
f: \begin{bmatrix} \text{TOP} & h: [\text{``Ann''}] \\ \text{SUBJ} & [\text{``I''}] \\ \text{PRED} & \text{`think } \langle (f\,\text{SUBJ})(f\,\text{COMPL}) \rangle\text{'} \\ \text{COMPL} & g: \begin{bmatrix} \text{SUBJ} & [\text{``he''}] \\ \text{PRED} & \text{`like } \langle (g\,\text{SUBJ})(g\,\text{OBJ}) \rangle\text{'} \\ \text{OBJ} & f' \end{bmatrix} \end{bmatrix}
$$

(The phrases in double quotation marks abbreviate the actual f-structure contents where they are not relevant to the discussion.) Hence, the f-structure (69) satisfies the functional description in (68) provided that we set $f_x = f$ and $x = \text{COMPL OBJ}$:

(70) $(f\,\text{COMPL OBJ}) = f'$
$(f\,\text{TOP}) = f'$

The functional description in (67) thus adds to (69) the information needed to identify the complement object function with the topic function:

(71)
$$f:\begin{bmatrix} \text{TOP} & h, f': [\text{``Ann''}] \\ \text{SUBJ} & [\text{``I''}] \\ \text{PRED} & \text{`think } \langle (f \text{ SUBJ})(f \text{ COMPL}) \rangle\text{'} \\ \text{COMPL} & g: \begin{bmatrix} \text{SUBJ} & [\text{``he''}] \\ \text{PRED} & \text{`like } \langle (g \text{ SUBJ})(g \text{ OBJ}) \rangle\text{'} \\ \text{OBJ} & f' \end{bmatrix} \end{bmatrix}$$

Functional uncertainty has been used in modelling anaphoric binding relations (Dalrymple 1993), extractions (Kaplan and Zaenen 1989a, Kroeger 1993), and a type of scrambling or extraposition of complements (Matsumoto 1992, 1996a). We employ it in modelling extraction and binding in this work.

The formal model of extraction developed in this work makes use of inside-out functional uncertainty by stating simply that the f-structure of a gap in the c-structure is identified with the value of a higher nonargument function DF (DF here refers to TOP or FOC):[21]

(72)   Annotate XP → e with $((x \uparrow)\text{DF}) = \uparrow$.

Other models of extraction in LFG employ "constituent control" metavariables (Kaplan and Bresnan 1982) and "outside-in" functional uncertainty (Kaplan and Zaenen 1989a).[22]

To see how (72) applies to an example of topicalization in English, consider (73):

(73)

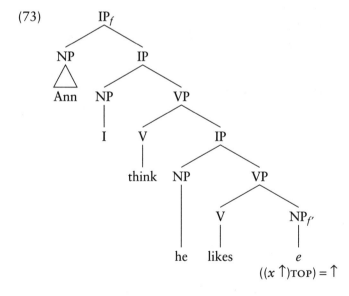

$$((x \uparrow)\text{TOP}) = \uparrow$$

The functional schema associated with the gap NP in (73) comes from (72). By uniformly instantiating this schema in the same way as all of the other functional schemata of English (omitted here for simplicity), and solving the identity as outlined above, we arrive at the f-structure in (74):

(74)
$$
f: \begin{bmatrix} \text{TOP} & h: [\text{``Ann''}] \\ \text{SUBJ} & [\text{``I''}] \\ \text{PRED} & \text{'think } \langle (f\ \text{SUBJ})(f\ \text{COMPL}) \rangle \text{'} \\ \\ \text{COMPL} & g: \begin{bmatrix} \text{SUBJ} & [\text{``he''}] \\ \text{PRED} & \text{'like } \langle (g\ \text{SUBJ})(g\ \text{OBJ}) \rangle \text{'} \\ \text{OBJ} & \end{bmatrix} \end{bmatrix}
$$

The f-structure in (74) is derived by assuming the standard annotation of functions to X′ structures for English (chapter 6): the NP sister to IP is annotated with (↑ TOP) = ↓; the NP sister to VP, with (↑ SUBJ) = ↓; the IP sister to V, with (↑ COMPL) = ↓; the NP sister to VP, with (↑ SUBJ) = ↓, the NP sister to V, with (↑ OBJ) = ↓; and all other categories, with ↑ = ↓. The reader may find it a useful exercise to derive the f-description from (73) and solve it, comparing the result to (74).

Observe that a single f-structure *h* in (74) is the same value of two different attributes, the TOP and the OBJ. These are the two functions whose values are identified by the schema in (73). This identity is represented graphically by an arrow connecting the two values. This example illustrates how a single constituent, in this case the NP *Ann*, can simultaneously have two different syntactic functions in the f-structure: here the syntactic topic and the object functions. In this case, the two functions correspond to two distinct phrase structure positions, but functions are not always expressed by c-structure positions, as we will see in part III. Without the identification of TOP and OBJ provided by the functional uncertainty equation, the f-structure would be incomplete and incoherent: incomplete because the value of the OBJ attribute would lack a PRED, and incoherent because the TOP function would not be integrated into the f-structure.

There are, however, alternative ways to satisfy the extended coherence condition, without employing functional uncertainty. One is to use anaphoric linking to connect the DF to another function.[23] This alternative is illustrated by the example in (75):

(75)   Ann, I think he likes her.

In this example, there is no extraction configuration: although *Ann* is in a clause-initial, "displaced" position, the remaining portion of the sentence *I think he likes her* is fully complete and coherent on its own. What allows *Ann* to satisfy the extended coherence condition is that the following clause is understood to be about Ann, the topic. This type of topic is sometimes referred to as a dislocated topic, or "external topic" (Aissen 1992, King 1995), to distinguish it from the (internal) topic of the preceding example. When dislocated topics are anaphorically linked to a pronominal element within the clause, what is identified is not the f-structure value of the DF and clause-internal function (which would cause a functional uniqueness violation), but the referential index of the two functions. This linkage too can be formally modelled using inside-out functional uncertainty, as developed by Dalrymple (1993). Even anaphoric linking is not required in cases where the dislocated or external topic is simultaneously an adjunct:

(76) As for Ann, I don't think Roger likes women.

In this case, the clause-initial phrase appears simultaneously to be both an adjunct to the following clause and its topic. Bearing the double functions of adjunct and topic allows the phrase to satisfy extended coherence without either anaphoric linking or a functional uncertainty chain.[24]

4.9 Sets of f-structures

The nonargument functions TOP, FOC, and ADJUNCT all allow multiple instances without violating functional uniqueness (Bresnan 1980, Bresnan and Mchombo 1987, Simpson 1991, King 1995). There are various ways of accounting for this property, but a simple formal device that has been employed since the earliest LFG work is the membership connective $\in$: $f_1 \in f_2$ means that the f-structure f_1 is an element of the set of f-structures f_2. For example, the schema $\downarrow \in (\uparrow \text{TOP})$ means that $\downarrow$ is an element of a set of f-structures which is the value of TOP. Sets of f-structures are discussed in detail in Kaplan and Maxwell (1988b) and Dalrymple and Kaplan (1997).

An example is provided by Russian topicalization (chapter 9). The annotated c-structure shown in (77), augmented with the case conditionals shown in (78) and the morpholexical information given in (79), yields the f-structure shown in (80). The case conditionals are assumed to be freely annotated to c-structure nodes:

(77)

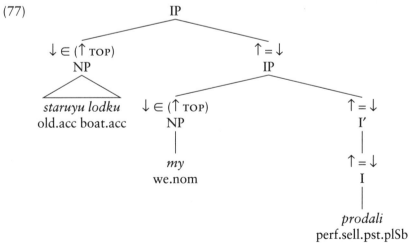

'The old boat, we sold'

(78)   a. $(\downarrow$ CASE$)$ = NOM $\Rightarrow$ $(\uparrow$ SUBJ$)$ = $\downarrow$
        b. $(\downarrow$ CASE$)$ = ACC $\Rightarrow$ $(\uparrow$ OBJ$)$ = $\downarrow$

(79)   *lodk-*: N $(\uparrow$ PRED$)$ = 'boat'
      -u: infl$_N$ $(\uparrow$ CASE$)$ = ACC
      my: Pron $(\uparrow$ CASE$)$ = NOM
                   $(\uparrow$ NUM$)$ = PL
                   $(\uparrow$ PERS$)$ = 1
                   $(\uparrow$ PRED$)$ = 'PRO'
      proda-: V $(\uparrow$ PRED$)$ = 'sell $\langle(\uparrow$ SUBJ$)(\uparrow$ OBJ$)\rangle$'
                   $(\uparrow$ ASPECT$)$ = PERF
      -li: infl$_I$ $(\uparrow$ TENSE$)$ = PAST
                   $(\uparrow$ SUBJ$)$ = $\downarrow$
                       $(\downarrow$ NUM$)$ = PL

(80)

$$
f: \begin{bmatrix}
\text{TOP} & \left\{ \begin{bmatrix} \text{PRED} & \text{'boat'} \\ \text{CASE} & \text{ACC} \end{bmatrix} \begin{bmatrix} \text{PRED} & \text{'PRO'} \\ \text{CASE} & \text{NOM} \\ \text{NUM} & \text{PL} \\ \text{PERS} & 1 \end{bmatrix} \right\} \\
\text{TENSE} & \text{PAST} \\
\text{OBJ} & \\
\text{SUBJ} & \\
\text{PRED} & \text{'sell } \langle(f \text{ SUBJ})(f \text{ OBJ})\rangle \text{'}
\end{bmatrix}
$$

To verify the f-structure, assume that the case conditionals (78) are annotated to all NPs in the c-structure (77). It is a useful exercise to derive the functional description and solve it, observing how functional uniqueness is satisfied.

4.10   Conclusion

We have now examined the basic formal architecture of LFG. The reader of this chapter is equipped to begin to exploit LFG ideas in the analysis and solution of syntactic problems, such as those in problem set 2, and to advance to most of the theoretical ideas built upon this framework in parts III–IV. A formal architecture is also of interest for its epistemological implications – the way in which it models linguistic knowledge. Some epistemological aspects of the design principles of LFG are discussed in the next chapter.

Further Reading

A clear, practical guide to using the LFG formalism is Wescoat (1989). Dalrymple et al. (1995) collects together a number of articles on the formal architecture of LFG, including the original Kaplan and Bresnan (1982) paper, and Kaplan's (1995) updated overview of the formal system.

Notes

1. Regular expressions are formed with the boolean operators ('and', 'or', and 'not'), together with the Kleene star operator S*, which forms the set of all strings created by concatenation of elements of S, including the empty string.
2. See Inkelas and Zec (1990) and the references cited therein.
3. See Dalrymple (1993: chapter 4).
4. Peters and Ritchie (1981) define an extension of phrase structure grammars that allow this type of multiple domination.
5. This equation is read "f_1's SUBJ equals f_2."
6. In (10a) the equation $(f_1$ SUBJ NUM$) =$ SG is read "f_1's SUBJ's NUM equals SG." Example (10c) may look like a formal oddity: why would we want to identify an attribute with a value? This formal possibility was invented for the situation in which one may wish to test for the presence of an attribute within a phrase (say a PP), which then can be used to name the whole phrase. For example, the function of a PP might depend upon the type of preposition within it.
7. The parentheses around the nodes in (26) and (27) abbreviate two alternative structures, one with the node in parentheses and the other without it.
8. The equations $(\uparrow$ SUBJ$) = \downarrow$ and $\uparrow = \downarrow$ are read "up's SUBJ equals down" and "up equals down," respectively. 'up' refers to the f-structure of the mother node and 'down' refers to the f-structure of the annotated node. If we imagine ourselves in the position of the annotated node, looking "up" at its "mother" in the tree, the equations can be given an intuitive interpretation: "the f-structure of my mother's node has a SUBJ attribute whose value is identified with the f-structure of me" and "the f-structure of my mother's node is identified with the f-structure of me."
9. The $\uparrow$ arrows in these lexical entries are taken to refer to the (f-structure of the) preterminal node (N in the case of (31)). The $\downarrow$ arrows then refer to the (f-structure of the) terminal node.
10. On the index of the PRED value, see the discussion of semantic features in section 4.2. We adopt here the convention of choosing as PRED index the unique f-structure index of the mother node; see the index '4' in (33) for an example.
11. Annotations of terminal nodes (words) are written below the word rather than above it, dropping a parallelism to annotations of nonterminal nodes, which are written above the node.
12. In fact, the grammaticality of any string of words of L is decidable (Kaplan and Bresnan 1982).
13. See, for example, Winograd (1983) for a pedagogical introduction.
14. An analysis of expletive subjects in several Germanic languages uses the difference between constraining and defining equations as a formal model of "weak" versus "strong" agreement (Berman 1999).
15. This definition is given in Andrews and Manning (1993).

16   To understand more precisely how this definition is interpreted, suppose that $\mathcal{D}$ is a purely conjunctive functional description containing no constraining equations, to which the conditional $A \Rightarrow B$ is added, obtaining $\mathcal{D} \wedge (A \Rightarrow B)$. By (56), this is equivalent to $\mathcal{D} \wedge (\neg A \vee (Ac \wedge B))$, which is in turn equivalent to $(\mathcal{D} \wedge \neg A) \vee (\mathcal{D} \wedge Ac \wedge B)$. This is a disjunction of two conjunctive f-descriptions, which are solved in the normal way to give us alternative f-structures. In particular, we construct the minimal f-structure satisfying the defining equations of the left disjunct (namely, $\mathcal{D}$), and then apply the constraining equation $\neg A$ to it; hence A must be false of this f-structure. Similarly, we construct the minimal f-structure satisfying the defining equations of the right disjunction ($\mathcal{D} \wedge B$) and subject the result to the constraining equation A_c; A must therefore be true of the alternative f-structure.

17   This much is required by formulating the function designators of PREDs as existential constraints.

18   All designators ($\uparrow$ GF) represented within the angled brackets $\langle \ldots \rangle$ correspond to semantic roles; nonsemantic arguments, such as expletive subjects, appear outside of the angled brackets (part IV).

19   Kaplan and Bresnan (1982) refer to these as "governable grammatical functions."

20   This development of functional uncertainty follows Dalrymple (1993).

21   The symbol e refers to the empty string, and is used to indicate the absence of a terminal symbol. It should not be taken to be a specific terminal symbol of itself.

22   Kaplan and Zaenen's (1989a) model of extraction assumes that there is no c-structure gap; a functional uncertainty chain associated with the topic constituent would identify it in initial position as also bearing its within-clause function. However, since CPs and locative PPs can be topicalized as well as DPs (Bresnan 1994a, 1995a), their approach violates the principle of canonical structural realization of functions (chapter 2) and is not adopted here. Some empirical consequences of the difference are discussed in Bresnan (1998c).

23   Recall from the definition of the extended coherence condition in section 4.7 that "A TOP or FOC function is integrated whenever it is identified with, *or anaphorically linked to*, an integrated function."

24   Another possible approach to external topics is to assume that they need not be syntactically integrated into the clause, but are related by looser constraints of discourse coherence.

5 Monotonicity and Some of its Consequences

As we have seen in chapters 1–4, the design principles for a formal model of universal grammar are motivated in part by a theory of linguistic knowledge: to explain in theory how knowledge of language can be acquired, the relation between the crosslinguistically invariant internal structures of language and the highly variable external structures must somehow be "transparent." Transparency is often taken to be sameness of form, entailing a configurational design of universal grammar in which transformational operations derive the external forms from the internal form. We have rejected this view as typologically unsound, adopting instead a principle of monotonicity. In this chapter we will examine more carefully what is meant by monotonicity and discuss some of its general consequences for our formal model of linguistic knowledge.

5.1 Monotonicity

In mapping from a c-structure to an f-structure, we accumulate local functional descriptions from parts of the c-structure to get a functional structure for the whole. As we add new functional equations to the functional description, the resulting f-structures that satisfy these descriptions become increasingly specific; they have more attributes. Intuitively, the mapping from c-structure to f-structure increases monotonically.[1]

Let us try to make this intuition a little more precise. What does it mean for one f-structure to be "more specific" than another? Intuitively, the more specific f-structure contains the same attribute–value pairs as the less specific one – and then some. Thus in (1), f_2 and f_3 are each more specific than f_1, and f_4 is more specific than all three.

(1)

$$f_4: \begin{bmatrix} a & b \\ c & d \\ e & f \end{bmatrix}$$

$$f_2: \begin{bmatrix} a & b \\ c & d \end{bmatrix} \qquad\qquad f_3: \begin{bmatrix} a & b \\ e & f \end{bmatrix}$$

$$f_1: [a \quad b]$$

But we also have the intuition that g in (2b) is more specific than f in (2a) –

(2)   a. $f: \begin{bmatrix} a & b \\ c & [e \quad f] \end{bmatrix}$

     b. $g: \begin{bmatrix} a & b \\ c & \begin{bmatrix} e & f \\ d & h \end{bmatrix} \end{bmatrix}$

– even though the pair $<c[ef]>$ in f is not also a member of g. In this case, however, (gc) *is* more specific than (fc). This suggests the following recursive definition: g is at least as specific as f if for every attribute a in f, either $(ga) = (fa)$ or (ga) is at least as specific as (fa). We will use the notation $g \sqsupseteq f$ or $f \sqsubseteq g$ to mean that g is at least as specific as f. We will also continue informally to use the term "more specific than" to refer to this relation, understanding that it does not exclude identity.

For each (consistent) functional description d, there are infinitely many functional structures that satisfy it – namely, the smallest one f that satisfies d, and all of the f-structures that are more specific than f. We define $\varphi(d)$ to be the *smallest* f that satisfies d. This gives us a mapping φ from functional descriptions D to functional structures F.

This mapping φ has the following property: as functional descriptions d_1, $d_2, \ldots$ get larger and larger, the functional structures $f_1, f_2, \ldots$ that satisfy them get more and more specific. In other words $\varphi : D \rightarrow F$ has the property that if $d \subseteq d'$ then $\varphi(d) \sqsubseteq \varphi(d')$. φ increases monotonically.

Notice that the smallest f-structure that is more specific than two f-structures f_1 and f_2 corresponds under φ to the smallest functional description that contains the respective functional descriptions d_1 and d_2 for f_1 and f_2. This smallest functional description is just $d_1 \cup d_2$, and $\varphi(d_1 \cup d_2)$ is called the *unification* of $\varphi(d_1)$ and $\varphi(d_2)$, notated $\varphi(d_1) \sqcup \varphi(d_2)$. Just as $d_1 \subseteq (d_1 \cup d_2)$, so $f_1 \sqsubseteq (f_1 \sqcup f_2)$. There is also an intersection operation on f-structures that corresponds under φ to the intersection of functional descriptions. Thus there is a lattice of f-structures ordered under specificity corresponding to the lattice of functional descriptions ordered under set inclusion.

Of course, it may happen that the union of two functional descriptions $d_1 \cup d_2$ contains an inconsistency not found in either d_1 or d_2:

(3)

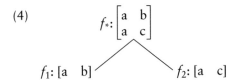

Here $d_1 \cup d_2$ corresponds to f_* in (4). f_* is a set of attribute–value pairs that is not itself an f-structure because it violates the uniqueness condition:

(4)

$$f_*: \begin{bmatrix} a & b \\ a & c \end{bmatrix}$$

$f_1: [a \quad b] \qquad\qquad f_2: [a \quad c]$

Whenever we have an inconsistent f-description d_* in the domain of f-descriptions D, we can set $\varphi(d_*)$ for any inconsistent f-description d_* to be some designated element added to the ordered set of all f-structures. Then φ will be defined over all descriptions, inconsistent or not. But an inconsistent functional description d_* has the peculiar property that for *any* description d, $d \cup d_*$ is also inconsistent. Hence $\varphi(d_*) = \varphi(d \cup d_*) = \varphi(d) \sqcup \varphi(d_*)$. Since for any f-description d $\varphi(d) \sqsubseteq (\varphi(d) \sqcup \varphi(d_*)) = \varphi(d_*)$, this means that $\varphi(d_*)$ must be more specific than any f-structure; it must be the "top" of the lattice of f-structures. This definition preserves the monotonicity of our mapping.

It may also happen that a functional description d contains finite disjunctions of functional equations. This arises in cases of ambiguity. In such cases $\varphi(d)$ will be a *set* of f-structures that satisfy the alternatives in the description. If in such a case d is contained in a larger description d', then we can still say that $\varphi(d')$ is more specific than $\varphi(d)$ if for each f-structure in $\varphi(d)$ there is a more specific f-structure in $\varphi(d')$. Our mapping φ has this property. When we add a new description to a disjunction of descriptions, we logically conjoin the new statement to the disjunction; the result is equivalent to distributing the new statement over the disjuncts, creating a disjunction of larger descriptions, each of which describes a more specific f-structure than the original.

Finally let us observe that our grammatical theory also provides us with a mapping π from the set S of strings of words into functional descriptions.[2] As the length of a string of words increases, so does the size of the functional description, so π is also monotonic. Now because of the fundamental relation between functional descriptions and f-structures given in chapter 4 ($(fa) = v$ iff $<a\ v> \in f$), the content of the f-structures in terms of attribute–value pairs increases or stays the same as the size of the functional description increases. Hence the composite mapping $\varphi \circ \pi : S \to F$ is also monotonic. All of this is by way of clarifying the following property of our grammars: they are designed so that as you increase the length of a string of words, you monotonically increase the information about the f-structure of the string.

What is the linguistic significance of this formal property of monotonicity? F-structures are formal models of the internal structures of language, and these reflect meaningful grammatical relations, how words are mapped into semantic arguments. Thus the monotonicity of our mapping from strings to f-structures implies that the grammatical relations of *parts* are preserved in the whole. Our mapping cannot destroy or change these grammatical relations, and this is the sense in which the mapping between internal and external structures in our formal model in *transparent*. What is preserved in the external structure is not the form of the internal structure, but the specification of its contents.

5.2   Relation Changes and Monotonicity

There is an apparent problem with this model of syntactic structure: in natural languages there are certain cases where grammatical relations *do* appear to change, cases where the initial mapping of words into semantic arguments appears not to be preserved in the external structure. For example, the subject *Mary* of the passive construction (5b) is interpreted like an object, not a subject, of the active construction (5a):

(5)   a.   Mary kissed the child.
      b.   Mary was kissed by the child.

Note that the verb *be* is not essential to this remapping:

(6)   a.   I imagined Mary kissed the child.
      b.   I imagined Mary kissed by the child.

In many theories of grammar this phenomenon has been viewed as a remapping of grammatical relations in the syntax: for example, the external structure of the passive sentence might be mapped onto an internal structure similar to that for the corresponding active sentence. But our theory excludes such an analysis, for in our theory, grammatical relations cannot be destroyed or changed by the syntactic mapping $\varphi \circ \pi$, which can only add information.

How then can we solve the problem posed by (5) and (6)? In early LFG it was assumed that grammatical relations cannot be changed by the syntactic mapping between sentences and internal structures, but that they can be remapped in the lexicon, by creating alternative lexical predicates for active and passive verbs. As we have seen above, the existence of finite disjunctions in our functional descriptions does not alter the monotonicity of the syntactic mapping. The following was thus adopted as a postulate of LFG:

(7) **The Principle of Direct Syntactic Encoding:**
All grammatical relation changes are lexical.

Thus early LFG (Bresnan 1982c) achieved monotonicity by removing all relation changes from syntax into the lexical component, where they could be expressed by alternative lexical forms. This move is possible just because relation changes are lexically governed: they affect only lexically related arguments and so are local in their syntactic effects.

This idea requires that active and passive verb forms (and those of other relation changes) be lexically available, related by lexical redundancy rules (Bresnan 1980, 1982a). This idea was discussed informally in chapter 3, where the same underlying predicate argument structure is lexically associated with, or mapped to, alternative sets of grammatical functions:[3]

(8)   active   passive
$$R < \quad x \qquad y \quad > \quad \Leftrightarrow \quad R < \quad x \qquad y \quad >$$
$$\qquad \quad | \qquad \; | \qquad \qquad \qquad \qquad \; | \qquad \; |$$
$$\qquad \text{SUBJ} \;\; \text{OBJ} \qquad \qquad \quad (\text{OBL}_\theta) \;\; \text{SUBJ}$$

In the notation used for semantic forms, the argument role positions are filled by function designators, so (8) is written as in (9):

(9) 'live $\langle (\uparrow \text{SUBJ})(\uparrow \text{OBJ}) \rangle$' $\Leftrightarrow$ 'live $\langle ((\uparrow \text{OBL}_{ag}))(\uparrow \text{SUBJ}) \rangle$'

In essence, the grammar is factored into relation changing lexical regularities like (9) and relation preserving syntactic regularities. The latter consist of word order alternations (such as we see in verb movement, scrambling, topicalization, and the other phenomena of part III) and principles for associating surface structures with syntactic functions. All of these syntactic regularities are monotonic in the sense defined above.

Although relation changes are lexical alternations, they induce syntactic alternations in forms of expression through the principles of completeness and coherence. For example, the verb *kissed* has the alternative semantic forms given in (10)–(10a) for the active past tense verb, (10b) for the passive participle:

(10) a. *kissed*: 'kiss $\langle (\uparrow \text{SUBJ})(\uparrow \text{OBJ}) \rangle$'
      b. *kissed*: 'kiss $\langle ((\uparrow \text{OBL}_{ag}))(\uparrow \text{SUBJ}) \rangle$'

In syntactic contexts where (10b) is chosen, completeness will require a SUBJ and optionally an OBL$_{ag}$, and coherence will exclude an OBJ. Where (10a) is chosen, completeness will require a SUBJ and OBJ and coherence will exclude an OBL$_{ag}$. Thus different c-structures will be required to support the alternative semantic forms, as illustrated in (11) for the active and (12) for the passive:

(11)

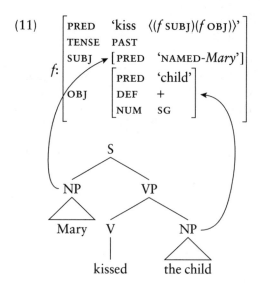

(An auxiliary verb is required with the passive in (12) because the past participle is not a finite verb form.)

(12)

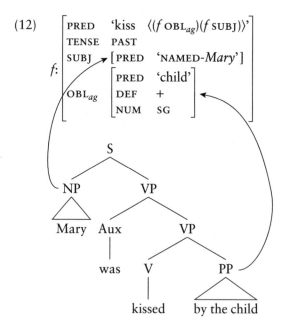

A strong point of the early LFG theory of relation changes was that it captured the undeniable lexicality of these processes (chapter 3).[4] However, rule-based theories are explanatorily weak and this theory has been replaced by a new, monotonic theory of relation changes known as the lexical mapping theory. That theory and some of its implications are discussed in part IV.

5.3   Information and Form

We now observe several other very general consequences of the design features built into the formal architecture of LFG.

5.3.1   *The fragmentability of language*

Because information about the functional structure is locally distributed through-out the word and phrase structure under these principles, it is easy to explain the "fragmentability of language" – the fact that we can infer the internal structural relations of arbitrary sentence fragments as easily as we can those of complete sentences, and the supporting fact that sentence fragments are so extensively used in actual discourse contexts.

Fragments give partial, or incomplete, specifications of f-structures. For example, the verb *seem* in the following fragment gives the partially specified f-structure shown in (14):[5]

(13)   ... seems to ...

(14)   *F-structure of fragment (13)*

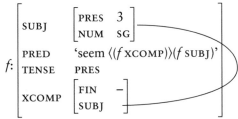

The f-structure in (14) satisfies the partial functional specifications provided in the c-structure fragment (15). Note how the functional information is localized in individual words and pieces of c-structure:

(15)   *Annotated C-structure and lexicon of fragment (13)*

a.   ...

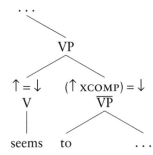

   b.   seem $(\uparrow \text{PRED}) = \text{'seem} \langle(\uparrow \text{XCOMP})\rangle(\uparrow \text{SUBJ})\text{'}$
                    $(\uparrow \text{SUBJ}) = (\uparrow \text{XCOMP SUBJ})$
       -s $(\uparrow \text{TENSE}) = \text{PRES}$
                    $(\uparrow \text{SUBJ}) = \downarrow$
                        $(\downarrow \text{PERS}) = 3$
                        $(\downarrow \text{NUM}) = \text{SG}$
       to $(\uparrow \text{FIN}) = -$

Although (15) depicts only a fragment of structure, and one that is not even a complete constituent, observe that it determines the skeletal function–argument relations of a full clause and embedded complement construction as shown in (14). Compare to this fragment the c- and f-structure for the full sentence (16), given in (17) and (18):

(16)   He seems to agree.

(17)   *Annotated C-structure and lexicon of (16)*
     a.

   b.   he $(\uparrow \text{PRED}) = \text{'pro'}$
                   $(\uparrow \text{NUM}) = \text{SG}$
                   $(\uparrow \text{PERS}) = 3$
                   $(\uparrow \text{GEND}) = \text{MASC}$
      seem   (as in (15)b)
      -s   (as in (15)b)
      to   (as in (15)b)
      agree $(\uparrow \text{PRED}) = \text{'agree} \langle(\uparrow \text{SUBJ})\rangle\text{'}$

(18)   *F-structure of* (16)

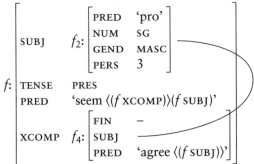

Observe the relation between the fragment f-structure (15) and the full f-structure (18). The c-structure context in which the fragment is embedded simply adds further information about the subject and the complement of *seems*. In actual discourse contexts this information may be redundant, and can easily be eliminated:

(19)   [Speaker A:] And he agrees?
       [Speaker B:] – seems to.

A fragment containing a word which is the main predicator of its phrasal context (that is, a word which is the "head") will specify, in skeletal form, an f-structure for that entire phrasal context. Thus a verb like *seem* carries a great deal of information about the global f-structures of the sentences it can be used in. However, not all fragments are as informative about the possible internal relations of their syntactic contexts, as the following example illustrates:

(20)   . . . to by for . . .

This fragment occurs embedded in the English sentence (21):

(21)   The one he should be spoken <u>to by, for</u> God's sake, is his mother.

The three prepositions are not grammatically related to each other in the internal structure of this sentence. What we can infer from them in (20) is just three unrelated f-structures containing the lexical features of each preposition. Thus fragmentability does not mean that arbitrary sentence fragments are easy to understand; it means that the internal structures of fragments can be inferred as easily as those of sentences. The inferred internal structures of fragments may cohere to a greater or lesser degree, depending on how closely related are the words of the fragment in their syntactic context.

5.3.2   The nonconfigurationality of language

Another pervasive property which these principles support is the nonconfigurationality of language – the fact that the functions and arguments of internal
structures are not canonically externalized in phrase structure configurations across
languages. The reason is that the same kinds of functional descriptions can be
carried by word structure as by phrase structure, and languages may differ typologically in the extent to which they localize information about internal structures in morphology or in phrasal syntax.

Within a language, too, functional specifications of the same elements of internal structure may be carried by the morphology of words, by the phrasal syntax,
or by both together. For example, although English is relatively poor in the
amount of functional information carried in its morphology, we can see even in
English that a functional specification of the subject is carried by the verbal
inflection in (22) and by the surface constituent configuration shown in (23):

(22)   -s: $(\uparrow$ TENSE$) =$ PRES
            $(\uparrow$ SUBJ$) = \downarrow$
               $(\downarrow$ PERS$) = 3$
               $(\downarrow$ NUM$) =$ SG

(23)   S
                        /
    $(\uparrow$ SUBJ$) = \downarrow$
            NP

It follows that the functional information carried by word structure and by
phrase structure can interact, even though the internal constituency of words and
phrases is relatively independent, or modular. As we will see in subsequent chapters, this consequence enables us to explain the existence of syntactic "bracketing
paradoxes" in natural languages – cases where the f-structure bracketing of a
sentence does not correspond to the c-structure bracketing.

On our theory, the existence of both nonconfigurationality and syntactic bracketing paradoxes arises from the fact that f-structure is a parallel, co-present
structure that corresponds imperfectly to c-structure.

5.3.3   Apparent information flow through external structure

The third general property of language explained by these principles is the
apparent flow of information through external structure. In (24), for example,
information about the singular number of *the boy* seems to flow between the
subject NP and the V:

(24)

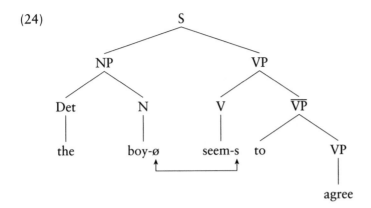

In general, syntactic features seem to propagate across nodes of the phrase structure and morphology. Most linguistic theories have recognized this phenomenon and incorporated it into explicit conventions of feature propagation. These theories provide various mechanisms for describing this flow of information, but they do not explain it: *why* do features propagate in external structures?

The design principles of our theory provide an explanation: the mapping between external and internal structure is not an isomorphism, but a many-to-one relation. Thus in (24), a single functional constituent, the SUBJ *the boy*, corresponds to information given in two different c-structure positions, as shown in (25) – that of the verbal inflection and that of the initial NP:

(25)

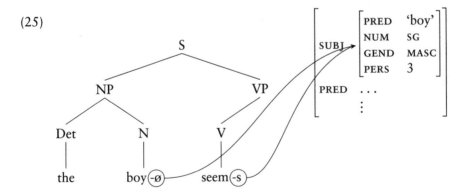

The initial NP carries information about the subject, as shown in the annotated c-structure in (23); and the verbal tense inflection -*s* also carries information about the subject, as shown in the morphological entry in (22). By functional uniqueness, this information must agree.

In general, the locality relations on f-structure are not identical to the locality relations on c-structure. Hence, information projected from the f-structure onto the c-structure will often be discontinuous. This imperfect correspondence between the two parallel structures is what gives rise to the illusion of feature propagation and movement.

5.3.4 Noncompositionality

Finally, observe that LFGS are noncompositional, in the sense that the f-structure of a constituent is not solely a function of the f-structures of its immediate daughter constituents. To see this, consider the f-structure f of the VP in (26) (it happens that f is an incomplete f-structure, because it lacks the SUBJ required by the PRED 'kiss'):

(26)

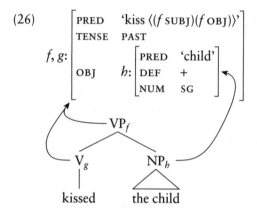

Given that every c-structure node corresponds to a unique f-structure, we have labelled each of VP, V, and NP with a unique f-structure index, f, g, and h, respectively. Recall that these f-structures are not necessarily distinct; for example, because the V is the head of the VP (annotated $\uparrow = \downarrow$), $f = g$. In (26), where VP is the root of its own tree, f-structure f consists entirely of the attribute–value pairs collected from the functional descriptions of VP's immediate constituents V and NP.

Now compare the same VP dominated by the S in example (11), repeated here:

(27)

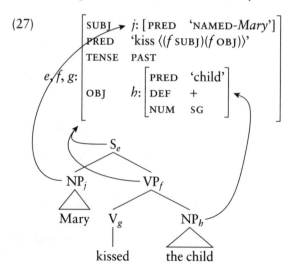

In (27) we find that the f-structure of VP also contains attribute–value pairs collected from the f-structure of its mother node S – namely, those of the subject NP. This result follows from the annotation $\uparrow = \downarrow$, which means precisely that the f-structure f of this VP is identified with the f-structure e of its mother node S. In isolation, the VP specifies an incomplete f-structure which contains no information about the subject other than that it must exist (inferred from the lexical specification of *kissed*). The fact that the f-structure of the VP may vary with the sentential context in which it is embedded, while its internal constituents remain invariant, illustrates very clearly the noncompositionality of the LFG architecture. In general, the f-structure of a constituent may depend on its surrounding syntactic context, and not merely on its internal constituents. Indeed, this is how discontinuous constituents, such as we find in Warlpiri (chapter 1), are unified. In a sense, our analysis of English treats the VP as a potentially discontinuous constituent, whose f-structure contents may be dispersed across the sentence.

Compositionality of predication relations in the constituent structure is a defining property of many grammatical architectures. However, LFG has been deliberately designed as a noncompositional grammatical architecture, for the reason that the typological diversity of syntactic structures we find across languages motivates a more flexible design of grammar than strict compositionality allows. Grammatical phenomena motivating noncompositionality can be found in chapters 1, 7, and 9 and problem sets 2, 3, 4, and 5.

5.4   Conclusion

Interpreted epistemologically, LFG represents knowledge of language as localized, partial knowledge that is synthesized by constraint satisfaction. Because of its distinctive architectural properties – monotonic, lexicalist, parallel, and constraint-based – and its explicit mathematical model, LFG has attracted interest beyond linguistics proper, and has been incorporated into psychological theories of language acquisition, perception, and production, as well as into computational systems of language processing (see the LFG Bibliography, http://www-lfg.stanford.edu/lfg/). The reader of chapters 1–5 is well equipped to pursue further readings in these areas.

Notes

1   A function $f : A \rightarrow B$ increases monotonically if A and B are partially ordered by relations $\leqslant_A$ and $\leqslant_B$ and whenever $a \leqslant_A a' \; f(a) \leqslant_B f(a')$.
2   This is the c-structure parsing algorithm together with the instantiation procedure.
3   Optionality of the oblique agent function is indicated by parentheses.
4   This idea was subsequently adopted within other frameworks to a greater or lesser degree. The previous transformational view was that passivization is a purely structure-

dependent syntactic operation on phrase markers, considered to be insensitive to the lexical relation between the verb and the NP to be moved (e.g. Chomsky 1973: 233).

5   In fact, there is a set of f-structures for this fragment, arising from its ambiguity. For example, *to* could be the infinitival marker, as in . . . *seems to V* . . . , or it could be the preposition marking an experiencer, as in . . . *seems to NP*. . . . The f-structure in (14) arises from the former analysis.

Part III Inflectional Morphology and
Phrase Structure Variation

Introduction

The formal model given in part II allows us to analyze a wide range of syntactic phenomena and to develop some central principles of syntactic theory.

We can now see explicitly how the syntax of language is modelled as linked parallel structures, each of a different formal character. We can also see how the grammar and lexicon consist of a set of local, codescriptive constraints on partial structures. There are no serial operations involved: grammatical structures are defined by constraint satisfaction. If grammar is taken to represent knowledge of a language, then a lexical-functional grammar represents this knowledge as *localized, partial knowledge* – an epistemologically distinctive conception with very different implications from the conventional generative view.

However suggestive this formal architecture of grammar may be, it does not by itself answer a number of substantive questions of syntactic theory. Perhaps the central questions are, *Where do the annotated c-structure constraints come from?* and *What gives c- and f-structure the properties of variability and invariance they are supposed to model?* The purpose of part III is to sketch the outlines of an answer, focusing particularly on the source of variability.

Chapter 6 addresses the first question by proposing general principles for annotating c-structures with functional schemata. This theory prevents arbitrary structure–function mappings, and thereby gives one solution to the problem posed by the existence of "monsters" of c-structure/f-structure correspondence (problem set 1). At the same time it allows for very substantial variation in modes of expression across languages, permitting what is possibly the richest syntactic typology of all current generative theories.

The problem of variability is also addressed in chapter 6, beginning with the principles of economy of expression and lexical integrity, which create competition between words and phrases expressing the same f-structure information. In a kind of lexical bias, LFG gives preference to lexical over syntactic representations of equivalent f-structures. Extensive illustrations of the interplay between lexically and configurationally expressed information are given in chapters 7, 8, and 9 (on head movement, pronominal incorporation, and scrambling/extraction).

6 A Theory of Structure–Function Mappings

Why, in principle, should phrase structure vary across languages? It is a surprising fact that virtually all generative theories of universal grammar are completely compatible with the absence of all variation across languages.[1] We may stipulate that there are alternative universal schemata for phrase structure, or different parameters of variation or choices of formal features, but we do not thereby explain this fact, or relate it to other properties of language. In contrast, functionalists have long argued that language variability reflects conflicting functional constraints such as iconicity and economy (e.g. Haiman 1985), which may be resolved differently by different languages. Yet they have found it difficult to relate these constraints systematically to generative theories of linguistic structure, perhaps because the functional constraints are "output-oriented," applying to overt, "surface" forms of expression rather than to underlying structures. In most generative theories of universal grammar, all of the linguistically significant properties of surface forms are completely derivative from underlying structures by means of the generative mechanisms. No independent theoretical status is accorded to "surface" forms of expression.

The formal architecture of LFG suggests a distinctive theoretical answer to these questions: the parallel structures of LFG do have an independent status and may be subject to conflicting constraints. For example, as we have already seen in chapter 4, the principles of completeness and coherence require full representation of grammatical relations in f-structure, and this induces the presence of certain c-structure constituents through the correspondence mapping. Hence full representation might be thought of as a universal *iconicity* requirement between syntax and semantics. In contrast, principles of lexical integrity and economy of expression, to be discussed directly, universally require elimination of unnecessary syntactic constituents from c-structure. The elimination of syntactic complexity has an equally valid functional motivation, minimizing effort in computing forms of expression. Thus, these parallel c- and f-structures are subject to conflicting principles related to their roles within the overall grammar as a system of transduction between meaning and form. Hence, the correspondence between them cannot be perfect. There will be possible mismatches between the parallel structures and redundancies between types of forms of expression. In this setting, principles of conflict resolution can play an explanatory role in accounting for variation in forms of expression.

In the present work, we will adopt the specific economy principle stated in (1):

(1)   **Economy of Expression:**
      All syntactic phrase structure nodes are optional and are not used unless
      required by independent principles (completeness, coherence, semantic
      expressivity).

Here the restriction to *syntactic* phrase structure nodes is meant to exclude both
terminal nodes, which are morphological words, and preterminal nodes, which
immediately dominate words. In (2) NP and N' are syntactic phrase structure
nodes: *big* and *lions* are terminal nodes; A and N are preterminal nodes.

(2)

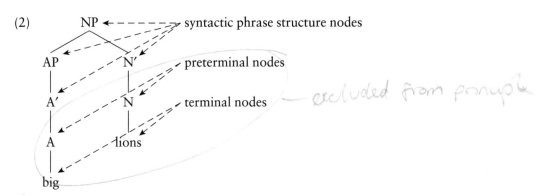

Thus "syntactic phrase structure nodes" refers to those nonterminal nodes which
do not immediately dominate a lexical element. The restriction of economy of
expression (1) to syntactic phrase structure nodes privileges lexical over phrasal
expression where possible, as we will see. Economy of expression requires that if
a syntactic phrase structure node does not contribute to completeness, coherence,
or semantic expressivity, then it is not allowed. "Semantic expressivity" allows
for the use of nodes like the AP *big* in (2). Adjuncts like this AP are not required
by completeness and coherence; yet they are retained because *big lions* differs
from *lions* in semantic expressivity.
     Now the principle of economy of expression implies that if a syntactic phrase
structure node provides *only* redundant information, it is not allowed. Within
the scope of our study, we can model relative information by the lattice of
f-structures described in chapter 5: a phrase structure node is omitted if the
f-structure arising in its absence is at least as specific as the f-structure arising in
its presence.[2] In each case we will compare c-structures of a given sentence for
which the lexical choices have antecedently been made. Under these assumptions,
the satisfaction of the economy principle is clearly decidable, and follows from
the decidability of grammaticality in LFG (chapters 4 and 5). An immediate
consequence is that an empty c-structure category dominating no terminal element and providing only redundant f-structure information will not be allowed.
For example, the nodes labelled N and N' in (3) would be rejected by economy of
expression:

(3)   NP

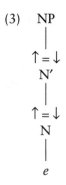

The N node dominates no terminal node[3] and so does not contribute to semantic expressivity; it also adds no new functional information of its own, being annotated only with the $\uparrow = \downarrow$ schema which simply identifies the f-structures of the mother and daughter nodes (chapter 4). The same is true of the N′ node. Thus both N′ and N will be rejected by economy of expression in favor of a similar structure without these nodes. Whether or not the node labelled NP in (3) is allowed depends on whether its annotations provide information needed for completeness and coherence of the sentence of which it is a part. In isolation as in (3) it would simply be rejected by economy of expression. In the present framework (following Bresnan 1998c, Choi 1996, 1997, 1999, Berman 1997), empty categories can appear as a "last resort" in highly configurational languages which lack other means of specifying functions. Examples are discussed in chapter 9.

Economy of expression may be viewed as a special case of the functionalist economy principle articulated by Haiman (1985: 158–9) as the avoidance of syntagmatic redundancy, or "the tendency to economize on the length or complexity of any utterance or message." However, it is structural complexity rather than length in words that is economized by (1). Although not articulated explicitly in these terms, something like this principle has been implicit in analytic work in LFG, which has always avoided empty categories or structures empirically unmotivated by overt forms.[4] Another way to think of the principle is to see that it requires each c-structure node to contribute to the overall f-structure; from this point of view it may be better to regard it as a **principle of functionality of c-structure**.

Economy of expression creates potential competition between different forms of expression that carry overlapping information within the same sentence or phrase. When we consider a further principle, explicit in LFG from the beginning (Bresnan 1982c, Simpson 1983a), the elements of our theoretical explanation of phrase structure variation fall into place. This is the principle of lexical integrity:[5]

(4) **Lexical Integrity:**
     Morphologically complete words are leaves of the c-structure tree and each
     leaf corresponds to one and only one c-structure node.

(4) implies that the structural formation of words is independent of the structural formation of phrases.[6] We see this difference clearly in Warlpiri c-structure: while

the relative order of words in sentences is extremely free (chapters 1 and 9), the relative order of stems and inflections in words (such as the case and tense markers) is fixed. It is quite generally true across languages that morphemic order within words is rigidly encapsulated from the kind of scrambling and free orderings seen in word-external structures. Not only the order of word-internal elements but their structural type also differs from that of c-structure phrases. Even in cases of word formation that appear to interact with the structure of the clause, such as West Greenlandic noun incorporation (problem set 2), where a verb-internal noun stem may specify an f-structure complement of the clause, the incorporated noun is a bound stem which lacks the structural properties of syntactic noun phrases (such as case morphology). This difference reappears in other noun incorporation languages (T. Mohanan 1994, 1995). Such structural differences have further consequences which can be traced to the fundamental requirement that words be composed of lexical materials (stems and affixes), which exclude purely syntactic constructs such as empty categories and phrasal configurations (T. Mohanan 1994, Bresnan and Mchombo 1995). Thus while it is possible that certain types of words may be compounded from elements which are arranged in a word-internal morphemic tree structure whose constituents may even have f-structure functions, these word trees still give evidence that they are not subject to the c-structure principles or rules (such as extraction configurations) that we find in the structural formation of syntactic phrases.

Lexical integrity within LFG differs from other formulations of lexical integrity which assert that the internal structure of words is invisible to all syntax. (4) keeps the internal structural formation of words invisible to c-structure principles, but it allows the f-structures specified by words to unify with the f-structures of the syntactic contexts.

This conception of lexical integrity has close parallels in prosodic phonology. The phonological word is the minimal element in sentential prosodic structure, and it is well known that phonological words may mismatch and overlap c-structure words (Inkelas and Zec 1990). Similarly, within a morphological word, prosodic units such as syllables and feet may mismatch the morphemic units, giving rise to prosodic infixation. In the same way, the morphologically complete word is a minimal element in c-structure, but it may correspond to several "functional words"; conversely, a single "functional word" may correspond to several morphologically complete syntactic words.[7] We have already seen examples of such mismatches: the Greenlandic verb can be analyzed as a single c-structural word that may incorporate different f-structure "words" (an object and the main predicator), each corresponding to a different PRED attribute; similarly, the synthetic verbal forms of Ulster Irish are morphologically complete c-structure words that correspond to distinct f-structure "words" (a pronominal subject and the main predicator).[8]

As we have just seen, LFG's lexical integrity principle implies that while morphemic words and syntactic phrases are different types of forms of expression in c-structure, they may carry the same types of information in f-structure. In other words, these different forms of expression – words and phrases – may be functionally equivalent (in terms of f-structure content). In such cases of equivalence, economy of expression privileges words over syntactic phrase structure nodes: it is only the syntactic nodes whose presence must be justified by economy of expression. In effect, words are considered more economical than phrases. It then follows that within a sentence morphological forms will compete with and pre-empt phrases that carry no additional information. If the syntactic phrase structure nodes do not bear additional functions that distinguish them from the morphological structures, they must be omitted. Morphologically rich languages thus potentially exert a strong competitive pressure on their syntactic phrase structures, and given the historical changes that lead to morphological elaboration and erosion, this result can provide a theoretical explanation for the existence of phrase structure variation within our formal model of universal grammar.[9]

The present chapter outlines a particular theory of c-structure to f-structure mappings based on these principles. In the subsequent chapters of part III we apply this theory to several types of phrase structure variation seen crosslinguistically: head movement (chapter 7), pronominal incorporation (chapter 8), and scrambling (chapter 9). In chapters 9 and 10 we examine the consequences of this theory for pronominal binding, and we discover independent evidence for the thesis that morphology competes with syntax in the way proposed here.

In relation to part II, the theory developed in the subsequent chapters is a metatheory. The LFG architecture is compatible with a range of differing substantive theoretical conceptions of grammatical functions, c-structure categories, morphology, and c-structure to f-structure mappings. If we think of each grammar as a formal theory of the language it generates, the substantive linguistic principles under discussion here constitute a metatheory – a theory of theories.

6.1   Grammatical Functions

A theory of c-structure to f-structure mappings begins with the definition of the f-structure functions. We will therefore outline the basics of the theory of grammatical functions assumed here; functions are further analyzed in part IV.

6.1.1   *Basics of grammatical functions*

Grammatical functions are characterized in chapter 1 as the "relators" of c-structure to a-structure. Each function – e.g. SUBJ, OBJ, ADJ(unct) – maps a class of expressions to argument structures in a characteristic way; hence each function can be defined as a class of c-structure expressions which are equivalently mapped. Syntactic functions are thus a useful abstraction from the variability of c-structures. This property holds regardless of the particular inventory of functions defined by the metatheory.[10]

For example, the SUBJ function has no single universal structural form. Instead there is a class of varying forms of expression that participate in the mappings to argument structures in the same way. Structural expressions of the subject include NPs in a certain phrase structure configuration (English), discontinuous nominals bearing a specific case (Warlpiri, chapter 1), verbal inflectional morphology alternating with syntactic NPs (Ulster Irish, problem set 2), and zero pronouns lacking any c-structure representation. These expressions are schematically represented as $c\text{-}s_1$, $c\text{-}s_2, \ldots, c\text{-}s_n$ in (5), which depicts their shared mappings to argument structures $a\text{-}s_1$, $a\text{-}s_2, \ldots, a\text{-}s_n$ (e.g. monadic, dyadic, triadic, passive of dyadic, etc.):

(5)
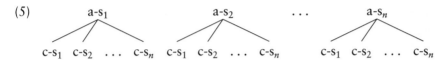

The "SUBJ" abstraction allows us to avoid separately stating the same argument structure mappings for each type of expression, which would make their equivalence accidental:

(6)
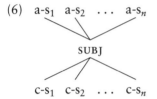

The characteristic mappings of the SUBJ function onto arguments vary typologically along several dimensions. In the basic case (i.e., without special verbal morphology), the subject may map onto the semantically most prominent available role in the argument structure (as in accusative languages), or onto the argument in control of the eventuality (as in active languages), or onto the argument most affected by the eventuality (as in ergative languages). The subject may also map onto the most prominent argument on a person or animacy hierarchy (as in inverse systems – see chapter 8). What these possibilities have in common is the prominence of the subject argument on the selected dimension compared to other arguments.

As with the SUBJ function, the OBJ function has no single universal structural form. Instead there is a class of varying forms of expression that all participate in the OBJ mappings to argument structures in the same way. Structural expressions of the object include NPs in a certain phrase structure configuration (English), discontinuous nominals bearing a specific case (Warlpiri, chapter 1), noun stems morphologically bound to the verb (in some noun-incorporating languages; cf. Greenlandic, problem set 2), verbal inflectional morphology alternating with syntactic NPs (Moroccan Arabic, problem set 2), and null pronominals lacking any c-structural expression at all. In the Bantu language Kichaga, an SVO language, topical pronominal objects are prefixed to the verb stem as part of the verb morphology, free pronoun objects appear at the right edge of the VP (doubled by the verbal object prefix), and nominal objects are NPs immediately following the verb (Bresnan and Moshi 1990). All three of these different structural expressions of OBJ behave alike under lexical operations that alter argument structure (e.g. applicatives, causatives, passives). The "OBJ" abstraction allows us to avoid restating the same argument-structure mappings for each type of expression, exactly as in the case of the SUBJ (6). The OBJ function is thus an equivalence class of c-structure expressions that share these characteristic mappings to argument structure.

Among objects typologists have made several classifications, distinguishing direct and indirect objects on the one hand, and primary and secondary objects on the other (Dryer 1986). Researchers in LFG have generally adopted the latter classification, using the names "OBJ" and "OBJ$_\theta$" for primary and secondary objects, respectively.[11]

The subject and objects are the **core functions** associated with the central participants of the eventuality expressed by the verb.[12] They are usually formally distinguished from noncore functions, such as obliques (designated OBL$_\theta$ and indexed to their thematic role), predicate complements (the latter of which we will designate by "COMPL" for now), and adjuncts, which are not argument functions at all. In English, for example, core arguments have canonical c-structure positions which can be occupied only by NPs/DPs; noncore arguments are generally expressed by other c-structure categories (obliques by PPs, other complements by VPs, APs, or CPs, etc.). In Zazaki (a variety of Zaza, an Anatolian language belonging to the northwest subgroup of Iranian languages), core arguments are all marked by the same direct case, while noncore arguments receive the same oblique case (Sandonato 1994). In Malayalam only core arguments can be expressed as zero pronouns (K. P. Mohanan 1982a).

The core and noncore functions are arranged in a **relational hierarchy** (Keenan and Comrie 1977), shown in (7):

(7) **Relational Hierarchy:**

core			noncore		
SUBJ >	OBJ >	OBJ$_\theta$ >	OBL$_\theta$ >	COMPL >	ADJUNCT

Argument functions are all more prominent than adjuncts, and these prominence relations play a role in pronominal binding theory (chapters 10 and 11).

In addition to adjuncts there are other nonargument functions that do not map directly to a-structure roles:

(8) **Nonargument Functions:**
TOP, FOC, ADJ

As discussed in section 4.9, all nonargument functions allow multiple instances without violating the uniqueness condition on f-structures.[13]

Like the argument functions, the nonargument functions can be defined as equivalence classes of c-structure expressions under the mapping to argument structures. All of the nonargument functions bind their expressions to something other than an argument role. ADJ binds to the PRED itself, while TOP and FOC bind to argument structure through other syntactic functions.

The ADJ(unct) function binds to a PRED rather than to one of its arguments: an ADJ satisfies completeness and coherence (section 4.7) by occurring in the same f-structure as the PRED it modifies. As with the argument functions, there is no universal structural form taken by all ADJs. They may be of any category type and they may occur in a variety of configurations or case-marked forms.

The TOP and FOC functions indirectly map to the argument structure by being identified with, or anaphorically linked to, another syntactic function. For example, the preposed phrase *Rosie* in (9) is both the FOC and the OBJ$_\theta$ of its sentence:

(9)   ROSIE I named her.

English topicalizations can have either FOCUS or TOPIC functions, as shown by the *wh-* question test (Gundel 1974, Kroeger 1993). The answer to an interrogative is focused with respect to the (topical) residue that remains after subtracting the interrogative phrase. By this test the construction called "topicalization" in English can either focus the initial constituent or make a (new) topic of it:[14]

(10)   Q: What did you name your cat?
       A: ROSIE I named her. (*Rosie* = FOC)

(11)   Q: What did you name your pets?
       A: My dog, I named Harold. My cat, I named Rosie.
            (*my dog, my cat* = TOP)

However, TOP and FOC often diverge in their formal expressions, occupying different phrase structure positions or bearing different morphological marking.

Note that f-structure is not meant as a model of the pragmatics of discourse functions, but only as one dimension of grammatical structure, which includes the syntactically represented ("grammaticalized") functions. These functions, whether TOP, FOC, SUBJ, or OBJ, all have much richer, more complex, and variable discourse uses. Similarly, a-structure is not meant as a model of semantic structure.

6.1.2   Classification of grammatical functions

For the theory of structure–function mappings, the grammatical functions may be cross-classified according to several properties. First, we may distinguish the **argument functions** from the **nonargument functions**, as discussed above. The argument functions are labelled *a-fns* in (12):

		a-fns					
(12) TOP	FOC	SUBJ	OBJ	OBJ$_\theta$	OBL$_\theta$	COMPL	ADJUNCT
non-a-fns							*non-a-fns*

Next we may distinguish the grammaticalized **discourse functions**, referred to as *d-fns* in (13):

$$\overbrace{\hphantom{xxxxxxxxxxxxxxxxxxxx}}^{\textit{d-fns}}$$

(13) TOP   FOC   SUBJ $\underbrace{\text{OBJ}\quad \text{OBJ}_\theta\quad \text{OBL}_\theta\quad \text{COMPL}\quad \text{ADJUNCT}}_{\textit{non-d-fns}}$

These functions are the most salient in discourse and often have c-structure properties that iconically express this prominence, such as preceding or c-commanding other constituents in the clause. In addition the SUBJ is often identified as the default TOP of the clause.[15]

Note that the **subject**, according to this classification, has the unique property of being both an argument function and a grammaticalized discourse function. The nondiscourse argument functions are the **complement functions** (CF), and the nondiscourse nonargument functions are the **adjuncts**.

The argument functions are further distinguished by primitive features that play a role in the lexical mapping theory, which projects nuclear f-structures from a-structures (chapter 14). This theory imposes fairly narrow limits on the possible alternations of syntactic functions for a given lexical role, both within and across languages, and so may be regarded as a major explanatory source of the relative invariance of f-structures across languages.

Thus, while f-structure functions are not defined by c-structure categories, and hence are irreducible or "primitive" in categorial terms, they may be derived from more primitive functional properties, and so are not primitives of syntactic theory. In the same way the c-structure phrasal categories are decomposable into primitive categorial features.[16]

6.2   The Organization of C-Structure Categories

C-structure categories can be organized **endocentrically** and **lexocentrically**. Endocentric organization appears in highly hierarchical c-structures, such as we find in English. Lexocentric organization appears in flat c-structures with all arguments (including subjects) sisters of the verb, such as we find in Warlpiri, Jiwarli, and other nonconfigurational languages of Australia; it requires the specification of syntactic functions by morpholexical means, such as case and agreement.[17] Consistent with our model of the grammar as localized constraints on partial structures, many languages have a mixture of both types of structures.

6.2.1   Endocentricity and X′ structures

The endocentric organization of c-structure is embodied in X′ theory. The reader is assumed to be familiar with some version of X′ theory, but a brief self-contained review of X′ theory, establishing the notation and terminology used here, can be found in the appendix to this chapter. Empirical exemplifications of the X′ theory assumed here will be given in subsequent chapters of part III.

Recall from chapter 4 that we are interpreting our c-structure schemata as tree admissibility conditions (constraints on possible tree structures), rather than as rules for rewriting, generating, or "projecting" structures. We continue to use the "rule" notation as in (14) rather than tree structure notation, in order to keep clearly separate the objects of the model, which are structures, from the grammar, which consists of constraints on structures:

(14) a. $X′ \rightarrow X^0$, YP
       b. XP $\rightarrow$ YP, X′

An important development in X′ theory is the extension of the principle of endocentricity to closed classes of grammatical categories – to "minor" categories such as complementizers, finite auxiliary verbs, or determiners. These belong to a subdivision of "functional" F^0 categories, which are generally closed classes of "function words" distinguishable from the "lexical words" which project the levels of (lexical) categories seen above. In some languages the functional categories may include inflectionally defined subclasses of lexical categories (such as all finite verbs). In English, for example, I^0 (read: "infl") is the category of temporal/aspectual finite auxiliary and modal verbs; C^0 is the category of complementizers; D^0 is a category of determiners, demonstratives, and pronouns. Each of these is assumed to be the head of endocentric phrasal projections such as IP, CP, DP, I′, etc., as in (15):[18]

(15)

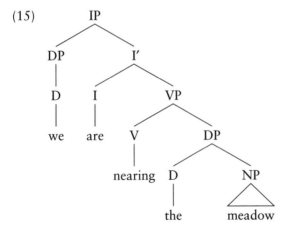

In a thoroughly endocentric language, the sentence itself can be identified with IP, possibly dominated by CP. As Kroeger (1993: 6) observes, the idea that a sentence (IP) is the projection of I^0 captures the widespread generalization that the finite verbal element occupies a unique position in the sentence and functions as its (categorial) head.[19] As remarked above, in English only a subset of finite verbs (the auxiliaries and modals) can occupy the I position. This subset of verb forms has special syntactic properties, inverting with the subject (*Is she sleeping?* vs. **Sleeps she?*), preceding sentential negation *not* (*She is not sleeping* vs. **She sleeps not*), permitting contracted negation (*She isn't sleeping* vs. **She sleepsn't*), and the like. D^0 is a functional category of determiners and pronouns in English, but is not present in all languages. (Warlpiri, for example, has been argued to lack determiners: Bittner and Hale 1995.) Thus we adopt the following inventory of X^0 categories, which project X′ and X″ phrases:

(16) a. F^0: C^0, I^0, D^0 ("functional" categories)
      b. L^0: N^0, V^0, A^0, P^0 (lexical categories)

An interesting relation between the lexical and functional categories has been observed: in many languages I and C are occupied by verbal elements or verbs while D is occupied by nominal elements (Grimshaw 1998). This leads to the idea (proposed by Grimshaw 1998) that **functional categories share the categorial features of lexical categories**: I is a verbal category, D is a nominal category, and C – we will assume here – may be verbal or nominal (Webelhuth 1992, Bresnan 1995a).

Formally, X′ categories can be analyzed as triples consisting of a categorial feature matrix (17), a level of structure (18), and a third, privative feature F, which flags a category as "functional" (F) or unspecified as functional (lexical) (ØF). The features and levels are discussed in the appendix to this chapter. We allow up to two levels of distinct functional projections F1 and F2, which can be used, for example, to distinguish IP and CP (Grimshaw 1998).[20] This permits us to state constraints on the combination of functional projections with other categories (Grimshaw 1998):

(17) **Kinds of Categories:**

	"predicative"	"transitive"	
V	+	+	verbal
P	–	+	pre- or postpositional
N	–	–	nominal
A	+	–	adjectival

(18) **Levels of Categories:**

type:	0	1	2
	V	V′	V″ (VP)
	P	P′	P″ (PP)
	N	N′	N″ (NP)
	A	A′	A″ (AP)

(19) Examples:
      V^0:   <[+ predicative, + transitive], 0, ØF>
      VP = V″:   <[+ predicative, + transitive], 2, ØF>

I^0:   <[+ predicative, + transitive], 0, F1>
CP = C″:   <[+ predicative, + transitive], 2, F2>
DP = D″:   <[− predicative, − transitive], 2, F1>

In what follows we assume the following categorial combination constraint:

(20) **Combinatorial Constraint on Functional Heads:**
      A category C can be the complement of a functional head $\mathcal{F}$ only if $\mathcal{F}$'s categorial feature matrix is less marked than C's.
      ("Less marked" means differing only in having a minus feature value instead of a plus feature value, referring to the values in (17).)

This will allow the verbal categories to be embedded in both nominal (DP, CP) and verbal (CP, IP) functional projections, while nominal categories can be embedded only in nominal functional projections.

Each functional projection FP, then, provides a grammatically specialized category and position for specific subclasses of words that have a special (syncategorematic) grammatical role such as marking subordination, clause type, finiteness, and the like. As we will see, the extension of X′ theory to functional categories FP enables us to capture significant structural generalizations about syntactic typology and word order that are familiar from the transformational framework. In the present framework, of course, X′ theory is not a theory of the input structures to syntactic transformations, but part of the theory of overt forms of expression (c-structure). As such, our X′ must conform to the principle of *structural integrity of words*, the lexical integrity principle of (4): X^0 categories are categories of morphologically complete words. Hence "bare affixes or disembodied morphological features," as Kroeger (1993: 6) puts it, cannot be independently generated in phrase structure. This principle holds for both lexical L^0 and functional F^0 categories. In English, for example, C^0 is the category of *that* and *if*, I^0 is the category of *is*, finite *do*, and *must* (finite auxiliary and modal verbs), and V^0 is the category of all other verbs. In Russian C^0 is the category of *čto* 'that' and interrogative *li*, I^0 is the category of all finite verbs, and V^0 is the category of infinitives (King 1995). In other words, **functional categories are specialized subclasses of lexical categories which have a syncategorematic role in the grammar (such as marking subordination, clause type, or finiteness).**

The types of c-structure constraints used in chapter 4 as tree admissibility conditions can now be derived from these more abstract universal c-structure constraints given by the principle of endocentricity. Any c-structure pattern can be considered unmarked if it is an instantiation of these universal endocentric constraints. By this means our theory allows the presence of marked constructions of irregular form and content alongside of instantiations of the universal endocentric patterns.

The functional component of these constraints (the "rule annotations" of chapter 4) may also be derived from the following proposed universal principles of endocentric structure–function association.[21] Because the head relation in LFG is modelled through the identification of a node's f-structure with the f-structure of its mother, the term "f-structure head" does not refer to an attribute such as HEAD, but to an f-structure. Again because of the imperfect correspondence between structure and function permitted in LFG, f-structure heads need not correspond only to c-structure heads:

(21) a. C-structure heads are f-structure heads.
      b. Specifiers of functional categories are the grammaticalized discourse functions DF.
      c. Complements of functional categories are f-structure coheads.
      d. Complements of lexical categories are the nondiscourse argument functions CF.
      e. Constituents adjoined[22] to phrasal constituents are nonargument functions $\overline{\text{AF}}$ or not annotated.[23]

Each statement in (21a–e) licenses a particular type of annotation to a c-structure configuration, as illustrated in (22a–e), respectively:

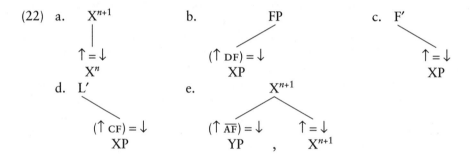

Observe that (22d, e) allow the same configuration of X′ immediately dominating X′ and YP to define YP as a complement function (d) and as an adjunct (e). We will interpret these two possibilities as nondeterministically chosen alternatives.

Let us now define the intuitive statements in (21) and their accompanying diagrammatic illustrations in (22). The classic definitions of heads, complements, and specifiers given in (14) and in (59) in the appendix to this chapter assume that a zero-bar level lexical category X^0 is always present (at least at an underlying level) to project higher levels of structure. In the present setting, in contrast, any node may be optional, and functional ambiguities are allowed; we therefore need a more flexible and "surface-oriented" definition of these functions. For this reason the diagrams in (22) specify the functional annotations without reference to the presence of a sister category (except for adjunction structures, which are not purely endocentric in the classic sense of immediately dominating a categorial head which is one bar level lower). Building on this idea, the more precise formulation of the structure–function mapping principles given in (23) makes use of the following definitions. C-structure heads are defined as **projecting nodes**: nodes labelled X^0 and X′, as illustrated in (22a). A **projection** is any X^n category, for

$n > 0$, and a projection of the same kind as another node N matches the categorial features (including the functional category feature F) of N's category label. Specifiers, complements, and adjuncts are **nonprojecting nodes**, defined as nodes labelled by the maximal projections X″ (or by a nonprojective category S, to be discussed subsequently), as illustrated in (22b, d, e). A node **in** X refers to a node immediately dominated by a node labelled x. All of the preceding definitions are meant to exclude nodes to which constituents are adjoined, called **adjoined-to nodes**. The latter are defined to be a syntactic phrase structure node (as in (2)) immediately dominated by a node having the same label; this is illustrated in (22e).[24] With these definitions, the statements in (23a–e) correspond respectively to those in (21a–e) and the diagrams in (22a–e):

(23) a.   Annotate a projecting node in a projection of the same kind with ↑ = ↓.
 b.   Annotate a nonprojecting node in F″ with (↑ DF) = ↓.
 c.   Annotate a nonprojecting node in F′ with ↑ = ↓.
 d.   Annotate a nonprojecting node in L′ with (↑ CF) = ↓.
 e.   Optionally annotate a nonprojecting node and its adjoined-to sister node with (↑ A̅F̅) = ↓ and ↑ = ↓, respectively.

 These principles should be understood as giving us the predictable annotations of endocentric c-structure rules. (There may also be unpredictable annotations which would have to be fully specified.) To see their effects, let us examine an example c-structure:[25]

(24)

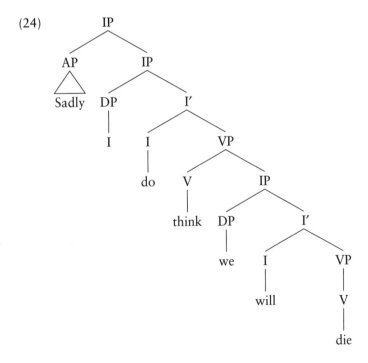

(23a) expresses the principle that the c-heads of all projections are f-structure heads; this generalization is captured by annotating ↑ = ↓ on all projecting nodes in a projection in the c-structure tree. Hence, in an endocentric system, the annotation ↑ = ↓ on the categorial head is implicit and need not be expressed. Applying this principle to (24), we can infer the following annotations from (23a):

(25)

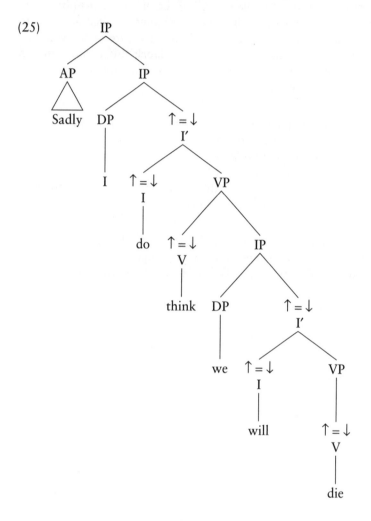

(23b) expresses the principle that the specifiers of functional projections are the grammaticalized discourse functions in (13): (TOP, FOC, SUBJ). The choice of discourse function for each FP varies across languages: for example, the specifier of IP in English is SUBJ, while in other languages it is TOP or FOC or even absent (Alsagoff 1992, Kroeger 1993, King 1995). Applying this principle to (24), with the specification of SUBJ for English, we infer the following additional annotations:

(26)

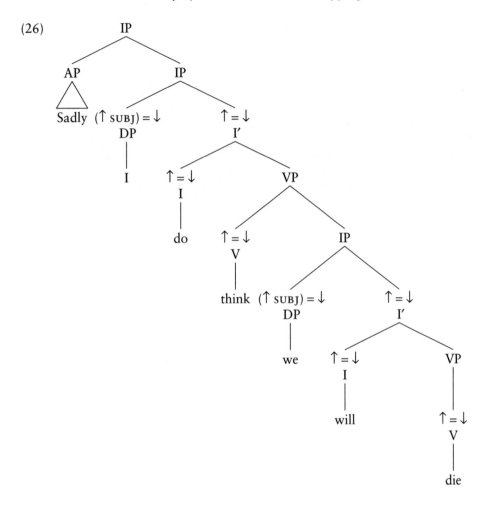

Now consider (23c), which expresses the principle that the complements of F′ are f-structure coheads with F⁰s. The effects are illustrated in (27):

(27)

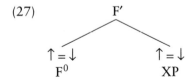

By (23a), F⁰ is both the c-structure head of F′ and an f-structure head, designated by $\uparrow = \downarrow$ in (27). By (23c), XP is also an f-structure head, hence an f-structure "cohead" of F⁰. Note that XP is *not* a c-head of F′. Thus (23c) captures the intuition that the relation of the functional F⁰ categories to their complements is not that of predicator to argument: either the F⁰ element is a function word

lacking descriptive content altogether, or it is an inflectionally defined lexical element such as a finite verb which is related to arguments within its phrasal cohead
at the level of f-structure. Observe how this principle of structure–function association crucially exploits the parallel architecture of LFG: because grammatical
relations are not *identified* with phrase structure configurations, but only associated with them through the correspondence mapping between parallel structures,
there can be mismatches between syntactic functions and the structural forms
that express them. Here the function of f-structure "head" systematically mismatches the categorial configuration of c-structure heads, with interesting consequences that we will examine in the next chapter. Applying this principle to our
example structure (24), we infer the following additional annotations on the
VPs:

(28)

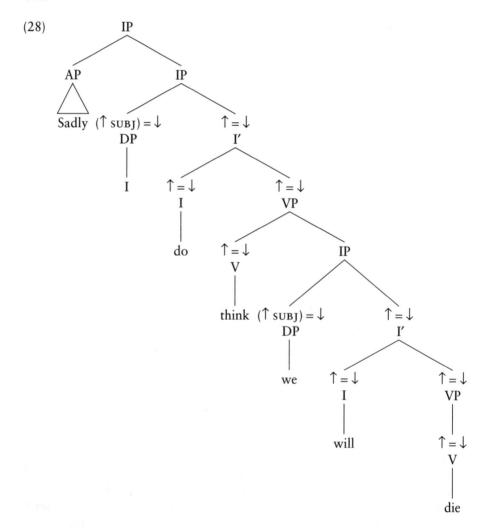

(23d) states that the complements of lexical projections (dominated by L′) are the nondiscourse argument functions – that is, the complement functions (OBJ, OBJ$_\theta$, OBL$_\theta$, COMPL) in (12) and (13). The choice of complement function is lexically determined. We have omitted the V′ nodes from our trees in accordance with a common abbreviatory convention (n. 18). Assume for the purposes of this illustration that V′ dominates V IP; then the annotation of the complement functions CF is licensed by (23d) (V′ itself would be annotated with ↑ = ↓ by (23a)):

(29)

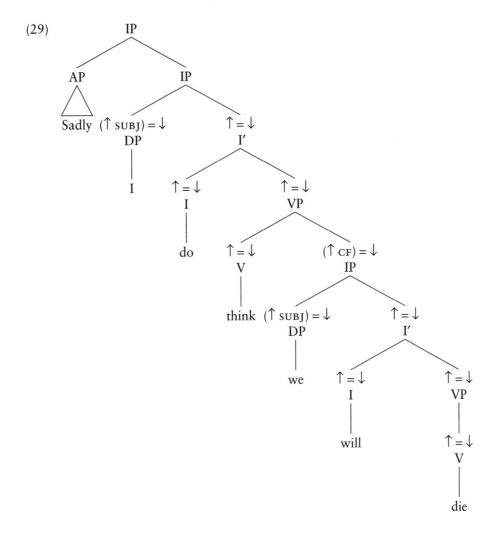

Finally, (23e) says that constituents adjoined to XP are nonargument functions: TOP, FOC, or ADJUNCT. This licenses the annotations on the AP and its sister IP shown in (30):

(30)

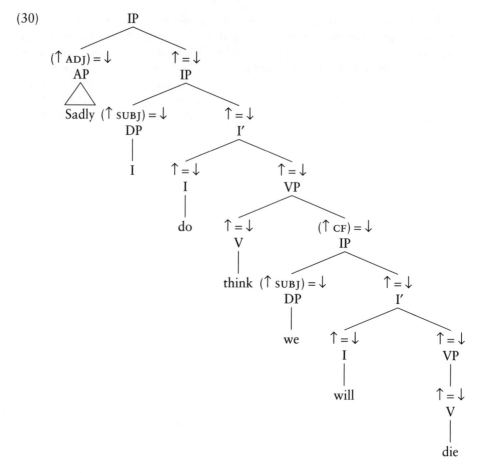

It must be noted that there is an implicit problem in this analysis of English auxiliaries as belonging to the category I, arising from the nonfinite forms of the auxiliaries *be, have*. Only the finite forms of the auxiliary verbs *be, have* in English are positioned in I, where they must precede standard sentence negation *not*:

(31) a. Mary is not running.
  b. *Mary not is running.
  c. *Mary is running not.

If *not* must follow I and precede nonfinite VP, then (31a, b) shows that *is* belongs to I, while (32) shows that *be* belongs to V, not I:

(32) Mary will not be running in that race.

Thus the nonfinite forms of the auxiliary are not in I, but appear to head the VP sister to I. Nevertheless, the lexical content of the verb *be* in these two forms appears the same: it is the same marker of progressive aspect. The absence of a PRED feature that permits it to appear in I cooccurring with the main verb in V can also be assumed for its occurrence in V. But this means that the complement of this V cannot have one of the complement functions CF; otherwise the coherence condition would be violated (because there would be no PRED designator of the CF in the highest f-structure for the sentence). This problem can be solved by extending the cohead principle optionally to V and VP.[26] General principles of the theory will cause the cohead option to be taken only when an appropriate auxiliary verb, rather than a main lexical verb, occupies V. Nonauxiliary verbs which take VP complements (discussed in chapter 12) will have their own PRED, which will require their VP complement to have a complement function by the complement mapping principle previously given (21d), together with completeness, coherence, and uniqueness. Only auxiliary verbs, lacking the PRED, will allow the cohead option.

We will therefore broaden our theory to extend the cohead principle optionally to the complements of lexical categories, as proposed by Alsina (1996b, 1997) and Sadler (1997):

(33) a. Complements of functional categories are f-structure coheads.
      b. Complements of lexical categories are the nondiscourse argument functions or f-structure coheads.

(34) a. F′   b. L′
                \\   \\
            ↑ = ↓   (↑ CF) = ↓ ∨ ↑ = ↓
            XP   XP

A nondeterministic choice may be made between the annotation possibilities given in (34b); completeness, coherence, and uniqueness will determine the correct outcome.

With these principles the grammar of a given language need not specify either the structures or the general structure–function associations of the endocentric pattern. A particular language may select from the available space of endocentric structures,[27] and the codescriptive constraints on partial c-structures and f-structures that constitute a lexical-functional grammar can be derived from these general principles as the instantiations of universal constraints. To this extent, annotated c-structure rules are eliminable.

6.2.2   Lexocentricity and S

Not all languages abide by endocentricity in all of their expression structures. An alternative mode of c-structure organization – *lexocentricity* – associates syntactic functions directly with features borne by words rather than with the configurational relations of phrases in syntax. This mode is evidenced in such typologically diverse languages as Tagalog (Kroeger 1993), Hungarian (Kiss 1987, 1994), Malayalam (K. P. Mohanan 1982a), Warlpiri (Simpson 1991), Jiwarli (Austin and Bresnan 1996), Wambaya (Nordlinger 1998b, Nordlinger and Bresnan 1996), Jakaltek, and others (Woolford 1991). Under this mode of c-structure organization, information about grammatical relations cannot be exclusively associated with the syntactic context of words in the form of distinct hierarchical phrase structure configurations, but must be "lexically localized" – that is, directly associated with the forms of words themselves (by case and agreement morphology, for example).

These languages reveal that universal grammar makes available **a nonprojective, exocentric category S** for clauses. S stands for "sentence" or "small clause," distinct from IP (Bresnan 1982b, Chung and McCloskey 1987, Kroeger 1993, Austin and Bresnan 1996, Choi 1999, Nordlinger and Bresnan 1996, Nordlinger 1998b, Sadler 1997, Sells 1998). Nonprojectivity means that S lacks a categorial head: its category cannot be identified with any fixed category X^0. Exocentricity means that S may have an f-structure head of a different category, whether V, N, A, VP, NP, AP, or other. The nonprojectivity of S implies that it may dominate multiple distinct categories C not bearing the typical branching relations of endocentricity, because it is not subject to the X′ schemata:

(35) S → C^*

In this radically nonconfigurational structure type, syntactic functions cannot be identified by phrase structural configuration – nor should they be. Instead, the functions are associated with information carried by words themselves. Let us assume that the categories C in (35) are freely associated with the annotations for f-structure head (↑ = ↓) and nonargument functions, but that c-structure does not associate argument functions with constituents; instead, these functions are characteristically associated with case and agreement features of the predicator and its arguments.

To see how the lexocentric mode works in principle, consider the c-structure in (36), and assume that configurational information about the grammatical function of the NP is lacking in S. We know only that it is not the head, but a dependent (argument or modifier) of the head:

(36)

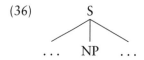

Suppose that the NP is headed by a nominal inflected for case, which carries the specification (↑ CASE) = ACC. [CASE ACC] will then be a feature of the NP's f-structure f_{np}. Suppose further that in the language in which (36) occurs, ACC is the case of objects OBJ. The latter generalization can be expressed by annotating the conditional functional schema in (37) to the NP in (36):

(37) (↓ CASE) = ACC ⇒ (↑ OBJ) = ↓

As explained in section 4.6, (37) will test for the presence of the accusative case feature in f_{np} (the f-structure of the NP), and if it is present, it will identify that f-structure as the value of the OBJ attribute in the containing f-structure of S, f_s. In this way, a case feature carried by a word can be used to construct the syntactic function of the NP. This mode of function identification is called **dependent-marking**, because the relation of the dependent to the head is marked on the dependent.

Alternatively, the language in which (36) occurs might be a **head-marking** language, in which the relation of the dependent to the head is marked on the head. Let us assume that this language is caseless, lacking dependent-marking altogether, as well as radically nonconfigurational. How can the grammatical function of NP be identified? Let us assume that the head of the S is a verb V, which is inflected to agree in person, number, and gender with both the subject and the object. The head will then specify, say, ($\uparrow$ OBJ GEND) = MASC, ($\uparrow$ OBJ PERS) = 3, etc. These verbal inflections will create an OBJ attribute in the f-structure of S, f_s, whose value will be a subsidiary f-structure containing just these agreement features. Now we can check the f-structure of NP, f_{np}, for the presence of the features [GEND MASC] and [PERS NUM], etc., and if they match the features of the object specified by the head, we can identify the grammatical function of the NP as OBJ. We can do this by annotating the following conditional constraint onto NP in (36):

(38) $((\downarrow \text{ PERS}) = (\uparrow \text{ OBJ PERS}) \ \& \ (\downarrow \text{ GEND}) = (\uparrow \text{ OBJ GEND})) \Rightarrow (\uparrow \text{ OBJ}) = \downarrow$

These two general types of lexocentric function specification – "dependent-marking" and "head-marking" – are schematized abstractly in (39)[28] (AGR is used here simply as a metavariable for attributes such as PERS, NUM, GEND, just as GF is used as a metavariable for function attributes such as SUBJ and OBJ):

(39)   **Types of Morphological Function Specification:**
   a.   dependent-marking:
        ($\downarrow$ CASE) = $\kappa \Rightarrow$ ($\uparrow$ GF) = $\downarrow$
   b.   head-marking:
        $((\downarrow \text{ AGR}) = (\uparrow \text{ AF AGR}) \Rightarrow (\uparrow \text{ AF}) = \downarrow)$

Assume free and optional annotation of the schemata to the NP in (36). Then (38a) means that (any instance of) the function GF can optionally be associated with NP if there is a case attribute with a certain value in NP's f-structure. Similarly, (38b) means that (any instance of) the argument function AF can optionally be associated with NP if there are agreement features in NP's f-structure which match the agreement features provided for that function (by the verbal inflections, for example). Constraints of this type, together with the principles of coherence and completeness, will select the correct function for each c.[29]

The crosslinguistic distribution of head-marking conditions generally follows the functional hierarchy for argument functions (Moravcsik 1974, Givón 1976):

OBJ is identified by head-marking only if SUBJ is, and more oblique arguments are rarely identified by head-marking. The dependent marking conditions appear to follow the same hierarchy in reverse, the more oblique functions being identified by dependent-marking before the less oblique functions are. Consequently, obique case-marked arguments rarely show verb agreement.

In the head-marking schema in (39b), agreement features borne by a head are used to specify the function of an external syntactic constituent that matches these features. "Head-marking" also refers to the situation in which the head itself fully specifies both the syntactic function and the semantic content of a dependent (which then must be omitted from phrase structure by virtue of uniqueness and economy of expression). We will study several examples of the latter in chapter 8. The dependent-marking schema (39a) will be exemplified in chapter 9.

The most dramatic examples of the structure type shown in (37) come from the Australian aboriginal languages, such as Warlpiri (Simpson 1991), Jiwarli (Austin and Bresnan 1996), and Wambaya (Nordlinger 1998b). Because these are discussed in chapter 1, problem set 1, and chapter 7, we will not provide a further illustration here.

6.2.3 *S and endocentricity*

The exocentric category S is not everywhere nonconfigurational, however, if by "nonconfigurational" we mean "lacking a VP" or other projection distinguishing subject position from complement position. Many languages have subject predicate constructions of the form in (40), where XP may be a predicate phrase of any of a range of categories VP, NP, AP, or PP:[30]

(40)

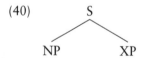

The very fact that the predicate XP, the functional head, may be one of a range of categories indicates that its parent category is not endocentric. Nevertheless, both NP and XP in this example are hierarchical categories organized by endocentricity. A language with this structure may or may not make use of lexocentric means of function identification; it is possible that the subject and predicate simply correspond to the structural configuration. Thus we add to our principles of structure–function correspondence the following simple addition:

(41)   The daughters of S may be subject and predicate.

We understand (41) as licensing the annotation of ($\uparrow$ SUBJ) = $\downarrow$ and $\uparrow$ = $\downarrow$ to NP and XP in (40). An example of the configurational S is discussed in chapter 7 in the analysis of Welsh verb positioning.

6.3 Toward a Typology

Because the LFG architecture of grammar consists of localized constraints on partial structures, languages may freely mix endocentric and lexocentric modes of categorial organization. This produces a typology of possible syntaxes much closer to a continuum than to a small, discrete parameterization. In her study of nonconfigurationality in Australian languages, Nordlinger (1998b) proposes the following typology to illustrate this important point:

(42) **Basic Typology of Expression of Grammatical Relations** (Nordlinger 1998b):

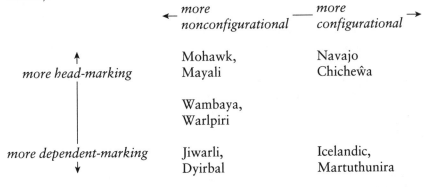

The column on the left shows the lexocentric mode of organization, with head-marking at the top of the scale and dependent-marking at the bottom. The horizontal row at the top shows the endocentric mode of organization, with extreme endocentricity at the right (designated as greater configurationality) and no endocentricity at the left (designated as greater nonconfigurationality). The languages situated in this typological space include Mohawk (an Iroquoian language of northeastern North America), Mayali (a non-Pama-Nyungan language of northern Australia), Jiwarli (a Pama-Nyungan language of western Australia), Dyirbal (a Pama-Nyungan language of northeastern Australia), Navajo (an Athapaskan language of western North America), Chicheŵa (a Bantu language of southern central Africa: see references in chapter 8), Icelandic (an insular Scandinavian language), and Martuthunira (a western Australian language). Finnish (a Finno-Ugric language of northern Europe), is a candidate for a possibly configurational language showing both head- and dependent-marking, according to the analyses of Niño (1997) and Toivonen (1996, 1997, in press.)

We can further refine Nordlinger's typology by adding languages which have endocentrically organized functional projections FP but lack endocentrically organized lexical projections such as VP, using lexocentric S instead (see the references in section 6.2.2). Such languages will fall between the nonconfigurational and configurational ends of the horizontal continuum, in having one or more mixtures of the structural types, as illustrated schematically in (43). Through choices of various FPs and their embeddings, and choices of S-internal categorial organization, a range of varying structures mixing S and FP is available:

(43) Points on the endocentricity scale:

According to our theory of structure–function mapping, languages in the range of the second structure from the left in (43) will show a fixed hierarchical arrangement of the grammaticalized discourse functions DF but will show non-configurational arrangements of argument functions. Such languages are classified as **discourse configurational languages** (Kiss 1995), and include the head-marking Mayan languages (Aissen 1992, Woolford 1991) and the head- and dependent-marking languages Wambaya (Nordlinger 1998b) and (possibly) Hungarian (Kiss 1987, 1994). Again, this is not a rigid, discrete classification: discourse configurational languages may mix together both more and less configurational structures for argument functions (Kroeger 1993, Sells 1998), and may differ in the number and kinds of embedded functional projections. Tagalog, according to Kroeger (1993), falls between this and the second structure from the right (with order of subject and predicate reversed under S).

Nordlinger (1998b) provides a careful and detailed study of Australian non-configurational languages within the present theoretical framework, showing that morphology takes over many of the functions of syntactic configuration in some languages, while coexisting harmoniously with others. In subsequent chapters we will investigate the interactions of morphology and configurational syntactic structures.

6.4 Effects of Economy of Expression

The principle of economy of expression (1) interacts with the principles of structure–function mapping. For a simple English sentence like *Mary swims*, several c-structures are possible. (The internal structure of NP is omitted in these illustrations). The following selection assumes the presence in English of both endocentric XPs (section 6.2.1) and endocentrically organized S having subject and VP predicate (section 6.2.3):

(44) a.

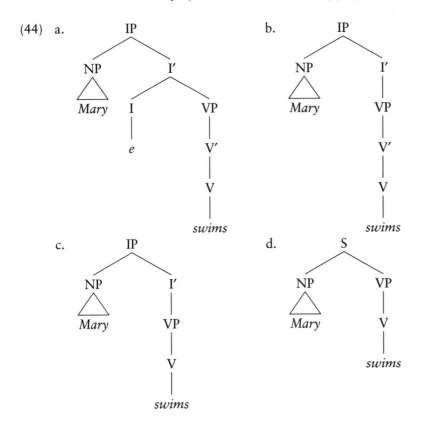

By our structure–function mapping principles (23), together with the subject–predicate principle for S (41), all of these c-structures support the same f-structure (as the reader can check). These c-structures are thus functionally equivalent. Economy of expression requires us to select the c-structure having the fewest syntactic phrase structure nodes, which is (44d).

Observe that for given lexical content, economy of expression can prune away only as much structure as can be eliminated from the structural resources of the language without violating completeness and coherence. The following structure for our example sentence *Mary swims* has fewer nodes than (44d), but it does not support a complete and coherent f-structure by our structure–function mapping principles, given that by hypothesis English has only endocentric structure–function mapping (for XP and S):

(45)

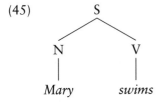

Let us further illustrate the interaction of these principles by re-examining the English topicalized CP structure given in chapter 2, repeated here:

(46)

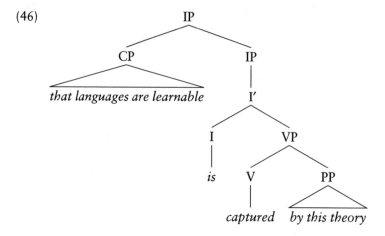

From general principles we can infer the following functional associations:[31]

(47)

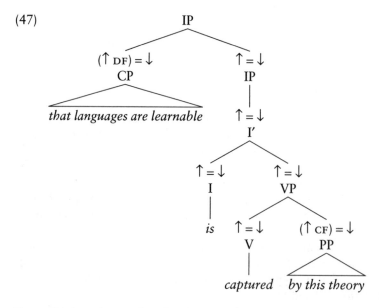

From (23e) we know that the CP must have a nonargument function: TOP, FOC, or ADJUNCT. CP cannot be ADJUNCT in this example, because it would lead to an incomplete f-structure, as the reader can check. Therefore, CP must be either TOP or FOC: DF for short. We also know that if the PP is a daughter of V′, it must have a complement function (CF), whose type is lexically determined by the verb. Let us assume for purposes of illustration that passive verb V and the auxiliary verb I in this example include the following functional schemata in their lexical entries:[32]

(48) *captured*: V   ($\uparrow$ PRED) = 'capture $\langle(\uparrow \text{OBL}_{ag})(\uparrow \text{SUBJ})\rangle$'
      is: I   ($\uparrow$ TENSE) = PRES
                       ($\uparrow$ SUBJ) = $\downarrow$
                          ($\downarrow$ PERS) = 3
                          ($\downarrow$ NUM) = SG

Our theory then gives us the following correspondence between the c-structure and f-structure of this example:[33]

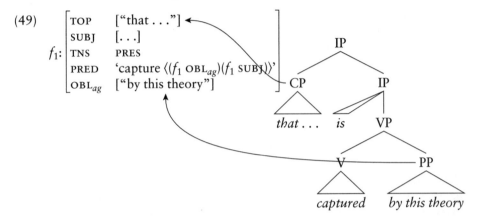

To secure completeness and coherence we must assume that the nonargument DF in (49) is identified with the SUBJ. This connection comes from the universal default that optionally identifies SUBJ and TOP.[34] An alternative would be to postulate an empty category DP in subject position as specifier of IP, identifying SUBJ with TOP by means of an extraction chain modelled by inside-out functional uncertainty (section 4.8 and chapter 9). But in this situation, such an empty node would provide only the redundant information that there is a SUBJ identifiable with TOP; this information is already given by the c-structure context without the empty node (from the universal default), and so by economy of expression (1) this option is excluded. (Elsewhere, however, extraction gaps in topicalization are possible. See section 4.8 and chapter 9.) The result is shown in (50):[35]

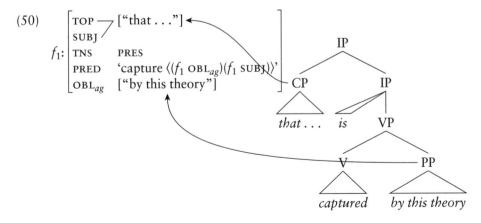

We have seen that because economy of expression must preserve completeness and coherence, its effects are constrained by the structure–function mappings available in a given language, and hence by the theory of structure–function mapping. In our theory of endocentric structure–function mapping we have assumed the classic definition of X′ complement as immediately dominated by X′. However, instead of defining a complement to be a nonprojecting category immediately dominated by X′, as we have in (23c, d), we could define it as in (51):

(51)   **Flexible Definition of an Endocentric Complement:**
         A c-structure complement is a nonprojecting node which is the sister of no non-projecting node.

This definition generalizes the earlier definition of complement assumed in (23c, d), repeated in (52a, b):

(52)   a.   Annotate a nonprojecting node in F′ with $\uparrow = \downarrow$.
         b.   Annotate a nonprojecting node in L′ with $(\uparrow \text{CF}) = \downarrow$.

The earlier definition requires a c-structure complement to be immediately dominated by a category of one bar level (either lexical L′ or functional F′) in order to receive the lexical or functional complement annotations (respectively, $(\uparrow \text{CF}) = \downarrow$ or $\uparrow = \downarrow$). Our flexible definition of complement drops the requirement of immediate domination by X′, and requires only that there be no sister node which is nonprojecting. Since it is only nonprojecting nodes that may receive GF specifications by (23), the new requirement is simply defining a complement to be a phrase that does not have as a sister something that could be a complement.[36]

With our new flexible definition (51) we may restate the annotation principles for endocentric complements (52a, b) as in (53a, b):

(53)   a.   Annotate a nonprojecting complement node dominated by any functional category F″ with $\uparrow = \downarrow$.
         b.   Annotate a nonprojecting complement node dominated by any lexical category L″ with $(\uparrow \text{CF}) = \downarrow$.

(53) allows the same configurations for c-complements as our previous principles (52) [(23c, d)], but in addition it allows complement configurations like (54a, b) while still excluding those like (54c):

(54)   a.   b.   c.

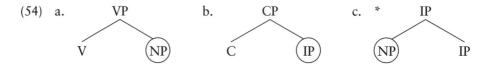

Interacting with economy of expression, the principle (53) will cause more extensive pruning of X′ nodes, because there are now alternative structural configurations that support the same functions. In particular, X′ nodes will be pruned when they are either dominated by or dominate nonbranching nodes of the same category type (cf. n. 18).

Thus the important point to bear in mind about economy of expression is that it economizes the resources for function mapping available to a given language; it does not create new resources. Consequently a highly configurational language like English will inevitably show fewer effects of the economy principle than languages which have richer exocentric and lexocentric resources for structure–function mapping. This point will be illustrated in subsequent chapters.

In conclusion, let us summarize here the endocentric c-structure to f-structure mapping principles we will assume. These mapping principles are of course supplemented by the non-X′ principles in sections 6.2.2 and 6.2.3:

(55)   **Endocentric Mapping Principles:**
    a. **Heads:** Annotate a projecting node in a projection of the same kind with $\uparrow = \downarrow$.
    b. **Specifiers:** Annotate a nonprojecting node in F″ with $(\uparrow \text{ DF}) = \downarrow$.
    c. **Coheads:** Annotate a nonprojecting complement node (51) dominated by any category X″ with $\uparrow = \downarrow$. (Recall (33).)
    d. **Complements:** Annotate a nonprojecting complement node (51) dominated by any lexical category L″ with $(\uparrow \text{ CF}) = \downarrow$.
    e. **Adjuncts:** Optionally annotate a nonprojecting node and its adjoined-to sister node with $(\uparrow \overline{\text{AF}}) = \downarrow$ and $\uparrow = \downarrow$, respectively.

Further Reading and Discussion

Although extended X′ theory is often associated with works in the transformational tradition, functional projections were originally motivated by research in nontransformational frameworks. The category CP as a projection of C was first introduced into LFG by Fassi Fehri (1981: 141ff; 1982: 100ff) in his analysis of Arabic syntax.[37] The analysis of English pronouns as determiners first proposed by Postal (1966). The hypothesis of a category DP as the projection of a category of determiners is originally due to Brame (1982). The hypothesis that the sentence is a projection of a functional head (the IP hypothesis) is due to Falk (1984), using 'M' for 'I', in his analysis of auxiliaries within LFG. All of these works are worth reading to understand some of the original empirical motivations for hypothesizing functional projections. For a standard exposition of the X′ theory of lexical categories in English, see Jackendoff (1977). The innovation of factoring apart the linear ordering of X′ categories from their dominance relations is due to Falk (1983).

Two further works on lexocentricity and phrase structure variation can be highly recommended: Kroeger (1993) and Nordlinger (1998b). These provide detailed studies of nonconfigurational and mixed configurational/nonconfigurational languages in LFG.

Appendix: X′ Theory

Many versions of X′ theory are compatible with the present theoretical framework, and we will not attempt to distinguish among them empirically here. For concreteness, we outline one set of X′ theoretic assumptions here, without attempting careful empirical justification of each point.[38] Subsequent chapters (7, 8 and 9) and problem sets will provide more detailed examples of extended X′ structures and the kinds of evidence that motivate their presence in a grammar.

The simple formal model of phrase structure categories given in chapter 4 is adequate for descriptive purposes, but it leaves many questions unanswered about the relations among categories, and permits "monstrous" tree structures (as in problem set 1). Because the category labels are simple, unanalyzed symbols, there is no necessary relation expressed between VP and V or NP and N, a problem originally pointed out by Lyons (1968: 234–5), which led to the development of X′ theory. For although "VP" (for verb phrase) is written as a composite name containing "V" (for verb), in fact it is treated within the formal theory of context-free phrase structure rules as an unanalyzed symbol (just as the function names in chapter 4 are treated as unanalyzed symbols denoting f-structure attributes). X′ theory hypothesizes an internal structure to the category labels which permits their relations to be captured (just as current theoretical work on grammatical relations attributes an internal structure to the functions). LFG's X′ theory, like the theory of grammatical functions, is a metatheory with respect to the grammars permitted by the theory of formal structures presented in chapters 4 and 5.

Under X′ theory c-structure categories are decomposed into a **level** of structure (represented by an integer) and called the "bar level," and a **kind** of category (represented by a feature matrix of categorial features). The kinds and levels of categories assumed here are based on Jackendoff's (1977) and Bresnan's (1982b) theories of categories.[39] Two basic properties of categories are hypothesized, **predicative** and **transitive**. "Predicative" categories are those which cannot stand alone as arguments, but require an external subject of predication. Adjective and verb are predicative categories; noun and preposition are not. "Transitive" categories are those which may take an object or direct complement function. Verb and preposition/postposition are transitive categories; noun and adjective are not. This analysis is shown in (17) and (18), repeated here as (56) and (57), respectively:[40]

(56) **Kinds of Categories:**

	"predicative"	"transitive"	
V	+	+	verbal
P	−	+	pre- or postpositional
N	−	−	nominal
A	+	−	adjectival

(57) **Levels of Categories:**

type:	0	1	2
	V	V′	V″ (VP)
	P	P′	P″ (PP)
	N	N′	N″ (NP)
	A	A′	A″ (AP)

The categorial features "predicative" and "transitive" of (56) can be defined in terms of the syntactic functions subj and obj (Bresnan 1982b). They capture the widespread generalizations (i) that (some) lexical elements of categories V and P can take direct object complements, while those of the categories N and A cannot, and (ii) that the phrases headed by P and N can serve as complete arguments while those headed by V and A cannot, but must have a subject of predication.[41] The categories of level 0 are called **lexical categories**; the categories of levels 1 and 2 called **projections**; projections of the highest level (i.e., level 2 in (57)) are call **maximal projections.**

X′ theory allows us to capture relations between different categories. It postulates that phrases are related to heads in a uniform way, as shown in (58), where the comma indicates no specification of relative order of the categories it separates, and the arrow is read "immediately dominates:"

(58) a. $X′ \rightarrow X^0$, YP
       b. $XP \rightarrow YP$, X′

In this, the endocentric pattern, X^0 is the (c-)head of X′, and X′ is the (c-)head of X″.[42] A phrase and its c-head have the same feature matrix. Thus endocentricity guarantees that the (c-)**head** of every phrase is a category having the same feature matrix but of a lesser level of structural complexity. The YP in (58a) is the **complement**, the YP in (58b) is the **specifier**. Specifiers and complements are maximal projections in the endocentric mode. They need not share the category features of their mother category. Multiple complements are sometimes treated by adding the recursive pattern of (59a) to (58a), which preserves binary branching, or by replacing (58a) with (59b), which creates a flatter complement structure. We will adopt here the analysis in (59a):[43]

(59) a. $X′ \rightarrow X′$, YP
       b. $X′ \rightarrow X^0$, YP*

Adjuncts are often analyzed as sisters to XP dominated by XP or as sisters to X′ dominated by X′.[44]

Some examples of cross-categorial parallelism in English are given in (60):[45]

(60) a. We are *nearing the meadow.*   VP
       b. *Nearness to the meadow* is the great virtue of our house.   NP

c. The house was *much nearer to the meadow* after the tornado. AP
d. *Near the meadow*, we built a house. PP

Although the italicized phrases belong to different categories, they show striking parallelisms. Each phrase is headed by a category having the same feature matrix: the VP by the verb *nearing* in (60a), the NP by the noun *nearness* in (60b), the AP by the adjective *nearer* in (60c), and the PP by the preposition *near* in (60d).[46] Each head has a complement and precedes it. In contrast, in a head-final language like Navajo (chapter 8), complements precede their heads in each category. At the same time, the categories show differences reflecting their different featural composition. The verb *nearing* and preposition *near* take direct NP complements, while the noun and adjective take indirect PP complements. This reflects the categorial analysis of V and P as [+ transitive] and N and A as [− transitive] in (56). Further, the NP and PP categories need not have a subject of predication, as in (60b, d), while the AP and VP categories must have a subject of predication, as they do in (60a, c). This contrast reflects the feature [± predicative].

Notes

1 An important exception is Optimality Theory (OT) (Prince and Smolensky 1993), which defines grammars to be the language-particular prioritizations of conflicting universal constraints. Since universal constraints conflict, they cannot simultaneously be satisfied. In this framework variation could be eliminated only with the extrinsic stipulation of a single, universal prioritization. LFG is actively being developed in an OT setting by a number of researchers. See Bresnan (1998a, 1998b, to appear, and references) and Sells (forthcoming).
2 Clearly, this idea can be generalized to other dimensions of information than that represented by f-structure, but we will not take this further step in the present study.
3 The familiar symbol *e* originating in formal language theory denotes the empty string; it thus stands for the absence of a terminal node, not for the presence of a special "empty" terminal node.
4 Compare Zaenen's (1989) WYSIWYG ("what you see is what you get") principle, which is close in spirit though not identical in consequence.
5 See Bresnan and Mchombo (1995), T. Mohanan (1995), Sells (1995), Matsumoto (1996a), Niño (1997), Nordlinger (1998b), and the references cited in these for recent discussion.
6 Compositionality effects of word formation on the syntactic context do occur, because the order in which valence-adding and valence-reducing morphological components are utilized affects the valence of the resulting word: see Alsina and Mchombo (1990) and Alsina (1999) for discussion.
7 On the functional word as a PRED-bearing unit, see Webelhuth and Ackerman (1999), Matsumoto (1996a), T. Mohanan (1995); on the functional word as an element of a paradigm sharing f-structure features, see Börjars et al. (1997) and Bresnan (1998b).
8 See problem set 2.
9 These principles do not of course exhaust the relevant constraints which may come into conflict in the parallel structures architecture. See Bresnan (1998b) for a more recent discussion and references.

10 Some alternatives are to employ a coarser-grained inventory of core functions, such as SPEC (specifier), COMP (complement) (e.g. Bresnan 1998a), or of object functions (Joshi 1993, Alsina 1996b); a finer-grained inventory of core functions distinguishing transitive subject (A) from intransitive subject (S) (e.g. Dixon 1972, Kiparsky 1997a); a coarser inventory of discourse functions using the concept of PIVOT (e.g. Manning 1996); and different primitive classifications of functions (e.g. T. Mohanan 1994, Alsina 1996b, Joshi 1993, Zaenen 1994).

11 In this scheme indirect objects are analyzed as primary or secondary objects which have a specific type of argument role associated with dative case (recipient, beneficiary). Special syntactic properties of indirect objects are then derived from conditions on their argument role or the effects of dative case marking (Alsina 1994b, 1996b). "OBJ$_\theta$" designates any secondary object; secondary objects are indexed to some thematic role. See Alsina (1994b, 1996b) for an alternative representation of secondary objects.

12 Core functions are characterized as "semantically unrestricted" functions in Bresnan (1982b) (see also Kroeger 1998), but in later work (e.g. L. Levin 1985, Bresnan and Kanerva 1989, Bresnan and Moshi 1990) the terms "restricted" and "unrestricted" are used in a different sense. To avoid confusion, the term "core" is adopted here. "Term" is also used for core functions in LFG by T. Mohanan (1994), Alsina (1994b, 1996b), Arka (1998).

13 It is possible to preserve uniqueness by adopting a more fine-grained sortal theory of nonargument functions.

14 Examples of this particular type were pointed out by Paul Kroeger (personal communication).

15 See the discussion and references in Andrews (1985) and in Manning (1996). We may formally express this by postulating that the optional constraint (($\downarrow$ SUBJ) = ($\downarrow$ TOP)) is associated with root sentential nodes, in a slight extension of the formalism of chapter 4. See n. 34 below.

16 In fact, we can reduce categories to primitive functional properties, following Jackendoff (1977) and Bresnan (1982b). See below.

17 But the converse does not hold: endocentricity does not require the absence of morpholexical means of function specification.

18 We have omitted the V$'$ and D$'$ nodes in this example. A common convention is to omit X$'$ when either it or its mother XP fails to branch. Any ambiguities introduced are easily resolved by completeness, and uniqueness. Below, in section 6.4, we will show that the structures represented by this notational convention follow from economy of expression.

19 Kroeger characterizes the finite element of Tagalog as "the fixed point around which the other elements are arranged." Recent LFG work in support of IP and CP include (in addition to Kroeger 1993) Alsagoff (1992), King (1995), Austin and Bresnan (1996), Nordlinger and Bresnan (1996), Niño (1997), Choi (1996), Berman (1996, 1997, 1998), Sadler (1997), Sells (1998), Nordlinger (1998b), Arka (1998).

20 For Grimshaw (1998) IP and CP are respectively the first (F1) and second (F2) functional projections of VP. She argues that PP is the F2 projection of NP; for evidence against this analysis, see Bresnan (1995a). We assume that not all functional projections need occur, just as not every lexical projection appears in every language. English may simply lack a nominal F2 category.

21 See Sadler (1997) and Sells (1998) for further development of the theory of functions for "small" phrases consisting of the adjunction X^0 categories. Also, specifiers of lexical categories are not utilized here; as shown below, S provides phrase-internal subjects.

22 $\mathcal{A}$ is adjoined to $\mathcal{B}$ when $\mathcal{A}$ and $\mathcal{B}$ are immediately dominated by a node labelled $\mathcal{B}$. In (22e) YP is adjoined to X^{n+1}.

23 Optional annotation allows for lexocentric specification of an argument function (section 6.2.2).

24 See Sadler (1997) and Sells (1998) on the theory of adjunction to preterminal nodes.

25 To reduce the size and complexity of this example, the internal structure of the DP is omitted, and the V′ nodes have been omitted in accordance with the tree abbreviatory convention in n. 18.

26 We do not deal here with the detailed cooccurrence restrictions between English auxiliaries and their complements. One approach within LFG postulates a morphological projection for this purpose (Butt et al. 1996). Another LFG approach uses parameterized c-structure rules, which would allow more fine-grained expansions of different subtypes of verbal projections, such as participial or infinitival (Frank and Zaenen 1998). An auxiliary or modal verb could then locally select for its verbal complement subtype, without any extension of the overall formal power of the system (Peters and Ritchie 1972).

27 This selection constitutes parametric variation. For example, English sets specifier of IP to be only one of the available DFS: SUBJ. Other languages may set the specifier of IP function to be any or all of TOP, FOC, or SUBJ. As we will see in chapter 7, in Welsh specifier of IP is omitted altogether, and in Wambaya it is optional.

28 Cf. Nichols (1986). Our use of the terms in this text is related to the typological characterization given by Nichols. Note that verbal forms not morphologically marked for agreement may nevertheless carry agreement information by virtue of their paradigmatic relation to marked verbal forms; usually the unmarked form carries the complement of the features carried by the marked forms (Andrews 1990a). This is the case with the English present tense verbal forms and the conditional verb paradigm of Ulster Irish (problem set 2).

29 See Andrews (1996), Nordlinger (1998b), Sadler (1997), Barron (1998), Sells (1999a), Lee (1999a, 1999b), and Sharma (1999) for an alternative formal model of the morphological construction of f-structures making use of inside-out function application (chapter 4).

30 Both predicate-final structures like (40) and predicate-initial structures having the typical order XP NP occur. See Kroeger (1993) for arguments that Tagalog has clause-initial predicate phrases of all types *except* VP in predicate-initial structures.

31 ADJ is an alternative to DF by our principles, but it will be excluded in the current example by the principle of completeness.

32 As remarked in chapter 2, *captured* is a passive participle. The linkages between lexical roles and functions follows from the lexical mapping theory (part IV) and need not be stipulated.

33 Here again we follow the convention of using double quoted strings to abbreviate the content of subsidiary f-structures where it is not relevant to the discussion.

34 We can assume that this option is carried only by the root clause. The functional specification is given in n. 15.

35 See n. 33.

36 Hence, the flexible definition requires the binary branching analysis of multiple complements given in (59a) and adopted subsequently.

37 Fassi Fehri (1981: 164, 1982: 118) attributes the original (unpublished) proposal to Ken Hale, who used it to analyze auxiliary inversion in English.

38 This version is based on Bresnan (1977, 1982b), Jackendoff (1977), Falk (1983), Grimshaw (1998), Webelhuth (1992), Kroeger (1993), King (1995), Nordlinger (1998b), and Sadler (1997).

39   Other categorial analyses are of course compatible with the general framework.

40   "A" is here used to cover the category of adverb as well as adjective, as in Emonds (1976).

41   These generalizations are not exceptionless, however. See Simpson (1991).

42   By taking the transitive closure of this relation ("being an immediate c-head of"), we can define the sense in which N is the head of NP, V of VP, and the like.

43   See n. 36 for one motivation.

44   Given (59a), this proposal creates functional ambiguity for a constituent which is a sister to X′: it may be either a complement or an adjunct. However, because of the general imperfect correspondence between structures and functions in our framework, the functional ambiguity of structural form is harmless. (In fact it may play an explanatory role in the historical change of syntax, as conjectured in Bresnan and Mchombo 1987, and discussed more fully in Börjars et al. 1997 and Toivonen 1997, in press.) The solution algorithm in chapters 4 and 5 treats alternative annotations on the same c-structure rule as case of nondeterministic choice.

45   These are from Bresnan (1977).

46   These categories are morphologically distinguishable: the verb can have verbal tense/aspect inflections -s, -ed; the adjective can have comparative and superlative inflections -er, -est; the noun bears nominalizing derivational morphology; the preposition is uninflected and underived.

7 Endocentricity and Heads

The structure–function mapping principles of chapter 6 entail that large regions of categorial structure, for example a VP and its dominating IP and CP, may be mapped into a single f-structure. Let us refer to this region as a single **functional domain** under the correspondence mapping from c-structure to f-structure.[1] The imperfect correspondence between c-structure and f-structure explains two types of interesting phenomena that have been observed within a single functional domain: **head mobility** and **distributed exponence**. Both phenomena can be seen as consequences of the same general principles for sharing f-structure head properties in a complex c-structural domain.

7.1 Head Mobility

The mapping principles of chapter 6 entail the noncompositionality of f-structures in c-structures. That is, the f-structure of a node is not only a function of the f-structures of its immediate constituents, but also depends upon the surrounding syntactic structure in the functional domain. For example, the English VP (as discussed in section 5.3.4) has an f-structure subject whose contents come from the higher S or IP in which the VP is embedded. This follows from the principle that the complement of a functional category is an f-structure cohead (chapter 6). By this principle the contents of a VP f-structure could be distributed across the entire functional domain of the VP (i.e., the higher S, IP, and CP structures). This is true not only for verbal dependents such as subjects and objects, but also for the head itself. The noncompositionality of LFG thus implies that VPs can be discontinuous phrases whose heads may appear external to the rest of the phrase. A number of languages exhibit this phenomenon, which is commonly known as "head movement" but perhaps more accurately termed "variable head positioning." One such case of head mobility we will examine in this chapter is thought to occur in Welsh.

7.1.1 Verb order in Welsh

As pointed out in chapter 6, Welsh is one of the many languages employing subject predicate constructions of the form in (1), where XP may be a predicate phrase of any of a range of categories VP, NP, AP, or PP:

(1)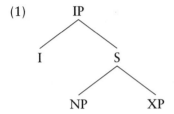

The specifier of IP is taken to be null (omitted) in Welsh, as a parametric choice.

In Welsh, the finite verb is clause-initial, yielding $V_{fin}SO$ word order. However, the SVO order appears when V is a "verbal noun," a nonfinite verbal complement to a finite auxiliary verb which occupies the clause-initial position: $Aux_{fin}SV_nO$. These alternative orders are illustrated by (2a, b) from Sproat (1985: 176):

(2) a. *Gwelodd   Siôn ddraig.*
        saw-3.SG.PAST John dragon
        'John saw a dragon.'
     b. *Gwnaeth   Siôn weld   draig.*
        do-3.SG.PAST John see.VN dragon
        'John saw a dragon.'

Example (2b) illustrates the structure of (1) very clearly. Here the finite auxiliary verb *gwnaeth* 'did' appears in the I position, with the nonfinite form of 'see', the uninflected verbal noun *gweld*,[2] in V position in the VP:[3]

(3)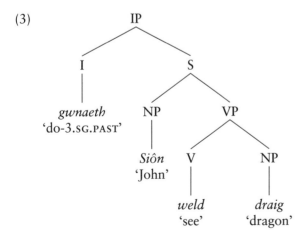

Evidence for the presence of a VP containing the nonfinite verb and its complements includes the fact that this constituent may be fronted, a characteristic of the Celtic languages (Tallerman 1998a: 24–5, 1998b). In the cleft construction of (4), for example, the main verb 'built' and its complement 'houses' and adjunct 'in Bangor' are all fronted together in their normal order as a unit in front of the sentence (Tallerman 1998a: 245):

(4) [$_{VP}$ *Adeiladu tai   ym Mangor*]$_{VP}$ *a   wnaeth   o.*
         build   house.PL in Bangor   PRL do:PST:3SG he
     'He BUILT HOUSES IN BANGOR.'

The c- to f-structure mapping principles of chapter 6 yield the annotations to (3) shown in (5):[4]

(5)

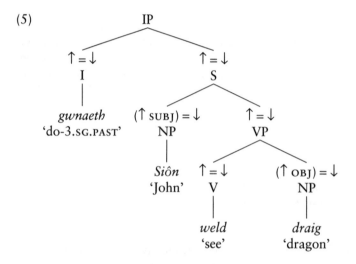

From this we can see that the nodes I, IP, S, VP, and V belong to the same functional domain. In this example the tense inflection is carried by the auxiliary verb *gwnaeth* 'did'. We will assume that this verb serves merely as a tense and agreement carrier without a PRED attribute to conflict with that of the V in VP. We will therefore provide it with the following morpholexical specifications (which are created by the inflectional morphology):

(6) *gwnaeth*: I   ($\uparrow$ TENSE) = PAST
                 ($\uparrow$ SUBJ) = $\downarrow$
                   ($\downarrow$ PERS) = 3
                   ($\downarrow$ NUM) = SG

The PRED attribute of example (2b) is carried by the nonfinite verb form *weld* 'see' in V:

(7) *weld*: V   ($\uparrow$ PRED) = 'see $\langle(\uparrow$ SUBJ)($\uparrow$ OBJ)$\rangle$'

Together, these constraints yield the following correspondence between the c-structure and f-structure:[5]

(8)

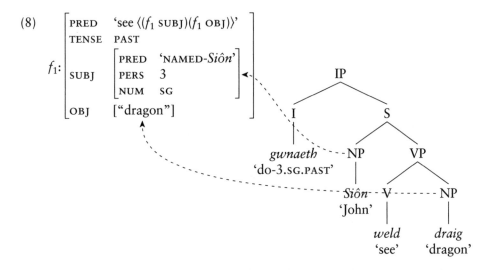

Now the main verb *weld* 'see' of (2b) also has a finite inflected form, based on the inflecting stem *gwel-*. Since all finite verbs in Welsh appear in initial position (represented by I in our structure (3)), we simply assume that the rules of Welsh inflectional morphology produce the following form for lexical insertion into an I:

(9) *gwelodd*: I   ($\uparrow$ PRED) = 'see $\langle(\uparrow$ SUBJ)($\uparrow$ OBJ)$\rangle$'
    ($\uparrow$ TENSE) = PAST
    ($\uparrow$ SUBJ) = $\downarrow$
     ($\downarrow$ PERS) = 3
     ($\downarrow$ NUM) = SG

If we insert *gwelodd* 'saw-3sg' into the I position of the structure (3), thereby replacing the auxiliary with this particular I verb, there will be two instances of 'see' in the same clause, giving rise to a violation of the functional uniqueness principle. By our general principles of structure–function correspondence together with the transitivity of equality, the VP f-structure is identified with the IP f-structure containing the finite verb features, and consequently the PRED attribute would have two values, one for each instantiation of a verb (the finite I in IP, the nonfinite V in VP). Therefore, inserting *gwelodd* 'saw-3sg' into structure (3) produces an inconsistency in the value of the PRED attribute (because of the property of unique instantiation of semantic features – section 4.2, section 4.4, n. 10). Could we resolve this clash of values by omitting the lexical content of V, creating an empty category? An empty category V counts as a syntactic node for the principle of economy of expression (chapter 6), because it dominates no terminal lexical node. Hence it would be eliminated because it provides no information that is not already available from the syntactic context without it. Economy of expression thus forces us to eliminate V when we insert *gwelodd* 'saw-3sg' into I, as in (10):[6,7]

(10)

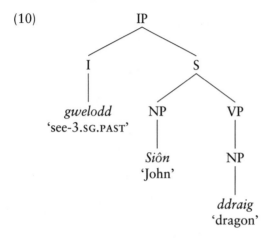

Observe that this structure closely resembles a transformationally derived structure in which the finite verb has been moved from V to I, except that there is no trace of movement in the form of an empty category V in VP. However, the absence of the V does not affect our principles of structure–function correspondence (the annotation principles that produced (5) above). The result is shown in (11):[8]

(11)

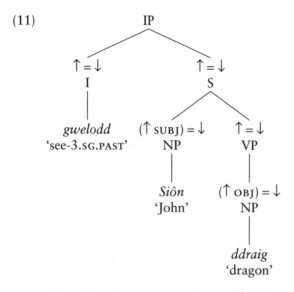

These constraints yield the following correspondence between the c-structure and f-structure:

(12)

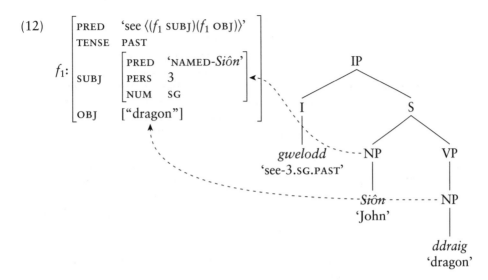

Note that (10) and (3) have the same f-structures, displayed in (12) and (8) respectively. The functional equivalence of (10) and (3) has suggested to many that the head "moves" from one position to the other. But we can now see that the apparent mobility of the head arises nonderivationally from general principles governing the imperfect correspondence between c-structure and f-structure.[9] A much fuller discussion of the theory of structure–function mapping in relation to Welsh syntax can be found in Sadler (1997).

7.2 Endocentricity and Extended Heads

The mobility of heads within their functional domains naturally raises questions about the status of the phrases with missing heads.

One question is this: why does the VP in (11) escape elimination by economy of expression? Welsh permits XPs other than VP in S, so it is a possibility within the structural resources of the language that the headless VP could be replaced by an NP. But these XPs are interpreted as the "predicate" (f-structure heads) of their S, and must be annotated with "↑ = ↓," as discussed in section 6.2.3. In the case of examples like (11), eliminating the VP would require annotating the NP immediately dominated by S with ↑ = ↓, leading to an inconsistent f-structure: functional uniqueness would be violated, because the verb 'saw' already provides the main predicator for the sentence.

Another question is: why does economy of expression not eliminate the structure in (5) as having too many nodes compared to the functionally equivalent structure in (11)? If these two c-structures have identical f-structures, there is no appeal to semantic expressivity to distinguish them. Notice, however, that although it is true that (5) has more c-structure nodes than (11), the extra nodes are preterminal nodes dominating lexical material, and these are exempt from economy of expression, as pointed out in chapter 6.

A more fundamental question that we must consider is why our analysis of Welsh verb order does not violate the basic principle of endocentricity which X′ theory was designed to embody: that every category has a head which determines its properties. In (12) the embedded VP lacks an internal V constituent. In our framework, however, it is incorrect to say that VP lacks a head: after all, the finite verb in I functions as its head in f-structure. Because of the imperfect correspondence between c-structure and f-structure, the head of a constituent cannot in general be fixed in a unique structural configuration (indeed, this is why variable head positioning can occur at all, within the present framework); but the head can be recovered from looking at the set of nodes that are mapped into the same f-structure as VP under the correspondence function ϕ. In other words, we use the **inverse function** to ϕ, called ϕ^{-1}, which takes each f-structure f into the *set* of nodes that correspond to f under ϕ.[10] Within the **inverse image** of $\phi(VP)$ (that is, within $\phi^{-1}(\phi(VP))$) will be all of the nodes that are mapped to VP's f-structure by ϕ. Among these nodes, the closest nondominating node to VP can be identified as the head. This will be the internal c-structure head if it is present, otherwise the next higher nondominating node in the functional domain. The well-known tree relation of **c-command** can pick out both these cases: $\mathcal{A}$ c-commands $\mathcal{B}$ if every node properly dominating $\mathcal{A}$ also dominates $\mathcal{B}$.[11] Therefore, to find the extended head of a given node (call it VP), we look in the inverse image of VP under ϕ, throw out all of the nodes therein that dominate VP, and pick a node which c-commands VP and is c-commanded by any other node that also c-commands VP. This gives us our definition of extended head:

(13)   **Definition of Extended Head** (based on Jar n.d., Zaenen and Kaplan 1995: 221–2, Bresnan 1998a): Given a c-structure containing nodes $\mathcal{N}$, C, and c-to f-structure correspondence mapping ϕ, $\mathcal{N}$ is an **extended head** of C if $\mathcal{N}$ is the minimal node in $\phi^{-1}(\phi(C))$ that c-commands C without dominating C.

Consider how this definition applies to our previous example (8). Taking VP to be C, the node requiring an extended head, we see that V and VP are mapped into the same f-structure, V does not dominate VP, and every node that properly dominates V also dominates VP. As for I, I and VP are mapped into the same f-structure, I does not dominate VP, and every node that properly dominates I also dominates VP. However, only V counts as the extended head of VP. The reason is that V is the *minimal* node c-commanding VP, because I c-commands V (every node that properly dominates I also dominates V). In this same figure (8) it is also true that VP cannot be the extended head of V (because VP dominates V), and VP cannot be the extended head of I (because it does not c-command I). Referring now to (12), the reader can check that I is the extended head of both IP and VP.

Thus (13) amounts to saying that X is an extended head of Y if X is the X′ categorial head of Y (by the definitions of chapter 6), or Y lacks a categorial head but X is the closest element higher up in the tree that functions like the f-structure head of Y. It is easy to see that under this definition there is a many-to-one relation between categories and extended heads: categories have unique but not necessarily distinct heads. For example, in (12), each category including IP and VP has one and only one extended head, but the same finite verb I in (12) serves as the head of two distinct categories, the I′ and the VP.

By replacing "head" with "extended head," we can state a preliminary version of the endocentricity principle of the present framework:

(14)   **Endocentricity (Preliminary):**
       Every category has an extended head.

As it stands, however, (14) is false. There are many instances where categories lack even extended heads. A well-known example is the case of interrogative complements in (Standard) English, where either the complementizer of CP (*if* or *whether*) or the specifier of CP (the *wh*-phrase) is present, but not both:

(15)   a.   I wonder [$_{CP}$ [$_C$ if] [$_{IP}$ I am tall enough]]
       b.   I wonder [$_{CP}$ [$_{AP}$ how tall] [$_{IP}$ I am]]
       c.   *I wonder [$_{CP}$ [how tall] [$_C$ if] [$_{IP}$ I am]]

The same is true for DPs in English; either the determiner of DP (*the* or *a(n)*) or the specifier of DP (the possessive phrase) is present, but not both:

(16)   a.   [$_{DP}$ [$_D$ the] [$_{NP}$ house]]
       b.   [$_{DP}$ [$_{NP}$ Mary's and Lily's] [$_{NP}$ house]]
       c.   *[$_{NP}$ [Mary's and Lily's] [$_D$ the] [$_{NP}$ house]]

Of course, endocentricity is violated in this way only under the assumed analyses. If the *wh*-phrase in (15) and the possessive phrase in (16) were not assumed to be specifiers of functional projections, but perhaps simply alternative realizations of the same category as the interrogative complementizer and the determiner, respectively, there would be no missing heads to worry about (though the alternative violates the basic X′ theory patterns). But there is reason to analyze these elements as occupying positions distinct from the complementizer and determiner. Observe that the specifiers of CP and DP in these examples (15)–(16) allow ellipsis of their complements (IP and NP, respectively): *She's tall. I wonder how tall (she is)* and *Is this your house? No, it's Mary's and Lily's (house).* In contrast, the functional heads C and D, even when heavily stressed, do not allow this kind of ellipsis: *They say she'll do it, but I wonder* IF *(she'll do it)* and *Is this a house of yours? No, it's* THE *(house of mine).*

If we think of (14) as a kind of recoverability condition, requiring us to recover an extended head for every category from its syntactic context, we can see why certain functional projections FP, such as the CP and DP in (15)–(16), might be exempted from the endocentricity requirement. If the category is headed by a sufficiently small closed class of grammatical elements, recoverability is trivial and the contribution of the head often redundantly encoded. English complementizers carry limited grammatical information about finiteness and sentence type; with an interrogative specifier, an interrogative complementizer is redundant. The English determiners likewise carry limited grammatical information about definiteness, and the definite feature is redundant with the possessive specifier. We can therefore replace (14) with (17):

(17) **Endocentricity:**
      Every lexical category has an extended head.

In (17) 'lexical category' picks out the L″ categories of chapter 6, excluding the "functional categories" F″. Note that the converse of (17) is not true: there are lexical categories that are not the heads of lexical projections, as when a lexical verb in a nonconfigurational language like Warlpiri is immediately dominated by S. Finally, observe that (17) can be applied even to lexical categories L^0: the terminal node dominated by L^0 will count as its extended head by our definition (13).

   In sum, the problem that head mobility poses for endocentricity can be resolved by recovering the head of a locally headless phrase from the inverse image of the f-structure of the phrase.

7.3   Distributed Exponence

We have seen that according to the principles of the mapping theory in chapter 6, the f-structures of functional heads F are identified with those of their c-structure complements. By the transitivity of identity, it follows that all of the c-structure heads within the same functional domain will share their f-structure attributes. Hence, if a functional head contributes f-structure information to the clause, it must be consistent with that of all other heads in the same functional domain. In this way, for example, complementizers and verbs may be seen to agree, even though they may be widely separated in their c-structure tree positions:

(18)

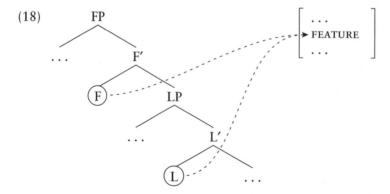

An interesting case of this sort may be found in West Flemish (problem set 3).

Now looking at the same correspondence mapping from the point of view of the f-structure (reversing the arrows in (18)), we see that information about the same functional property (meaning an f-structure attribute such as TENSE) may appear distributed in c-structure across multiple heads. This is what is meant by distributed exponence, an exponent of a "functional" feature (such as TENSE, NUM, PERS) being an expression of that feature in c-structure. The structure–function mapping principles make it possible to have syntactically distributed exponents of the same morphosyntactic category. This phenomenon occurs in a number of languages. We will examine here the case of Wambaya (Nordlinger 1998a), an Australian language where tense marking occurs simultaneously on both auxiliary (I) and main verb (V):

(19)

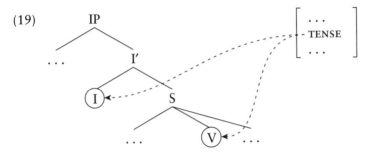

In Wambaya, the tense values of a clause arise compositionally from the individual inflections on I and V which have overlapping values, and thus are not a simple matter of feature copying.[12]

7.3.1 Wambaya c-structure

The c-structure of Wambaya is outlined in Nordlinger (1998b) and is similar to that which has been proposed for Warlpiri (e.g. Simpson 1991, Kroeger 1993, Austin and Bresnan 1996). In this structure a nonprojective, nonconfigurational constituent S is generated as a sister to I. I is the locus of the second position auxiliary, while the main verb appears in V (within S) or in I (under circumstances discussed below). The order of constituents within S is completely free and all constituents are optional. Since S is exocentric, its head may be either a verbal predicator (as in (20)), or a nominal predicator (as in (21)):

(20) *Naniyawulu   nagawulu   baraj-bulu   wurlu-Ø-n*
    that.DU.II.NOM female.DU.II.NOM old.person-DU(NOM) 3DU.S-NP-PROG
    duwa.
    get.up(UNM)
    'The two old women are getting up.'

(21) *Iligirra   buyurru.*
    river(NOM) dry(NOM)
    'The river is dry.'

All permutations of the constituents are possible (although some may be more pragmatically marked than others) as long as the auxiliary remains in second position:

(22) *Dawu   gin-a   alaji   janyi-ni.*
      bite(UNM) 3SG.M.A-PST boy(ACC) dog-ERG
      'The dog bit the boy.'
      Alaji gin-a dawu janyi-ni.
      Alaji gin-a janyi-ni dawu.
      Dawu gin-a janyi-ni alaji.
      Janyi-ni gin-a alaji dawu.
      Janyi-ni gin-a dawu alaji.

Like Warlpiri (chapter 1), Wambaya also has discontinuous NPs and lacks a VP. The contrast between (20) and (23) shows that while the auxiliary can follow a NP constituent (20), it cannot follow the main verb and its object (23). This suggests that the verb and its object do not form a constituent in Wambaya since, if they did, we would need to explain why it is that the VP constituent cannot appear before the auxiliary, while other constituents can:

(23) **Daguma janji   ng-a   ngawurniji.*
      hit(UNM) dog(ACC) 1SG.A-PST 1SG(ERG)
      'I hit the dog.'

    The specifier of IP position is optional and can be filled only by a maximal projection; thus in Wambaya it is limited to NPs and subordinate clauses (since there is no VP, as discussed above). The structure of a simple sentence is given in (24) (auxiliary placement is discussed below). The annotations shown follow from the theory of structure–function mapping in chapter 6:[13]

(24)

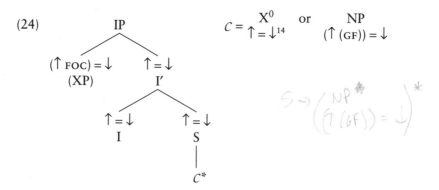

    Since S is a nonconfigurational category, the assignment of grammatical functions to NPs within S is not determined by annotations in the phrase structure rules (as it is in a configurational language such as English, for example), but by lexocentric case principles whereby lexical predicators select for the case features of their arguments.[15] Each NP can be assigned a set of possible functions by means of dependent-marking conditional annotation schemata of the form in (25):[16]

(25) $(\downarrow \text{CASE}) = \kappa \Rightarrow (\uparrow \text{GF}) = \downarrow$

The general principles of functional uniqueness, completeness, and coherence will ensure that the correct NPs in the c-structure are associated with the correct grammatical functions in the corresponding f-structure. For example, a transitive verb such as *dawu* 'bite' in (22) will require that its subject have ergative case, and its object accusative case, thus specifying an f-structure such as the following:

(26) $\begin{bmatrix} \text{PRED} & \text{'bite} \langle \dots \rangle \text{'} \\ \text{SUBJ} & [\text{CASE ERG}] \\ \text{OBJ} & [\text{CASE ACC}] \end{bmatrix}$

The only f-structures for the sentence that satisfy completeness and coherence will be those in which an accusative NP (*alaji* in (22)) is identified with the OBJ grammatical function and an ergative NP (*janyini* in (22)) is identified with the SUBJ grammatical function. In a situation in which the specifier of IP is filled with a NP (as in (20)), the NP is identified both with the FOC function in the f-structure (by virtue of its position) and with the grammatical function determined by its case marking (i.e., SUBJ in (20)). (See Simpson 1991, Austin and Bresnan 1996, and Nordlinger 1998b for further discussion.)

Evidence for the existence of S as a constituent separate from the auxiliary comes from (at least) two sources: clauses with nominal predicates, and coordination. First, clauses with nominal predicates, such as (21), can never contain an auxiliary and, thus, can only be of category S:

(27)

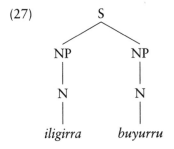

This follows from the fact that there is a dependency between verbs and auxiliaries, both being inflected for tense, while nominal predicates lack tense inflection. Verbs may not appear in auxiliary-less sentences, except when two Ss are conjoined as a single c-structure complement of the same auxiliary I.

The possibility of conjoining Ss under I constitutes the second piece of evidence for the I–S constituent structure of (24). It is possible to coordinate either IPs (e.g. (28a)) or Ss (e.g. (28b)). In the latter case there is no auxiliary in the coordinated clause(s):

(28) a. *Manjungu ngirr-a   angbardi,   nguya   ngirr-a*
         shade(ACC) 1PL.EXC.A-PST build(UNM) dig(UNM) 1PL.EXC.A-PST
         jamba,   wugbardi ngirr-a   mayinanji.
         ground(ACC) cook(UNM) 1PL.EXC.A-PST goanna(ACC)
         'We built a shade, (and) we dug (a hole in) the ground (and) we
         cooked the goanna.'
   b. *Manjungu ngirr-a   angbardi,   nguya   jamba,*
         shade(ACC) 1PL.EXC.A-PST build(UNM) dig(UNM) ground(ACC)
         wugbardi mayinanji.
         cook(UNM) goanna(ACC)
         'We built a shade, (and we) dug (a hole in) the ground (and we) cooked
         the goanna.'

This analysis accounts for all of the structural aspects of a simple Wambaya
clause considered so far, except for one: the possible appearance of the verb
before the auxiliary, shown in (22). The reason is that by our endocentric principles, only nonprojecting categories can appear in the specifier of IP position, and
the only pre-I position we have defined so far is the optional specifier of IP. The
auxiliary belongs to the c-structure category I. However, it is actually an enclitic
(despite the convention of writing it as a separate word), and its placement is
prosodically conditioned; it needs to follow another word to which it can cliticize.[17]
When the optional specifier of IP is omitted, the enclitic auxiliary requires a host.
In this situation we will assume that the main verb can be generated in I to the
left of the auxiliary.[18] Thus we assume that the Wambaya I has the structure
shown in (29). Since the specifier of IP is annotated with the FOC function, we
can express the incompatibility of having V in I together with specifier of IP by
means of a negative existential constraint $\neg(\uparrow \text{FOC})$ attached to the I categorization
of verbs:[19]

(29)   I

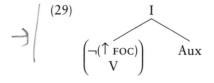

Across languages, there are often dependencies between elements in a head position and the specifier of the head. The constraint in (29) is simply a formalization
of the idea of a specifier-head dependency.
    Wambaya main verbs are lexically categorized as V, then, and V may appear
either in the nonconfigurational S or in I:

(30) *dawu*: V: 'bite $\langle(\uparrow \text{SUBJ})(\uparrow \text{OBJ})\rangle$'

The structure of the initial sentence in (22) above is given in (31). The annotations follow from the chapter 6 structure–function mapping theory, together
with (29).[20] Economy of expression has eliminated I'; the case conditionals (25)
are simplified to their true consequents.

(31)

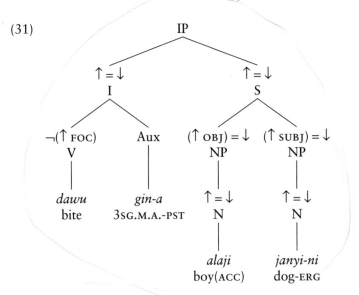

What is interesting about Wambaya to us here is that both the auxiliary and the verb are inflected for tense and share tense attributes regardless of their structural positions in I and V.

7.3.2 The Wambaya tense system

The Wambaya auxiliary has no morphological head/base, but simply is a cluster of clitics and suffixes marking some combination of tense, aspect, mood, directional information, and subject and object information. The auxiliary maximally makes a three-way tense distinction, distinguishing past, present, and future tenses. In addition to the tense marking in the auxiliary, tense marking is also found on the main verb; however, the system of marking on each element is different. Thus, rather than redundantly marking information already provided by the auxiliary, the verbal inflection works in conjunction with the auxiliary marking, the ultimate combination defining the tense category for the clause as a whole. Verbs in Wambaya have two forms: the -*ba* form, which occurs in positive future tense clauses and in imperative clauses, and the unmarked form (also the citation form), which occurs in all other contexts.[21] The marked form -*ba* carries the information that the speaker is uncertain as to whether the (as yet unrealized) event will actually occur, yet predicts it to be likely to occur. The unmarked verb form (in the absence of incompatible information) carries the meaning that the speaker is certain about the occurrence or likelihood of occurrence of the event.

An example of the role of these inflections is shown by the contrast between (32) and (33). In (32) the future tense suffix in the auxiliary cooccurs with an unmarked verb, giving the clause a meaning of immediate or definite future tense, similar to 'be going to' or 'be about to' in English:

(32)   *Daguma-Ø gunu-ny-u   ninki!*
       hit-UNM   3SG.M.A-2.O-FUT this.SG.M.ERG
       'He's going to hit you!'

In (33) (from Nordlinger 1998b: 232) the future tense suffix in the auxiliary cooccurs with a *ba*-marked verb, giving a simple future tense meaning:[22]

(33)   ...*ngawu   ng-u   ini   dudiyarri-j-ba.*
       1.SG.ERG 1.SG.A-FUT this.1.SG.ACC spear-TH -FUT
       'I'll spear this one.'

Nordlinger and Bresnan (1996) propose that the Wambaya tenses are composites of three primitive binary features: [± PAST], [± FUTURE] and [± UNCERTAIN]. The various compatible combinations of features give rise to the various tense values of Wambaya. This is illustrated for future and immediate future in (34):[23]

(34)   a.
$$\text{FUTURE:}\begin{bmatrix} - & \text{PAST} \\ + & \text{FUTURE} \\ + & \text{UNCERTAIN} \end{bmatrix}$$

       b.
$$\text{IMMEDIATE FUTURE:}\begin{bmatrix} - & \text{PAST} \\ + & \text{FUTURE} \\ - & \text{UNCERTAIN} \end{bmatrix}$$

The different auxiliary and verb inflections encode various combinations of these features, as illustrated in (35) and (36); here (35) is an example featural specification of the auxiliary tense morphology, while (36) is one of the verb tense morphology:

(35)   Sample auxiliary tense inflection:

$$\textit{-u:}\begin{bmatrix} - & \text{PAST} \\ + & \text{FUTURE} \end{bmatrix} \quad (= \text{Future})$$

(36)   Sample verb tense inflections:
       a.   *-ba:* [+   UNCERTAIN]
       b.   *-bi, -Ø:* ([−   UNCERTAIN])

Thus, from the general principles of structure–function association mentioned above, the different future tenses are arrived at by combining the information provided by the auxiliary suffix with that provided by the verbal suffix.[24]

   In (37) the combination of the auxiliary suffix and the verbal suffix fully specifies the category of future tense, and thus this is the only possible interpretation for the clause:

(37) a. ... *ngawu   ng-u*   *ini*   *dudiyarri-j-ba.*

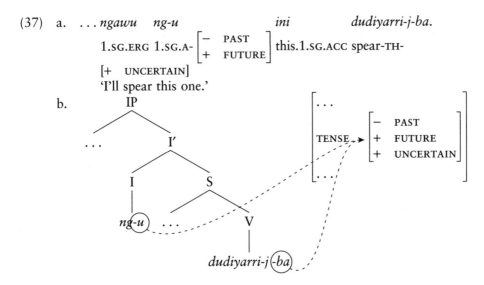

b.

As described at the outset, by the theory of structure–function mapping both the auxiliary in I and the main verb in V are f-structure heads of the clause. Their respective f-structures are unified with each other, and with the f-structure of the clause as a whole. This fact, along with the lexical integrity principle, which ensures that each word is inserted fully inflected into the syntax, allows in principle for a situation in which both the auxiliary and the verb are inflected with the same inflectional feature.

7.4   Conclusion

We now see that the phenomenon of distributed exponence can be explained by the same theory of structure–function mapping that explains the mobility of heads. The difference is that with distributed exponence each head is filled and contributes partial information to the whole, while with head mobility the same information that is distributed across several heads elsewhere is lexicalized in a single word that fills a single head position within the multi-phrasal domain.

Problems

The reader is now equipped to solve the first problem of problem set 3 (German word order).

Notes

1   Grimshaw's (1991) "extended projection" corresponds closely to the functional domain in LFG.

2 Consonant mutations affect the verbal form in context.

3 The Welsh verbal noun has both nominal and verbal properties, and could be categorized in alternative ways without affecting the essential point here. See Awbery (1976), Sproat (1985), and below for some discussion.

4 The principles of chapter 6 actually tell us only that the rightmost NP has a complement function CF; the lexical requirements of the verb (part IV) select exactly what type of complement function it is – OBJ in this case. In this illustration we have anticipated which of the possible complement functions (CF) on the NP in VP will match that of the PRED attribute, satisfying completeness and coherence.

5 The actual attribute–value pairs for *ddraig* are abbreviated by "dragon" in (8), following our convention for abbreviating the content of subsidiary f-structures where it is not relevant to the discussion.

6 This analysis of Welsh VSO structures is adopted from Kroeger (1993: 8–9). Previous work on head movement phenomena in LFG includes Netter and Kärcher (1986), Netter (1988), Meier (1992), Frank and Kärcher-Momma (1992), Kroeger (1993), King (1995), Berman and Frank (1996). Recent work includes King (1995), Choi (1996, 1999), Berman (1996, 1997, 1998, forthcoming), Sadler (1997), Sells (1998), Bresnan (1998a), among others.

7 We could also choose to solve the problem by eliminating I, but I is presumably required because of the need for tense or other attributes to be present in the sentence.

8 In this illustration we have again anticipated which of the possible complement functions (CF) on the NP in VP will match that of the PRED attribute, satisfying completeness and coherence.

9 Alternative analyses of these Welsh and (more generally) Celtic structures are possible and have been given (see, e.g., Borsley 1989, 1990). We have also set aside for expository purposes the very real possibility that auxiliaries may have semantic content forming a composite PRED with the main verb (Butt 1995, Alsina 1997, T. Mohanan 1994, Webelhuth and Ackerman 1999, Frank 1996, Andrews and Manning 1999).

10 Recall that ϕ is a many-to-one function from c-structure nodes to f-structures. Hence the inverse mapping from f-structures to nodes is not a well-defined function, because a single f-structure f is not associated with a unique c-structure node. However, the *set* of all c-structure nodes mapped by ϕ into f does give a unique value for f, and that allows the inverse of ϕ to be well defined.

11 The "dominates" relation is reflexive, antisymmetrical, and transitive: every node dominates itself and its daughters, its daughters' daughters, etc., but it properly dominates only its daughters, its daughters' daughters, etc. Accordingly, $\mathcal{A}$ c-commands itself and all of the nodes dominated by its mother (including that mother).

12 The following account closely follows Nordlinger and Bresnan (1996), for which permission from the publisher is gratefully acknowledged.

13 The phrase in the specifier of IP position is represented here as having a focus function. While this appears to be a reasonable characterization of its function, the discourse function of this initial position in Wambaya has not yet been studied in any detail and this may, therefore, turn out to be a simplification of the facts. "GF" can be any function but FOC.

14 There may also be a small class of X^0 elements that have an adjunct function, such as adverbs.

15 In the majority of cases this is predictable from the argument structure of the verb.

16 The account given in Nordlinger and Bresnan (1996) differs from this. The present account follows Simpson (1991) and resembles the treatment of grammatical functions

in problem set 1; see Nordlinger (1998b) for a full discussion of the theory of dependent-marking function specification in nonconfigurational languages using "constructive case" – inside-out function application – rather than case conditionals.

17 This is supported by the fact that the auxiliary never constitutes a phonological word of its own (for example, its first syllable never receives primary stress), but forms a phonological word with the element to its left. When the auxiliary is monosyllabic it is completely unstressed; when it is polysyllabic, it constitutes its own stress domain, as do all polysyllabic morphemes in Wambaya (Nordlinger 1998a), having secondary stress on the first syllable.

18 Nordlinger and Bresnan (1996) and Nordlinger (1998b) adopt a different analysis, based on 'prosodic inversion' (Simpson 1983a, 1991, Halpern 1995, and Austin and Bresnan 1996).

19 On existential constraints and negation, see section 4.6.

20 The annotation of X^0 adjunction structures is not discussed in chapter 6. Presumably both V and Aux must be annotated $\uparrow = \downarrow$ under I, because all are verbal categories.

21 Regular verbs belong to one of two phonologically determined verb classes which differ slightly in the forms of their unmarked inflections and in the nature of the stem to which the -ba suffix attaches.

22 A = transitive subject, TH = thematic consonant

23 Other values of the possible combinations are not discussed here; see Nordlinger (1996) and Nordlinger and Bresnan (1996) for details.

24 Nordlinger and Bresnan (1996) further assume that unspecified UNCERTAIN features are given the unmarked (i.e., negative) value by default. The idea of default feature specification can be expressed in LFG in various ways, including morphological blocking (Andrews 1990a) and type hierarchies (Markantonatou and Sadler 1996). Restricting ourselves to the formal architecture of chapter 4, we could provide (36b) with a conditional schema: $\neg(\uparrow \text{UNCERTAIN}) \Rightarrow (\uparrow \text{UNCERTAIN}) = -$. The condition is a negative existential constraint testing for the presence of the UNCERTAIN attribute, and the consequent provides a negative value to this attribute if it is not otherwise specified.

8 Pronoun Incorporation and Agreement

In the architecture of LFG, as we have seen, morphological words may determine the same kinds of functional structures as syntactic phrases. There is typological variation in the degree of functional specification provided by word structure versus phrase structure. In the grammars of some languages bound morphemes carry as much functional information as syntactic c-structure constituents. A widespread typological phenomenon called *pronoun incorporation* or *pronominal inflection* can be analyzed in this way: an incorporated pronoun or pronominal inflection is a bound morpheme that specifies a complete pronominal f-structure. The functional specification of a pronoun is incorporated with the functional specifications of the stem to which the morpheme is bound.[1]

The functional specification of a pronoun includes its semantic feature(s), binding features which constrain the range of possible syntactic antecedents (part IV), and case and agreement features. The latter features are shared by lexical nominals, and include gender, person, number, animacy, and specificity features. Only pronouns carry the pronominal binding and semantic features. In (1) the attributes PRED, *bind*, *agr*, and CASE respectively represent these four types of features. (*agr* is a metavariable over PERS, NUM, and GEND features; likewise, *bind* is a metavariable over the actual binding features (part IV). (CASE might also be taken as a metavariable over a more primitive decomposition of case features, but we will not pursue this possibility here. See Neidle 1988.) The actual features for the English pronoun *she* specify a nominative third person singular feminine definite personal pronoun:

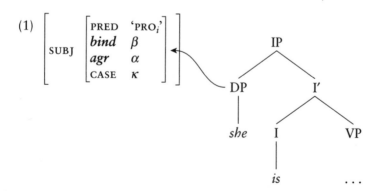

The PRED attribute, as a semantic feature, is uniquely individuated with each instantiation, as represented by the subscripted 'PRO$_i$'.

A pronominal inflection morphologically bound to a verb stem can specify the same type of f-structure as the pronominal DP shown in (1). An example is shown in (2), based on the Ulster Irish problem in problem set 1. The actual values for the Irish inflection specify a nominative first person singular definite personal pronoun ('I'):[2]

(2)

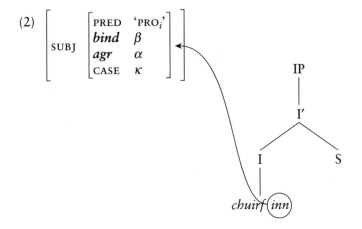

Because of the principle of functional uniqueness, if we are given an incorporated pronoun, it will pre-empt the appearance of any c-structure constituent of the same function having a conflicting semantic feature (PRED value), within the functional domain of the head to which the pronominal inflection is bound. (Recall from chapter 7 that the functional domain of a head is just the set of phrases which are mapped into the same f-structure as the head; in example (2) it includes I', IP, and S.) Absent further constraints, a pronominal inflection will therefore be in complementary distribution with a headed syntactic phrase of the same function. Independent (headed) NPs that cooccur with these pronominal inflections must then have nonargument functions, like the dislocated topics in *My mother, she's a really good sport* and *She's a really good sport, my mother*. The incorporated pronoun will agree with such nominals anaphorically, in just the way a pronoun agrees with its antecedent. An empty c-structure constituent of the same function as the inflection will not be ruled out by functional uniqueness, but – infsofar as it contains no information required for completeness, coherence, or semantic expressivity – it will be excluded by economy of expression (chapter 6).

At the level of f-structure, the similarities between incorporated pronouns and grammatical agreement inflections in our theory are striking. Verbal agreement morphology carries a subset of the kinds of features carried by pronouns (animacy, specificity, person, number, and gender). Thus, the inflected auxiliary verb *is* specifies a nominative third personal singular subject (as well as clausal present tense, not shown in (3)):

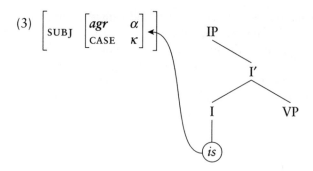

(3)

Because of the absence of the semantic and binding features of pronominals in (3) in contrast to (2), functional uniqueness will allow the expression of a syntactic subject DP or NP within the same clause (provided that its agreement features are compatible with those of the inflection), and the principle of completeness will require such a syntactic subject, because the verbal predicator will not be satisfied by a subject argument devoid of a semantic feature. Thus, absent other complicating constraints, a grammatical agreement inflection will obligatorily cooccur with a headed syntactic phrase of the same function. The agreement inflection thus "doubles" a syntactic argument, in the sense that the f-structures of the two are identified.

Verbal agreement systems evolve historically from the morphological incorporation of pronouns into verbs or other heads.[3] One trace of this historical evolution is the frequently found formal similarity between bound pronominal inflections and syntactically independent pronouns in the same language: the former tend to be reduced forms of the latter, although the different forms acquire distinct properties (Givón 1976, 1983, Bresnan and Mchombo 1987). Another trace of this evolution is the fact that the categories of verbal agreement across languages – person, number, and gender – are precisely the referentially classificatory properties of definite personal pronouns (see Bresnan and Mchombo 1987 for discussion). Yet another trace is the fact that in many languages the agreement system is in a transitional state between grammatical agreement and pronominal inflections, the same forms having both uses.

These transitional states can be naturally characterized in our theory: the obligatory semantic and binding features of the pronominal inflection become optional. The optionality of features represents a step in their gradual erosion and loss. When the semantic and binding features are present, the inflection behaves like an incorporated pronoun (2), showing complementary distribution with a corresponding syntactic argument. When these feature are absent, the inflection behaves like a grammatical agreement inflection (3), doubling a corresponding syntactic argument. This situation is often referred to as "pro-drop."[4]

Still finer transitional states are naturally characterized within this framework. If, for example, only the semantic feature of the inflection becomes omissible, but the pronominal binding features are retained, then the agreement inflection will double only syntactic pronouns, not NPs, because lexical nominals are incompatible with pronominal binding features.[5] Agreement with or doubling of syntactic pronouns is common; it may be restricted by person and number. For example, in some dialects of Irish, some of the personal inflections may double an overt syntactic pronoun (Andrews 1990a: 532–3, McCloskey and Hale 1984: 528–9). In the Bantu language Kichaga, the verbal object agreement prefix is in complementary distribution with lexical object NPs but obligatorily doubles object pronouns (Bresnan and Moshi 1990: 151–2). In Spanish, clitic doubling of accusative object pronouns is obligatory, while doubling of lexical accusative objects is restricted to certain dialects (Andrews 1990a: 539–42, Suñer 1988).[6] Object agreement in a number of Bantu languages is restricted to animate or specific objects (Givón 1976, Wald 1979, Allan 1983); clitic doubling of accusative objects in dialects of Spanish shows similar restrictions (Suñer 1988); and so does clitic doubling of subjects in northern Italian dialects (Suñer 1992).

Verbal clitics have an interesting status within this theory. While such clitics form a phonological word with their verbal host, they nevertheless have often been analyzed as syntactically independent phrase structure nodes (as in the analysis of Spanish clitics in problem set 2). Eventually, through diachronic processes of syntactic change, such clitics may become morphologically bound affixes (Givón 1976, Bresnan and Mchombo 1987, 1995, Börjars et al. 1997, Toivonen 1997, in press). What happens at the stage when a syntactically independent clitic loses its semantic feature (PRED value) and becomes merely an agreement marker, as has been argued to happen in Spanish? The clitic is no longer required for completeness or coherence. Consider the structures depicted in (4) for the accusative clitic-doubling dialects discussed in problem set 2. The question is, why does (4b) not replace (4a), by economy of expression?

(4) a.   b.

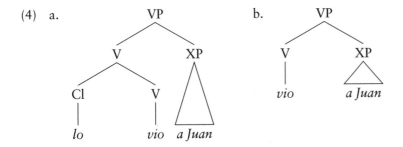

Recall that the principle of economy of expression (chapter 6) requires that all syntactic phrase structure nodes contribute to completeness, coherence, or semantic expressivity; nodes that immediately dominate lexical material are exempt. In (4a) the clitic node Cl is therefore not directly affected by economy of expression, because it dominates a terminal element. However, its mother node V does come under the pressure of the principle when compared to structure (4b), which yields the same f-structure with one fewer syntactic node (the V node dominating Cl and V). So by the principle of economy of expression the clitic structure shown in (4a) should be omitted from the c-structure as completely redundant. But it is not omitted. There are two alternative explanations for this within the present theory. One possibility is that when used as a grammatical agreement marker the clitic still bears some kind of information not available elsewhere, and hence satisfies "semantic expressivity." The other possibility is that the clitic agreement marker is in fact voided of nonredundant information, but is no longer counted as an independent syntactic node; it is reanalyzed as part of the verbal host. The fact that optional clitics become obligatory, like morphological inflections, when used as grammatical agreement markers seems to support the reanalysis hypothesis.[7] The reanalysis idea is illustrated by (5a, b):

(5) a.   b.

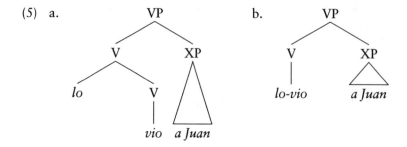

In this chapter we will apply this theory of pronoun incorporation and agreement to two head-marking languages, Chicheŵa and Navajo, and briefly compare the latter to the inverse agreement system of Plains Cree. In the conclusion, we will examine some implications of the theory for the principle of economy of expression.

8.1   Chicheŵa

Chicheŵa, a Bantu language of Malaŵi and neighboring areas of eastern central Africa, is a configurational, head-marking language.[8] Like most Bantu languages Chicheŵa has a rich concord system based on gender; Chicheŵa has 18 gender classes (or noun classes), and no morphological case. Chicheŵa is also strictly head-initial: every XP begins with X. Thus V is initial in VP, N in NP, P in PP, and A in AP (though prepositions and adjectives are small, closed-class categories). There is no evidence for IP in Chicheŵa: there is no positionally distinct category of finite verbs, auxiliary verbs, or particles with clausal scope.

In Chicheŵa the subject is external to the VP, and may precede or follow it and other sentential constituents. This constitutes an exception to the head-initial character of XP. One way of explaining this exception is to analyze the subject and VP as daughters of the nonprojective category S, which lacks a c-structure head. As we saw in chapter 6, S is not an XP projection for any X. Thus it can be hypothesized that the simple sentence of Chicheŵa has the following structure, where the comma indicates no order, NP is the subject, and VP is the "predicate" or f-structure head (as in section 6.2.3, (40) and (41)):

(6)   S
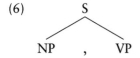
      NP ,   VP

As we will see below, Chicheŵa also admits nonargument XPs under S, so the basic sentence schema is like (7), where the daughters of S are XPs including a subject NP, a predicate VP, and nonargument XPs:

(7) S → C*

The verbal inflectional morphology of Chicheŵa is quite transparent, simple finite verbs having the sequence of prefixes shown in (8):[9]

(8) SM-T/A-(DIR)-(OM)-V$_{stem}$

The subject and object markers may historically have arisen from pronominal clitics which were at first phonologically bound to the verb, and subsequently morphologically bound, as Givón (1976) suggests for Bantu.[10] The agreement prefixes for the noun classes have formal resemblances to syntactically independent demonstrative pronouns, as shown in (9):[11]

(9) P/N/CLASS   SM   OM   PRONS   DEMS

P/N/CLASS	SM	OM	PRONS	DEMS
1stSg	ndi-	ndí-	ine	
2ndSg	u-	kú-	iwe	
1stPl	ti-	tí-	ife	
2ndPl	mu-	kú-...=ni	inu	
1, 1A	a-, u-	mú-	ĭye	uyu
2	a-	wá-	ĭwo	awa
3	u-	ú-		uwu
4	i-	í-		iyi
5	li-	lí-		ili
6	a-	á-		awa
7	chi-	chí		ichi
8	zi-	zí-		izi
9	i-	í-		iyi
10	zi-	zí-		izi
12	ka-	ká-		aka
13	ti-	tí-		iti
14	u-	ú-		uwu
15	ku-	kú-		uku
16	pa-	pá-		apa
17	ku-	kú-		uku
18	mu-	mú-		umu

Despite their probable historical origin as independent forms, the subject and object markers are part of the word structure of verbs in the synchronic grammar of the language. First, they are tightly bound to the word: the prefixes cannot be split off from the verb stem in conjunctions, ellipsis, or gapping, and syntactic clitics cannot be inserted between them (see Bresnan and Mchombo 1995). Second, there is allomorphy in the imperative and "associative" forms, which is phonologically conditioned by the foot structure of the stem, including the DIR and OM prefixes (Bresnan and Mchombo 1985). In short, the inflectional prefixes have morphological status in c-structure.

Chicheŵa has obligatory subject–verb agreement and optional object–verb agreement. The subject NP can always be omitted, giving rise to a definite pronoun interpretation ("pro-drop"):[12]

(10) a. *Njûchi zi-ná-lúm-a   a-lenje.*
          10.bee 10.s-PST-bite-FV 2-hunter
          'The bees bit the hunters.'
      b. *Zi-ná-lúm-a   a-lenje.*
          10.s-PST-bite-FV 2-hunter
          'They bit the hunters.'

Hence, we can associate the following functional specifications with the subject agreement inflection of the verb:[13]

(11) SM-: V_{infl} ($\uparrow$ SUBJ) = $\downarrow$
                        ($\downarrow$ *agr*) = α
                        (($\downarrow$ PRED) = 'PRO')

These specifications give rise to the structural correspondence shown in (12):

(12) $\left[\text{SUBJ} \begin{bmatrix} (\text{PRED} & \text{'PRO}_i\text{')} \\ agr & \alpha \end{bmatrix} \right]$

In the representation in (12), the parenthesized feature abbreviates two f-structures – one with the [PRED 'PRO'] feature, the other without it.

The object marker is only optionally present, as shown by (10a) and (13a), but when it is present, the object NP may also be omitted, as shown in (13b). Without the object marker, the object cannot be omitted, as shown in (13c):

(13) a. *Njûchi zi-ná-wá-lum-a   a-lenje.*
          10.bee 10.s-PST-2.o-bite-FV 2-hunter
          'The bees bit them, the hunters.'
      b. *Njûchi zi-ná-wá-lum-a*
          10.bee 10.s-PST-2.o-bite-FV
          'The bees bit them.'

c. **Njûchi zi-ná–lúm-a.*
   10.bee 10.s-st-bite-fv
   'The bees bit.'

Thus the object marker, like the subject marker, permits "pro-drop." But why is it optional? Optional elements are those which involve some pragmatic or semantic choice. What choice is involved in the Chicheŵa speaker's decision to use an object marker? Bresnan and Mchombo (1986, 1987) hypothesize that the Chicheŵa object marker, unlike the subject marker, is a full-blooded incorporated pronoun. That is, it has the functional specifications in (14):[14]

(14)   OM-: V_{infl} $(\uparrow$ OBJ$) = \downarrow$
   $(\downarrow \textit{agr}) = \alpha$
   $(\downarrow$ PRED$) =$ 'PRO'

These specifications give rise to the structural correspondence shown in (15):

(15) $\begin{bmatrix} \text{OBJ} & \begin{bmatrix} \text{PRED} & \text{'PRO}_i\text{'} \\ \textit{agr} & \alpha \end{bmatrix} \end{bmatrix}$ $\longleftarrow$ V
   |
   (OM)-*verb*

According to this analysis, the choice involved in using the object marker is simply the choice to use an anaphoric pronoun (which in this language is expressed as a pronominal inflection). The "object" with which the object marker agrees in (13a) is actually a dislocated topic, as indicated in the English translation, not a direct object NP in the VP. And the agreement in gender class between the object marker and this dislocated topic is simply the anaphoric agreement with its referent that a pronoun normally shows.

This hypothesized difference between grammatical agreement with an argument of the verb and anaphoric agreement with a topic explains a number of systematic differences between the subject- and object-agreement markers of the language. Tests based on (i) interactions of word order and agreement, (ii) the use of independent prnouns in discourse, (iii) contrastive focus, (iv) interrogatives and relatives, and (v) other syntactic and phonological differences show that the object prefix to the verb differs from the subject prefix in this way.[15]

8.1.1   Word order

Word order in Chicheŵa is affected by the presence of the object prefix. In simple, stylistically neutral, transitive sentences, when there is no object prefix on the verb, the object immediately follows the verb, while the subject may be reordered, as shown in (16):

(16) a. S V O: *njûchi zi-ná-lúm-a a-lenje*
                10.bee 10.s-PST-bite-FV 2-hunter
                'The bees bit the hunters.'
      b. V O S: *zinálúma alenje njûchi*
      c. O V S: **alenje zinálúma njûchi*
      d. V S O: **zinálúma njûchi alenje*
      e. S O V: **njûchi alenje zináluma*
      f. O S V: **alenje njûchi zináluma*

But when the object prefix is present, all six orders are possible:

(17) a. S V O: *njûchi zi-ná-wá-lum-a alenje*
                10.bee s-PST-O-bite-FV 2.hunter
                'The bees bit them, the hunters.'
      b. V O S: *zináwáluma alenje njûchi*
      c. O V S: *alenje zináwáluma njûchi*
      d. V S O: *zináwáluma njûchi alenje*
      e. S O V: *njûchi alenje zináwáluma*
      f. O S V: *alenje njûchi zináwáluma*

This difference follows from the hypothesized analysis above. Object NPs in Chicheŵa occur in postverbal position in a VP constituent, while the constituents of S include an optional subject NP, a VP, and an optional topic NP, all unordered with respect to each other (as indicated by commas separating them):

(18) S → (NP) , VP , (NP)
                SUBJ   TOP

(18) is an instance of (7). Note that while Chicheŵa's head-initial VP allows only the single order V O, its S allows six different orders of the subject NP, the VP, and the topic NP.[16]

    Given these assumptions, the word order facts can be understood in the following way. In (17) we have a transitive verb with an object prefix. The object argument role of the verb can be satisfied by the postverbal NP in the VP. An NP object can only occur in the VP. Therefore the subject NP in S can be reordered before or after the VP, but not inside it. If a topic NP were also generated under S, the extended coherence condition would require that it be linked to the lexical argument structure. This can be done in Chicheŵa by employing the pronominal object prefix of the verb, which is anaphorically linked to the topic NP. The object prefix precludes an object NP by functional uniqueness. Thus, the free-floating NP that agrees with the object prefix in (17) is not really an object, but a topic. As such, it is freely orderable with respect to the subject and the VP. Thus, (17) should be replaced with the more accurate description (19):

(19) a. SUBJ [$_{VP}$ V] TOP: *njûchi zi-ná-wá-lum-a alenje*
        10.bee S-PST-O-bite-FV 2.hunter
        'The bees bit them, the hunters.'

   b. [$_{VP}$ V] TOP SUBJ: *zináwáluma alenje njûchi*
   c. TOP [$_{VP}$ V] SUBJ: *alenje zináwáluma njûchi*
   d. [$_{VP}$ V] SUBJ TOP: *zináwáluma njûchi alenje*
   e. SUBJ TOP [$_{VP}$ V]: *njûchi alenje zináwáluma*
   f. TOP SUBJ [$_{VP}$ V]: *alenje njûchi zináwáluma*

In sum, the apparent cooccurrence of the Chicheŵa object prefix and an object NP with which it agrees is analyzed as the anaphoric linking of an object pronoun incorporated in the verb to a topic NP in S. The agreement of the object prefix in person, number, and gender class with the topic NP is simply anaphoric agreement: person, number, and gender class are universally the categories of pronominal agreement (Lehmann 1982).

The subject prefix contrasts with the object prefix in failing to interact with word order. While the choice of an object prefix precludes the presence of a syntactic NP object, the presence of the subject prefix is obligatory.

8.1.2 *Independent pronouns*

Further evidence of the difference between grammatical and anaphoric agreement can be found in the use of independent pronouns in discourse. It has been observed that all languages have two kinds of pronominals that can be used anaphorically, those used for reference recoverable in discourse and those used for contrast, emphasis, or focus, the former having less phonetic content than the latter (Givón 1983). In English the contrast arises between unstressed and stressed independent pronouns. In Chicheŵa the object prefixes are phonetically reduced relative to the independent pronouns, so the prefixes would be the topic-anaphoric pronominals, and the independent object pronouns would be contrastive. It is a striking fact about Chicheŵa, and appears to be a general property of languages of this type (Bresnan and Mchombo 1987), that the analytic object pronouns (that is, the pronouns that are independent phrasal constituents in the object NP position) are used only to introduce new topics or for contrast. They cannot be used anaphorically to refer to a topic in the preceding discourse, nor can they be anaphorically linked to a grammaticized topic. This is illustrated by examples (20) and (21):

(20) *Fîsi   a-na-dyá   chí-manga. Á-tá-chí-dya,*
   1A.hyena 1ASu-PST-eat 7-corn   1A.s-SERIAL-7.o-eat
   a-na-pítá   ku San Francîsco.
   1A.s-PST-go to S.F.
   'The hyena ate the corn. Having eaten it, he went to S.F.'

(21) *Fîsi   a-na-dyá   chí-manga. Á-tá-dyá*
1A.hyena 1A.s-PST-eat 7-corn   1A.s-SERIAL-eat
icho, a-na-pítá   ku San Francîsco.
7.it   1A.s-PST-go to S.F.
'The hyena ate the corn. Having eaten it (something other than corn), he
went to S.F.'

The discourse fragment in example (20) is fine. Here the incorporated pronoun –
the *chi-* prefixed to the verb stem for 'eat' – is used. In contrast, the discourse
fragment in (21) is bizarre. The independent pronoun *icho*, though it agrees in
gender class with *chímanga* 'corn', refers to something *not* mentioned in the
previous discourse. For the same reason, the independent pronoun cannot be
anaphorically linked to a grammaticalized topic in the same sentence:

(22)?* *M-kángó uwu fîsi   a-na-dyá   íwo.*
3-lion   3.this 1A.hyena 1.s-REC.PST-eat 3.it
'This lion, the hyena ate it.'

Again, the subject prefix contrasts with the object prefix. Serving as a grammatical agreement marker, the subject prefix fails to provide a topic-anaphoric
counterpart to the independent subject pronoun, and permits the independent
pronoun to take on both communicative functions, like the independent pronouns of English. Thus, the independent pronoun *when it is a subject* can be used
for anaphoric reference to both grammaticalized and discourse topics. The following examples illustrate this:

(23) *M-kângo u-na-gúmúla   khólá lá   mbûzi koma*
3-lion   3.s-REC.PST-pull.down 5.corral 5.ASSOC 10-goat but
íwo u-ma-fúná   ku-gúmúla   nyumbá yá   mfûmu.
3.it 3.s-PST.HAB-want INF-pull.down 9.house 9.ASSOC 9.chief
'The lion pulled down the goats' corral, but it really wanted to pull down
the chief's house.'

(24) *M-kángó uwu, ndi-ku-gáníza kutí íwó*
3-lion   3.this, i-PRES-think   that 3.it
u-ma-fúná   ku-gúmúla   nyumbá yá   mfûmu.
3.s-PST.HAB-want **inf**-pull.down 9.house 9.ASSOC 9.chief
'This lion, I think that it wanted to pull down the house of the chief.'

In both (23) and (24) the subject pronoun *íwo* is anaphorically linked to the
topic *mkángo* 'lion'.

This opposition in the pronominal system of Chicheŵa is quite systematic.
Bresnan and Mchombo (1987) show that it extends to prepositional objects as
well. One preposition has an alternate form that occurs with contracted pronominal objects; the contracted form is topic-anaphoric, and the uncontracted
counterpart is contrastive. Pronoun objects of all the other prepositions, which
lack contracted forms, are used ambiguously, like the subject pronoun.

8.1.3 Contrastive focus

Susceptibility to contrastive focus is another difference between grammatical and anaphoric uses of the agreement prefixes in Chicheŵa. Observe first that contrastive focus is possible with the independent object pronoun but not with the object prefix pronoun. Thus, example (25) has a contrastive object reading which (26) lacks, because the prefixed object pronoun *ndi-* 'me' in (26) is the non-contrastive pronominal.

(25) *M-dyerekezi a-ku-fúná   ine, osatí iwe.*
      1-devil   1.s-pres-want me not   you
      'The devil wants me, not you (i.e., he doesn't want you).'

(26) *M-dyerekezi a-ku-ndí-fúna,   osatí iwe.*
      1-devil   1.s-pres-i.sg.ø-want not   you
      'The devil wants me, not you (i.e., you don't want me).'

Now observe the contrast between examples (27) and (28). (27) shows that the object NP 'devil' can be a focus of contrast when there is no object prefix. The unacceptability of (28) is predicted if the presence of the object prefix makes the postverbal NP 'devil' not an object, but a topic, just as we hypothesize. Because a topic is ineligible to be a focus of contrast, the sentence is bizarre:

(27) *Ndi-ku-fúná   m-dyerekezi, osatí iwe.*
      i.SG.s-PRES-want 1-devil   not   you
      'I want the devil, not you (i.e., I don't want you).'

(28)?? *Ndi-ku-mú-fúná   m-dyerekezi, osatí iwe.*
      i.SGS-PRES-1O.ø-want 1-devil   not   you
      'I want him, the devil, not you (i.e., I don't want you).'

Finally, consider the contrast between (29) and (28). (29) shows that contrastive focus of the subject is possible with the subject prefix present, while (30) (further below) shows that contrastive focus of the object is not possible with the object prefix present:

(29) *M-dyerekezi a-ku-ndí-fúna,   osatí iwe.*
      1-devil   1.s-PRES-i.SGø-want not   you
      'The devil wants me, not you (i.e., you don't want me).'

This is explained by our hypothesis that the subject prefix, unlike the object prefix, can be a grammatical marker of subject–verb agreement. Thus a subject that agrees with the verb can be clearly distinguished from a topic that is linked anaphorically to an incorporated pronominal subject. Here then is another systematic difference between grammatical agreement and anaphora to a topic by a morphologically bound pronoun.

8.1.4 Interrogatives and relatives

Further differences between grammatical and anaphoric agreement derive from three postulates Bresnan and Mchombo (1987) make about the grammaticalized TOP and FOC functions. The first postulate is that in relative clauses the relative pronoun or relativized constituent bears the TOP function. The second is that in interrogative clauses the interrogative pronoun or questioned constituent bears the FOC function. And the third is that the same constituent cannot be both focus and topic of the same level of (functional) clause structure.

Given our analysis of the Chicheŵa object and subject prefixes, a consequence of these postulates is that a direct object should be able to be questioned in place, but only when there is no object prefix on the verb. For by hypothesis the questioned constituent is a focus, while the NP related anaphorically to the object prefix must be a topic, producing a clash of functions. The facts of Chicheŵa bear out this prediction:

(30) (*Kodí*) *mu-ku-fúná   chí-yâni?*
     Q   you-PRES-want 7-what
     'What do you want?'

(31)?? (*Kodí*) *mu-ku-chí-fúná   chí-yâni?*
     Q   ii.SGS-PRES-7.ø-want 7-what
     'What do you want (*it)?'

A further consequence is that a subject, in contrast, should be able to be questioned in place with subject agreement. For the focused interrogative constituent would not clash with the subject function, which grammatically agrees with the verb. This prediction is also true:

(32) (*Kodí*) *chi-ná-ónéka   chí-yâni?*
     Q   7.S-PAST-happen 7-what
     'What happened?'

Still another consequence is that this asymmetry in subject–object agreement with interrogatives should disappear with relatives. For by hypothesis the relative pronoun constituent is a topic, not a focus, so no clash of functions should arise. The facts bear this prediction out as well. An interesting further result is that questions that are formed with apparent movement of the interrogative pronoun should differ from questions formed with the interrogative pronoun in place, because in Chicheŵa the former are cleft constructions, in which the interrogative pronoun is the focus of the main clause but relativized in the subordinate clause. It follows that cleft questioning of both the subject and the object should be possible with agreement, in contrast to the questioning in place illustrated here.[17]

8.1.5 *Other syntactic and phonological differences*

In fact many other syntactic differences between the incorporated pronoun and the grammatical agreement marker are predicted in out theoretical framework. One is that only the anaphoric agreement relations can be nonlocal to the agreeing predicator – that is, span several clauses. Another is that in contrast to local subjects, the nonlocal NPs with which the subject prefix agrees should not allow questioning in place. Still another is that there should be subject–object asymmetries in the occurrence of cognate objects, idiomatic objects, and other NPs that do not easily topicalize: these NPs should allow agreement with the subject prefix but not the object prefix. And finally, verbally governed case on the full nominal is inconsistent with anaphoric, but not with grammatical, agreement. All of these predictions are borne out in Chicheŵa.[18]

Finally, there is phonological evidence that the object NP lies within the VP, while the NP we are calling the dislocated topic lies without (Bresnan and Mchombo 1987, Bresnan and Kanerva 1989, Kanerva 1990). Several phrasal phonological phenomena (tonal retraction, vowel lengthening, and high tone doubling) can be interpreted as indicators of the presence of a VP boundary, and they clearly show that the presence of the object marker on the verb forces the NP it agrees with outside of the VP.

8.1.6 *Functional ambiguity of subject and topic*

Clearly, then, there are systematic differences between grammatical agreement with a verb and the anaphoric relation between a morphologically bound pronoun and a discourse topic. Chicheŵa has both types of agreement relations, as shown by a variety of tests. The same tests reveal that the subject prefix of Chicheŵa is used for both grammatical and anaphoric agreement.

Like the object prefix, the subject prefix can be used anaphorically when the subject NP is omitted (10). Also like the object prefix, the subject prefix can agree with a floating topic NP several clauses above, as is characteristic of pronominal anaphoric relations:

(33) *Mkángó uwu, a-lenje   a-ku-gáníza   kutí ú-ma-fúná*
      3.lion   3.this 2-hunter 2.s-PRES-think that 3.s-HAB-want
      ku-gúmúla   nyumbá yá   mfûmu.
      INF-pull.down 9.house 9.ASSOC 3.chief
      'This lion, the hunters think that it wants to pull down the chief's house.'

And just in such nonlocal agreement relations with the subject, the floating NP cannot be questioned in place – in contrast to the case of grammatical agreement between a subject NP and the subject prefix in the same clause.

In sum, the subject prefix behaves like a grammatical areement marker, while the object prefix behaves like an incorporated pronoun. Yet in circumstances where grammatical agreement is excluded, the subject prefix also behaves like a morphologically bound pronoun. Thus there is ample evidence that the subject prefix in Chicheŵa is ambiguously used as a marker of grammatical agreement and as a morphologically incorporated pronoun that agrees anaphorically with a topic NP.

Two basic ideas underlie this theory. One is functional uniqueness: regardless of where it is expressed in the word and phrase structure, information about the same function must be consistent, and in the case of meaning, unique. Hence when an incorporated pronoun – such as a subject or object prefix – loses its pronominal reference, it no longer blocks the cooccurrence of an NP subject or object; but the grammatical information the marker carries – person, number, and gender – remains and by functional uniqueness must be consistent with that carried by the subject or object NP that cooccurs with it. In other words, by functional uniqueness the features of the subject or object marker must merge with those of the subject or object NPs. Nothing has to be added to our theory to derive this result: grammatical agreement follows immediately upon the loss of pronominal reference.

The second basic idea is the functional ambiguity of structural form. In our theory, functional information is related to surface structural form – the concrete word and phrase structure that is phonologically interpreted – by a many-to-one mapping. Consequently, one functional relation, such as that between a topic and an incorporated pronoun, may look exactly like another functional relation – subject–verb agreement – in all of its *structural* properties (word order and constituency relations), as illustrated in (34) and (35):

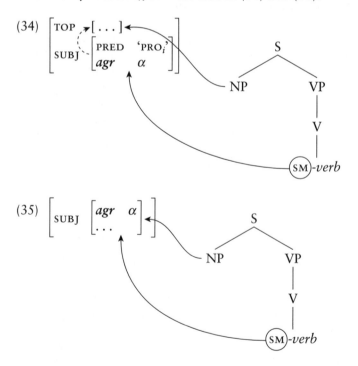

Diagram (34) shows the incorporated pronominal subject anaphorically agreeing with the topic (anaphoric agreement is indicated by the broken-lined arrow), and diagram (35) shows the subject marker agreeing grammatically with the syntactic subject with which its f-structure has been unified through functional uniqueness. Because these alternative functional possibilities correspond to identical expression structures, the alternation between the anaphoric and grammatical agreement is induced by the minimal possible change: the presence or absence of the semantic attributes of the subject inflection. The very minimality of this difference suggests a path of historical change through the gradual loss of semantic attributes of a pronominal element.

Thus the minimal difference between an agreement marker and a morphologically incorporated pronoun is the presence or absence of a referential attribute in the lexical content of the affix. Similarly, the minimal difference between the subject NP and the topic NP is the function, and not the phrase structure attributes of dominance, precedence, and category. In our framework, in other words, functional ambiguity between subject and topic does not imply structural ambiguity, for structure and function are independent planes of grammatical organization.

There is clear syntactic evidence for this crucial idea of functional ambiguity of structural form. In our analysis of Chicheŵa, the subject and topic NPs appear at the same level of structure in the S, with exactly the same ordering possibilities. An alternative hyothesis is that the structural position of the subject is fixed in Chicheŵa as [NP VP], and the post-VP subject is really a postposed (right-dislocated) topic anaphorically linked to the subject agreement marker (which is optionally pronominal, as we have seen).[19] The latter analysis would predict that the subject in VP-final position cannot be questioned in place, for in that position the apparent subject is by hypothesis a postposed topic, and hence incompatible with the question word's FOC function. But in Chicheŵa, the question word *can* follow the VP, as we saw in an earlier example, repeated here:

(36) (*Kodí*) *chi-ná-ónéka   chí-yâni?*
      Q   7.s-PST-happen 7-what
      'What happened?'

This confirms that the subject NP in Chicheŵa is unordered with respect to the VP.

Another alternative analysis is that both the subject and topic NPs are postposable, but the topic lies outside of the subject structure at a higher level of S (or FP):

(37) S   →   NP   , S
                (↑ TOPIC) = ↓

      S   →   NP   , VP
                (↑ SUBJ) = ↓

Because of the independence of structure and function in LFG, grammatical functions need not be represented by distinctive phrase structural configurations in this way. If the topic NP were generated either initially or finally, at a higher S level that the subject NP, then the subject would always be adjacent to the VP. The [V TOP SUBJ] order could therefore be generated only by analyzing the final SUBJ as an *apparent* subject. The apparent subject would actually be another topic NP generated at the topmost level of S structure and anaphorically linked to the subject prefix, which optionally functions pronominally, as we have seen:

(38) [s [s [s SU- OB- V] TOP] TOP]

Since interrogative words cannot be topics, this hypothesis predicts that in *in situ* questions, questioning the subject should be possible only when the subject is adjacent to the VP. Our analysis, in contrast, predicts that in such cases questioning the subject should be possible even when the subject is separated from the VP by a topic NP. In fact the question word subject can be separated from the verb phrase by a topic NP linked anaphorically to the object prefix:

(39) a. (*Kodí*) *chi-ku-í-fúná*   *mí-chírá yá*   *mbewa*   *chi-yâni?*
          Q   7.S-PRES-4.O-want 4-tail   4.ASSOC 10.mouse 7-what
          'Mouse tails, who wants them?' [V TOP SUBJ]
      b. (*Kodí*) *chí-yâni mi-chírá yá*   *mbewa*   *chi-ku-í-fúna?*
          Q   7-what 4-tail   4.ASSOC 10-mouse 7.S-PRES-4.O-want
          'Mouse tails, who wants them?' [SUBJ TOP V]

This confirms that the subject NP is at the same level as the topic NP, as in our analysis.

We see, then, that although the SUBJ function is grammatically distinguishable from the TOP function in Chicheŵa, the subject NP is indistinguishable from the topic NP in its *phrase structure* properties. The evidence suggests that it is functional ambiguity in the structural form of topic and subject constructions in Bantu that has led to the evolution of the incorporated subject pronominal into a grammatical agreement marker.

This theory leads us to expect that we might encounter languages in which the subject pronominal inflection is like the Chicheŵa object inflection, a pure incorporated pronoun without the option of grammatical agreement. Among the Bantu languages, Setawana, a northern dialect of Setswana, spoken in southern Africa, has been argued to exemplify this possibility (Demuth and Johnson 1989).[20] There are also instances where the object marker has acquired or is beginning to acquire the properties of a grammatical agreement marker: in Kichaga the object marker can double syntactic pronouns only (Bresnan and Moshi 1990: 151–2), the Kiswahili object marker can double animate NP objects (Wald 1979, Allan 1983) and the Makua class 1/2 object markers obligatorily double all NPs of their class (see Bresnan and Mchombo 1987: 777 and the references cited there).

8.2 Navajo

Like Chicheŵa, Navajo is a configurational head-marking language with no morphological case.[21] Navajo is strictly head-final, with V final in VP, N final in NP, and P final in PP. There is some positional evidence for a final I in IP, which can be occupied by a class of uninflected postverbal particles that express propositional attitude or (with a class of defective verbs) temporal reference (Speas 1990: 276–8). Taking the subject as specifier of IP, endocentricity entails a rigidly SOV word order pattern, and this is generally true of Navajo.[22] Examples are given in (40) and (41), taken from Speas (1990: 203):

(40)

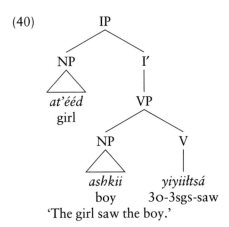

'The girl saw the boy.'

(41)

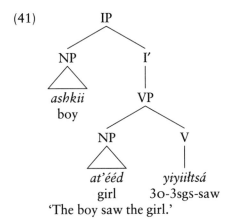

'The boy saw the girl.'

The only difference between the two sentences (40) and (41) is the c-structure position of the nouns 'boy' and 'girl'; reversing their order reverses their interpretation as subject or object.

When the NPs in (41) are omitted, a definite pronominal interpretation arises (Speas 1990: 260):

(42)   V

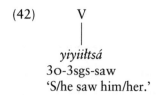

yiyiiłtsá
3o-3sgs-saw
'S/he saw him/her.'

The pronominal interpretation stems from the inflectional morphology of the verb.
   The morphology of the Navajo verb is often described as having 10 "position classes," which are numbered as they appear in the word from left to right:

(43)   NAVAJO VERB POSITION CLASSES
        1   Adverbial (including indirect object)
        2   Iterative
        3   Distributive
        4   Direct object
        5   Deictic subject
        6   Adverbial/Aspectual
        7   Mode
        8   Subject
        9   Class
        10 Stem

Positions 1–3 are referred to as "disjunct prefixes," and positions 4–9 are called "conjunct prefixes." The disjunct prefixes are more loosely bound to the verb than the conjunct prefixes.
   Here we are particularly interested in the conjunct prefixes in positions 4 and 8, which include the subject and object agreement markers:[23]

(44) | | 4: OM | 8: SM |
| --- | --- | --- |
| 1sg | *shi-* | *-sh-* |
| 2sg | *ni-* | *-ni-* |
| 3sg | Ø/*yi*/*bi* | Ø |
| 4th person | *ha-* | |
| 1du/pl | *nihi-* | *-iid-* |
| 2du/pl | *nihi-* | *-oh-* |

These agreement markers bear a close formal resemblance to the syntactically independent pronouns:

(45) INDEPENDENT PRONOUNS
1sg	*shí*
2sg	*ní*
3sg	*bí*
4th person	*ho*
1pl	*nihí*
2du/pl	*nihí*

Notwithstanding the formal similarity between these inflections and the independent pronouns, the agreement markers are morphologically bound components of the verb. McDonough (1990) argues from phonological and morphological evidence that the Navajo verb stem is a bipartite compound consisting of the verbal base (positions 9 and 10) and the cluster of other conjunct prefixes (positions 4 through 8), while the disjunct prefixes are a syntactically separate clitic group. She argues that the mode and subject morphemes in positions 7 and 8 have fused into portmanteau morphs.

With this picture of the verbal pronominal inflections, it is natural to ask whether they are grammatical agreement markers (as implicitly assumed in the representation of 'boy' and 'girl' as subject and object) in (40) and (41), or whether they should be analyzed as incorporated pronouns with the NPs as adjuncts. Speas (1990: 238–40) gives a number of arguments in favor of the agreement analysis.

The more convincing arguments are these. First, Speas argues that the rigid SOV order of NPs in Navajo would follow from their being arguments of a strictly head-final language; if they were loosely connected adjuncts or topics linked to pronominal arguments, this strict ordering would require additional explanation.[24] Second, Speas cites evidence of long distance question extraction in Navajo, which is inconsistent with the adjunct analysis. In the following example the verb 'hear' shows third person agreement with the complement clause. If that complement clause were an adjunct to a pronominal object argument, then extraction from it should be ill-formed, because extraction paths are blocked by such adjuncts (compare *Mary would love it, a picture of a cat* and * *What would Mary love it, a picture of?*):

(46) *Háágóólá   Bíl Mary íiyáa-go   yidiizts'áá'?*
      where.to.Q B. M.   3.P.came.comp 3.3.P.hear
      'Where did Bill hear that Mary went?' (Schauber 1979: 292)

Since the example is good, it supports the agreement analysis. However, Schauber (1979: 13–4) notes problems with the examples of leftward long distance extraction (which is typologically very unusual in an SOV language): "It is quite clear that many of the crucial grammatical examples are considered less than natural by at least some of the Navajos consulted." Apparently it is more typical for question words to appear within their local clause, and speakers disagree about the acceptability and interpretation of examples with extracted question words, as Speas (1990: 284) acknowledges.

We can add to these arguments a third, based on the fact that (according to Speas) Navajo shows a constraint on pronominal binding characteristic of arguments and not adjuncts.[25] The following examples are from Speas (1990: 213):

(47) a. *T'áá 'altso bimá   'ayóí 'áyó'ní.*
          everyone   his/her-mother really loves
          'Everyone$_i$ loves his/her$_{i/j}$ mother.'

b. *Bimá*   *t'áá 'altso 'ayóí 'áyó'ní.*
his/her-mother everyone really loves
'His/her.$_{i/j}$ mother loves everyone$_i$.

Example (47b) shows that a pronoun within the subject cannot be bound by a quantified object. Contrast (47b) with a corresponding Mohawk example from Baker (1995: ex. 15), where coreference is possible:

(48)   *raoti-skare' wa'-t-huwati-norukwanyu-' akweku*
      MpP-friend fact-dual-MpI/3II-kiss-punc all
      'Their$_i$ girlfriends kissed all (of them$_i$).'

Baker (1995) argues that the Mohawk quantifiers are referential expressions, which are not subject to the pronominal binding constraint exhibited by true quantifying expressions. Pronominal argument languages (that is, languages in which all of the direct arguments of predicators are incorporated pronouns) must make use of this type of quantification (Baker 1995, Jelinek 1995), because nonreferential phrases cannot be linked anaphorically to pronominal arguments, as we saw in chapter 2 ("Further Reading and Discussion"). Thus if Navajo does systematically show this effect, it would support the agreement analysis over the pronominal incorporation analysis.[26]

Speas's other arguments for the agreement analysis of Navajo are less convincing, and will not be discussed here. The main point is that even though several of Speas's arguments are inconclusive and some data must be treated with caution, on balance the evidence favors the agreement anaysis, especially the rigid SOV word order in a head-final language, the possibility for some speakers of extracting question words out of complements with which the verb agrees, and the weak crossover (n. 25) phenomenon with quantifiers. In terms of the present theory, we can therefore analyze *yi-* as in (49) (omitting the binding features – part IV). Here the PRED attribute is optional, meaning that *yi-*will be used as an agreement marker, and "pro-drop" will occur in the absence of a syntactic NP object. The final specification captures the fact that *yi-* is used only with a third person subject:

(49)   *yi-:* $(\uparrow \text{OBJ}) = \downarrow$
             $(\downarrow \text{PERS}) = 3$
             $(\downarrow \text{NUM}) = \text{SG}$
             $((\downarrow \text{PRED}) = \text{'PRO'})$
        $(\uparrow \text{SUBJ PERS}) = 3$

However, this is far from the whole story.

The use of the third person object markers is associated with an animacy hierarchy in Navajo:

(50)   **Animacy Hierarchy:**
      humans > animals > insects > natural forces > plants, inanimate objects > abstract notions

This hierarchy is described as follows (Uyechi 1990: 9):[27]

> Humans are highest in the animacy hierarchy and other NPs, animate and inanimate, follow. The other items are grouped according to what Creamer identified as status-giving qualities: "capacity for having intent or purpose; intelligence; strength, vigor, aggressiveness, or special potency; usefulness to man or relatedness to man; animation, or capacity for motion" (1974: 30). In accordance with those factors, animals are subdivided into three categories, large (e.g., bears, horses), medium (e.g., sheep, fox), and small (e.g. squirrels, snakes). Natural forces include phenomena such as windstorms, floods, sunshine, and fires from natural causes, and abstract notions encompassing concepts like old age, hunger, emotions, and disease. Within the group of plants and inanimate objects, Creamer notes that moving inanimate objects, e.g. a rolling log, take preference over stationary inanimate objects, e.g. a stone, . . .

While reversal of the c-structure positions of subject and object changes the grammatical relations of the sentence in (40) and (41) above, this is only because both boy and girl are human, ranking equally high on the animacy hierarchy. The expression of the subject and object is constrained by the animacy hierarchy. In (51a) (from Hale et al. 1977: 381) the subject is more prominent on the hierarchy than the object; in (51b, c) (from Uyechi 1990: 9, 2) it is less prominent:

(51) a. *'ashkii tsé   yiztał.*
        boy   stone 3o-3sgs-kicked
        'The boy kicked the stone.'
  b. **dzaanééz 'ashkii yiztał.*
        mule   boy   3o-3sgs-kicked
        'The mule kicked the boy.'
  c. **tsís'ná na'ast'oosí yishish.*
        bee   mouse   3o-3sgs-stung
        'The bee stung the mouse.'

Various formulations of this constraint have been given in the literature. Our characterization here is due to Uyechi (1990), who draws on the fact that the initial NP in Navajo is considered to be more topical (for reasons considered below):

(52) **Third Person Topicality Condition:**
The referent of the third person topic of the sentence must be of equal or higher rank on the animacy hierarchy than other referents of third person arguments in the clause.

To this we need only add that the *yi-* object marker is used in the unmarked case when the clausal subject is identified with the topic. We thus modify our entry for *yi-* in (49) above to (53):[28]

(53) *yi-*: ($\uparrow$ OBJ) = $\downarrow$
    ($\downarrow$ PERS) = 3
    ($\downarrow$ NUM) = SG
    (($\downarrow$ PRED) = 'PRO')
    ($\uparrow$ SUBJ PERS) = 3
    ($\uparrow$ SUBJ) = ($\uparrow$ TOP)

Then examples like (51b, c) will violate (52), because the initial NP is the subject and topic, but is of lesser rank than the object. In contrast, (51a) and both of examples (40) and (41) will pass the condition, because in all three cases the initial NP is the subject and topic, and is of rank greater than or equal to the object.

To express events in which a mule kicks a boy or a bee stings a mouse, Navajo employs the *bi-* object marker instead of *yi-* (from Uyechi 1990: 9, 2):

(54) a. *'ashkii dzaanééz biztał.*
        boy   mule   3o-3sgs-kicked
        'The boy, the mule kicked him.'
    b. *na'ast'oosí tsís'ná bishish.*
        mouse   bee   3o-3sgs-stung
        'The mouse, the bee stung it.'

Again, following Uyechi (1990) and Speas (1990), we analyze *bi-* as an incorporated pronoun which is anaphorically linked to a marked topic – not the subject, but a dislocated NP adjoined to IP:[29]

(55) *bi-*: ($\uparrow$ OBJ) = $\downarrow$
    ($\downarrow$ PERS) = 3
    ($\downarrow$ NUM) = SG
    ($\downarrow$ PRED) = 'PRO'
    ($\uparrow$ SUBJ PERS) = 3
    ($\uparrow$ SUBJ) $\neq$ ($\uparrow$ TOP)

The c-structure and f-structure of example (54a) under this analysis are as follows:

(56) 'The boy, the mule kicked him.'

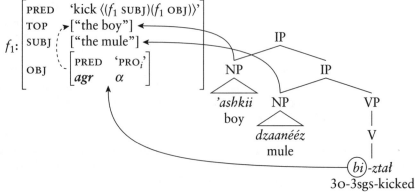

It follows from the topicality condition (52) that the referent of the left-dislocated NP must be of rank on the animacy hierarchy greater than or equal to the referent of the subject. This analysis predicts that *bi-* is obligatory when expressing situations in which a lesser subject acts on a higher object (with respect to the animacy hierarchy), optional when subject and object are of equal rank on the animacy hierarchy, and ill-formed when the subject outranks the object on the hierarchy. All three predictions are true (Hale et al. 1977).

Independent evidence for this analysis comes from a variety of sources. First, the syntactically independent pronouns differ from the pronominal inflections in being constrastive (Willie 1989: 411–12):

(57) a. *Yisháál.*
          1sg.walking
          'I am walking'
    b. *Shi yisháál.*
          I   i.sg.walking
          'I am walking.'

(58) a. *Yisháásh.*
          du.walking
          'We (two) are walking.'
    b. *Nihi yisháásh.*
          dual i.du.walking
          'WE (two) are walking.'

The third person independent pronoun *bí* is also contrastive, as Uyechi (1991: 438) notes:

(59) *ashkii bí yiyiiltsá*
      boy her *yi*-saw
      'The boy saw HER.'

The same contrast is found with the object prefixes and independent pronoun objects in Chicheŵa (section 8.1).

Second, researchers on Navajo have often noted a difference in the "aboutness focus" of the *yi-* and *bi-* sentences, in that the sentence is felt to be "about" the initial NP. This is partly captured in the translation used by Barss et al. (1989: 321):

(60) a. *Ashkii at'ééd yi-yiiltsá.*
          boy   girl   *yi*-saw
          'The boy saw the girl.'
    b. *At'ééd ashkii b-iiltsá.*
          girl   boy   *bi*-saw
          'The boy saw the girl (speaking of the latter).'

Platero (1974: 210) also comments that "the higher ranking nominal appears in initial, or 'topic', position" and notes that a contrasting pair of *yi-/bi-* sentences differ in that the former is primarily about the agent while the latter is primarily about the patient. Uyechi (1991) notes that a similar observation is made for Jicarilla Apache, a closely related Athapaskan language, by Sandoval and Jelinek (1989):

(61)   a.   *'ishkiyíí chékéé yaa'í*
            boy   girl   *yi*-sees
            'The boy sees the girl.'
       b.   *chékéé 'ishkiyíí baa'í*
            girl   boy   *bi*-sees
            'The girl is seen by the boy.'

They observe that (61a) answers the question 'What did the boy do?', while (61b) answers the question 'What happened to the girl?' Uyechi (1991: 438) observes, "[i]n each case, the sentence initial noun phrase refers to who the sentence is about and the remainder of the sentence responds to the question. In this sense, the sentence initial positions of both of these sentences function as discourse topics (Dik 1978)."

Third, the NP linked to *bi-* need not occur in the same clause, but can appear in a higher clause separated by a pause, according to Uyechi (1991: 437):

(62)   *Kii,* [s *Mary aníigo* [s *łíí'   biztał] ní].*
        K.   M.   recently horse *bi*-kick said
       'Kii, Mary said that recently the horse kicked him.'

Fourth, a topic question enclitic can attach to the initial NP linked to *bi-*:

(63)   *ashkii=sha' łíí'   nabíítgo'*
        boy=Q   horse 3.3.P.throw
       'Was the boy thrown by the horse?' (Schauber 1979: 111)

A fifth source of support for the incorporated pronoun analysis is the distribution of the *yi-* and *bi-* inflections elsewhere in the grammar of Navajo. In fact, nouns and postpositions may be inflected for *yi-/bi-* as well as verbs. The following examples from Speas (1990: 272, 266) show some of the effects:[30]

(64)   a.   *Hastiin Baa' yilíí'   yizloh.*
            man   B. POSS-horse 3sgO-3sgS-roped
            'The man roped Baa's horse.'
       b.   *Hastiin Baa' bilíí'   yizloh.*
            man   B. POSS-horse 3sgO-3sgS-roped
            'Baa' roped the man's horse.'

With the possessive inflection *bi-* in (64b), there is a reversal of meaning from (64a). The meaning change follows on the analysis given here, as shown in (65a, b):

(65) a.

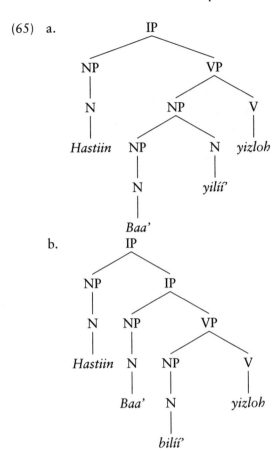

b.

Exercise

Provide f-structures that correspond to these two c-structures (65a, b), and explain the meaning reversal. Is the PRED the same? What is its lexical entry? Although we have not analyzed the functions of NP-internal constituents, you can assume for convenience that the possessor is the specifier of NP, and designate it simply as POSS in the f-structure; assume further that the POSS function is an optional argument of the nominal PRED: 'horse-of<(↑ POSS)>'. (See chapter 12).

The following pair of examples involve inflected postpositions (from Speas 1990: 266):

(66) a. *Ashkii at'ééd yichi'i' yáłti'.*
         boy   girl   yi-to   3s-talking
         'The boy is talking to the girl.'
     b. *At'ééd ashkii bichi'i' yáłti'.*
         girl   boy   bi-to   3s-talking
         'The boy is talking to the girl.'

Exercise

Provide c-structures and f-structures for (66a, b). Include the PRED and its lexical entry/ies.

Hint: Although *yi-* and *bi-* have different syntactic functions in their possessive and postpositional uses, their functional content (set of f-structure features) can be kept invariant across these uses by assuming that they take their functions from the morphological context. For example, position 4 of the V inflection specifies the OBJ function for any morphemes that appear there; the inflected postpositional stem also specifies the OBJ function for whatever morphemes are selected; but nominal stems specify the SPEC (or POSS) function for their inflections. The SUBJ and TOP designators in (53) and (55) must then be expressed using inside-out functional uncertainty: $((\dots\uparrow)\text{SUBJ}) = ((\dots\uparrow)\text{TOP})$; see sections 4.8, 10.4, and 11.6, and chapter 7.

Still further evidence for the topic status of the initial NP agreeing with *bi-* is given by Jelinek 1997.

In addition to the animacy hierarchy, Navajo provides evidence for a hierarchy of inherent lexical content:[31]

(67) **Hierarchy of Inherent Lexical Content:**
       null/incorporated pronominals > pronouns > common nouns

The choice of topic in Navajo is conditioned by the inherent lexical content of the topic designator as well as by animacy (Uyechi 1991). The basic idea is that those elements designated by reduced or null pronominals are inherently more topical than those designated by free-standing NPs, including pronouns:

(68) **Third Person Topicality Condition (Part II):**
       Expressions designating a third person topic of the sentence must not be outranked on the hierarchy of inherent lexical content by a null or incorporated pronominal designating another third person referent of the same clause.

Formulating the third person topicality condition to reference both the animacy hierarchy (50) and the hierarchy of inherent lexical content (67) enables us to explain the contrast between (59), repeated here as (69a), and the same example without a free-standing object pronoun (69b)[32] (recall from (45) that *bí* is the independent form of the third person pronoun):

(69) a. *ashkii bí yiyiiłtsá*
          boy   her *yi*-saw
          'The boy saw HER.'
      b. *ashkii yiyiiłtsá*
          boy   *yi*-saw
          'She/he saw the boy.'
          Not: 'The boy saw him/her.' (Speas 1990: 314)

In (69a) 'the boy' is the subject and the pronoun 'her' is the object. The incorporated pronoun (69b), in contrast, cannot be the object because the incorporated pronominal is highest on the hierarchy of inherent lexical content and so is required to be the topic by (68). (Recall from (53) that *yi-* is used when the clausal subject is identified with the topic.) Similarly, only one reading is available with *bi-* and a single NP argument in (70) (Speas 1990: 216, 260):

(70) *At'ééd b-iiłtsá.*
     girl   *bi-*saw
     'The girl saw him/her.'
     Not: 'He/she saw the girl.'

Under our analysis *bi-* requires the subject not to be the topic (see (55)), but this fact is still consistent with interpreting the NP 'the girl' in (70) as a dislocated object topic resumed by the incorporated pronominal *bi-*. However, the latter interpretation would violate (68), because the null pronominal subject would outrank the dislocated topic on the hierarchy of inherent lexical content. Only if we interpret 'the girl' in (70) as the subject can we satisfy this condition.

8.3 Plains Cree and Inverse Agreement

It is instructive to compare an inverse agreement system with the topic condition effects that we see in Navajo (52). Plains Cree is a member of Algonquian, perhaps the best-studied group of inverse agreement languages. In Algonquian morphology there are direct and inverse verbal makers distinct from the person agreement inflections, as illustrated in (71):[33]

(71) a. *ni- wi:cih-a: -na:n -ak*
       1   help   dir (1)pl (3)pl
       'We help them.'
    b. *ni- wi:cih -iko -na:n -ak*
       1   help   inv (1)pl (3)pl
       'They help us.'

These examples illustrate a morphological property which is quite characteristic of inverse systems of agreement. Dahlstrom (1984: 198–9) describes it as follows: "the affixes marking person and number features are not specified for subject and object. Instead, special suffixes called theme signs are used with transitive verbs to indicate which argument is subject and which object."

The inverse markers of some Algonquian languages have been analyzed as involving a remapping of grammatical relations to semantic roles. On one such analysis (cf. Rhodes 1976 on Ojibwa), the first person prefix *ni-* in (71a, b) would invariantly specify features of the subject; likewise, the third person suffix

-*ak* would specify object features. The direct theme marker (glossed 'dir' (71a)) would link the SUBJ to the agent and the OBJ to the patient (or beneficiary), while the inverse theme marker (glossed 'inv' in (71b)) would link the SUBJ to the patient/beneficiary and the OBJ to the agent.[34] This analysis is diagrammed in (72):

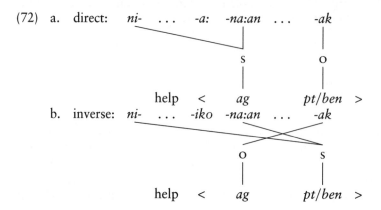

However, Dahlstrom warns us of the riskiness of arguing from morphology or discourse to syntactic conclusions: "a syntactic analysis cannot be motivated solely by inflectional patterns and contexts of use. The analysis of inverse verbs must rest instead on syntactic evidence" (1984: 105–6). She provides convincing evidence against the inverse mapping of syntactic functions to semantic roles (illustrated in (72b)) in Plains Cree: three syntactic tests for subject/object status converge on identifying the patient argument of transitive verbs, whether direct or inverse, as a syntactic object, and not a subject.[35] Dahlstrom's analysis, which (according to her) accords with that of most Algonquianists (including Bloomfield), is diagrammed in (73):

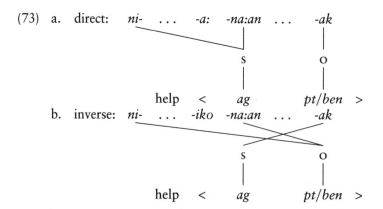

Observe that (73) differs from (72) in that the s and o links to the roles do not differ between direct and inverse forms.

    If we accept the syntactic arguments against remapping the grammatical functions to semantic roles in Plains Cree, how can we capture the inverse morphological pattern illustrated in (73)? Dahlstrom provides a simple model of this type of inflectional morphology. She assumes that the person inflections are unspecified for grammatical functions, and that the theme markers fix the person of one of the functions, allowing the others to be deduced by the general principles of uniqueness, completeness, and coherence. Her lexical entries for the verbal inflections in the examples of (71) are given here (with minor modifications for formal consistency with chapter 4):

(74)   *-ni-*

$(\downarrow \text{PERS}) = 1$

-na:n

$(\downarrow \text{NUM}) = \text{PL}$

$(\downarrow \text{PERS}) =_c 1$

-ak

$(\downarrow \text{NUM}) = \text{PL}$

$(\downarrow \text{PERS}) =_c 3$

-a:

$(\uparrow \text{OBJ PERS}) = 3$

-iko-

$(\uparrow \text{SUBJ PERS}) = 3$

wi:cih-

$(\uparrow \text{PRED}) = \text{'help } \langle(\uparrow \text{SUBJ})_{(agent)}(\uparrow \text{OBJ})_{(ben)}\rangle\text{'}$

$(\uparrow \text{OBJ GEND}) = \text{ANIM}$

She explains: "The grammatical information may be combined using the same mechanisms which are needed for constituent structure. The grammatical features listed in the lexical entries of *ni-*, *-na:n*, and *-ak* may be associated with subject or object by letting the annotation rule of 'Assign GF freely' apply to positions within the inflectional template of the verb." Because the theme sign *-a:-* or *iko-* already specifies person information about a fixed grammatical function, it constrains the functions that can be assigned to the other morphemes. Thus, "in *niwi:ciha:na:nak*, the theme sign *-a:-* indicates that the object is third person. Since the object is known to be third person, the first person affixes must be contributing information about the subject. If the first person argument were interpreted as the object, the resulting clash of features would rule out this f-structure." Dahlstrom states that this basic model (extended to include paradigmatic information) can account for the entire Cree verbal inflection system.[36]

Exercise

Work out the morphological structure and f-structure implicit in Dahlstrom's analysis of the Cree examples (71a, b).

As Cree illustrates, inverse agreement systems characteristically split inflectional position from syntactic function. One and the same inflection may specify person/

number information about the subject or the object, depending on the form of the verb. Navajo does not share this typical morphological property of inverse languages.

Yet Navajo and Cree do have a tantalizing typological similarity in their agreement systems (Jelinek 1990, Klaiman 1991). Part of what makes the Cree agreement system "inverse" is that although the subject outranks the object on the hierarchy of syntactic functions, the object may be more prominent on a distinct hierarchy of discourse participants which ranks first and second person above third person, and proximate third persons (roughly, those salient in the discourse) above obviative third persons (those less salient, morphologically marked on nominals designating them). When the object is more prominent than the subject on this hierarchy, the verb must bear the inverse theme marker. Here the analogy to Navajo is close: when the Navajo third person object is more prominent than the third person subject on the animacy hierarchy, the *bi-* pronominal inflection must be used, dislocating any object NP to topic position. In this way the most "topical" NP (a dislocated object, else the subject) is highest on the animacy hierarchy. In neither Plains Cree nor Navajo does the grammatical function of the object change under the "inverse" condition where the object outranks the subject in person/obviation or animacy. In both, an "inverse" association of syntactic and discourse/ontological functions is morphologically marked.[37]

8.4   Conclusion

The phenomenon of pronoun incorporation strikingly illustrates one way in which morphology competes with syntax within our framework and theory. Morphologically bound pronouns may pre-empt syntactic constituents from c-structure subject or complement positions. However, as the semantic and other pronominal features of these bound pronouns erode, they lose this pre-emptive power and begin to cooccur with external constituents in argument positions, thus functioning as grammatical agreement markers. Phonologically bound syntactic pronouns – clitics – undergo a similar process (as suggested by Givón 1976), but as soon as they provide only redundant grammatical information, economy of expression imposes pressure on them to change, either by differentiating their features or by undergoing reanalysis with their host and losing their status as independent syntactic constituents. Thus, it seems that economy of expression imposes a pressure both to prune away informationally empty syntactic phrases and to elaborate words.

Problems

The reader may now wish to solve the problem "Person and Number Marking in Wambaya" in problem set 3.

Further Reading and Discussion

A range of evidence in Navajo supports the analysis of *bi-* (in contrast to *yi-*) as a pronominal inflection, or incorporated pronoun. The analysis is not unproblematic, however. One problem not mentioned by Speas (1990) or by Uyechi (1991) is the fact that the NP linked to *bi-* can be questioned. The following examples illustrate this possibility:

(75) a. *háílá łíí' nabíílgo'*
       who.Q horse 3.3.P.throw
       'Who got thrown off the horse?' (Schauber 1979: 117)
    b. *háílá Jáan biiłtsá*
       who.Q John 3.3.P.see
       'Who was it that John saw?' (Schauber 1979: 220)

Normally topics cannot be questioned in place (** Who, he loves you?*); this fact formed part of the evidence given in section 8.1 for the pronominal status of the Chicheŵa object marker, in contrast to the subject. Bresnan and Mchombo (1987) show that questioning of topics is possible in cleft constructions, however, where the focus is external to a relative clause (*Who is it that loves you?*). The relative element is topical and permits cooccurrence with a pronominal object marker. There is no evidence for a syntactic cleft of this sort in the Navajo examples (75), but it is possible that the Navajo question words may allow similar presuppositions of referentiality. Schauber (1979: 220) comments that example (75b) may differ in meaning from the parallel *yi-* example in (76), as reflected by the difference in the translations of the two:

(76) *Jáan háílá yiyiiłtsá*
     John who.Q 3.3.P.see
     'Whom did John see?' (Schauber 1979: 197)

Thus questioning of *bi-*linked nominals may be consistent with their topical status, if Navajo interrogative words can be interpreted as referential, as discussed above in connection with weak crossover. There is some indication that this might be the case, in the appearance of the topic enclitic /*-sha'*/ on question words (63). Further research is needed.

Another problem noted by Barss et al. (1989: 321–2) is that in certain *bi-*marked postpositional constructions with conjoined NPs, "the 'topic' is not fully extracted from its clause in syntax." Speas (1990: 269ff) discusses this problem further, suggesting that in certain constructions (the "conjunctive postposition"), *bi-* may differ from its other uses. It is possible that *bi-*, like *yi-*, alternates between a pronominal argument and an agreement marker, and that other factors force the pronominal alternative in certain situations.[38]

Finally, Navajo *bi-* has been widely analyzed as a voice marker, either passive (Comrie 1989: 193) or inverse (Klaiman 1991, Jelinek 1990, 1997). In both of these types of voice analyses, it is assumed that the NP linked to *bi-* is syntactically a subject, not a topical dislocated object; the analyses differ in that the agent is expressed as a demoted or oblique argument with the passive, and as an object with the inverse. The passive analysis does not satisfactorily explain the relations of a voice marker *bi-* to the independent pronoun *bí*, and to the postpositional and nominal inflections. These nonverbal inflections pose difficulties for the inverse analysis, too. For their inverse analysis of Jicarilla Apache, Sandoval and Jelinek (1989) analyze all possessive and postpositional *bi-* inflections as inverse markers of complex transitive verbs made up of the verb and its nominal object or postpositional complement. Thus in (64), the possessive *bi-* on the nominal object 'horse' would be treated as an inverse object marker of a complex transitive verb 'rope horse'. While complex verbs may well exist in Navajo as in other languages, this analysis seems implausible as a general explanation of the distribution of *bi-*. For transitive verbs often form complex predicates with their objects and other complements, but they seldom, if ever, do so with their agent subjects (chapter 1). Yet possessive *bi-*inflections can appear on subject NPs in Navajo (see (47)).

Also telling against the voice analyses of *bi-* is the observation that the fourth person object inflection behaves as an incorporated pronoun, exactly like the third person (Uyechi 1990).[39] Both the subject *ji-* (which appears in position 5 in the verbal morphology) and object *ha-* fourth person inflections refer to humans or personified animals. (Note that the fourth person object inflection *ha-* resembles the fourth person independent pronoun *ho*.) Uyechi (1990) cites the following data in support of this analysis:

(77) a. *'at'ééd 'ashkii jiztał*
          girl   boy   ji-kicked
          'The girl$_4$ kicked the boy$_3$.'
      b. *'ashkii 'at'ééd haztał*
          boy   girl   ha-kicked
          'The boy$_4$, the girl$_3$ kicked him$_4$.'

(78) a. *'at'ééd łíí' jiztał*
          girl   horse ha-kicked
          'The girl$_4$ kicked the horse$_3$.'
      b. **łíí' 'at'ééd haztał*
          horse girl   ha-kicked
          'The horse$_4$, the girl$_3$ kicked him$_4$.'

(79) a. **łíí' 'at'ééd jiztał*
          horse girl   ji-kicked
          'The horse$_4$ kicked the girl$_3$.'
      b. *'at'ééd łíí' haztał*
          girl   horse ha-kicked
          'The girl$_4$, the horse$_3$ kicked her$_4$.'

(80) a. *łı̨́ı̨́   dzaanééz jiztał
         horse mule   ji-kicked
         'The horse₄ kicked the mule₃.'
     b. *dzaanééz łı̨́ı̨́   haztał
         mule   horse ha-kicked
         'The mule₄, the horse₃ kicked it₄.'

This pattern of data immediately falls out of the analysis of the fourth person subject as an agreement marker with optional [PRED 'pro'] and the fourth person object as an incorporated pronoun with obligatory [PRED 'pro'], together with the assumption that both are [HUMAN +]. Many languages have pronouns restricted to humans, but it seems less plausible to assume that Navajo has two voice morphemes with identical syntactic consequences associated with different animacy hierarchies.

These facts suggest that it may be a mistake to identify the pronominal inflections of Navajo as voice markers signalling a remapping of the grammatical relations of transitive verbs.

Notes

1 The term "pronoun incorporation" is frequently assumed to refer to the transformational movement of a syntactic element into a head (as in Baker 1988). This conception stems from the configurational design of universal grammar, wherein grammatical functions are represented in terms of syntactic phrase structure configurations (chapter 1). In the alternative design of LFG, there is no such implication: pronoun incorporation involves the incorporation of the *function* of a pronoun within an inflected word, not the incorporation of the *phrase structure* of a pronoun into a word. No (synchronic) movement is involved.

2 The functional specifications that give rise to this correspondence are these:

$$-inn: \mathrm{V}_{infl} \quad (\uparrow \text{ SUBJ}) = \downarrow$$
$$(\downarrow \text{ PRED}) = \text{'PRO'}$$
$$(\downarrow \textbf{\textit{bind}}) = \beta$$
$$(\downarrow \textbf{\textit{agr}}) = \alpha$$
$$(\downarrow \text{ CASE}) = \kappa$$

3 See Givón (1976), Greenberg (1977, 1978), and for qualifications and criticism, Chafe (1977), Moravcsik (1978), Russell (1984). For more recent work within an LFG perspective on this evolution, see Börjars et al. (1997) and Toivonen (1996, 1997, in press).

4 Like the term "pronoun incorporation," the term "pro-drop" is often interpreted to refer to an operation on phrase structure, in this case the transformational deletion of a syntactic pronoun or the "licensing" of a phonologically null syntactic phrase representing the pronominal argument. Again, this conception stems from the configurational design of universal grammar, in which syntactic functions are equated with syntactic phrase structure configurations. In the alternative design of LFG, "pro-drop" refers to the functional specification of a pronominal argument by a head; this entails the absence of the structural expression of the pronoun as a syntactic NP or DP.

5 Lexical nominals are subject to "Principle C," not to "Principle B," of the binding theory (see chapter 10); for present purposes let us assume that pronominals have a feature *bind* for which nominals are negatively constrained.

6 Instances where pronouns but not lexical NPs are excluded by pronominal inflections also occur (e.g. in Palauan: Georgopoulos' 1991: 52–4). These might be accounted for in terms of an incompatible grammatical feature of the syntactic pronoun and the pronominal inflection; further investigation is required.

7 For evidence bearing on the morphological status of clitics in Catalan and French, see Alsina (1994b) and Miller (1991). For an alternative model of obligatory clitic doubling in LFG, see Sadler (1997) on Welsh.

8 The present section closely follows the exposition given in Bresnan (1993), for which permission from the publisher is gratefully acknowledged.

9 SM = "subject marker," T/A = "tense/aspect," (DIR) = "optional directional," (OM) = "optional object marker." This depiction of the sequence of morphemes is not meant to endorse a template ("slot and filler") morphological structure.

10 Similarly, the T/A markers may have historically arisen from auxiliary-like verbal forms (Tabor 1992).

11 Some of the classes which are not formally distinct in the verbal concords are distinguished elsewhere in the concord system. 1A designates a subclass of noun stems that take the usual class 1 concords but lack the class 1 nominal prefix *m(u)-*.

12 The numerals used in glosses refer to noun classes, with 1A designating a subclass of class 1; S = SUBJ, O = OBJ; FV = final vowel; PST = past, REC.PST = recent past, PRES = present, HAB = habitual, PST.HAB = past habitual; ASSOC = "associative" (adnominal) marker; INF = infinitive; small roman numerals = persons; SG = singular.

13 Binding features are omitted. See part IV.

14 The Chicheŵa verb has an internal structure not developed here, in which the object marker and suffixed verbal stem form one morphological unit, while the outer prefixes form another (Bresnan and Mchombo 1985). Presumably the instantiation of the ↓ metavariable for the object prefix is thus indepedent of that for the subject prefix.

15 The following sections closely follow the exposition in Bresnan (1993).

16 Recall that the topic NP in (18) is a grammaticalized topic. Grammaticalized topics – constituents that bear the TOP function – designate discourse topics, but not all discourse topics are grammatically marked, and the same holds for focus. The discourse topic is what is under discussion, whether previously mentioned or assumed (cf. Chafe 1976, Givón 1976, Wald 1979, and Bresnan and Mchombo 1987).

17 See Bresnan and Mchombo (1987) for a detailed discussion of these results and data illustrating them.

18 See Bresnan and Mchombo (1987) for detailed discussion.

19 Such an analysis has been suggested for Kihaya by Byarushengo and Tenenbaum (1976).

20 Outside of Bantu, languages in which pronominal inflections provide the core arguments of a predicator have been argued for by Foley and Van Valin (1984), Jelinek (1984, 1989, 1990, 1995), and Baker (1991, 1995), among others.

21 The analysis of Navajo presented here draws on Speas (1990: chapter 4) and Uyechi (1990, 1991).

22 Kaufman (1974: 508) shows that with complex sentential arguments, word order is freer; for example, a sentential subject of a transitive verb can follow the object or even the verb. In addition, certain NPs and relative clauses may be right-dislocated, appearing postverbally (Platero 1978: 44ff, Perkins 1982).

23 The third person marker in position 4 is null if the subject is other than third person, and *yi-* or *bi-* if both subject and object are third person. The choice between *yi-* and *bi-* is discussed below. The fourth person pronouns are discussed below.

24 Jelinek (1997) proposes that additional constraints on topic/focus structure limit word order possibilities in Navajo under the pronominal argument hypothesis.

25 This constraint is referred to as "weak crossover," because (i) it occurs when the binder must "cross over" the bound pronoun in terms of word order, and (ii) the effect is weaker than when the pronoun is superordinate in the tree structure to the binder.

26 The reason that true (nonreferring) quantifiers show weak crossover effects is discussed in chapter 9.

27 Some authors have described the hierarchy in terms of control rather than animacy. See Klaiman (1991) for discussion and further references.

28 Uyechi (1991: 445, n. 4) notes that there is speaker variation which can be explained in terms of whether *yi-* explicitly marks the subject.

29 The fact that *bi-* is anaphorically linked to a marked topic other than the subject could be characterized as part of its binding features: [subject –, topic +].

30 There appears to be some variation in the use of *bi-* with kinship nouns. Speas claims (1990: 272–3) that *bi-* is obligatory with kinship nouns, but Uyechi (1990) cites a counterexample from Young and Morgan (1980: 9). There could well be speaker variation in the use of these morphemes. Further investigation is required.

31 This version of the hierarchy is due to Uyechi (1991: 441). Her hierarchy is a revision of Silverstein's (1976) hierarchy, to take account of the difference between free-standing and incorporated pronominals in Navajo.

32 This analysis is based on Uyechi (1991), though she explicitly discusses only its application to Navajo relative clauses. A similar idea is employed in Aissen (1999) within a more general theory of obviation (Aissen 1997). See section 8.3 on Cree below.

33 Our analysis of Plains Cree is taken from Dahlstrom (1984). Vowel lengthening is indicated by a colon here, where Dahlstrom has a raised dot, and plural is marked here as pl, where Dahlstrom has p.

34 A similar voice-changing model of inverse morphology for Mapudungun is described by Arnold (1994) within the framework of lexical mapping theory (part IV).

35 The tests are copying-to-object (anaphoric control of a finite clause subject by a matrix object), floating quantification, and control of secondary predication.

36 For other person combinations of subject and object, different "theme" morphemes are used. For example, *-i-* is used with transitive active verbs for second person subject, first person object (Dahlstrom 1984: 47ff).

37 See Aissen (1999) for a formal articulation of the insight that the Navajo *yi-/bi-* alternation expresses obviation as found in Plains Cree.

38 Suppose, for example, that all Navajo main clauses had to have a topic. Then by the third person topicality condition given above, if a third person subject were lower on the hierarchy than a third person object, the subject could not be the default topic, and that would force the pronominal alternative of *bi-*. The scope of the topicality constraint might not extend over certain subsidiary arguments, such as the conjunctive postposition construction, accounting for variations in the domain in which *bi-* had to be pronominal.

39 According to Uyechi (1990), the fourth person "is similar to third person in that it refers to someone outside the realm of the speaker and the hearer but it is unique in that its referent must be human or an anthropomorphized being; it is also similar to first and second person in that the referent is understood unambiguously by the speaker and hearer in the context of discourse."

9 Topicalization and Scrambling

The previous chapter described one way in which morphological words may determine the same kinds of functional structures as syntactic phrases. There we saw how pronominal inflections of a head can specify a complete pronominal f-structure for dependents of the head, and further, how the progressive erosion of these functional specifications gives rise to "pro-drop" and grammatical agreement phenomena. In the present chapter we examine a different way in which inflectional morphology determines the same kinds of functional structures as syntactic categories, through dependent marking. (If the reader has not yet done so, this would be a good point to read sections 4.8 and 4.9.)

9.1 English Topicalization

Consider the English c-structure given in (1):

(1)

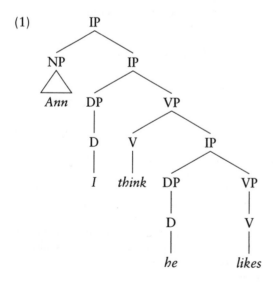

The endocentric principles of structure–function association for English tell us that *Ann* has the TOP or FOC function, that the sentential complement to *think* has a complement function, and that *I* and *he* have the SUBJ functions of their respective f-structures. However, the f-structure of the sentential complement is incomplete, because the verb *likes* requires an OBJ. Furthermore, the matrix f-structure violates the extended coherence condition (chapter 4), because the TOP is not integrated into the f-structure. The topic must be identified with some element which is functionally integrated. The default identification of TOP with SUBJ cannot be appealed to here, because the subjects are syntactically expressed in their canonical phrase structure positions, and cannot be identified with the TOP without violating functional uniqueness.

How does English secure completeness and coherence in such cases? The language has meager morpholexical resources for specifying syntactic functions: head-marking pronominal inflections are absent, a zero pronominal is available only for the subjects of nonfinite verbs (as in control constructions – chapter 13); and except for personal pronouns, which bear the vestiges of Germanic case inflections, the language is morphologically caseless. Thus, given the typology of the language within the endocentric principles of structure–function association proposed in chapter 6, it seems natural for English to utilize a structural means of function identification: the presence of a c-structure gap, to which is anchored a connecting chain of functions to the TOP in f-structure.

Recall from chapter 4 that our formal model of extraction makes use of inside-out functional uncertainty by stating simply that a gap in the c-structure is identified in f-structure with a higher discourse function (DF here refers to TOP or FOC):

(2) **Principle for Identifying Gaps:**
     Associate XP $\rightarrow$ *e* with $((x \uparrow)\text{DF}) = \uparrow$.

We take the functional specification in (2) to be annotated to the empty string dominated by XP. English (and some other Germanic languages) impose the additional restriction on (2) that for DF = TOP, XP = DP/NP (see below).

Let us recall how this principle applies to the example of topicalization given in (1), which was briefly discussed in section 4.8:

(3)

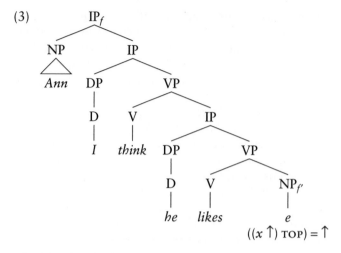

$$((x \uparrow)\ \textrm{TOP}) = \uparrow$$

The functional schema associated with the gap NP in (3) comes from the principle for identifying gaps (2). By uniformly instantiating this schema in the same way as all of the other functional schemata provided by the other principles of structure–function association, and solving the identity as outlined in chapter 4, we arrive at the f-structure in (4):

(4)
$$f: \begin{bmatrix} \text{TOP} & [\text{``Ann''}] \leftarrow \\ \text{SUBJ} & [\text{``I''}] \\ \text{PRED} & \text{`think} \langle(f\ \text{SUBJ})(f\ \text{COMPL})\rangle\text{'} \\ \text{COMPL} & g: \begin{bmatrix} \text{SUBJ} & [\text{``he''}] \\ \text{PRED} & \text{`like} \langle(g\ \text{SUBJ})(g\ \text{OBJ})\rangle\text{'} \\ \text{OBJ} & \underline{\hspace{2cm}} \end{bmatrix} \end{bmatrix}$$

For our second illustration of this model of extraction, let us use the example of CP topicalization discussed in chapter 2(3):

(5)

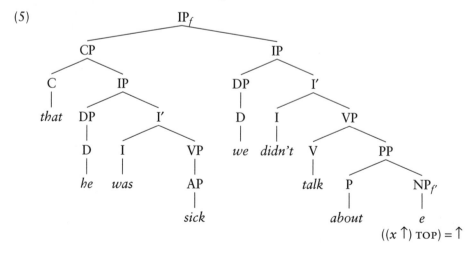

$$((x \uparrow)\ \textrm{TOP}) = \uparrow$$

Again, the principles of structure–function association for English tell us that the adjoined CP is TOP, the PP is a complement function (determined to be an OBL$_\theta$ by the preposition and the lexical properties of the verb *talk*), and the DP/NP gap is an OBJ of the preposition. Again, the principle for identifying gaps (2) adds the information that the TOP f-structure can be identified with the OBL$_\theta$ OBJ f-structure. Consequently the f-structure in (6) is a complete and coherent solution to the functional description of (5), with inessential details omitted (it would be a useful exercise for the reader at this point to check how the f-structure for (5) is derived):

(6)
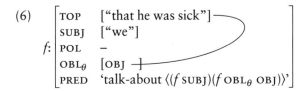

$$f: \begin{bmatrix} \text{TOP} & [\text{``that he was sick''}] \\ \text{SUBJ} & [\text{``we''}] \\ \text{POL} & - \\ \text{OBL}_\theta & [\text{OBJ} \quad] \\ \text{PRED} & \text{`talk-about } \langle(f\,\text{SUBJ})(f\,\text{OBL}_\theta\,\text{OBJ})\rangle\text{'} \end{bmatrix}$$

The fact that there is a mismatch of c-structure category type between CP and DP/NP in (5) is no problem for f-structure identification of the topic and prepositional object functions. The CP is never moved from the DP/NP position, as in (7), but is simply generated in place by the principles of c-structure:

(7) *We didn't talk about that he was sick.

It is natural to ask how the empty categories in this theory satisfy the endocentricity condition of chapter 7, which requires that every lexical category have an extended head. It is not difficult to see that the topicalized phrase itself serves as the extended head of the gap: it is mapped into the same f-structure and it c-commands the gap without dominating it. No closer phrase has these properties.

Further constraints of various types can be imposed on the possible paths x that connect the DF to the syntactic function of a gap, but constraints on extraction are not our concern here. Rather, we are interested in the typological difference underlying the extraction model of topicalization and an alternative scrambling model.

9.2 Russian Topicalization

Languages need not employ extraction to identify a DF with a non-DF function, if they make use of nonconfigurational means of function specification. Russian, for example, employs both configurational and case-marking principles of function specification.[1] Russian is an internal subject language, meaning it has two subject positions, in S and as specifier of IP. In our framework, S is the sister of I, where I is the category of finite verbs and V is the category of infinitives. King

(1995) argues that in Russian the specifier of IP has the TOP function; by our default identification of subject and topic (chapter 2), this position is therefore also a subject position. Two examples are given in (8) and (9):[2]

(8)

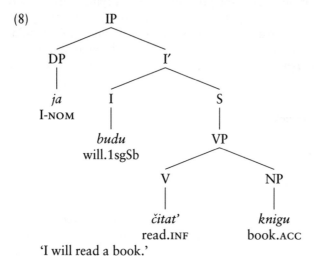

'I will read a book.'

(9)

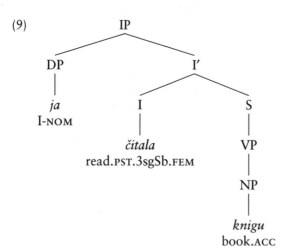

'I was reading a book.'

The existence of an I position for finite verbs outside of VP is supported by the contrast in (10) in colloquial Russian:

(10) a. *Ja [učit'sja   v novoj škole] slyšal, on budet.*
          I [study.INF in new school] heard he will
          'I heard that he will study in a new school.'
      b. **Ja [pošel v školu] skazal, (čto) on.*
          I [went to school] said   that he
          'I said that he had gone to school.'

As in (2), only maximal projections can be extracted. The finite verb–object sequence constitutes not such an XP, but an I′, as we see in (9). In contrast, the infinitive verb–object sequence does constitute a maximal VP, as we see in (8).[3]

Further evidence for a distinct category of the finite verb in Russian comes from the interaction of negation and conjunction. According to the IP/VP analysis, if we conjoin an infinitive verb with its complement as in (11), we are conjoining VPs:

(11)

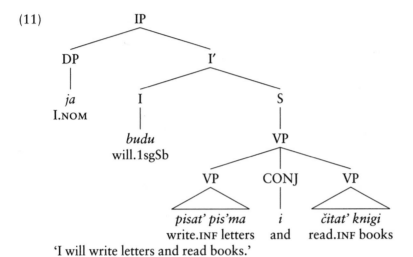

'I will write letters and read books.'

But if we conjoin a finite verb with its complement as in (12), we are conjoining I′s:

(12)

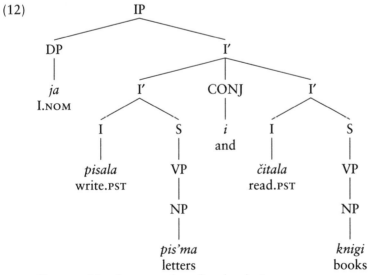

'I was writing letters and reading books.'

Now the negative proclitic *ne* attaches to finite verbs and not infinitives, with scope over the VP. One signal of the scope of negation in Russian is the "genitive of negation:" within the scope of negation, an accusative object can bear genitive case instead. Under the IP/VP analysis, *ne* attaches to I and not V. Hence it is predicted that a single *ne* will suffice to negate the conjunction in (11) but not in (12), and this difference should show up in the possible case marking of the objects. This prediction is borne out:

(13) a. *Ja ne budu pisat'   pisem   i   čitat'   knig.*
          I   not will write.INF letters.gen and read.INF books.gen
          'I will not write letters and read books.'
      b. **Ja ne pisala pisem   i   čitala knig.*
          I   not write letters.GEN and read books.GEN
          'I did not write letters and read books.'
      c. *Ja ne pisala pisem   i   ne čitala knig.*
          I   not write letters.GEN and not read books.GEN
          'I did not write letters nor read books.'

See King (1994, 1995) for further evidence in support of the IP/VP hypothesis for Russian.[4]

Given the structures in (8) and (9), our endocentric principles of function specification, with the specified parameter settings for Russian, will identify the initial DP as a DF and the final NP as OBJ in both of these examples; for concreteness, let us take the initial DP to be TOP. To secure completeness and coherence, a subject is required. A default principle identifying the TOP with SUBJ will not suffice in Russian, because the specifier of IP position may be filled by a nonsubject:

(14)

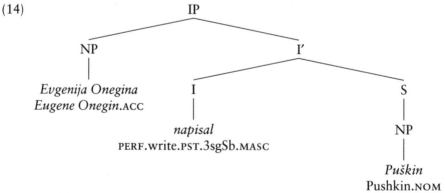

'Pushkin wrote *Eugene Onegin*.'

Russian solves this problem by using case (dependent-marking) principles of function specification in addition to configurational principles. In particular the following two principles hold in Russian (among others):[5]

(15) $(\downarrow \text{ CASE}) = \text{NOM} \Rightarrow (\uparrow \text{ SUBJ}) = \downarrow$
      $(\downarrow \text{ CASE}) = \text{ACC} \Rightarrow (\uparrow \text{ OBJ}) = \downarrow$

These principles can be applied to (11), (12), and (14) to associate grammatical functions with the TOP NP: nominative case yields the SUBJ function and accusative case yields the OBJ function. Because both configurational and nonconfigurational means of function association are simultaneously employed by the language, double functions are associated with a single constituent. Thus the f-structure of (14) will be as in (16):

(16)
$$f: \begin{bmatrix} \text{TOP} & \text{["Eugene Onegin"]} \\ \text{OBJ} & \\ \text{PRED} & \text{'write } \langle (f \text{ SUBJ})(f \text{ OBJ}) \rangle \text{'} \\ \text{SUBJ} & \text{["Pushkin"]} \end{bmatrix}$$

Even though the object is displaced from the canonical (endocentric) object position, it is nevertheless successfully associated with the object function by the nonconfigurational means of (15). However, this means of function association is possible only within the region of c-structure which is mapped into the f-structure of the verb or other predicator. Otherwise the principles of completeness and coherence could not be satisfied. Hence, this kind of function specification, which does not involve extraction, is bounded by the functional domain of the predicator. This type of "reordering" must therefore be local. In contrast, extractions, which employ a connecting chain of functions anchored to a gap, are not necessarily bounded in this way.[6]

While the specifier of IP can be a TOP or FOC, phrases adjoined to IP are topics in Russian.[7] Observe now the differences between the parallel English and Russian examples of topicalization in (17) and (18):

(17)

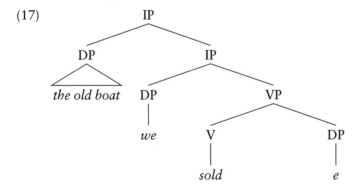

(18)

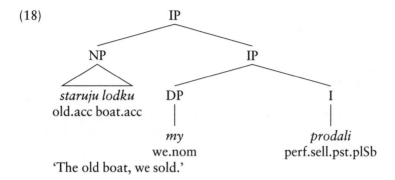

'The old boat, we sold.'

Given our typological hypotheses (chapter 6), the empty category representing the gap is essential in the English structure (17) to provide a means of identifying the topicalized DP with the OBJ function. In Russian, in contrast, an extraction gap is not necessary, because the language has an additional, morphological means of function specification. This is not to say that English has no case morphology, but merely that the case morphology English does have plays a different role in its syntax than case does in Russian. English relies on structural means of syntactic function specification rather than morphological means such as those illustrated in (15). Otherwise we would find that pronouns – the sole case-marked forms in English – would scramble.

9.3   Economy of Expression

Let us carefully examine the effects of economy of expression in the two cases above. We have assumed (chapter 6) that all c-structure categories are optional and are present only if required by general principles such as completeness or coherence. We have further hypothesized that the presence or absence of c-structure gaps in the English and Russian examples of topicalization, illustrated in (17) and (18), is typological. Russian has no need for the empty category in its clause-internal topicalizations, because it employs lexocentric principles of function specification in addition to the purely configurational endocentric principles. English, in contrast, cannot do without the endocentric principles. Empty categories are pressed into service in English as a "last resort," to secure completeness and coherence when there is no other means of function specification available.

What allows the occurrence of an empty category in the example of English topicalization (17) but excludes its occurrence in the example of Russian topicalization (18) is the principle of economy of expression, repeated here:

(19)   **Economy of Expression:**
       All syntactic phrase structure nodes are optional and are not used unless required by independent principles (completeness, coherence, semantic expressivity).

It follows from (19) that every syntactic node in c-structure must add new information to the f-structure. (Recall that the relative information provided by a category C and its context C' can be compared by means of the lattice of f-structures (chapter 5).) Economy of expression (19) rules out the empty NP in (20), since the information added by the empty NP – that there is an OBJ – is already provided by the initial NP, through the case-marking principles of function specification. In this way Russian contrasts with English. Vestigial case marking does exist in English, but (we hypothesize) it does not have the typological role of function specification that we find in Russian and other languages. If it did have this typological role, then the case marking itself would be sufficient to associate a pronoun with its syntactic function, regardless of its configurational position in the c-structure. Phenomenologically, the result would be pronoun "scrambling" in English – that is, the optional appearance of pronouns in multiple positions outside of the endocentric structures where their functions would be configurationally defined:

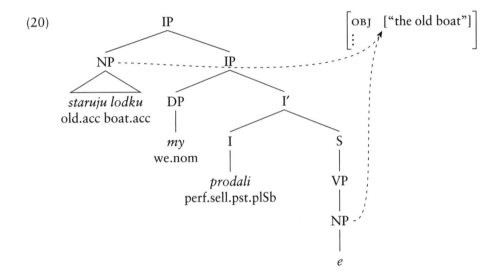

As we saw in chapter 8, the same principle rules out an empty category for instances of null or incorporated pronominals. In these cases the inflected verb or other head fully specifies the function and contents of a pronominal argument. Given the principle of economy of expression, the redundancy of an empty phrase structure category in such cases is sufficient to eliminate it.

This discussion offers some insight into the typological shift that a language may undergo when it loses its case system and abandons the dependent-marking schemata for function specification. When the case system has eroded to a sufficient extent, the f-structure information carried by words (i.e., the CASE features) is no longer recoverable. At this point case-based principles of function specification cannot be employed. The loss of these principles will leave scrambled structures functionally disconnected (violating coherence and completeness). As a result, the language may shift typologically to more rigid word orders and a greater reliance on endocentric principles of function specification – as appears to have happened in the history of English.

Of course, languages may take other avenues of change. The word order flexibility we see in Russian is generally shared by the Slavic languages, among them Bulgarian and Macedonian, which have lost case marking on nouns. However, in Bulgarian and Macedonian clitic doubling is associated with the noncanonical word orders (and pronouns are case marked). This point is illustrated by the contrast in Bulgarian between (21a, b) (Siewierska and Uhlířová 1998: 108):

(21)   Bulgarian:
    a.   *Tanja vidja Marija.*
        Tanja saw   Marija
        'Tanja saw Marija.'
    b.   *Tanja ja vidja Marija.*
        Tanja her saw   Marija
        'Marija saw Tanja.'

Here clitics apparently serve as head-marking specifications of argument function.

Problems

The reader may now wish to solve the remaining problem of problem set 3 (Subject Agreement in West Flemish).

9.4   Topicalization vs. Scrambling

An important question is how topicalization differs from scrambling under the present theory. Both processes order constituents out of their canonical (endocentrically defined) argument positions. Topicalization involves a constituent appearing in a fixed prominent position, usually sentence- or clause-initial. In contrast, scrambling involves the ordering of argument constituents in a variety of medial adjunct positions. As illustrated in (22), English lacks scrambling:

(22)   a.   Ann and Louise, Roger doesn't talk about. (topicalization)
    b.   *Roger Ann and Louise doesn't talk about. (scrambling)
    c.   *Roger doesn't Ann and Louise talk about. (scrambling)
    d.   Roger doesn't talk about Ann and Louise. (canonical word order)

If English made use of lexocentric function specification, it would be possible to derive such scrambling structures in the way illustrated in (23):

(23)

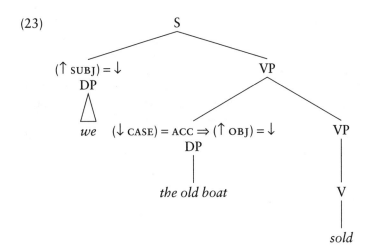

In (23) we have the object DP adjoined to the VP, which is not a position for objects by the endocentric principles of chapter 6, but a position for optional annotation of the adjunct function. However, the dependent-marking lexocentric principles of chapter 6 do allow free annotation of DPs with case conditionals, which can specify the f-structure function as illustrated. Because English lacks such lexocentric function specification, examples like (23) are not possible.

One might think initially that the absence of scrambling in English follows from the absence of lexocentric function specification. That is part of the story, but not all of it. For nothing in our theory thus far would rule out using extraction to mimic scrambling. For example, we could associate a DF with medial adjunct positions such as those in (22b) and (22c); then the gap-identification principle (2) could identify these DFs with the prepositional object, satisfying completeness and coherence. The structure in (24) illustrates this general point:

(24)

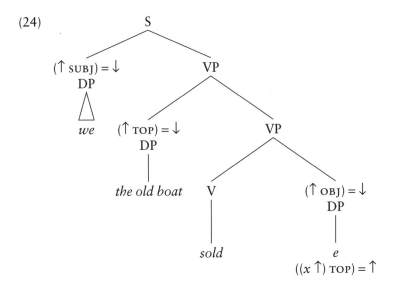

The theory of chapter 6 associates DFs with specifier of FP positions, which are prominent in the tree structure of clauses. The same theory also associates non-argument functions (including DFs) with adjunct positions; for example, a topicalized NP is an IP adjunct DF in English in section 9.1 (3) and an IP adjunct of Russian in section 9.2 (18). However, the theory does not express the fact that DF adjuncts are more prominent than other adjuncts: they appear in fixed positions, either at the edge of the clause preceding other maximal projections, or adjacent to the head (as with pre- or postverbal focus). Let us state this generalization as a further constraint on the structure–function mapping theory of chapter 6:[8]

(25) **Clause-Prominence of DFs:**
       DF adjuncts must be clause-prominent, occurring either at an edge of the clause or adjacent to the head of the clause.

In conjunction with the rest of the theory developed in chapters 6–9, the clause-prominence of DFs explains the absence of scrambling in English.

Another consequence of (25) within the present theory is that extraction antecedents ("gap fillers") do not scramble. If a language employs gaps for extractions, then it lacks other resources to identify the argument functions of the extracted element. Hence, these functions can only be recovered by the principle for identifying gaps (2), which targets a DF; DFs, however, are restricted in their distribution by (25) to prominent fixed (nonscrambling) positions.

The clause-prominence of DFs has another consequence. In the present theory almost all function specification is local to a single clause. This follows from the structure–function mapping theory, which specifies only the functions within a single functional domain. The possibilities for designating functions across clauses are quite limited. One is the principle for identifying gaps (2), which allows for nonlocal identifications of clause-internal functions with DFs in a higher clause, as we saw in the case of English topicalization (section 9.1). Another possibility is functional control (chapter 12), where a head may identify the SUBJ of its complement. These are the only nonlocal (clause-crossing) GF specifications permitted by the present theory, and both involve identification with the grammaticalized discourse functions DF: SUBJ, TOP, and FOC. Thus, the only function specifications which cross clausal boundaries are those which designate DFs.[9] Now, as we have just remarked, these syntactic functions are more salient than all others, in that crosslinguistically they appear in prominent structural positions. In this way they are distinguished from scrambling structures in our theory. Scrambling must lexocentrically specify all argument functions occuring in medial (nonprominent) adjunct positions. It follows then that while topicalization and other extractions (such as *wh-* questions) may or may not cross clauses (depending on what constraints are imposed on the inside-out variable (2)), scrambling must always be local to the clause:

(26) **Locality of Scrambling:**
       Extractions may cross clauses, but scrambling is clause-bounded.

9.5   Detecting Empty Categories

According to the present theory, empty categories in c-structure will appear only where other means of function specification are not available, because they are a "last resort" penalized by economy of expression. English, lacking lexocentric resources for function specification, uses empty categories for nonsubject extractions within a clause and for all extractions across clauses.[10] Scrambling languages, in contrast, do not use empty categories for extractions within a clause, because of the availability of alternative lexocentric means of function specification. But even in these languages, empty categories may be used as a last resort in just those situations where lexocentric function specification is unavailable – namely, in nonlocal extractions.

Is there is an empirical means of testing this theory by detecting empty categories? A clue is provided by an observation originally due to Mohanan (K. P. Mohanan 1981, 1982a, 1983, Bresnan 1984, 1994b, 1995, 1998c): *in Malayalam, linear order constrains the binding of overt pronouns, but not null pronouns.* This pattern is illustrated in (27)–(30) from Bresnan (1998c: 62). Each example is provided with a schematic representation of its annotated c-structure.[11] Examples (27)–(28) show binding from a quantified subject into an object relative clause. In (27) the subject precedes the object and in (28) the object precedes the subject. The generalization is that the overt pronoun may not precede its binder, while the null pronoun may:[12]

(27)   a.

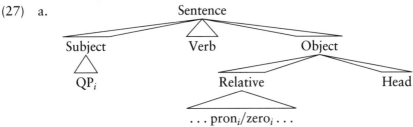

    b. *inna   ooṟoo kuṭṭiyum sahaayiccu*
        today each   child.N   helped
        [*innale   (awaṟe/awanawane) šakaaṟicca striikaḷe*]
        yesterday (they.A/he.REDUP.A) scolded.REL woman.A
        'Today each child$_i$ helped the women who scolded him$_i$ yesterday.'

(28)   a.

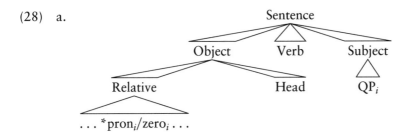

b. [*innale*   (*awaṟe/*awanawane) *ṣakaaṟicca sṭriikaḷe*]
yesterday (they.A/he.REDUP.A)   scolded.REL woman.A
innə   ooṟoo kuṭṭiyum sahaayiccu
today each   child.N   helped
'Today each child$_i$ helped the women who scolded him$_i$ yesterday.'

In (29) we see binding from a preposed object (accusative) quantified NP into a subject (nominative) relative clause that follows it. In (30) the object binder follows the subject it binds into. While both the overt and the null pronoun can be bound in (29), in (30) the overt pronoun cannot be bound preceding the binder, but the null pronoun can:

(29) a.

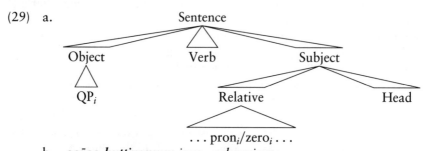

b. *ooṟoo kuṭṭiyeeyum innə   sahaayiccu*
each   child.A   today helped
[*innale*   (*awaṟə*)   *ṣakaaṟicca sṭrii*]
yesterday (they.N/he.REDUP.N) scolded.REL woman.N
Lit.: 'The woman who he$_i$ scolded yesterday helped each child$_i$ today.'

(30) a.

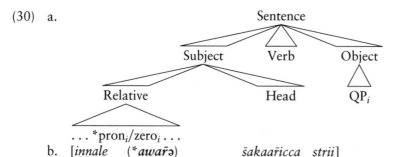

b. [*innale*   (*awaṟə)   *ṣakaaṟicca sṭrii*]
yesterday (they.N/he.REDUP.N) scolded.REL woman.N
innə   ooṟoo kuṭṭiyeeyum sahaayiccu
today each   child.A   helped
Lit.: 'The woman who he$_i$ scolded yesterday helped each child$_i$ today.'

Again, the overt pronoun must not precede the quantifier that binds it, while a null bound pronoun may. This generalization holds regardless of the relative hierarchical prominence of binder and bound. Thus, it is pure linear order that constrains pronominal binding by quantifiers in Malayalam:[13]

(31)   **Binding Generalization for Malayalam:**
       A pronoun cannot precede its binder.

Why are only overt pronouns and not null pronouns affected by (31)? One could of course simply stipulate this result as a special property of null pronouns. But Mohanan observes that this result already follows from the LFG assumption that null pronouns are functional elements without any c-structure expression. Linear order is a relation native to c-structure, not f-structure. If null pronominals are not represented in c-structure at all, then their lack of linear order relations follows from the basic architecture of LFG. Malayalam belongs to a language type in which null pronominals are provided as a lexical default to core arguments of verbal argument structures (K. P. Mohanan 1981, Bresnan 1982b, Simpson 1983a, Hale 1983, Austin and Bresnan 1996); see chapter 13. From the principle of economy of expression it then follows that empty categories cannot represent these null arguments in c-structure.[14] Hence, they cannot bear linear order relations to c-structure constituents.

In short, by completeness and coherence all pronominals, whether overt or null, are represented in f-structure, but by economy of expression and lexical integrity, only some are represented in c-structure. Hence f-structure is the natural domain of binding relations. Exactly how then can c-structure relations such as linear order exert any influence on binding? They do so through the correspondence mapping between c-structure and f-structure. We can determine the linear order relations of two f-structure constituents (such as a binder and a pronominal) very simply by looking at their correspondents in c-structure to determine which one is rightmost. This is the intuitive content of the formal relation of **f-precedence** (Kameyama 1985, Bresnan 1984, 1994b, 1995b, 1998c):

(32)   **Definition of f-Precedence:**
       Given a correspondence mapping ϕ (defined as in chapters 4–5) between a c-structure and its f-structure, and given two subsidiary f-structures α and β, α f-precedes β if the rightmost node in $\phi^{-1}(\alpha)$ precedes the rightmost node of $\phi^{-1}(\beta)$.

In other words, we simply look at the inverse images in c-structure of two f-structure constituents to see which one has the rightmost exponent: that one will be f-preceded by the other. A null pronominal which has no c-structure expression at all will fail to f-precede anything. Condition (33) therefore explains why null pronominals are not excluded from binding in Malayalam, where overt pronouns are:

(33)   **Precedence Condition on Pronominal Binding:**
       The domain of a binder excludes any pronominal that f-precedes it.

Malayalam null pronominals are not an isolated case. In Korean, Japanese, Mandarin, and South Min it has also been shown that linear order constrains pronominal binding and that null pronominals mitigate the binding constraints that hold for overt pronouns (Choi 1996, 1999, Kameyama 1985, Cole 1974).[15]

When the correspondence between f-structures and c-structure constituents is one-to-one, f-precedence (32) reduces to simple linear order in the string. However, when two discontinuous contituents correspond to the same f-structure, f-precedence relations become less transparent. Observe, for example, that in (34) the f-structure for the quantifier *everyone* corresponds to discontinuous c-structure constituents, consisting of the contents of the adjunct to IP and complement of VP:

(34)

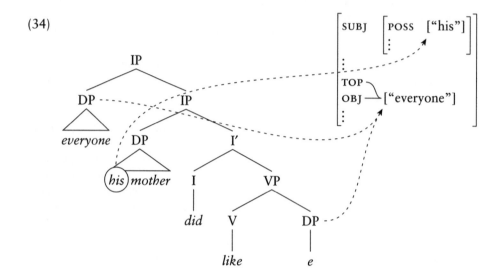

In (34) the f-structure quantifier ["everyone"] is realized in c-structure positions both preceding and following the pronoun. Applying the definition (32) to (34), we see that the subject possessor ["his"] f-precedes the topicalized object ["everyone"], because the rightmost node in the inverse image of ["his"] (namely, [*his*]$_{DP}$) is to the left of the rightmost node in the inverse image of ["everyone"] (namely, [*e*]$_{DP}$). Hence the pronoun f-precedes the binder. Here then is an empirical consequence of the presence of an empty category in c-structure: it can reverse the apparent linear order relations of pronouns and binders.

Hindi is a language which, like Malayalam, imposes the precedence condition (33) on the binding of pronominals by quantifiers, interrogative words, and other variable binding operators (Bresnan 1994b, 1995b, 1998c). Unlike Malayalam, Hindi has both scrambling and crossclausal extractions. It is therefore a test case for our theory that scrambling languages do not use empty categories for extractions within a clause, because of the availability of alternative lexocentric means of function specification, but do use empty categories as a last resort in nonlocal extractions.

In fact, clause-internal and crossclausal reorderings in Hindi do give rise to different pronominal binding effects (Gurtu 1985, Mahajan 1990, Dayal 1994,

Dwivedi 1994). Because a locally scrambled, topicalized, or questioned binder leaves no empty category, its function is determined by the lexocentric principles of function specification; hence, an empty c-structure node is not required, and by the principle of economy of expression is not present. In such cases, the relative f-precedence relation of binder and pronoun constituents reduces to their simple linear order in the string, and binding can occur as long as the pronominal is not ordered to the left of the binder. This situation is illustrated by the Hindi example in (35) from Mahajan (1990):[16]

(35) [*kis-ko$_i$/sab-ko$_i$*　　　*uskii$_i$ bahin*　　*pyaar kartii*　　*thii?*]
　　who-(DO)/everyone-(DO) his　　sister.(SUB) love　do.IMP.F be.PST.F
　　'Who$_i$/Everyone$_i$ was loved by his$_i$ sister?/.'
　　Lit.: *'Who$_i$/everyone$_i$ (did) his$_i$ sister love?/.' (Mahajan 1990: 25)

In (35) the pronoun does not f-precede its binder, and so is not excluded from the binding domain. If the fronted binder were associated with a gap, the structure would be similar to (34) and the pronoun would f-precede the operator, preventing binding.

　　In contrast, extracting a constituent out of its clause eliminates the means of local function specification. To secure completeness and coherence, the binder must therefore have a corresponding empty category within the lower clause, which belongs to the inverse image of the binder under the correspondence mapping. In this case by (32) the pronominal may f-precede the binder even though the binder precedes the pronominal in the string, as illustrated in (36):[17]

(36) *[Op$_i$]OBJ ... [... **pron**$_i$ ...]SUBJ ... [e_i] ...

A violation of the precedence condition on pronominal binding (33) arises in Hindi in just this situation, as shown by the following example from Mahajan (1990: 39, 41):

(37) *[*kis-ko$_i$/sab-ko$_i$*　　　*uskii$_i$ bahin-ne*　*socaa*　[*ki*　*raam-ne*　[*e*]$_i$
　　who.(DO)/everyone.(DO) his　　sister-(SUB) thought　that　Ram-(ESUB)
　　dekhaa thaa]?]
　　seen　be.PST
　　'Who$_i$ was it that his$_i$ sister thought that Ram had seen him$_i$?'
　　'Everyone was such that his sister thought that Ram had seen him.'

If, however, the pronominal belongs to the same clause as the gap corresponding to the extracted constituent, no binding violation occurs, as expected, because the possibility of scrambling varies the possible orders of the gap with respect to the pronominal within the clause, keeping the pronominal within the binding domain.[18] This explains another generalization about Hindi pronominal binding, illustrated in (38) (Mahajan 1990: 42):

(38) [*kis-ko$_i$/sab-ko$_i$*   raam-ne   *socaa*   [*ki* [*e*]$_i$ ***uskii$_i$***
     who.(EDO)/everyone.(EDO) Ram.(SUB) thought that   his
     bahin-ne   dekhaa thaa]?]
     sister.(SUB) seen   be.PST
     'Who$_i$ did Ram think was seen by his$_i$ sister?'
     Everyone$_i$, Ram thought was seen by his$_i$ sister.

By taking the precedence condition on pronominal binding (33) as a probe for the presence of c-structure gaps, we see that Hindi illustrates the "last resort" behavior of the c-structure empty category: it is used only where no other means of function specification is available. This behavior is just what economy of expression leads us to expect.

Not all languages make use of a precedence condition on pronominal binding. In Chicheŵa complements follow their heads; but Chicheŵa allows the subject to be ordered before or after the VP, as we saw in chapter 8. Regardless of linear order, the subject can bind into the object (39a, b), but not vice versa (40a, b) (Bresnan 1998c):

(39) a. ***Mu-nthu á lí yĕnse$_i$*** *á-ma-lemekézá*   *ma-kóló ăke$_j$*.
         1-person 1 every   1 S-PRES.HAB-respect 6-parent 6 POSS.iii.SG
         'Every person$_i$ respects his$_j$ parents.' (possibly $i = j$)
     b. *Á-ma-lemekézá*   *ma-kóló ăke$_j$*   ***mu-nthu á lí yĕnse$_i$***.
         1 S-PRES.HAB-respect 6-parent 6 POSS.iii.SG 1-person 1 every
         'Every person$_i$ respects his$_j$ parents.' (possibly $i = j$)

(40) a. *Ma-kóló ăke$_j$*   *á-ma-lemekézá*   ***mu-nthu á lí yĕnse$_i$***.
         6-parent 6 POSS.iii.SG 6 S-PRES.HAB-respect 1-person 1 every
         'His$_j$ parents respect everyone$_i$.' ($i \neq j$)
     b. *Á-ma-lemekézá*   ***mu-nthu á lí yĕnse$_i$*** *ma-kóló ăke$_j$*.
         6 S-PRES.HAB-respect 1-person 1 every   6-parent 6 POSS.iii.SG
         'His$_j$ parents respect everyone$_i$.' ($i \neq j$)

The operator binding condition in Chicheŵa is based on syntactic rank, as defined in (41)–(42):

(41) **Rank Condition on Pronominal Binding:**
     The domain of a binder excludes any pronominal contained in a constituent that outranks the binder.

We define syntactic rank as in (42):

(42) **Syntactic Rank:**
     Given the relational hierarchy
     SUBJ > OBJ > OBJ$_\theta$ > OBL$_\theta$ > COMPL > ADJUNCTS,

> α **outranks** β if α and β belong to the same f-structure and α is more prominent than β on the functional hierarchy or α outranks some γ that contains β.

According to this definition the subject outranks the object and every subfunction of the object in f-structure. Thus in (39) the quantified subject can bind the possessive pronoun in the object, regardless of their relative linear order. Conversely, when the possessive pronoun is part of the subject, as in (40), it is excluded by (41) from being bound by a quantified object. Kiswahili is another Bantu language like Chicheŵa, which has an order-free condition on operator binding of pronominals (Bresnan 1998c).

What do the precedence condition (33) found in Malayalam and Hindi and the syntactic rank condition (41) found in Chicheŵa and Kiswahili have in common? It appears that there is a fundamental unifying principle constraining pronominal binding relations in f-structure (Bresnan 1998c: 75):[19]

(43) **Prominence Principle:**
A binder excludes from its domain any personal pronouns more prominent than it.

(44) The **domain** of a binder is the minimal clause or predication structure containing it (formally modelled as the minimal f-structure).

Binder and bindee are both represented in parallel, nonhomogeneous structures, which model different dimensions of linguistic substance. Linear order is a prominence relation native to c-structures (which model the ordering of overt, perceptible expressions). Syntactic rank is a prominence relation native to f-structures, which model the grammatical relations among all syntactic functions, whether expressed or unexpressed.[20] Because the linked parallel structures of this framework can mismatch in the ways illustrated, the prominence principle translates into distinct relations which do not necessarily converge. An element may be of low syntactic rank and at the same time highly prominent in the linear order, or it may be of the highest rank but unexpressed and therefore lacking in any linear order relations at all. It has been hypothesized that languages select their binding conditions by adopting these universal but conflicting dimensions in different combinations or prioritizations (Bresnan 1998c, Choi 1997).

An interesting illustration of the latter possibility comes from German. German has been argued to have both precedence and syntactic rank conditions on operator binding of pronouns (Haider 1989, Choi 1997, Berman 1997). The following are examples of German scrambling in subordinate clauses.

(45) a. *daß jeder$_i$ seine$_i$ Mutter   mag*
that everyone.NOM his   mother.ACC likes
'that everyone likes his mother'

    b.   *daß jeden$_i$*   *seine$_i$ Mutter*   *mag*
        that everyone.ACC his   mother.NOM likes
        'that his mother likes everyone'
    c.   *daß seine$_i$ Mutter*   *jeder$_i$*   *mag*
        that his   mother.ACC everyone.NOM likes
        'that everyone likes his mother'
    d. *daß seine$_i$ Mutter*   *jeden$_i$*   *mag*
        that his   mother.NOM everyone.ACC likes
        'that his mother likes everyone'

The only example which lacks a bound reading is (45d). The Hindi equivalent of (45c) would not permit binding, but in German a pronoun can precede its binder within the same clause as long as the constituent it is contained in does not have greater hierarchical prominence than the binder.[21] Binding is possible in (45c) because the binder is a subject and the preceding pronoun is contained in an object. In (45d), the binder is an object and the preceding pronoun is contained in a subject, which outranks the binder on the relational hierarchy. Thus we have the following binding condition:[22]

(46)   **Precedence-Rank Condition on Pronominal Binding:**
       A pronominal that both f-precedes a binder and is contained in a constituent that outranks the binder is excluded from the domain of the binder.

Syntactic rank is defined as before by (42).
   To see clearly how this condition applies to the examples (45), consider the structure of (45b):

(47)

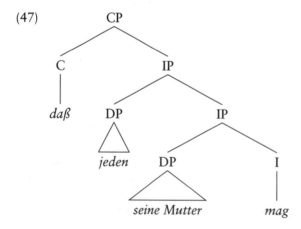

(47) shows the *seine Mutter* in the subject (specifier of IP) position, with the accusative object *jeden* adjoined to the IP. The endocentric and lexocentric principles of function specification will yield full annotations, including those shown in (48):

(48)   'that his mother likes everyone'

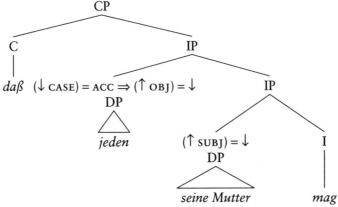

The precedence-rank condition on operator binding (46) does not exclude the possessive pronoun *seine* in (48) from the binding domain of the quantifier *jeden*. The reason is that though the pronoun is contained in the subject, which does outrank the object binder, the pronoun fails to precede that object. Exclusion in German requires high prominence along the dimensions of both precedence and syntactic rank. Binding of *seine* by *jeden* is therefore possible in (48). Example (45c) has the same c-structure, except that the roles of 'his/her mother' and 'everyone' are interchanged. Again, the pronoun fails to meet both prominence conditions and is not excluded from the domain of the binder.

Clause-internal topicalization and question formation in German show exactly the same gapless pattern of operator binding that we see with scrambling (45) (Berman 1997):

(49) a. *Jeder$_i$/Wer$_i$ mag seine$_i$ Mutter.*
          everyone.NOM/who.NOM likes his   mother.ACC
          'Everyone likes his mother'/'Who likes his mother?'
      b. *Jeden$_i$/Wen$_i$ mag seine$_i$ Mutter.*
          everyone.ACC/whom.ACC likes his   mother.NOM
          'Everyone is liked by his mother'/'Who is liked by his mother?'
          Lit.: *'Everyone$_i$, his$_i$ mother likes'/*'Whom$_i$ does his$_i$ mother like?'
      c. *Seine$_i$ Mutter   mag jeder$_i$.*
          his   mother.ACC likes everyone.NOM
          'His mother, everyone likes.'
      d. **Seine$_i$ Mutter   mag jeden$_i$.*
          his   mother.NOM likes everyone.ACC
          'His mother likes everyone.'

This result is in accordance with our theory: because dependent-marking function specification can apply to NPs/DPs in any position within the clause, economy of expression will exclude gaps for any of the clause-internal NPs/DPs, whether they are ordered according to scrambling, topicalization, or question formation.

Now in German as in Hindi, clause-internal and crossclausal reorderings have been reported to give rise to different pronominal binding effects (Haider 1989, Frey 1993, Berman 1997). When topicalization or question formation in German crosses a clause, the present theory predicts that a gap must be present in the lower clause to permit the identification of the within-clause function of the preposed constituent. This gap will necessarily follow a pronoun argument of the matrix verb, altering the f-precedence relations of the binder and pronoun. The pronoun will be excluded from the domain of the binder by (46):

(50) *$Jeden_i$/Wen_i sagte $seine_i$ Mutter,   habe sie getröstet.
     everyone.ACC/whom.ACC said   his   mother.NOM has   she consoled
     Lit.: *'$Everyone_i$, his_i mother said she consoled.'/
     *'$Whom_i$ did his_i mother say she consoled?'

The possessive pronoun *seine* both f-precedes the binder (by virtue of preceding the object gap left by extraction of the binder) and is contained in a constituent (the matrix subject) which outranks the binder as object, because the subject is higher on the relational hierarchy than the clausal complement which contains the object.

In contrast, an extracted binder can bind a pronoun within the subject of the complement clause it is extracted from in German, just as in Hindi:

(51) $Jeden_i$/Wen_i sagte sie, habe $seine_i$ Mutter   getröstet.
     everyone.ACC/whom.ACC said   she has   his   mother.NOM consoled
     Lit.: *'$Everyone_i$, she said his_i mother consoled.'/
     'Of $whom_i$ did she say that his_i mother consoled him_i?'

The reason again is that the gap can be positioned within the complement clause before the bound pronoun, so that (46) is not violated.

Finally, let us consider English as a Germanic language without scrambling. The following examples are parallel to the examples of topicalization in German (49):[23]

(52) a. $Everyone_i$ should like his_i mother. [possibly $i = j$]
     b. *$Everyone_i$, his_j mother should like. [$i \neq j$]
     c. His_j mother, $everyone_i$ should like. [possibly $i = j$]
     d. *His_j mother should like $everyone_i$. [$i \neq j$]

In English, unlike German, clause-internal topicalization of an object binder over a subject constituent containing a possessive pronoun (52b) prevents binding. Given that English is not a scrambling language, this pattern is exactly what we expect from the precedence-rank condition on operator binding (46). The lack of bound interpretations in (52b, d) has a uniform explanation: the pronominal both f-precedes the binder and is contained in a constituent which syntactically outranks the binder. In (52b) the pronoun *his* is contained in a constituent, the subject, that outranks the object *everyone*. Here *everyone* is extracted from its within-clause position as object of the verb *likes* by topicalization as illustrated in (53):

(53)

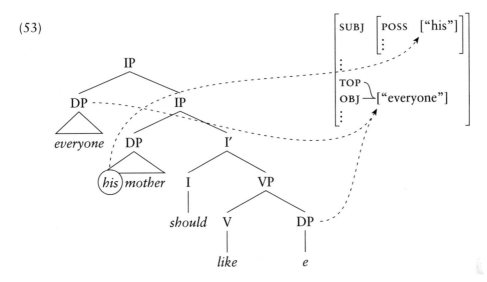

Hence there is a gap represented by an empty DP/NP in the object position, and the f-structure operator is expressed by a discontinuous constituent, made up of the contents of the adjunct to IP and complement of VP. In (53) the pronoun f-precedes the binder.[24]

Given that English and German share the precedence-rank condition on binding (46), the differing binding patterns of topicalized quantifiers can be traced directly to the presence of the gap in English and its absence in German:

(54) a. *Everyone*ᵢ, his*ᵢ* mother likes.
   b. *Jeden*ᵢ   *mag seine*ᵢ *Mutter*
      everyone.ACC likes his   mother.NOM
      'Everyone is liked by his mother.'
      Lit.: 'Everyone, his mother likes.'

If the quantifier *jeden* 'everyone (accusative)' were identified with a gap in (54b), the possessive pronoun would fail the constraint on operator binding, just as the English example does in (53). But this, the extraction analysis of (54b), is ruled out by economy of expression, because of the availability of the nonconfigurational means of function specification. Without a gap, *jeden* under this analysis is a single continuous constituent which the pronoun cannot f-precede. Binding is therefore possible.

Exercise

Draw the annotated c-structure and the f-structure for the German example (54b). Explain in detail why the pronoun does not f-precede the binder in (54b), but does in (54a). *Hint*: Consider the analysis of German word order in problem set 3.

Further Reading and Discussion

Bresnan (1998c) is recommended. There are many additional sources of variation in judgments of weak crossover examples in English and other languages; see Bresnan (1994b, 1995b, 1998c) for relevant discussion and references.

Two Types of Null Pronominals

In some languages it has been argued that null pronominals pattern with overt pronouns with respect to linear ordering constraints on binding. In Navajo, for example, null pronominals seem to show a precedence effect for noncoreference (Platero 1974, 1978). But there is an obvious typological difference between Navajo and the Malayalam-like languages discussed in the text above. Navajo, as we saw in chapter 8, has pronominal inflections. These are overt morphological exponents of f-structure pronouns, expressed in c-structure as head-marking morphology. Hence, according to our theory, the latter null pronominals are not actually "null" at all, but have c-structure correspondents – not empty categories, which are ruled out by economy of expression, but the pronominal inflections themselves. Bresnan (1998c) argues that it is these morphological exponents whose linear order relations determine pronominal binding in Navajo. In contrast, Malayalam has no verbal agreement morphology, but allows its direct argument functions (subjects and objects) to be unexpressed, giving rise to a definite pronominal interpretation. Formally, the null pronominals of Malayalam are simply analyzed as default f-structure arguments provided to the nucleus of the verb, as noted above. The same is true for the other languages of this type. See Bresnan (1998c) for further discussion.

Generalization to Operator Complexes

The term "operator" is commonly used for both quantifiers and interrogative words. Operators in this sense have a special property with respect to the binding theory. In English, but not all languages, an operator binder can inherit the syntactic rank of an operator complex it is embedded in.[25] A simple characterization of operator complex is that it is a phrase that "pied pipes" (Ross 1967) with an operator, as illustrated in the following example:

(55)

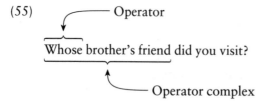

Whose brother's friend did you visit?

What counts as an operator complex varies across languages and may be somewhat variable across speakers of the same language.[26] Common English operator complexes include phrases whose specifiers are (true) variable-binding quantifiers (e.g. *every woman, no man, what book*), possessors (e.g. *no man's children, whose sister's friend*), and prepositional phrases dominating operator-complex objects (e.g. *to every woman*, etc.). In the case of simple NP (or DP) operators such as *who, whom, everyone, no one*, which are not dominated by pied piping material, we can take the phrase itself to be its own operator complex.

The crucial property of operator complexes is this: an operator O which by itself does not outrank a pronoun can bind that pronoun if O belongs to an operator complex that does outrank the pronoun.[27] This phenomenon is illustrated in (56) and (57), where the binder in the (a) examples does not outrank the pronoun it binds, but the complex it is contained in does.

(56) a. Everyone$_i$'s mother loves his$_i$ cute ways.
      b. Everyone's mother$_j$ loves her$_j$ free time.

(57) a. Whose$_i$ mother loves his$_i$ cute ways?
      b. Whose mother$_j$ loves her$_j$ free time?

It is straightforward to generalize the relation of outranking to operator complexes:[28]

(58) If O is an operator, O outranks B if O's operator complex outranks B.

Finally, note that ordinary DP specifiers which are not operators are not affected by (58). This accounts for the contrasts in (59) noted by Wasow (1979) and referred to in the recent literature as "secondary crossover" (cf. Postal 1993, Safir 1996):

(59) a. John$_i$'s mother, his$_i$ friends adore.
      b. *Everyone$_i$'s mother, his$_i$ friends adore.
      c. *Whose$_i$ mother do his$_i$ friends adore?

Other Factors

Other factors are known to affect operator binding, including thematic prominence, intonation, and focus structure. See Bresnan (1994b, 1998c) for further discussion and references.

Notes

1 The analysis of Russian given here follows King (1993, 1994, 1995) with minor modification to fit the present framework: we assume S where King has a VP-internal subject.

2   We assume here that Russian pronouns and demonstratives belong to the category DP, while common nouns are N. Economy of expression forces the minimal c-structure for NPs without determiners; so the objects of the verb are NPs and not DPs in (8)–(9).

3   King (1995: 28–30) cites these examples from Yadroff (1992). Comrie (1973: 295), however, notes an example from recorded colloquial Russian speech of extraction of a finite verb and its object out of a *čto* 'that' complement, leaving a PP complement behind:

(i)   *No ja ix   postavila   pomnju   čto v škaf.*
      But I them PERF.put.PAST.3sgS.FEM remember.PRES.1sgS that in cupboard
      'But I remember that I put them in the cupboard.'

This could be an instance either of extraction of a finite VP (contrary to the V-to-I analysis) or of an IP (consistent with the V-to-I analysis). In either case the PP would have to be scrambled away from the extracted constituent. The position of the complement subject would indicate which node is extracted, but that cannot be determined from this example because one of the finite subjects is unexpressed. Only the V-to-I analysis is consistent with both (10) and (i).

4   Strictly speaking, King's evidence from negation shows only that the finite verb is a distinguished category for the negative proclitic, not that the finite verb must appear outside of the VP in declarative sentences. However, King shows that a class of uninflected verbs called "predicate adverbs" (e.g. *možno* 'can', *nado* 'must') can be generated in V, I, or C.

5   See Neidle (1988), King (1995), and Bloom (1999) for discussions of the syntactic distribution of other Russian cases within the general LFG framework.

6   The phenomenon of extraposition or detachment of constituents from a predicate complement into a higher clause may represent a distinct type of ordering phenomenon involving functional uncertainty without gaps (Matsumoto 1992, 1996a, 1996b, 1998, Kaplan and Zaenen 1989b). Compare the English example *John took up exercising recently on the stairmaster*: the taking up is recent, the exercising is on the stairmaster, but *on the stairmaster* appears in the matrix clause outside of the gerund phrase *exercising* . . . which it modifies. This phenomenon departs in various ways from the two types of topicalization processes considered here.

7   See King (1994, 1995) for details. Multiple adjoined topics are allowed by the schema $\downarrow \in (\uparrow \text{TOP})$ (section 4.9), which creates a set of f-structures as the value of the TOP attribute.

8   Individual languages can parametrically select among the positions for specific DFs permitted by (25): for example, in English TOP and FOC would be available for left IP adjuncts (yielding topicalizations) and FOC for right VP adjuncts (yielding heavy NP shift, or right focus, complements: *She gave to each of us our own autographed photo*), but not for V adjuncts, left VP adjuncts, or I′ adjuncts.

9   The locality of function specification is a property of the substantive linguistic (meta)theory over formal grammars which is proposed here; it is not an inherent limitation in the formal architecture of LFG. Indeed, some other work within LFG makes much greater use of nonlocal function specification. See the references in n. 6. In addition, recent work on complex predicates extends the functional domain across several c-structure projections of main verbs. See Andrews and Manning (1999) for a review.

10 Some subject extractions within a clause – such as the topicalized CP construction discussed in chapters 2 and 6 – utilized the default identification of SUBJ and TOP, thereby removing the need for an empty category subject, by economy of expression.

11 In all the examples, the overt pronoun has both a collective interpretation (implying that a single woman was involved with a group of children) and a distributive interpretation (implying that different women were involved with different children). When the overt pronoun is omitted, a null pronominal interpretation arises, with either the group or distributive reading. Note that the examples are starred only on the bound interpretation; the overt pronoun is grammatical if interpreted as referring to others.

12 Here and throughout this section, "binding" refers to the referential dependence of a (nonreflexive) personal pronoun on a quantifier or interrogative expression. The relations of reflexive pronouns and other "bound anaphors" to their antecedents is discussed in chapters 10 and 11.

13 Here and throughout this section, we are referring to the binding of (nonreflexive) pronouns by quantifiers, question words, and other variable binding operators.

14 An interesting issue is what additional information is provided by overt pronouns that prevents their elimination in favor of null pronominals. Crosslinguistically, null and overt pronominals differ in topic anaphoricity and agreement features (Bresnan 1997a).

15 Note that pronominal inflections (chapter 8) are not considered null pronominals in our theory, because they have overt morphological exponents in c-structure, as morphological head marking. See "Further Reading and Discussion" below.

16 Mahajan's own theory of the Hindi binding patterns does not directly involve linear order; linear order is encoded in c-command relations. See Bresnan (1998c) for comparative discussion and review of order-free theories of operator binding.

17 "Op" here refers to a variable binding operator such as a quantifier (*everyone, no one*) or substantive interrogative expression (*who, what*).

18 The function of a scrambled empty category can be determined by applying the lexocentric case principles of function specification to it; these principles associate a syntactic function with a constituent conditional upon the CASE attributes of the constituent in f-structure. Though an empty category of course lacks any functional attributes in itself, it corresponds to the same f-structure unit as the binder, through which its CASE attribute appears.

19 "Binder" here and below refers to a variable binding operator such as a quantifier (*everyone, no one*) or substantive interrogative expression (*who, what*).

20 Thematic prominence is native to a-structures, which model the grammatically expressible participants of eventualities. Interactions of thematic prominence with pronominal binding are noted in Jackendoff (1972), and many subsequent references including Bresnan (1998c). For further references, see chapters 11 and 14.

21 There is some speaker variation in the exact prominence conditions applicable; some speakers only have a subject/nonsubject asymmetry, while others show asymmetries with multiple objects as well. See Choi (1997), Berman (1997), and Bresnan (1998c) for discussion and references.

22 This account is based on Bresnan (1994b, 1995b, 1998c), Choi (1996, 1997, 1999), Berman (1997), and discussions between Berman and the author in the fall of 1997.

23 As noted in Bresnan (1998c), judgments of the English data by some other researchers vary from those reported in Bresnan (1994b, 1995b). The present account is both a reanalysis and re-evaluation of the relevant English data.

24 Note that in (52c) the possessive pronoun f-precedes the quantifier, even though the topicalized phrase containing the pronoun does not f-precede the quantifier: the topicalized object is a discontinuous constituent with two exponents, but the possessive pronoun within it is not discontinuous. Though *his* f-precedes its quantifier binder, it is not contained in a constituent which outranks that binder: instead, the

subject *everyone* outranks the object *his mother*. Binding is therefore not ruled out by
(46).

25 Some material in this section is taken from Bresnan (1994b).

26 In Malayalam (K. P. Mohanan 1981), in Chinese (Higginbotham 1980), and in
Hungarian (Kiss 1987), it appears that an operator complex is limited to the operator phrase itself.

27 It is possible that *every*, *which*, and the other variable-binding operators are "un-
selective" quantifiers or polyadic operators over all of the predicates in the operator
complex:

(i)   every man's mother: $(\forall x, y)((x \text{ a man})(y \text{ the mother of } x) \rightarrow \ldots)$

28 Bresnan (1994b) has an operator inherit the domain rather than simply the rank of
its operator complex. This broader generalization is not taken here because of differences in the linear order effects of operators and their operator complexes.

Part IV On Functional Structures: Binding, Predication, and Control

Introduction

In the preceding chapters of part III – on endocentricity and its alternatives (chapter 6), head positioning (chapter 7), pronominal incorporation (chapter 8), and scrambling (chapter 9) – we have seen that hierarchical phrase structure is diminished or pre-empted in varying ways by the presence of rich morpholexical specifications. After this exploration of phrase structure variation we now turn to functional structure.

F-structure models the abstract (not always overtly expressed) predication relations that grammars systematize. One overt index of abstract subject–predicate relations is the binding of reflexive pronouns, which is the topic of chapters 10 and 11. Chapter 12 takes up the LFG model of predication and functional control, chapter 13 distinguishes anaphoric from functional control, and chapter 14 outlines the lexical mapping theory of how skeletal f-structures are projected from argument structures. The LFG literature on these topics is too large to permit full discussion here of all of the various theoretical developments and empirical results. Instead, the aim of part IV is to enable the reader to understand the fundamental issues that have guided work in LFG and to read critically the LFG literature, to which references will be given.

10 Basic Binding Theory

The binding theory of textbook generative grammar refers to a selected class of phrase structure positions (argument and nonargument positions), a relation of relative prominence among them (c-command), a typology of the elements that enter into binding relations (anaphors, pronominals, referring expressions), and designated regions of phrase structure within which the binding relations hold for these elements (e.g. governing category). All of the definitions of the theory presuppose the configurational design of universal grammar (chapter 1). In LFG, in contrast, binding theory is defined at the level of functional structure (and a-structure – chapter 14), because anaphors, pronominals, and referring expressions are not uniformly represented in c-structure positions across languages or even within the same language, as we have seen.

10.1 Basic Concepts

The basic concepts of binding theory in LFG abstract away from phrase structure. In place of argument and nonargument positions in phrase structure, we have argument and nonargument functions (chapter 6). In (1) the functions are arranged according to the relational hierarchy, with the SUBJ as the most prominent function:

(1) **Relational Hierarchy:**
    SUBJ > OBJ > OBJ_θ > OBL_θ > COMPL > ADJUNCT

Note that this hierarchy excludes grammaticalized discourse functions TOP and FOC. These are the only syntactic functions which are not directly associated with a PRED by the coherence condition (chapter 4): to satisfy coherence, they must be identified with one of the functions on the relational hierarchy (1).

In place of c-command, a relation of relative prominence on phrase structure,[1] we have syntactic rank, a relation of relative prominence on functional structure based on the relational hierarchy (1) (chapter 9):

(2) **Syntactic Rank:**
A locally outranks B if A and B belong to the same f-structure and A is more prominent than B on the relational hierarchy (1). A outranks B if A locally outranks some C which contains B.

The concept of syntactic rank can be formalized using the concept of inside-out functional uncertainty (section 4.8). See section 10.4 below.

In place of governing category, defined in terms of X' theory,[2] we have the concept of the nucleus of an f-structure:

(3) **Nucleus:**
Given an f-structure f, the nucleus of f is the subset of f consisting of the PRED element and all of the elements whose attributes are functions designated by the PRED.

In other words, a nucleus is the subset of an f-structure consisting of its PRED and argument functions, and omitting any nonargument functions. This characterization of nucleus is equivalent to saying that the nucleus is the complete and coherent subset of f, using coherence and not extended coherence (chapter 4).

Finally, to characterize the typology of elements that enter into binding relations, we will assume the attributes of (personal) pronouns shown in (4). Here PERS, NUM, GEND, and NUCLEAR are the actual f-structure attributes of the types which were abbreviated by the metaclassifications *agr* and *bind* referred to in chapter 8. Thus, in (4) *agr* and *bind* are not attribute names, but simply metaclassifications which show the groupings of types of features. The feature values shown belong the pronoun *she*:

$$(4) \quad \begin{bmatrix} agr & \begin{cases} \text{PERS} & 3 \\ \text{GEND} & \text{FEM} \\ \text{NUM} & \text{SG} \end{cases} \\ bind & \begin{cases} \text{NUCL} & - \\ \text{INDEX} & i \end{cases} \\ \text{PRED} & \text{'PRO'} \\ \text{CASE} & \text{NOM} \end{bmatrix}$$

The feature [NUCLEAR +] is a lexical property of **nuclear pronouns** such as *herself, ourselves* and other reflexive pronouns and bound anaphors. The feature [NUCLEAR −] is a property of **nonnuclear pronouns** such as *her, us*, and other nonreflexive personal pronouns. Ordinary (nonpronominal) nominals will lack this feature, and can be characterized by a negative existential constraint $\neg(\uparrow \text{NUCLEAR})$ in their lexical specifications; this requires that there be no value for a NUCLEAR attribute in the f-structure.[3] NUCL will be an abbreviation of NUCLEAR.

We will begin with a preliminary version of binding theory which, although it is inadequate, illustrates certain essential concepts of a binding theory within the architecture of LFG. Notwithstanding the inadequacies of this theory, the exercise of reformulating it in the present framework is useful. It shows why the asymmetrical coreference patterns generated by principles A–C (see below) occur in the varying c-structure types discussed in part III.

10.2   A Toy Binding Theory

toy:
1: an artifact designed to be played with [syn: plaything]
2: a nonfunctional replica of something else (frequently used as a modifier); "a toy stove"
3: a copy that reproduces something in greatly reduced size [syn: miniature]
(from WordNet)

Our toy binding theory is modelled on the textbook binding theory of generative grammar.[4] It is based on the conception of the binding relation as given in (5):

(5)   *A* **binds** *B* if *A* outranks *B* and *A* and *B* are coindexed. *B* is **bound/free** if some/no *A* binds *B*.

For this binding theory it is assumed that there is an INDEX attribute whose value determines coindexing relations. The INDEX attribute is lexically specified by nominals heading referring expressions, and the values are arbitrary natural numbers (which we will designate by variables i, j, k). Coindexing between two referring elements, such as a pronoun and a proper name, represents (intended or stipulated) coreference (see section 10.3 below). Thus, we formulate the bind relation as in (6):

(6)   *A* **binds** *B* if *A* outranks *B* and $(A \text{ INDEX}) = (B \text{ INDEX})$.

In the f-structure of (7), the SUBJ binds the OBJ, but the OBJ does not bind the SUBJ. Binding requires both coindexing and outranking; the SUBJ outranks the OBJ, but not conversely (this binding relation is rejected as ill-formed by principle C, as we will see below):

(7)

$$
\begin{bmatrix}
\text{SUBJ} & \begin{bmatrix} \text{PRED} & \text{'PRO'} \\ \text{CASE} & \text{NOM} \\ \text{PERS} & 3 \\ \text{GEND} & \text{FEM} \\ \text{NUM} & \text{SG} \\ \text{NUCL} & - \\ \text{INDEX} & i \end{bmatrix} \\
\text{PRED} & \ldots \\
\text{OBJ} & \begin{bmatrix} \text{PRED} & \text{'NAMED-}Ann\text{'} \\ \text{GEN} & \text{FEM} \\ \text{NUM} & \text{SG} \\ \text{INDEX} & i \end{bmatrix}
\end{bmatrix}
$$

We will use the convention of referring to f-structures with double quotes around the English word they correspond to, with the index value simply subscripted. For example, the subsidiary subject and object f-structures of (7) will be abbreviated as in (8):

(8)

$$
\text{"she}_i\text{"} = \begin{bmatrix} \text{PRED} & \text{'PRO'} \\ \text{CASE} & \text{NOM} \\ \text{PERS} & 3 \\ \text{GEND} & \text{FEM} \\ \text{NUM} & \text{SG} \\ \text{NUCL} & - \\ \text{INDEX} & i \end{bmatrix} \qquad \text{"Ann}_i\text{"} = \begin{bmatrix} \text{PRED} & \text{'NAMED-}Ann\text{'} \\ \text{GEN} & \text{FEM} \\ \text{NUM} & \text{SG} \\ \text{INDEX} & i \end{bmatrix}
$$

Given this conception of binding, it is straightforward to state the binding principles given in (9a–c).[5] A definition of the binding principles in the formal constraint language of chapter 4 will be given in section 10.4:

(9) a. **Principle A:**
        A nuclear (reflexive) pronoun must be bound in the minimal nucleus that contains it.
     b. **Principle B:**
        A nonnuclear pronoun must be free in the minimal nucleus that contains it.
     c. **Principle C:**
        (Other) nominals must be free.

These binding principles have much the same effect as the binding principles of the configurational binding theory for English, as we will now see.

The following examples illustrate principle A:

(10) a.   Ann$_i$ saw herself$_i$.
      b. *Ann$_i$'s father saw herself$_i$.
      c. *Herself$_i$ yawned.
      d. *Ann$_i$ thinks that herself$_i$ is great.

In (10a) *Ann$_i$ saw herself$_i$*, the sentence is well-formed because the reflexive object *herself* is bound by the subject *Ann* in its nucleus: the subject outranks the object and is coindexed with it (by an abuse of notation, we use square brackets to enclose our double-quoted expressions introduced in (8) to emphasize that they are f-structures):

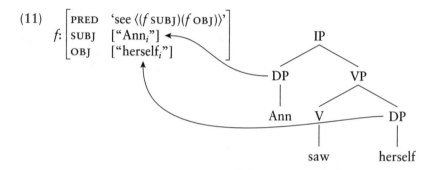

In (10b) **Ann$_i$'s father saw herself$_i$*, *Ann* is coindexed with the reflexive, but does not outrank it, so the reflexive is not bound in its nucleus:[6]

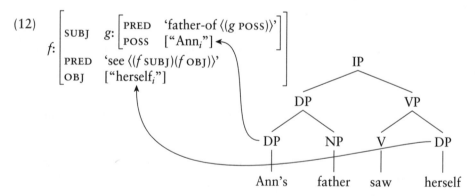

Note the reason that *Ann* does not outrank the reflexive object in (12). Because *Ann* is a subfunction of the subject *Ann's father*, it is not a member of the same f-structure as the reflexive object, nor is it a member of the same f-structure as any constituent that contains the reflexive object; hence it cannot be taken as the outranking element A in our definition (2). In (10c) **Herself$_i$ yawned*, the reflexive subject is not bound by any element of its nucleus, for no function outranks the subject:

(13) $f:\begin{bmatrix} \text{SUBJ} & [\text{"herself}_i\text{"}] \\ \text{PRED} & \text{'yawn} \langle (f\,\text{SUBJ}) \rangle \text{'} \end{bmatrix}$

Finally, in (10d) *Ann$_i$ thinks that herself$_i$ is great*, the reflexive subject is bound, but is not bound in its nucleus, which includes only the f-structure of the embedded complement.

Principle A accounts for cases of nonsubject binding of reflexives as well. Just as the subject outranks the complement and adjunct functions in (1), so the object outranks the restricted object, allowing examples like *I showed Ann$_i$ herself$_i$ (in the mirror)*.

Principle B of (9) accounts for examples such as (14a–c).

(14) a. *Ann$_i$ saw her$_i$.
  b. Ann$_i$ saw her$_i$ mother.
  c. Ann$_i$ thinks that she$_i$ is great.

Example (14a) is ill-formed under the given binding relation because the pronominal object *her* is bound by the subject *Ann* within its nucleus. Example (14b), in contrast, is allowed, because the possessor *her* does not occur in the same nucleus as the subject *Ann*. A nominal containing a possessor is mapped into its own nucleus, as seen in (12). Similarly, (14c) is allowed because the pronominal *she* occurs in a separate nucleus from its antecedent (namely, the nucleus of the embedded complement), where it is free as required by principle B.

It is evident that principles A and B as formulated above predict a complete complementarity between reflexive and nonreflexive pronouns within a nucleus: in any given pronoun–antecedent configuration, either the reflexive or the nonreflexive pronoun can be bound, but not both. Now consider (15a, b), where the possessive pronoun can be bound to the subject antecedent, but the possessive reflexive is ungrammatical:

(15) a. Mary admires her mother.
  b. *Mary admires herself's mother.

Assuming that the possessor is the most prominent function in the nominal nucleus, serving as the "subject" of the DP or NP, possessive reflexives are predicted not to exist by the binding theory above: for if the possessive pronoun *her* in (15a) is free to refer to *Mary* by virtue of being contained within the subsidiary nucleus corresponding to the object DP, then in (15b) that same nucleus would prevent *herself* from being bound to *Mary*, which lies outside it. However, there are languages which allow reflexive (nuclear) possessive pronouns in this situation; Faltz (1985: 201) cites Tagalog and Turkish as examples. Moreover, there is another possible explanation for the ungrammaticality of (15b): there could simply be a morphological gap in the case paradigm for reflexive pronouns. While personal pronouns have nominative, accusative, and genitive forms in Standard English (e.g. *he, him, and his*, respectively), the reflexive pronouns lack nominative and genitive cases: neither do distinct forms appear for these cases (e.g. *heself, *himself's), nor do reflexives occur where these cases are required, as shown by (15b) and by examples like *Mary thinks herself is great.*[7]

To solve this problem, an asymmetry is introduced into the definition of the domain for binding principles (C.-T. James Huang 1983). We can capture this asymmetry as follows in the present framework. Instead of requiring that a reflexive or pronoun be bound or free simply in its minimal nucleus, as in (9), we now require that it be bound or free in the minimal nucleus which could satisfy its binding requirements in principle. For a free form, this would simply be the minimal nucleus containing it. For a bound form, this would be the minimal nucleus containing it and another function that outranks it (a potential binder). We call this the **minimal complete nucleus**. We will simplify slightly by taking that potential binder to be a subject outranking the pronoun.[8]

Now in (15a), the minimal nucleus in which the pronoun *her* could be free is the minimal nucleus containing it, which is just the f-structure with the attributes of the object *her mother*. In (15b), in contrast, the minimal nucleus in which a genitive reflexive (ignoring the morphological gap in English) could be bound in principle is the minimal nucleus containing it and a subject outranking it. The f-structure of the object DP of the verb contains no such potential binder for a reflexive possessive, but the larger nucleus for the sentence does contain one: namely, the subject. Hence, a possessive reflexive would be bound in the larger f-structure. In general, when a reflexive is the highest ranking function of a nucleus, its binding domain will be the next most inclusive f-structure nucleus that contains a potential binder.

This revised version of principle A predicts that reflexive subjects can exist, but only when they are bound to an argument of a higher nucleus. In English reflexive subject pronouns do occur in nonfinite clauses, as shown in (16a, b, c):[9]

(16)   a.   I don't want myself getting stuck with all the work.
       b.   Mary wanted more than anything else for herself to be the one chosen.
       c.   What John would prefer is for himself to get the job. (Pollard and Sag 1992)

So far, so good. But why then are reflexive subjects ungrammatical in English finite clauses? This fact could be attributed to the absence of a nominative form of the reflexive pronoun, as noted above:

(17) *Mary is afraid that herself will get stuck with all of the work.

The idea that morphological case can constrain the distribution of reflexive pronouns in this way is supported by Maling (1984). She shows that the failure of the Icelandic reflexive pronoun to appear in subject position in subjunctive clauses can be attributed to a morphological gap. For Icelandic has both non-nominative subjects and nominative objects (Zaenen et al. 1985; see also part 2 of problem set 4). Interestingly, the reflexive pronoun can appear in the position of the former but not the latter:

(18) *Hún*ᵢ   *sagði að* *sér*ᵢ   *þætti*   *vænt um mig.*
     she.NOM said   that self.DAT was.SUBJN fond of me.ACC
     'She said she was fond of me.'

(19) **Honum*ᵢ *líkar*   *sig*ᵢ.
     he.DAT   like.PRES self.NOM
     'He likes himself.'

This pattern is exactly what the morphological gap proposal would predict.
Though nominative reflexives are lacking in English, Icelandic, and many of the
Indo-European languages to which they are related, such reflexives do exist elsewhere. K. P. Mohanan (1982c: 179), for example, cites the following case of
long distance reflexivization in Malayalam (the Dravidian language discussed in
chapters 3 and 9), in which both the pronoun *awan* and the reflexive *ṯaan* are in
the nominative case:

(20) *kuṭṭi ammayooṭə* [*ṯaan/awan*   *aanaye ṉuḷḷi   ennə*] *paraññu.*
     child mother   self.NOM/he.NOM elephant pinched that   said
     'The child told the mother that self/he pinched the elephant.'

(In chapter 11 we discuss the finite domain parameter, which restricts reflexive
binding to the minimal finite clause, allowing reflexivization into infinitival complements. This parameter provides an additional possible account of the contrast
between (16)–(17).)
   For all these reasons, we will revise the elementary binding theory (9) to incorporate the binding asymmetry between nuclear and nonnuclear pronouns. We
will adopt a version of Dalrymple's (1993) definition of the asymmetry:[10]

(21) **Principles of the (Toy) Binding Theory:**
   a. **Principle A:**
      A nuclear (reflexive) pronoun must be bound in the minimal nucleus
      that contains it and a subject outranking it (= the minimal complete
      nucleus).
   b. **Principle B:**
      A nonnuclear pronoun must be free in its minimal nucleus.
   c. **Principle C:**
      (Other) nominals must be free.

   With this modification relevant to principles A and B, let us now turn to principle C. Principle C is illustrated by (22a–c):

(22) a. **She*ᵢ saw *Ann*ᵢ.
     b. **She*ᵢ saw *Ann*ᵢ's mother.
     c. **She*ᵢ thinks that *Ann*ᵢ is great.

In (22a) the nominal *Ann* must be free, which means that there cannot be a coindexed element that outranks it; but the subject *she* is such an element, so the binding relation of the sentence is rejected. Exactly the same holds in (22b): the subject *she* outranks the possessor of the object, and so cannot be coindexed with it, making it a forbidden binder. Again, the same applies to (22c).

This familiar binding theory accounts for most of the well-known paradigm of examples within English, and in its configurational versions it has been widely adopted. In its present formulation, it has the advantage of explaining certain effects that do not fall out of the configurational formulation, such as the lack of contrast between (23a, b):[11]

(23)   a. *I convinced her$_i$ that Mary$_i$ should be my domestic partner.
       b. *I proposed to her$_i$ that Mary$_i$ should be my domestic partner.

In (b) *her* fails to c-command *Mary*, because the PP is a branching node that dominates *her* and not *Mary*, but the noncoreference effect is the same as in (a). The preposition in (b) functions to mark an oblique complement of the verb, and in this case, the extra structural embedding created by the PP over the NP is irrelevant to the noncoreference condition, which looks only at the functional relation. Another advantage is that it extends to more or less configurational languages without the imposition of rigid constituent structure requirements, such as the presence of a VP where there is language-internal lexical and syntactic evidence against it, such as the absence of "pro-VP" expressions (e.g. *do so* in English) and the failure of a verb and its complements to behave as a unit under word order variations.

Despite its textbook status, the familiar binding theory (21) is problematic. One reason for its inadequacy is typological: principles A and B provide too impoverished a typology of anaphoric elements (reflexives and pronouns) to explain the variety of anaphoric binding systems found across languages. In addition to nuclear and nonnuclear pronouns, languages have subjective/nonsubject pronominals, logophoric pronouns, and pronominals bound by the argument having the semantically most prominent role in the argument structure – all of which have been insightfully investigated and modelled in LFG works (such as K. P. Mohanan 1981, Kameyama 1984, 1985, Cho 1985, Saiki 1985, 1986, 1987, Sells et al. 1987, Joshi 1989, 1993, Tan 1991, Dalrymple and Zaenen 1991, Dalrymple 1993, T. Mohanan 1994, Manning 1996, and Toivonen 1996, 1997, in press). The typology of bound anaphors is discussed in chapter 11. A second reason for the inadequacy of (21) concerns principle C: the conception of binding that it presupposes is modelled on coreference (represented by coindexing). This aspect of the binding theory has been trenchantly criticized from within the general framework by Evans (1980) and Reinhart (1983a), and just as trenchantly criticized from without (Bickerton 1975, Kuno 1975, Bolinger 1979, McCray 1980, 1982), for reasons we turn to now.

10.3 Principle C

The idea that nominals are bound by elements that are coindexed with them creates obvious problems with identity statements (Evans 1980): why does *My mother is Marie Antoinette* not violate principle C? But even if one were to exempt all identity statements from the binding theory, principle C still rules out such perfectly good English sentences as (24a, b):

(24) a. Ann$_i$ told Mary that Ann$_i$'s mother is a spy.
    b. I know what John and Bill have in common. John thinks that Bill is terrific and Bill thinks that Bill is terrific. (Evans 1980: 356)

While English generally avoids repetition of coreferent lexical nominals, the presence of the "bound" nominal in these examples is required to avoid ambiguity. In Malayalam, Thai, and Vietnamese, nominals may appear much more freely in bound positions. (24a) is from K. P. Mohanan (1981), and (24b, c) are from Lasnik (1989: 153):

(25) a. *moohan$_i$ moohante$_i$ bhaaryaye nuḷḷi*
      M.NOM M.GEN   wife.ACC pinched
      'Mohan pinched Mohan's wife.'   Malayalam
    b. *cɔɔn khít wáà cɔɔn chàlaàt*
      John thinks that John is.smart
      'John thinks that John is smart.'   Thai
    c. *John tin   John sẽ thăng*
      believes   will win
      'John believes John will win.'   Vietnamese

It is interesting to observe that in the corresponding sentences with pronouns binding the nominal, coreferential readings are much harder to get in all four languages (K. P. Mohanan 1981, Lasnik 1989: 154):

(26) a. She$_i$ told Mary that Ann$_j$'s mother is a spy. $i \neq j$
    b. I know what John and Bill have in common. John thinks that Bill is terrific and he$_i$ thinks that Bill$_j$ is terrific. $i \neq j$
    c. *awan$_i$ moohante$_j$ bhaaryaye nuḷḷi*
      pronoun.NOM M.GEN   wife.ACC pinched
      'He$_i$ pinched Mohan$_j$'s wife.' $i \neq j$ Malayalam
    d. *khǎw$_i$ khít wáà cɔɔn$_j$ chàlaàt*
      he   thinks that John is.smart
      'He$_i$ thinks that John$_j$ is smart.' $i \neq j$ Thai
    e. *Nó$_i$ tin   John$_j$ sẽ thăng*
      he believes   will win
      'He$_i$ believes John$_j$ will win.' $i \neq j$ Vietnamese

From these facts we might conclude that while languages vary in their conditions on binding relations among nonpronominal referring expressions, the
universal core of principle C asserts that nominals must be "pronoun-free" – that
is, must not be bound by a pronoun (Lasnik 1989: 154). That this, too, is
inadequate is indicated by the existence of well-formed examples such as the following (Bolinger 1979, McCray 1980). In each of these cases a proper name is
coreferential with a pronoun that binds it in the sense of principle C:

(27) a. She$_i$ was told that if she wanted to get anywhere in this dog-eat-dog
          world, Mary$_i$ was going to have to start stepping on some people.
      b. The teacher warned him$_i$ that in order to succeed Walter$_i$ was going to
          have to work an awful lot harder from now on.
      c. It was rather indelicately pointed out to him$_i$ that Walter$_i$ would never
          become a successful accountant.
      d. It obviously surprises him$_i$ that John$_i$ is so well liked.
      e. What did John$_i$ do? – He$_i$ did what John$_i$ always does – he$_i$
          complained.

These examples cannot be distinguished from principle C violations such as (26a)
on the basis of their syntactic structure. For example, the c-structure of (27a)
clearly has the subject pronoun c-commanding the coreferential NP:

(28)

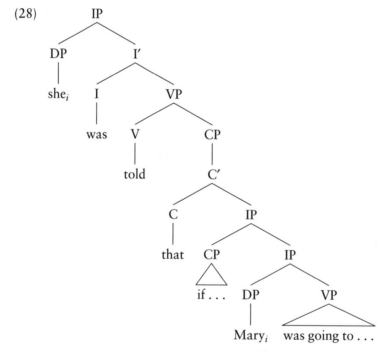

What seems to determine their acceptability, according to Bolinger (1979)
and McCray (1982), is that the preference in choosing between coreferential

pronouns and lexical nominals depends on what is important to the speaker, as conveyed in theme–rheme organization. The subject, as the default topic, has a special role in this organization, but one which can be overridden.[12]

These considerations all suggest that coreference is a relation that is not strictly subject to syntactic principles. This is the conclusion that both Evans (1980) and Reinhart (1983a, b) argue for: syntactic constraints on binding should not be about coreference relations among nominals in general, which are subject to pragmatic strategies and theme–rheme organization, but about the relation of referential dependence between pronominal elements and their antecedents (or binders in a semantic sense). How can pronominal binding in this sense be distinguished from pragmatic coreference? Reinhart's (1983a) proposal is that true binding creates **sloppy identity** effects. An example is given in (29):

(29)   Every woman admired her mother, and every girl did, too.

Here there are several possible readings of the sentence. In the strict identity reading, the mother of some particular woman – call her Mary – who was admired by every woman was also admired by every girl. The strict interpretation can be expressed as the property of x in which x admired her (= Mary's) mother; the referent of the pronoun *her* is strictly fixed for both conjuncts. In the sloppy identity reading, in contrast, every girl admired her own mother, and in doing so was doing the same thing as every woman in the first conjunct. "The same thing" in this case can be expressed as the property of x in which x admired x's mother. In this way the binding of a pronoun by a quantifier gives rise to a sloppy identity reading; the referent of *her* is not strictly fixed for both conjuncts, but sloppily varies with the antecedent. Reinhart (1983a) shows that the same is true for ordinary nonquantificational NPs, and argues that this fact can be explained if such NPs can also semantically bind pronouns. Thus (30) is ambiguous in the same way as (29):

(30)   Mary admired her mother, and Susan did, too.

In the strict readings Susan admires Mary's or someone else's mother, who is also admired by Mary; in the sloppy reading, Susan admired her own mother.

Sloppy identity is a necessary condition of semantic binding, but not a sufficient one. To see this, we must first distinguish bound pronouns from what Evans (1980: 339) dubs **"e-type"** pronouns:

(31)   a.   Few congressmen admire only the people they know.
            (bound pronoun)
       b.   Few congressmen admire Kennedy, and they are very junior.
            (e-type pronoun)

An e-type pronoun refers to a set or individual defined by its quantifier phrase antecedent, but not bound by that antecedent. E-type pronouns can be distinguished by the following tests. First, they lie outside the normal binding domain of their antecedents; thus, in (31b) *they* and *few congressmen* lie in separate sentential conjuncts, and could even occur in separate sentences. Second, one can sensibly ask what the e-type pronoun refers to, but this question is not sensible for quantificational binding. In (31b), for example, 'they' refers to the congressmen that admire Kennedy; in (31a), in contrast, the reference of 'they' cannot be fixed because it varies with the interpretation of the quantifier. Third, replacing the quantifier in the antecedent of an e-type pronoun by *no* renders the e-type pronoun nonsensical, but the bound pronoun continues to be interpretable:

(32)   a.   No congressmen admire only the people they know.
            (bound pronoun)
       b.?? No congressmen admire Kennedy, and they are very junior.
            (e-type pronoun)

Fourth, e-type pronouns yield different entailments from bound pronouns. They are interpreted, roughly speaking, as resumptive definite descriptions: "the congressmen who admire Kennedy" in the case of (31b). See Heim (1990) for a review of semantic issues concerning the e-type pronouns.

It seems, then, that e-type pronouns are not bound pronouns. Interestingly, though, e-type pronouns also give rise to sloppy identity effects:

(33)   Every man who owns a donkey beats it, and every man who owns a mule does, too

(33) can mean that every man who owns a mule beats the mule that he owns. Yet in the left conjunct *it* has all the earmarks of an e-type pronoun, so that pronoun is not bound in Evans's and Reinhart's sense.[13] Hence, while sloppy identity may be a necessary condition of pronoun binding, it is not a sufficient condition.

The important point made by both Evans (1980) and Reinhart (1983a) is that binding relations in the sense of referential dependence are much more narrowly constrained than coreference relations, and are subject to a syntactic condition. Observe that quantifier scope alone is insufficient to define the domain of possible pronominal binding. In (34a), for example, the quantifier phrase object *every candidate* can have scope over the subject *someone*, yielding the reading that for every candidate there were some, possibly different, voters. But in (34b) we see that the same object cannot easily bind a pronoun contained in the subject (Reinhart 1987: 131):

(34)   a.   Someone voted for every candidate.
       b.?? His$_i$ friends voted for every candidate$_i$.

Thus while it is undoubtedly necessary for a pronominal to lie within the semantic scope of the quantifier phrase that binds it, this condition is not sufficient. A syntactic condition that the pronominal lie in the syntactic domain of its binder is also required.

Further, if we go back to the Bolinger–McCray examples violating principle C (27) and replace the NP by a quantifier phrase, no binding relation is possible:[14]

(35)   a.   *She$_i$ was told that if she wanted to get anywhere in this dog-eat-dog world, every woman$_i$ in the group was going to have to start stepping on some people.
       b.   *The teacher warned him$_i$ that in order to succeed everyone$_i$ was going to have to work an awful lot harder from now on.
       c.   *It was rather indelicately pointed out to him$_i$ that each man$_i$ would never become a successful accountant.
       d.   *It obviously surprises him$_i$ that no one$_i$ is so well liked.
       e.   *What did everyone$_i$ do? – He$_i$ did what everyone$_i$ always does – he$_i$ complained.

Because these QPs are not referring expressions, both binding and coreference are ruled out in (35). When we reverse the QPs and the pronominals where possible in (35), we place the latter in the binding domains of the former, and binding is possible:

(36)   a.   Every woman$_i$ in the group was told that if she wanted to get anywhere in this dog-eat-dog world, she$_i$ was going to have to start stepping on some people.
       b.   The teacher warned everyone$_i$ that in order to succeed he$_i$ was going to have to work an awful lot harder from now on.
       c.   It was rather indelicately pointed out to each man$_i$ that he$_i$ would never become a successful accountant.
       d.   It surprises no one$_i$ that he$_i$ is well liked.

What is the domain in which personal pronouns can be bound, then? Evans (1980: 341) proposes that a pronoun can be bound by a quantifier phrase only if it precedes and c-commands the pronoun. In contrast to Evans, Reinhart (1983a) proposes that the binder only c-command the pronoun, dropping the precedence requirement of Evans's formulation. Both Evans and Reinhart restrict themselves to English data. But we saw in chapter 9 that a pronoun is excluded from the domain of a binder if the pronoun is more prominent than the binder along any of several dimensions that vary crosslinguistically (linear order, syntactic rank, or both, as well as thematic prominence). We will assume that the domain of pronominal binding is defined as in chapter 9 for personal pronouns (that is, pronouns that bear no positive binding constraints such as [NUCL +]). The definition is repeated here:

(37)   **Prominence Principle:**
       A binder excludes from its domain any personal pronouns more prominent than it (as defined in chapter 9).
       The **domain** of a binder is the minimal clause or predication structure containing it (formally modelled as the minimal f-structure).

Within this domain, any additional negative constraints lexically specified by the pronoun apply as defined in section 10.4 below. The restriction of the prominence principle (37) to nonreflexive pronouns is supported by divergences in the binding properties of reflexive and nonreflexive pronouns. For example, f-precedence is a prominence condition on the binding of personal pronouns but not reflexives in a number of languages; Malayalam is an example (K. P. Mohanan 1982c).

Are these considerations sufficient to eliminate principle C altogether? It would seem so at first sight: if construed as a condition on coreference, principle C has the counterexamples discussed above, especially sentences of the McCray–Bolinger type (27), which suggest that it is a matter of theme–rheme organization rather than of grammar. If construed as a condition on referential dependence (semantic binding), many cases that were covered by the old principle C simply fall out of the prominence-based domain constraints on semantic binding discussed in chapter 9. The failures of binding in (35), for example, all involve pronouns that both precede and (are contained in constituents that) outrank the quantifier phrase; the pronoun therefore cannot be bound by the quantifier phrase, and it makes no sense for the quantifier phrase to be bound by the pronoun.

However, there are other sources of referential dependence than binding, such as control (chapters 12, 13), which indicate a need for a version of principle C. Consider examples (38a, b). (38a) implies that the referent of *her*, if it is the one who visited Sally's farm, is not Sally:

(38) a. Visiting Sally's farm disturbed her.
          (her =/= Sally if her = the visitor)
      b. Visiting Sally's farm disturbed her friends.
          (possibly her = Sally)

In an example like (38a) under the interpretation that the referent of *her* is the visitor, the understood subject of *visiting* is referentially dependent on its controller *her*, which is taken to be coreferent with *Sally*; hence the subject of *visiting* is indirectly referentially dependent on *Sally*.[15] The binding domain constraints on referential dependence do not explain the contrast in (38a, b). But principle C does explain it, because the understood subject of *visiting* outranks the object of *visiting*: hence this subject cannot corefer with the object. If the controller of the subject is *her*, as in (38a), principle C is violated; if the controller is *her friends*, as in (38b), there is no violation of principle C.

The version of principle C we adopt here derives from Evans (1980). Evans (1980: 358) proposes a condition which states that a pronoun cannot be referentially dependent on a nominal if the pronoun precedes and c-commands the nominal. Translating this into our framework (dropping the precedence condition, which is inapplicable to null pronouns, as we saw in chapter 9), we can state the following "anti-binding" condition, which is hypothesized to be universal:[16]

(39) **Anti-binding:**
      A pronominal P cannot be referentially dependent on a nominal that it asymmetrically outranks.

According to anti-binding, the pronouns in (27a–d) are not referentially dependent on the nominals in their domain, although they corefer with these nominals. On the other hand, the controlled subject of (38a) is (indirectly) referentially dependent on the object, and so excluded by anti-binding.

Further Reading and Discussion

The present theory of binding, as we have seen, depends crucially on the relational hierarchy, in terms of which we have defined the f-structure relation of syntactic rank. But as part of a "survey of functional approaches to definite NP anaphora," Reinhart (1983b: 103–6), argues against a relational theory of non-coreference or anti-binding patterns based on the concept of a hierarchy of functions similar to the one proposed here (1). Her basic claim is that such a theory does not explain asymmetries in argument–adjunct coreference relations which depend on the exact phrase structure positions of the argument and the adjunct. For example, she claims that subjects and objects contrast in the possibility of referring to phrases within sentence-level adjuncts, because the subject c-commands these adjuncts, while the object in VP does not:

(40) a. *She$_i$ was last seen when Lola$_i$ graduated from high school.
    b. I saw her$_i$ last when Lola$_i$ graduated from high school.

Similarly, the contrast in (41a, b) she attributes to the point of phrase structure attachment of the PP, sentential in (a) and verb-phrasal in (b):

(41) a. People still regard him$_i$ highly in Carter$_i$'s home town.
    b. *Roslyn met him$_i$ in Carter$_i$'s home town.

Finally, she points out that the grammatical relations of phrases do not change when they are preposed, although their c-command relations do. Hence, rank-based functional accounts fail to explain contrasts like those in (42a, b, c):

(42) a. *With Ben$_i$'s peacock feather he$_i$ tickled Rosa gently.
    b. With Ben$_i$'s peacock feather, Rosa tickled him$_i$ gently.
    c. *Rosa tickled him$_i$ gently with Ben$_i$'s peacock feather.

The *with* phrase in (42c) is a VP adjunct, which is c-commanded by both subject and object. When this PP is preposed to sentence-initial position, it continues to be c-commanded by the subject, accounting for the ungrammaticality of (42a), but is no longer c-commanded by the object, accounting for the grammaticality of (42b).

However, a closer examination of the data shows that the generalizations they seem to support rather elegantly are false. First, compare (40a) with the following example from Bolinger (1979: 302):

(43) He$_i$'s impossible, when Ben$_i$ gets one of his tantrums.

The small capitals indicate a pitch peak in the intonation contour of the sentence. Here the subject can be coreferential with an NP in the temporal adverbial clause that it c-commands. Next, compare (41b) with (44):

(44) (Everyone knows that) his$_i$ wife first met him$_i$ in the little town of Plains, Georgia, where President Carter$_i$ grew up.

Here the object can be coreferential with an NP embedded in the locative phrase that it c-commands. Finally, compare the preposed adjuncts in (42a) with (45):[17]

(45) With the peacock feather that Ben$_i$ had brought with him all the way from Urbana, Illinois, he$_i$ began to tickle Rosa gently.

There is no difference in c-command relation between the subject and the preposed PP in (42a) and (45), yet the latter is perfectly acceptable.

These examples suggest that c-command is not the true source of the non-coreference effects in examples like (40)–(42). Instead, we must take into account the linear order of constituents, whether they contain given or new information, and the pragmatic effects of using nouns or pronouns. Several related proposals for the cases of English noncoreference considered here have been made by Kuno (1975), Bickerton (1975), and Bolinger (1979) from a functionalist perspective. See also Levinson (1987, 1991) for relevant commentary.

10.4 Formalization of the Binding Constraints

The grammatical binding constraints we have examined ([NUCLEAR +] and [NUCLEAR −]) can be expressed in the formal constraint language of LFG as lexical properties of pronouns and nominals (Dalrymple 1993).[18] The basic idea is that a pronoun or nominal can lexically specify its binding requirements by means of inside-out designators of the form in (46):

(46) ((DomainPath ↑) Antecedent)

The interpretation of this designator can be seen schematically in (47). This diagram depicts a pronoun with a lexical designator of the form (46) occurring in a tree structure as a D contained within a larger sentence structure S. The f-structure for S contains an antecedent. Where this antecedent comes from in the tree structure does not matter: among other possibilities, it could be realized as a pronominal inflection of the verb or auxiliary (chapters 7, 8), as a scrambled NP in a noncanonical subject position (chapter 9), or as an NP marked as the subject by agreement or case in a language lacking a VP (chapters 6, 7):

(47)

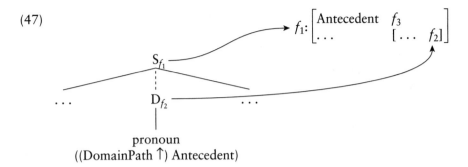

pronoun
((DomainPath ↑) Antecedent)

The expression "(DomainPath ↑)" is a schema for an inside-out functional uncertainty designator (section 4.6). When instantiated, it will designate an f-structure through which there is a path (determined by the attributes of the DomainPath) leading to the instantiation of "↑." In (47) the functional schema of the pronoun is part of its lexical entry. The "↑" will be instantiated as usual to refer to the f-structure of the mother node of the pronoun. Thus in (47) '((DomainPath ↑) Antecedent)' will be instantiated as '((DomainPath f_2) Antecedent)'. What does this expression refer to in (47)? Because there is a path of attributes in f_1 to f_2, it is true that $f_1 =$ (DomainPath f_2). Because (f_1 Antecedent) $= f_3$, we can infer that ((DomainPath f_2) Antecedent) $= f_3$. Of course, another choice of DomainPath might yield a different antecedent for f_2. In this way, an inside-out functional schema can designate possible antecedents for pronouns.

In general, the positive ([NUCLEAR +]) and negative ([NUCLEAR −]) binding requirements will have the structure in (48):[19]

(48) a. **Positive (Nuclear) Binding Constraint:**
((DomainPath ↑) Antecedent INDEX) = (↑ INDEX)
  b. **Negative (Nonnuclear) Binding Constraint:**
((DomainPath ↑) Antecedent INDEX) ≠ (↑ INDEX)

(48a) is true if there exists an antecedent satisfying the requirements of the equation. The negative equation in (48b) is true if there is no antecedent accessible from the given DomainPath which is coindexed with the pronoun or nominal bearing the constraint.

A further general property of these binding constraints is that the pronominal f-structure must be outranked by the antecedent f-structure. This condition is expressed by requiring the DomainPath to have a top attribute GF which is dominated by the antecedent on the relational hierarchy (1). We call this the "f-structure domainpath condition:"

(49) **f-Structure DomainPath Condition:**
All DomainPaths in positive and negative binding constraints (48) must be constructed so that (i) DomainPath = GF α for some possibly empty attribute string α, (ii) Antecedent = GF′, and (iii) GF′ > GF in the relational hierarchy (1).

These definitions are applied as follows. Consider the sentence *Mary likes her mother* with the f-structure illustrated in (50):

(50)
$$f: \begin{bmatrix} \text{SUBJ} & [\text{``Mary''}] \\ \text{TENSE} & \text{PRES} \\ \text{PRED} & \text{`like} <(f\,\text{SUBJ})(f\,\text{OBJ})>\text{'} \\ \text{OBJ} & g: \begin{bmatrix} \text{POSS} & f': [\text{``her''}] \\ \text{PRED} & \text{`mother-of} <(g\,\text{POSS})>\text{'} \end{bmatrix} \end{bmatrix}$$

The f-structure of the pronoun "her" in (50) will have a binding constraint of the general form in (48b). If we take the DomainPath from *her* to be OBJ POSS, then (OBJ POSS f') = f, which is the outer f-structure. (f SUBJ) designates the antecedent f-structure. So the antecedent = GF' = SUBJ, GF = OBJ, and α = POSS.[20] Now consider the sentence *Mary likes her* with the f-structure illustrated in (51):

(51)
$$\begin{bmatrix} \text{SUBJ} & [\text{``Mary''}] \\ \text{TENSE} & \text{PRES} \\ \text{PRED} & \text{`like} <(f\,\text{SUBJ})(f\,\text{OBJ})>\text{'} \\ \text{OBJ} & [\text{``her''}] \end{bmatrix}$$

Here the DomainPath = OBJ, and α = e is empty. Thus GF = OBJ, and the antecedent = GF' = SUBJ.

   To capture the minimality restriction, constraints can be imposed on those f-structures which are the values of the attributes in the DomainPath (Dalrymple 1993: 128ff). Such "off-path constraints" are notated with a "→" which is instantiated by the value of the attribute it is annotated to.[21] Consider the expression in (52):

(52)   (GF$_1$ f)
        ¬(→ PRED)

f is some f-structure that is the value of the attribute GF$_1$. In the off-path constraint, the expression "→" stands for the f-structure that is the value of GF$_1$, which is f. It requires that f not contain the attribute PRED. That is, the off-path constraint requires: ¬(f PRED). Off-path constraints permit the checking of properties of intermediate f-structures along the upward path to the antecedent. In particular, the constraint "¬(→ PRED)" is a negative existential constraint which can be associated with each attribute in the DomainPath, excluding the bound/free elements' own f-structure.

   Given off-path constraints, we can now formally define the minimal nucleus condition which was motivated in the discussion leading to the revised principles of the (toy) binding theory (21):

(53) **Minimal Nucleus Condition:**
A binding constraint designator $((\text{GF } \alpha \uparrow) \text{ GF}')$ in a nuclear (respectively, nonnuclear) binding constraint is subject to the minimal nucleus condition only if (i) GF and GF' are argument functions and (ii) if the attribute string α is nonempty, then setting $\alpha = xa$ for some attribute a and possibly empty string of attributes x, the off-path constraint $\neg(\rightarrow \text{SUBJ})$ (respectively $\neg(\rightarrow \text{PRED})$) holds for every attribute in GF x.

The restriction that both the antecedent and the top of the DomainPath be argument functions AF ensures that the domain of binding is a nucleus. We will see how a minimality restriction works below in the discussion of (56):

(54) **Nuclearity Constraints:**
a. A **nuclear pronoun** is lexically specified
$((\text{GF } \alpha \uparrow) \text{ GF}' \text{ INDEX}) = (\uparrow \text{ INDEX})$,
subject to the minimal nucleus condition (53).
b. A **nonnuclear pronoun** is lexically specified
$((\text{GF } \alpha \uparrow) \text{ GF}' \text{ INDEX}) \neq (\uparrow \text{ INDEX})$,
subject to the minimal nucleus condition (53).

Examples (55) and (56) illustrate the application of these constraints. Notice that all of the concepts are applicable to the f-structure without reference to the c-structure realization of the functions:

(55) a. (Her sister, she scorns.) . . . *Herself, she admires.*
b. f-structure of *Herself, she admires*:

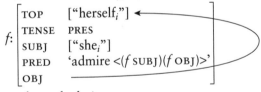

$$f: \begin{bmatrix} \text{TOP} & [\text{"herself}_i\text{"}] \\ \text{TENSE} & \text{PRES} \\ \text{SUBJ} & [\text{"she}_i\text{"}] \\ \text{PRED} & \text{'admire} <(f \text{ SUBJ})(f \text{ OBJ})>' \\ \text{OBJ} & \end{bmatrix}$$

c. nucleus of *admires*:

$$f: \begin{bmatrix} \text{SUBJ} & [\text{"she}_i\text{"}] \\ \text{PRED} & \text{'admire} <(f \text{ SUBJ})(f \text{ OBJ})>' \\ \text{OBJ} & [\text{"herself}_i\text{"}] \end{bmatrix}$$

The f-structure "herself$_i$" satisfies the nuclear pronoun condition because it is a nuclear pronoun bound by "she$_i$" in the nucleus shown in (55c). Referring to (54a), $\alpha = e$, GF = OBJ, GF' = SUBJ, and SUBJ and OBJ are coindexed. The f-structure "she$_i$" satisfies the nonnuclear pronoun condition because it is a non-nuclear pronoun and there is no element in the nucleus that binds it. Referring to (54b), we must make sure that there is no path to a coreferential outranking element. For $\alpha = e$, GF = SUBJ, GF' = OBJ. SUBJ and OBJ are coindexed, but

¬(OBJ > SUBJ) on the relational hierarchy (1), so it remains true that there is no antecedent outranking "she$_i$" and coindexed with it. No other coindexed element occurs in this f-structure.

Example (56) shows a violation of nuclearity:

(56) a. (Her sister, she knows we like.) . . . *Herself, she knows we love.*
      b. f-structure of *Herself, she knows we love*:

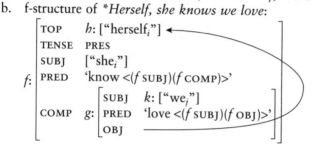

Here there are two f-structures, f and g, that contain "herself$_i$," and three possible paths to f-structures containing antecedents: the short path from OBJ to g, the long path from OBJ to f, and the short path from TOP to f. If $\alpha = e$, we have the two possible short paths to an antecedent: ((OBJ h) SUBJ) and ((TOP h) SUBJ). The first path takes us to the inner f-structure g, because (OBJ h) = g. But (g SUBJ INDEX) ≠ (h INDEX), so the nuclear binding condition (54a) is not satisfied.[22] The second path takes us to the outer f-structure f, because (TOP h) = f. Here there is a subject coindexed with the reflexive: (f SUBJ INDEX) = (h INDEX). But TOP is not an argument function, and so lies outside the nucleus of f; for this reason it fails to satisfy the condition on GF in (54a). Finally, we have the long path to an antecedent, taking α = OBJ and GF = COMP. Then (COMP OBJ h) = f and ((COMP OBJ h) SUBJ INDEX) = (h INDEX). But this path fails to satisfy the restriction that if α is a nonempty string of attributes xa, then ¬($\rightarrow$ PRED) for every attribute in the string GF x. Here $x = e$ and GF = COMP, so ($\rightarrow$ COMP) refers to g. It must then be true that ¬(g PRED) – that is, that there is no PRED attribute in g. But in (56b), the value of COMP does contain a PRED, so the negative existential constraint is false, eliminating this path to an antecedent. Intuitively, the negative off-path constraints prune away paths that take the search for an antecedent too high up: as soon as such a constraint becomes false, we know that the key domain attribute specified (PRED, SUBJ, or TENSE) occurs just below the current attribute in the path. We therefore know that we have gone outside the *minimal* f-structure needed, which could be the very f-structure that contains the key attribute which falsifies the off-path constraint.

Because of the structure-sharing property of f-structures, it may happen that a pronoun belongs simultaneously to more than one nucleus. An example would be a case of functional control (discussed in detail in chapter 12). In (57) the subject of *seem* is identified with the subject of *falling*, which has the f-structure shown in (58):

(57) *Herself$_i$ seemed to Mary$_i$ to be falling.

(58)

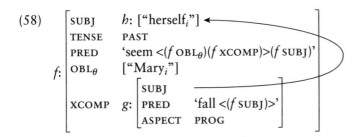

In such cases, the lexical binding features must be satisfied for each nucleus that the pronominal f-structure occurs in. Otherwise, (58) would be grammatical, for nuclearity as defined in (54a) requires only that there be some antecedent which satisfies the binding constraint. As the SUBJ of the XCOMP, "herself$_i$" would find its binding constraint satisfied by the oblique "Mary$_i$," which outranks it. Only if we also consider "herself$_i$" as the matrix subject can we see that it is not outranked by its antecedent.

This multiple satisfaction requirement is made explicit in (59):

(59) **Binding and Structure-Sharing:**
      All lexical binding constraints of a pronominal must be satisfied for each nucleus that the pronominal occurs in.

This interpretation of binding is perfectly compatible with the grammaticality of (60), as the reader can verify:

(60) Mary$_i$ seemed to herself$_i$ to be falling.

It is a natural consequence of our defining pronominals for purposes of the binding theory as the *elements of nuclei* – that is, as attribute–value pairs consisting of a nuclear GF and its value.

Finally, observe that a further consequence of nuclearity requiring the existence of an antecedent in the nucleus of the pronoun is to disallow examples like *Myself, I admire him* and *As for herself, she admires him*, where the reflexives occur as external topics outside of the nucleus of the sentence. Such examples do appear to be grammatical under contextually appropriate conditions. Because the external topics are contained in no nucleus, a possible explanation is that the distribution of reflexives when they belong to no nuclei is subject not to nuclearity, but to other conditions such as viewpoint.[23] We could capture this result if we wished to by conditioning the binding specifications on the existence of a nucleus containing the pronoun, using the conditionals defined in section 4.6. But we will leave aside this and other refinements of English binding because our focus is more general.

Notes

1   C-command is defined in chapter 7; several variant definitions are possible.

2   The governing category has gone through many formulations; for present purposes it can be thought of as the minimal sentential or nominal category that properly contains the element under consideration.

3   Culy (1996) gives evidence for a pronominality feature independent of our binding features, which could also serve to mark pronominality on nominal types.

4   See Lasnik (1989: chapter 1) for an overview of the various reformulations of binding theory within the configurational design of grammar.

5   This binding theory is somewhat oversimplified, in that there are certain asymmetries in the binding domains of reflexives and pronominals that are not captured. These are considered further on below.

6   Here we are taking the possessor function, designated POSS in LFG, to be the SPEC of DP analogous to the SUBJ as the SPEC of IP. The possessor outranks complements of nominals. We are also assuming that there is a lexical possessor template augmenting the lexical forms of nominals to take a possessor argument: 'mother' $\Rightarrow$ 'mother-of <($\uparrow$ POSS)>'.

7   Possessive expressions like *her own, their own* may be used to convey a reflexive meaning, but they are not bound anaphors themselves, because they need not have an antecedent within the sentence, as in *Her own mother agreed, I prefer to hear your own versions of what happened.*

8   This is an adaptation of Dalrymple's (1993) formalization of "minimal complete nucleus." See section 10.4.

9   The infinitival examples are best with some emphasis on the reflexive subject, possibly because of the availability of a control construction with the same meaning as the reflexive example without emphasis: *Mary wanted more than anything else to be the one chosen, What John would prefer is to get the job.*

10   Many variants are possible, having subtle empirical differences, which we will not pursue here. See Dalrymple (1993) for some further discussion of empirical consequences.

11   The problem posed by such examples is observed by Reinhart (1983a: 179) and Bach and Partee (1980: 13).

12   Sells (1987b) discusses these examples in terms of the discourse-based concept of "anti-logophoricity."

13   Reinhart (1987) extends her definition of binding to "specifier binding" in an attempt to assimilate e-type pronouns to bound pronominals.

14   If we replace the singular pronouns in examples (35a, b) with plural pronouns *they* or *them*, coreference seems possible, with the coreferent NP designating a group. The singular pronouns rule out the group reference, and so require binding.

15   Note that the control relation is one of referential dependence, for a quantifier can control an understood subject even in a configuration where direct binding of a pronoun by the quantifier is not possible:

    i. ??His$_i$ visiting Sally's farm disturbed everyone$_i$.
    ii. Visiting Sally's farm disturbed everyone.

16   This condition is given in Bresnan (1994b).

17   The contrast between examples like (42a) and (45) is observed by Lakoff (1976: 278–9).

18   We have adapted Dalrymple (1993) to the version of binding theory discussed here.

19 This is a simplification of Dalrymple's (1993) binding constraints, which refer to the semantic projection of the f-structure, rather than to the INDEX attributes of the toy binding theory.

20 The minimality condition to be given below will ensure that the binding constraint does not wrongly reject *Mary* as a possible antecedent for *her* in this example.

21 Off-path constraints are defined in section 4.8.

22 Even if "we$_j$" were coindexed with "herself$_i$," it would not agree in person and number, which would violate a general condition on anaphoric agreement (chapter 8).

23 See Pollard and Sag (1992, 1994), Dalrymple (1993), and Asudeh (1998) for arguments pro and con.

11 Types of Bound Anaphors

A major deficiency of the toy binding theory of chapter 10 is that it is based almost entirely on a conception of anaphoric binding that comes from English. Yet it turns out that among systems of bound anaphors across languages, English reflexives constitute a special case. As we have seen, English reflexives show local anaphoric dependencies, reflected in notions like "clause-mate," "minimal governing category," "minimal nucleus," and the like. But nonlocal reflexives occur in many languages, and these reveal other dimensions of anaphoric binding.[1]

11.1   Dimensions of Anaphoric Binding

Three dimensions play a central role in anaphoric binding systems. These are (i) the *subjective* dimension, which indicates whether or not the antecedent must be a grammatical subject, (ii) the *nuclear* dimension, which indicates whether or not the antecedent must lie in the same nucleus as the anaphor, and (iii) the *logophoric* dimension, in which the pronoun refers to one whose speech, thoughts, or feelings are represented in indirect discourse, from that person's own point of view.[2]

These three dimensions define a space of possible anaphors. Reflexive and nonreflexive pronouns can be conceived of as points in this space by assigning them a positive, negative, or zero coefficient for each dimension. For example, the English reflexive pronoun *himself* is 0 subjective, +nuclear, 0 logophoric, while the nonreflexive pronoun *him* is 0 subjective, −nuclear, 0 logophoric.[3] In other words, the English pronouns are degenerate in the subjective and logophoric dimensions, but positively or negatively specified for nuclearity.[4] This accounts for their complementary distribution in simple clauses. In contrast (as we will see), in the majority dialect of Icelandic (Maling 1982) the Icelandic pronouns *sig* and *hann* are positively and negatively specified in the subjective dimension, respectively, and degenerate in the nuclear dimension, while *sig* – but not *hann* – is also specified for logophoricity. Finally, the West Niger-Congo language Ewe has a pure logophoric pronoun (*yè-* in the third person) which is morphologically distinct from the reflexive pronoun and contrasts with the anti-logophoric personal pronoun (*e-* in the third person) (Clements 1975).

There is a natural grammatical representation for our concept of a multidimensional space of anaphoric elements. Because these dimensions are mutually irreducible properties that vary with the choice of pronoun, it is natural to represent them by means of grammatical features into which language-particular anaphors are lexically decomposed. We may think of these features informally as [sbj], [ncl], and [log] (for "subjective," "nuclear," and "logophoric," respectively) having positive or negative values. A pronoun that is degenerate in a dimension will be represented as unspecified for the corresponding feature. Different combinations and values of these features may be realized by different pronominal forms within and across languages. We define these features informally here:

(1) **subjective** – whether or not there must be an argument antecedent in the (minimal finite) clause
nuclear – whether or not there must be an argument antecedent in the minimal nucleus[5]
logophoric – whether or not the pronoun refers to one whose speech, thoughts, or feelings are represented in indirect discourse, from that person's own point of view.

The parenthesized condition in the description of subjectivity is called the **finite domain parameter**. It is a condition on subjective binding in some but not all languages. Subjectivity and logophoricity will be discussed in further detail below. Formal definitions of these concepts are discussed in section 11.6.

11.2 Icelandic: Subjective and Anti-Subjective Pronouns

Reflexive and nonreflexive pronouns in Icelandic illustrate the subjective dimension of the binding space. The following two basic generalizations of Icelandic reflexivization are due to Þráinsson (1976a), who is assuming in this work the early transformational theory of reflexivization.[6] There is dialect variation with respect to generalization (2ii); in particular, many speakers of Icelandic do not allow nonsubject antecedents (Maling 1982). For those that do allow it, as Maling (1982) notes, reflexivization from an object antecedent is restricted to simple clauses:[7]

(2) Basic generalizations (Þráinsson 1976a):
    i. Reflexivization is obligatory from a subject trigger within clauses and into infinitival clauses.
    ii. Reflexivization from an object trigger is optional within clauses, and impossible into infinitival complements.

Maling (1982, 1984) has clarified that there are two dialects of Icelandic which differ with respect to generalization (2ii). In what seems to be the majority dialect of Icelandic, reflexivization from objects is impossible, whether into an infinitival complement or within a simple clause. The minority dialect is that described in (2ii). These generalizations apply to the distribution of reflexives within a sentence that contains no more than one finite clause, as shown in (3) and (4). In (3) and (4) *sig* is a reflexive pronoun, and *hann* is a nonreflexive personal pronoun. We see that a reflexive cannot be bound to an antecedent outside of the finite clause containing the reflexive:[8]

(3) *Jón$_i$ veit   að   Mária elskar *sig$_i$/hann$_i$.*
    J.   knows that M.   loves   self-ACC/him-ACC
    'John knows that Mary loves him.'

(4) *Jón$_i$ skipaði mér   að raka   sig$_i$/*hann$_i$.*
    J.   ordered me-dat to shave-INFIN self-ACC/*him-ACC
    'John ordered me to shave him (John).'

At first sight, these generalizations appear quite different from the English system. The notion of "obligatory" reflexivization, in particular, seems to presuppose a system of rule application of the sort that is eschewed in modern constraint-based syntactic theories. Nevertheless, despite this striking difference in the observable binding behavior of Icelandic reflexives, the generalizations of (4) are immediate consequences of the binding theory, given the appropriate featural analyses of the Icelandic reflexive and personal pronouns. The reader is invited at this point to determine the featural analyses of the third person accusative reflexive *sig* 'self' and personal pronoun *hann* 'him':

(5) Featural analysis of Icelandic pronouns: (fill in)
      sig   *hann*
     $\begin{bmatrix} \quad \end{bmatrix}$ $\begin{bmatrix} \quad \end{bmatrix}$

Let us first consider generalization (2i). How can we express in our theory the property of *obligatory* reflexivization from a subject antecedent? Optional reflexivization from a subject would mean that both the reflexive *sig* and the nonreflexive *hann* could have the subject as antecedent. If reflexivization is obligatory from the subject, then the nonreflexive pronoun *hann* must not be able to take a subject antecedent. Hence, in terms of our theory, *hann* must be anti-subjective ([– sbj]). According to the interpretation of anti-subjectivity given in (1), it must then be true of *hann* that no subject binders can occur in its domain. Assuming that the finite domain parameter of (1) holds in Icelandic, we immediately account for the qualification "within clauses and into infinitival clauses" of (2i). What this means is that for *hann*, no subject binders can occur in the minimal finite clause portion of the domain. Outside of this restricted domain, *hann* should be free to have subject antecedents, and as the data below will illustrate, it is.

This featural analysis of the Icelandic nonreflexive definite pronoun *hann* has a further consequence that is remarkable from the point of view of English. It predicts that the pronoun is free to have nonsubject antecedents *within its own nucleus*. In other words, the so-called "disjoint reference" property of definite nonreflexive pronouns in English should not hold for the corresponding pronouns in Icelandic, and as we will see below, it does not.

Let us now consider generalization (2ii). In the majority dialect, as we noted above, reflexivization from objects is impossible, whether into an infinitival complement or within a simple clause. In terms of our theory, this means that *sig* is subjective ([+ sbj]). In the minority dialect, there is a second use of *sig* which permits nonsubject antecedents within clauses, just as the English reflexive does. In terms of our theory, this *sig* is nuclear ([+ ncl]). This analysis accounts for the fact that reflexivization from an object antecedent into an infinitival complement is impossible: the binders of this *sig* must be within its nucleus. It also accounts for the optionality of reflexivization from an object antecedent. Because the definite nonreflexive pronoun *hann* is [– sbj], nothing prevents it from having nonsubject antecedents within its clause nucleus, as noted above. Hence, *hann* and the second *sig* will be alternatives in just this situation.

Our featural analysis thus far is summarized in (6). Below we will make an addition to this basic system:

(6) Featural analysis of Icelandic pronouns:

sig	*hann*
$\left[+\text{sbj}\right]$	$\left[-\text{sbj}\right]$

   dialectal:

   sig

   $\left[+\text{ncl}\right]$

These pronouns are third person. Icelandic has morphologically distinctive reflexive forms only in the third person. *Sig* is unmarked for gender and number; it has accusative (*sig*), dative (*sér*) and genitive (*sín*) forms, but no nominative form. As we remarked in section 10.2, examples (18)–(19), this appears to be a morphological gap rather than a syntactic one: Icelandic has oblique case-marked subjects, and it turns out that oblique reflexives can occur as subjects. There is also a possessive reflexive (*sinn*), inflected for number, gender, and all four cases. As for the pronoun *hann*, it is a masculine, nominative or accusative, singular form.

Examples from Icelandic are given in (7)–(8). The "%" sign signifies that the form is grammatical in some, but not all, dialects. The reader is invited to explain the choice of pronouns and reflexives in each example on the basis of the subject

binding theory above. In analyzing these examples, recall the assumption of anaphoric agreement (chapter 8) and assume that pronouns must not disagree with
their antecedents in person, number, or gender. Hence, the reflexive pronoun *sig*
can have third person binders only. Finally, note carefully what assumptions
must be made about the understood subjects of the infinitives. These are controlled subjects, which will be the topic of chapters 12 and 13:[9]

(7) a. *Ég spurði Harald$_i$ um   hann$_i$ (sjálfan)/ %sig$_i$.*
         I. asked H.$_i$-ACC about him$_i$-ACC self-EMPH/ self$_i$
         'I asked Harold about himself.'

     b. *Haraldur$_i$ spurði mig   um *hann$_i$/sig$_i$.*
         H.-NOM   me-ACC
         'Harold asked me about himself.'

     c. *Haraldur$_i$ skipaði mér   að raka *hann$_i$/sig$_i$.*
         H.-NOM   ordered me-DAT to shave
         'Harold ordered me to shave him (Harold).'

     d. *Ég lofaði   Haraldi$_i$ að raka hann$_i$/*sig$_i$.*
         I   promised H.-DAT to shave
         'I promised Harold to shave him.'

     e. *Ég skipaði Haraldi$_i$ að raka *hann$_i$/sig$_i$.*
         I   ordered H.-DAT to shave
         'I ordered Harold to shave himself.'

Recalling the complex-appearing generalizations in (2), we see that they all
follow from the simple system of (6). The core of the Icelandic system is opposition along the dimension of subjectivity. Thus the Icelandic system appears on a
dimension orthogonal to that of the English system. This symmetry at the core of
the Icelandic system is clause-bounded, occurring only within the minimal finite
clause in accordance with the subjectivity finite domain parameter. This condition immediately accounts for (3) as well.

The pattern of Icelandic reflexives in subjunctive clauses differs from what we
have seen so far, and will be discussed below.

11.3   Norwegian: Subjective/Nuclear Pronouns

The Norwegian anaphoric binding system involves both subjectivity and nuclearity:
subject anaphors can be nuclear (*seg selv*) or nonnuclear (*seg*) and there is an
anti-subjective nuclear anaphor (*ham selv*). The resulting binding properties of
Norwegian anaphors differ markedly from those of both the English system,
with its simple contrast in nuclearity, and the Icelandic system, with its contrast
in subjectivity in the minimal finite clause:[10]

(8) Featural analysis of Norwegian pronouns:

$$\begin{array}{cc} seg & ham \\ \begin{bmatrix} +\text{sbj} \\ -\text{ncl} \end{bmatrix} & \begin{bmatrix} -\text{ncl} \end{bmatrix} \\[2em] segselv & hamselv \\ \begin{bmatrix} +\text{sb} \\ +\text{ncl} \end{bmatrix} & \begin{bmatrix} -\text{sb} \\ +\text{ncl} \end{bmatrix} \end{array}$$

There is also a local *seg* which has a different distribution, either occurring with a certain class of semantically reflexive lexical verbs such as *vaske seg* 'wash oneself', *kle på seg* 'dress oneself', or appearing with intransitive verbs such as *skamme seg* 'be ashamed', *knytte seg* 'get uptight'. Local *seg* is discussed in section 11.5 below.

Like Icelandic, Norwegian has morphologically distinctive reflexive forms only in the third person. *Seg selv* and *seg* are unmarked for both gender and number; *seg* has genitive forms *sin* (common gender, that is, masculine or feminine), *sitt* (neuter), and *sine* (plural), while the reflexives based on *selv*, like the English reflexive pronouns, cannot take genitive case. The pronouns *ham* and *ham selv* are masculine singular forms. We again assume that pronouns may not disagree in grammatical features of person, number, and gender with their antecedents; hence, *seg* and *seg selv* may have masculine or feminine, singular or plural antecedents, but not first or second person antecedents.

Norwegian instantiates in a morphologically distinctive way three of the four featural combinations of subjectivity and nuclearity. But the contrast between the nuclear reflexive pronoun component *selv* and the emphatic marker *selv* is not morphologically marked in Norwegian. The emphatic marker, however, is heavily stressed.[11] We exclude both the emphatic *selv* and the local *seg* from the examples discussed in this section.

How are combinations of the binding features interpreted? The formal definitions are given in section 11.6. Here we provide an informal description:

(9) [+sbj, +ncl] – The antecedent must be a subject in the minimal nucleus containing the pronoun.
[+sbj, –ncl] – The antecedent must be a subject in the minimal finite domain outside of the minimal nucleus containing the pronoun.
[–sbj, +ncl] – The antecedent must be a nonsubject in the minimal nucleus containing the pronoun.

In all cases, the antecedent in question is assumed to outrank the pronoun.

Let us now consider five sentence structure types that illustrate the basic properties of this anaphoric binding system. These are given in (10a–e). The theory determines which of the alternative anaphors are grammatical in each structure. The reader is invited at this point to predict the distribution of stars from the featural analyses, given the antecedent relations indicated by the translations. It is helpful to take note of the person features of pronoun and antecedent, which are required to agree, and also note what the understood subjects of the infinitival complements are. This information is crucial for application of the binding theory (Andrews 1976, 1982, 1990b).

Fill in the stars:

(10) a. *Ola overgår   seg selv/seg/ham selv/ham.*
         O.   surpasses
         'Ola surpasses himself.'
     b. *Ola bad   oss snakke   om   seg selv/seg/ham selv/ham.*
         O.   asked us   talk-INFIN about
         'Ola asked us to talk about him (Ola).'
     c. *Ola lovet   meg å snakke   om   seg selv/seg/ham selv/ham.*
         O.   promised me   to talk-INFIN about
         'Ola promised me to talk about himself.'
     d. *Vi fortalte Ola om   seg selv/seg/ham selv/ham.*
         We told   O.   about
         'We told Ola about himself.'
     e. *Ola vet   at   vi snakket om   seg selv/seg/ham selv/ham.*
         O.   knows that we talked   about
         'Ola knows that we talked about him (Ola).'

For the reader's reference, the following table provides the judgments of the pronominal forms in these examples:

(11)

	seg selv	*seg*	*ham selv*	*ham*
(10a)	√	*	*	*
(10b)	*	√	*	√
(10c)	√	*	*	*
(10d)	*	*	√	*
(10e)	*	*	*	√

11.4 Logophoricity vs. Subjectivity

Logophoric pronouns morphologically distinct from both personal and reflexive pronouns are found in a number of West African languages (see Culy 1994 for a comprehensive survey, and Stirling 1993 for a thorough analysis of the differences between logophoricity, switch reference, and obviation). These pronouns are used to refer to one whose speech, thoughts, or feelings are represented in indirect discourse, from that person's own point of view. In Ewe as in many other West African languages, a logophoric pronoun distinct from both the personal pronoun and the reflexive pronoun occurs (Clements 1975: 142):

(12) a. *Kofi be yè-dzo*
     K.   say LOG-leave
     'Kofi said that he (Kofi) left.'

   b. *Kofi be e-dzo*
     K.   say PRO-leave
     'Kofi said that he/she (≠Kofi) left.'

   c. *Kofi lɔ̃ e ɖokui*
     K.   love PRO self
     'Kofi loves himself.'

   d. *Kofi be yè-lɔ̃ yè ɖokui*
     K.   said LOG-love LOG self
     'Kofi said that he (Kofi) loves himself.'

The logophoric pronoun is itself a mark of indirect discourse, as we see from the following pair of contrasting sentences from Ewe (Clements 1975: 152):

(13) a. *Kofi gblɔ na wɔ be yè-a-dyi ga-a na wɔ*
     K.   speak to PRO that LOG-T-seek money-D for PRO
     'Kofi*ᵢ* said to them that he*ᵢ* would seek the money for them.'

   b. *Kofi gblɔ na wo be: ma-dyi ga-a na ni*
                       I.will-seek money-D for you
     'Kofe said to them: "I'll seek the money for you."'

Note that 'I' and 'you' in the direct discourse of (13b) are rendered by the logophor and 'them', respectively, in (13a). These are the usual rules governing indirect discourse, as Clements observes.[12]

Both Clements (1975) and Hyman and Comrie (1981) show that the antecedent of a logophoric pronoun need not be the subject of a clause, provided that the antecedent does indeed meet the condition of logophoricity. For example, Hyman and Comrie (1981: 22) give the following contrasting examples from Gokana (Nigeria):

(14) a. *mm̀ dã̄ lébàrè gã̄ kɔ aè dɔ-ὲ*
     I   heard Lebare mouth that he fell-LOG
     'I heard from Lebare*ᵢ* that he*ᵢ* fell.'

   b. **mm̀ kɔ́ nὲ lébàrè kɔ aè dɔ-ὲ*
     I   said give Lebare that he fell-LOG
     'I said to Lebare*ᵢ* that he*ᵢ* fell.'

In (14a) the logophoric pronoun (which is marked by the verbal suffix -ὲ) can have a nonsubject antecedent; in (14b) there cannot be a logophoric pronoun with the nonsubject antecedent. The contrast arises because in the first example, Lebare's speech is represented, while in the second, it is not.[13]

Clements (1975) also shows that logophoric pronouns can have nonsubject antecedents in a dialect of Ewe (Ghana), provided that the antecedents designate the one whose speech or point of view is reported. In (15) the antecedent *Kofi* is contained in the object of the prepositional verb *tso* (Clements 1975: 160):

(15) *Kɔmi xɔ   agbalẽ tso   Kofi gbɔ be   wò-a-va   me kpe   na yè*
      K.   receive letter   from K.   side that PRO-T-come cast block for LOG
      'Kwami got a letter from Kofi, saying that he should come cast blocks for him.'

In the preceding examples, the logophor is used to express self reference by the one whose speech is represented in an indirect discourse. But logophors are also used in complements of verbs that designate emotions or cognitive states, or take negated propositions or eventualities, as in the following Ewe examples (Clements 1975: 164, 170):

(16) a. *e-dzɔ   dyi   na Ama be   yè-dyi   vi*
          PRO-straighten heart to A.   that LOG-bear child
          'it made Ama; happy that she; bore a child'
      b. *Kofi nya   be   me-kpɔ yè*
          K.   know that PRO-see LOG
          'Kofi; knew that I had seen him;.'
      c. *Kofi me-nya   be   me-kpɔ yè*
          K.   NEG-know that PRO-see LOG
          'Kofi; didn't know that I had seen him;.'

In these cases, explicit self reference need not be involved. For example, (16a) could be true even if Ama did not say anything about her child and never referred to herself. Similarly, (16c) is true only if Kofi has no knowledge that the speaker had seen him; Kofi therefore cannot be the source of the information in the complement, and he cannot have been referring to himself as seen (or unseen) by the speaker. Nevertheless, logophoric reference to Kofi is possible. Here the logophor is used to show that the speaker takes Kofi's point of view in expressing Kofi's unawareness of the speaker's observation of him. Similarly, in (16a) the logophor is used to show that the speaker takes Ama's point of view in expressing Ama's happiness about having borne a child. The generalization governing logophoricity, then, seems to be that the logophor expresses not necessarily self reference by the antecedent in an indirect discourse attributing speech, thoughts, or feelings to the antecedent, but reference by the speaker to the antecedent in such a discourse *from the antecedent's point of view* (Sigurðsson 1990: 318–21).[14]

What does it mean precisely for the speaker to refer to someone from that person's point of view? An elegant explication of this concept is in terms of the "assigned epistemic validator" of a discourse ("validator" for short): "the individual to whom the speaker linguistically assigns responsibility for the discourse in question" (Stirling 1993: 282). In "objective" discourse, the speaker herself takes responsibility for her statements, and serves as their assigned epistemic validator. But in logophoric discourse, the speaker shifts validation for the statements to the logophoric referent. In (16c), for example, the speaker is identifying

Kofi as the validator of the proposition that Kofi did not know that the speaker had seen Kofi. In effect, the speaker, call her S, is suggesting that Kofi would say, if you asked him: "I didn't know that S had seen me."[15]

Logophoricity is not purely a matter of the semantics of viewpoint, however. There is a grammatical requirement for logophoric reference in Ewe: the presence of the complementizer *be*. Though (17a) is a paraphrase of (16a), it lacks *be* and does not allow the logophor.[16] Embedding (17a) in a *be* clause permits the use of logophor, as illustrated by (17b) (the expression *dzɔ dyi na* . . . – literally 'straighten heart to . . .' – is an idiom meaning 'make . . . happy'):

(17) a. *ye/*yè   wo   vidyidyi-a   dzɔ   dyi   na Ama*
          PRO/LOG GEN child-bearing-D straighten heart to Ama
          'her$_i$ having a child made Ama$_i$ happy.'
      b. *Ama gblɔ be   yè   wo   vidyidyi-a   dzɔ   dyi   na yè*
          A.   say that LOG GEN child-bearing-D straighten heart to LOG
          'Ama$_i$ said that her$_i$ having a child made her$_i$ happy.'

The generalization that the Ewe logophoric pronoun must occur in a clause marked by the complementizer *be* suggests that *be* is a formal marker of indirect discourse.

Other languages lack the morphologically distinctive logophoric pronouns found in Ewe but nevertheless exhibit logophoricity. According to Clements, logophoricity in Latin differs primarily from that in Ewe in being expressed by the reflexive pronoun rather than by a morphologically distinct pronoun type. In Latin examples like (18) (Cicero, *Epistulae ad Atticum* ii. 18, 3) the antecedent of the reflexive is sometimes called the "logical subject:"

(18)   *A Caesare . . . invitor . . . sibi ut sim legatus*
       'I am invited by Caesar$_i$ to be lieutenant to him$_i$ (*sibi*).'

It is tempting to explicate the "logical subject" in such examples as an underlying syntactic subject, as proposed by Chomsky (1965: 23, 70). But Clements cites other Latin examples showing that "a nominal standing in any relationship whatsoever to the main verb of the higher clause can be the antecedent of the 'indirect' reflexive, provided the semantic conditions (those appropriate to logophoric pronouns, as stated above) are met." In (19), for example (Cicero, *Oratio pro Milone* 44), the antecedent of the reflexive (Favonius) is the source/validator of reported speech, expressed by a base-generated prepositional phrase:

(19)   *Vos ex M. Favonio audistis Clodium sibi dixisse . . . periturum Milonem*
       'you heard from M. Favonius$_i$ that Clodius has said to him$_i$ (*sibi*) that Milo was to die'

In (20) (Cicero, *Oratio pro Cluentio* 135) the antecedent is again the source/validator of the reported speech, but is expressed as the embedded possessor of the will:

(20) *Elogium recitasti de testamento Cn. Egnati patris . . . idcirco se exheredasse*
      filium
      'you cited the passage from the will of the elder Egnatius$_i$ (stating) that for
      this reason he$_i$ (*se*) disinherited his son'

In (21) (Livius 32, 1) the reflexive refers to the source/validator of the complaint,
but is not directly expressed in the passage at all:

(21) *Legati ab Ardea questi . . . erant sibi in monte Albano Latinis carnem . . .*
      datam non esse
      'delegates from Ardea (i.e. from the Ardeans$_i$) had complained that the
      flesh (of the animals sacrificed) on the Alban Mount had not been given to
      them$_i$ (*sibi*)'

Thus these Latin reflexives are better analyzed as logophors than subject-bound
anaphors.

Icelandic is similar to Latin in that its reflexive pronoun is also used logophor-
ically, as we see in (22) (Þráinsson 1976a, Maling 1984, Sigurðsson 1990):

(22) *Haraldur$_i$ segir að   Sigga elski   sig$_i$/hann$_j$.*
      H.-NOM   says that S.   loves-SBJN self/him
      'Harold says that Sigga loves him (Harold).'

The subjunctive mood in Icelandic (glossed by -SBJN in (22)) is a grammatical
marker of indirect discourse, serving a similar function to that of the complementizer *be* in Ewe (Maling 1984: 232). In contrast, our earlier example (3),
parallel to (23), which barred reflexivization from an embedded finite clause,
involved an indicative complement:

(23) *Haraldur$_i$ veit   að   Sigga elskar   *sig$_i$/hann$_j$.*
      H.-NOM   knows that S.   loves-INDIC self-ACC/him-ACC
      'Harold knows that Sigga loves him (Harold).'

The verb 'know' in Icelandic does not select the subjunctive mood, and so does
not constitute part of an indirect discourse structure. It therefore bars logophoric
reference, in contrast to the Ewe verb *nya* 'know' that we saw in (16), which can
be part of an indirect discourse structure in Ewe.[17]

Icelandic also differs from the languages described by Clements (1975) and
Hyman and Comrie (1981) in that its logophoric pronoun is both logophoric
and subjective. The grammatical subject condition and the logophoric condition
must both be met simultaneously. This explains why the following examples
from Maling (1984: 233) are both ungrammatical for most Icelandic speakers:[18]

(24) a. **Ég sagði Jóni$_i$ að   Maria hefði   boðið   sér$_i$.*
         I   told J.   that M.   had-SBJN invited self
         'I told John that Maria had invited him (John).'

b. **Ég heyrði frá Jóni*ᵢ *að Maria hefði boðið sér*ᵢ.
  I heard from J. that M. had-SBJN invited self
  'I heard from John that Maria had invited him (John).'

In (24a) the antecedent meets neither the logophoric nor the subject condition, and in (24b) the antecedent meets the logophoric condition but not the subject condition. In (25a), in contrast, the antecedent meets the subject condition but not the logophoric condition, while in (25b) the antecedent meets both (Maling 1984: 232, 239)[19] (the expression *talin . . . trú um* is an idiom meaning "made to believe, convinced"):

(25) a. **Honum*ᵢ *var sagt að sig*ᵢ *vantaði hæfileika.*
        him-DAT was said that self-ACC lacked-SBJN ability
        'He was told that he lacked ability.'
    b. *Honum*ᵢ *var talin trú um, að sig*ᵢ *vantaði*
        him-DAT was convinced belief about that self-ACC lacked-SBJN
        hæfileika.
        ability
        'He was made to believe that he lacked ability.'

The crucial difference is that antecedent's speech, thoughts, or point of view are reported in the indirect discourse structure of (25b), but not in (25a). Predictably, the active counterpart of (25b) is ungrammatical because the antecedent meets the logophoric condition, but is no longer a subject, as we see in (26) (the active here, like the passive in (25b), involves an idiom *taldi . . . trú um* 'made . . . believe', 'convinced . . .'):

(26) **Ég taldi honum*ᵢ *trú um að sig*ᵢ *vantaði hæfileika.*
     I   convinced him-DAT belief about that self*ᵢ* lacked-SBJN ability.
     'I made him believe that he lacked ability.'

Examples like the following, cited by Maling (1984: 222), seem at first sight to contradict the subject condition on the logophoric reflexive:

(27) *Skoðun Siggu*ᵢ *er að hana*ᵢ/*sig*ᵢ *vanti hæfileika.*
     opinion Sigga's is that she/self lacks-SBJN talent
     'Sigga's opinion is that she (Sigga) lacks talent.'

Here the antecedent is the possessor of the NP 'Sigga's opinion', and the reflexive occurs in the postcopular subjunctive complement of the nominal. However, as Maling (1984: 222) points out, "In some sense, *Sigga* is the 'subject' of [(27)] . . .; "the NP *Sigga's opinion/belief* behaves like a matrix clause *Sigga believed that . . .* for the purposes of the antecedent–anaphor relations." Given our assumption in section 10.2 that the POSS function is the most prominent on the relational hierarchy within nominals, this intuition could be captured by analyzing (27) as a **focused complement extraposition** construction, sketched in (28):[20]

(28)

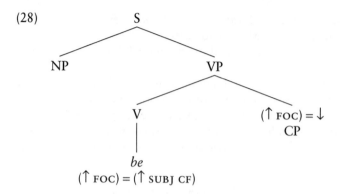

The focused postcopular CP 'that she lacks talent' is identified in f-structure with a complement function of the subject ('CF'; see chapter 6):

(29)
$$f: \begin{bmatrix} \text{FOC} & [\text{"that she lacks talent"}] \\ \text{SUBJ} & g: \begin{bmatrix} \text{POSS} & [\text{PRED} \quad \text{'NAMED-}Sigga\text{'}] \\ \text{PRED} & \text{'OPINION-OF} <(g \text{ POSS})(g \text{ CF})>\text{'} \\ \text{CF} & \end{bmatrix} \\ \text{PRED} & \text{'BE}<(f \text{ SUBJ})>\text{'} \end{bmatrix}$$

This analysis unifies the postcopular CP 'that she lacks talent' into the f-structure of the nominal containing 'Sigga's opinion', which is g in (29). The analysis predicts that the binding possibilities for (28) will be identical to those within a single NP-complement construction 'Sigga's opinion that she lacks talent': this example is good because both the logophoric condition and the subject antecedent condition are met (taking the possessor to be the 'subject' of the nominal). The possessor of the same nominal cannot bind the reflexive in a construction which does not represent the speech, thoughts, or feelings of the possessor, as shown by the following example from Maling:

(30) *Skoðun Siggu$_i$ fær*   *mig til að halda að hana$_i$/*sig$_i$*
      opinion Sigga's leads-INDIC me   to think that she/*self
      vanti   hæfileika.
      lacks-SBJN talent
      'Sigga's opinion leads me to think that she (Sigga) lacks talent.'

Here the finite 'that' clause is the complement of 'think', not 'opinion', and it represents the thoughts of the speaker, not Sigga.

A further very significant property of logophoric reflexives in Icelandic is their use to refer to antecedents in previous sentences in contexts of extended indirect discourse (Bresnan et al. 1983, Maling 1984, Sigurðsson 1990). The following example is from Gestur Pálsson's 'Tilhugalíf', chapter 6 (cited by Maling 1984: 239):

(31) [*Hann*] *var að hugsa um, hvað hún yrði, hissa, þegar hún kæmi á fætur*
næsta morgun, opnaði dyrnar og sæi sig á tröppunum; hún sæi sig ef til
vill öldungis ekki fyrst, en stigi bara út, ofan á sig; . . .
'[He] was thinking how she would be surprised when she got up the next
morning, opened the door and saw him (reflexive) on the steps; she would
see (subjunctive) him (reflexive) perhaps not at first, but would just step
(subjunctive) out, on top of him (reflexive); . . .'

Even in extended indirect discourse the subject condition appears to persist,
as we see in the following minimal pair of examples (Joan Maling, personal
communication):

(32) a. *Foreldrar mínir sannfærðu mig um að ég hefði verið latur. Ég hefði átt*
að skrifa sér oftar.
'My parents convinced me that I had been lazy. I should have written
(subjunctive) them (reflexive) oftener.'
b. *Af foreldrum mínum var ég sannfærður um það að ég hefði verið*
*latur. Ég hefði átt að skrifa þeim/*sér oftar.*
'By my parents I was convinced that I had been lazy. I should have
written (subjunctive) them (*reflexive) oftener.'

In both (32a) and (32b) the logophoric condition is met in the extended indirect
discourse, but only in (32a) is the logophoric antecedent also the subject of its
clause.
The contrast between the Icelandic and the Ewe logophor can thus be represented in our informal description as in (33):

(33) Icelandic logophor: [+log, +sbj]
Ewe logophor: [+log]

The formal interpretation of these features requires simultaneous reference to the
representation of extended indirect discourse and, in parallel, the f-structure of
the antecedent.[21]
Recall from section 11.2 (6) that the Icelandic personal pronoun *hann* 'him' is
anti-subjective within the minimal finite clause, but it is not anti-logophoric. For
this reason *hann* and *sig* are not in complementary distribution in nonclause-
bounded contexts. They may each be used in the same domain; indeed, they may
both be used in the same domain at the same time (Bresnan et al. 1983, Maling
1984: 238–9):

(34) *Jón$_i$ sagði* *að María hefði* *uppgötvað að læknirinn*
J.$_i$ said-INDIC that M. had-SBJN discovered that doctor-the
vildi *tala* *við sig$_i$ um* *hana$_j$.*
wanted-SBJN talk-INF with self$_i$ about her$_j$.
'John said that Mary had discovered that the doctor wanted to talk with
him (John) about her.'

In (34) the reflexive is bound to John, establishing that all three embedded clauses (the middle clauses headed by 'discovered' and 'wanted' and the bottom clause headed by 'talk') constitute a domain for the binding of the logophoric reflexive. But at the same time the nonreflexive pronoun is bound to Mary, establishing that the personal pronoun need not be free within the domain in which the logophoric reflexive is bound. Further examples are shown in (35a–d). In the last it is possible to have both a reflexive and nonreflexive pronoun bound to the same antecedent (this interpretation is assisted by the emphatic *sjálfan*; see nn. 9, 11 and section 11.5):

(35) a. *Jón$_i$ segir   að María$_j$ hafi   uppgötvað að ég*
          J.$_i$ says-INDIC that M.$_j$ has-SBJN discovered that I
          hafi   talað við sig$_i$ um   vandamál hennar$_j$.
          have-SBJN talked with self$_i$ about problem   her$_j$.
          'John says that Mary has discovered that I have talked with him (John) about her problem.'

      b. *Jón$_i$ segir   að María$_j$ telji   að ég*
          J. says-INDIC that M.   believes-SBJN that I
          hafi   lofað henni$_j$ bílnum sínum$_i$.
          have-SBJN promised her$_j$ car   his$_i$-REFL.
          'John says that Mary believes that I have promised her (Mary) his (John's) car.'

      c. *Jón$_i$ sagði   að börnin hans$_i$ ætluðu heimsækja*
          J. said-INDIC that children his$_i$ intended visit-INFIN
          sig$_i$ um jólin.
          self$_i$ for Christmas
          'John said that his (John's) children intended to visit him (John) for Christmas.'

      d. *Haraldur$_i$ sagði   mér   að ég skyldi   ekki*
          H.$_i$-NOM   said-INDIC me-DAT that I   should-SBJN not
          spyrja sig$_i$ um   hann$_i$ sjálfan.
          ask   self$_i$ about him$_i$ self-EMPH
          'Harold told me that I should not ask him (Harold) about himself.'

This evidence shows that the nonclause-bounded reflexives of Icelandic cannot merely be analyzed as analogues of English reflexives in a larger syntactic domain. It also clearly supports a central idea of our model, that binding properties are controlled by the lexical representations of pronominal elements along several independent dimensions.

As we have seen in section 11.2, the anti-subjectivity of the personal pronoun induces the complementary distribution of subjective reflexive and personal pronouns within the minimal finite clause, and hence the apparent obligatoriness of reflexivization in this domain. A language which unlike Icelandic possessed an anti-logophoric personal pronoun [–log] would show "obligatory logophoricization." Do such languages exist? Gokana is an example, as illustrated by the following pairs of sentences from Hyman and Comrie (1981: 19, 21, 22):

(36) a. *aè kɔ   aè dɔ̀*
      he said he fell
      'He$_i$ said that he$_j$ fell.'

    b. *aè kɔ   aè dɔ-ɛ̀*
      he said he fell-LOG
      'He$_i$ said that he$_i$ fell.'

(37) a. *mm̀ dá̆   lébàrè gá̆   kɔ   aè dɔ̀*
      I   heard Lebare mouth that he fell
      'I heard from Lebare$_i$ that he$_j$ fell.'

    b. *mm̀ dá̆   lébàrè gá̆   kɔ   aè dɔ-ɛ̀*
      I   heard Lebare mouth that he fell-LOG
      'I heard from Lebare$_i$ that he$_i$ fell.'

The (a) examples of each pair show the personal pronoun, which cannot be co-referential with the logophoric antecedent of the (b) examples. Now Hyman and Comrie (1981) show that Gokana logophors are not subjective, and this point is illustrated by (37b). Hence the complementarity of personal and logophoric pronouns in (36a, b)–(37a, b) cannot be attributed to anti-subjectivity, but appears to stem from the anti-logophoricity of the personal pronoun. The personal pronouns of Ewe, in contrast, are not obligatorily anti-logophoric in all contexts or in all dialects (Clements 1975). In addition, an anti-logophoric pronoun distinct in form from the personal pronoun is reported in Adioukrou (Hill 1995).

These considerations also indicate that the binding properties of personal pronouns are often highly grammaticalized: they cannot be completely explained in terms of pragmatic avoidance of the referents of bound anaphors.[22] Anti-logophoric, anti-subjective, and anti-nuclear pronouns all exist, each with a distinctive pattern of exclusion of possible antecedents, and they are not always complementary to positive binding elements as pragmatic avoidance would predict. This result is to be expected on our theory, because of the independence of the binding dimensions and the lexicality of the binding constraints.[23] For the same reason, our theory also allows for languages without reflexives (the pronouns have no positive binding constraints) and for personal pronouns without negative binding specifications. Fijian, as described by Dixon (1988: 255–6), is one example of a language lacking reflexives; personal pronouns are used to indicate coreference with coarguments of the same predicate. Old English is another example, discussed further below (Traugott 1972: 88–9, Faltz 1985, Levinson 1991: 133ff).

This discussion of the nuclear, subjective, and logophoric dimensions of anaphoric binding has taken us well outside of Principles A and B of the toy binding theory of section 10.2. Conceptually, an anaphoric binding system – that is, a set of reflexive and nonreflexive pronouns with their specific anaphoric binding properties – is a set of points in a discrete space generated by the independent dimensions of subjectivity, nuclearity, and logophoricity. By simple changes of coefficients, we can transform one system into another, creating complex variations in the observable binding behavior of elements of the systems. The complementary distribution of reflexive and nonreflexive pronouns is not an invariant property of this space; in fact, it can arise only in certain one-dimensional systems organized by simple symmetry.

Further Reading and Discussion

The term 'logophoricity' has been extended by some authors (e.g. Reinhart and Reuland 1993) well beyond its use in marking indirect discourse, to refer generally to all kinds of nonlocal reflexivization, including emphatics and any kind of "point of view" indicators. For arguments against this extension and in favor of a more coherent analysis of logophoricity, see Culy (1994, 1997). Sells (1987a) argues that there is no such thing as logophoricity, it being decomposable into three further primitive roles predicated of discourse referents in Discourse Representation Theory (DRT): SOURCE, SELF, and PIVOT. But as Stirling (1993: chapter 6) notes, Sells does not really provide an analysis of African logophoricity. Stirling (1993) does provide a formal analysis of African logophoricity within DRT, making use of only one primitive (the epistemic validator), and argues that her theory can be extended to non-African types of logophoricity as well, although she does not go into detail. She also notes that Sells's DRT analysis runs into problems with the scope of negation, which are not encountered under her analysis.

Culy (1994) observes that "pure" logophoric languages, which have special logophoric pronouns, addressee pronouns, or verbal markers of the logophoric domain, are found only in Africa, and provides a typological survey in support of Stirling's hierarchy of 'logocentric' verbs (verbs that introduce logophoric contexts):[24]

(38) **Logocentric Verb Hierarchy:**
     communication > thought > psychological state > perception (Stirling 1993: 259)

Culy (1997) argues that logophoric pronouns are primarily markers of indirect discourse, which may come to have secondary uses to express point of view, while reflexive pronouns may also express point of view but are never logophoric. As we have already seen, Icelandic logophoricity is crucially dependent on indirect discourse, including extended (intersentential) indirect discourse, all being marked by subjunctive mood. Culy's conclusions rest on a particular conception of "point of view" which does not seem applicable to Icelandic reflexives. He argues that in their core use as indirect speech markers, logophoric pronouns cannot express point of view, first, because they are obligatory and second, because they may have multiple occurrences in the same sentence. His conception of "point of view" (following Banfield 1982) is that it involves the narrator's choice and cannot be "dictated" by the grammar, so cannot be obligatory. Again following Banfield (1982), he assumes there can be only one point of view per (nonquoted) sentence. Taking the second argument first, it is true in Icelandic that logophoric *sig* cannot occur within the same nucleus as another *sig* (Bresnan et al. 1993):

(39) **Haraldur_i sagði mér   að   ég skyldi   ekki spyrja sig_i um*
     H.-NOM said me-DAT that I   should-SBJN not ask   self about
     (sjálfan)   sig_i.
     self-EMPH self
     'Harold told me that I should not ask him (Harold) about himself.'

But that restriction seems merely to be a sign of the nonnuclearity of logophoric *sig*, for multiple occurrences are possible when they do not occur in the same minimal nucleus.[25] In (40), for example, the adjectival predicate complement headed by 'fond of' comprises its own f-structure nucleus complete with subject (an 'XCOMP' in terms of chapter 12):[26]

(40) *Haraldur_i sagði að sér_i   þætti   aðeins vænt um (sjálfan) sig_i.*
     H.-NOM   said that self-DAT seems-SBJN only   fond of self-EMPH self
     'Harold said that he (Harold) seems fond only of himself.'

The same property holds of Ewe, which requires the reflexive base with a logophoric pronominal marker for clause-internal coreference between logophors (Clements 1975: 142, 156). Icelandic simply lacks a nuclear logophoric pronoun to complement the use of its nonnuclear, subjective logophoric reflexive.

As for Culy's first argument, it is unfortunately true that many categories which ought to be a matter of choice can be imposed by grammars: markers of humility, politeness, social level, and gender, for example,[27] and some possible choices of semantic content are ineffable within a single sentence in particular languages.[28] Whereas Culy takes obligatoriness to be an inherent property of logophors, in the present theory obligatory binding is a property of the *system* of pronouns, not of the logophor or anaphor by itself. Icelandic possesses an anti-subjective personal pronoun, but no anti-logophoric pronouns; hence, subjectivity is obligatory and logophoricity is optional. Across languages, there is probably a strong tendency for a personal pronoun to take on an anti-binding constraint in the domain in which a bound pronoun appears, as the grammaticalization of a pragmatic principle (Levinson 1987, 1991), so that in languages with pure logophoric, subjective, or nuclear pronouns, personal pronouns may be respectively anti-logophoric, anti-subjective, or nonnuclear. But when pronouns are as polyfunctional as the Icelandic reflexive *sig*, used for subjectivity as well as logophoricity, the personal pronoun need not be complementary to both functions (though it may be: see O'Connor 1993). Our examples (34) and (35a–d) also bear out that the personal pronoun in Icelandic is unmarked (neutral) for logophoricity, because it can have its antecedent within a logophoric domain, and even corefer to the logophoric antecedent.

11.5   The Typology of Reflexives and the Origins of Nuclearity

The subjective, nuclear, and logophoric dimensions recur in systems of anaphoric binding across languages, as shown by typologically oriented studies (e.g. Faltz 1985, Wiesemann 1986, Culy 1994, 1997, Comrie 1998), crosslinguistic theoretical works (especially Dalrymple 1993, Sells 1987a, Stirling 1993, Sells et al., 1987), and many language-particular studies (including, from an LFG perspective, K. P. Mohanan 1981, Kameyama 1984, 1985, Cho 1985, Saiki 1985, 1986, 1987, Hong 1987, Tan 1991, T. Mohanan 1994, and Toivonen 1996, 1997, in press.)

There is a very interesting correlation between the binding constraints and the morphological form of reflexive pronouns, discovered by Faltz (1985). Restricting our attention to reflexives that occupy the syntactic positions of nominal constituents, as opposed to reflexives expressed by verbal morphology as in head-marking languages (chapter 8), we find that these reflexives fall into two broad morphological types: simple and complex:

(41)   **Simple reflexives** consist of a pronominal stem which may or may not be inflected for case and agreement features; Icelandic *sig* is an example.
Complex reflexives consist of (i) a pronominal head together with an emphatic constituent (e.g. Norwegian *seg selv*), or (ii) a compound of these two (e.g. English *herself*), or (iii) a noun root with a meaning such as 'body', 'soul', or 'head' together with a pronominal marker.

The correlation between morphological form and binding constraints is stated in our terms in (42):

(42)   **Reflexive-Binding Typology:**
   i.   Simple reflexives are [+sbj]
   ii. Complex reflexives are [+ncl] (based on Faltz 1985)

These generalizations appear to have no exceptions in Faltz's (1985) typological survey, but there are exceptions to the reverse implications. Not all subjective reflexives are simple; Norwegian's *seg selv* is an example (see also Faltz 1985: 134ff). Some nuclear reflexives are simple; Czech reflexives are an example (Toman 1990), being nuclear and subjective. These possibilities are easily accommodated by our theory.

Exceptions to the implications as stated in (42i, ii) have also been reported. An important counterexample to generalization (42ii) is Chinese *ta ziji*, which permits long distance binding (and from nonsubject positions) despite being complex. Pan (1998) shows that *ta ziji* can be bound to a remote NP which is more prominent on a person/animacy hierarchy than all closer possible NPs, and argues that these properties of *ta ziji* can be explained in terms neither of logophoricity nor of contrast and emphasis. There are also counterexamples to (42i): there are simple reflexives bound, not to the subject, but to the most prominent argument on the thematic hierarchy (Marathi is an example, according to Joshi 1989, 1993, and Dalrymple 1993). Nevertheless, it seems that a great majority of languages bear out the truth of (42i, ii) as an implicational generalization of typology.

The implications expressed in (42i, ii) point to an explanation of the origins of nuclearity. Part of the explanation is given by Faltz. He proposes that complex reflexives incorporating emphatics arise historically from grammaticalization of the markedness of coreference between coarguments of the same predicate (Faltz 1985: 241ff, see also Comrie 1998). If a language lacks a reflexive pronoun, then an ordinary pronoun may be used for coreference, as in Old English (Traugott 1972: 88–9, Faltz 1985: 239):

(43) *swa hwa swa eadmedath   hine*
      whoever   humiliate+PRES him+ACC
      'whoever humiliates himself . . .'

As Faltz observes, the "Old English ancestor of the modern reflexive morpheme *self* was an NP emphatic *self* or *sylf*, which was placed after an NP and took endings marking gender, number, and case in agreement with it. Over time this morpheme was reinterpreted as a reflexive, thus providing English with its primary strategy" for reflexivization. The Old English *sylf* is directly cognate to the modern German emphatic *selbst*, and we can see in the modern languages that the function of the emphatic is "as a warning to the hearer that the intended referent of that NP is unusual or unexpected" (Faltz 1985: 240). Comparing (44a) and (44b), for example, we see that the former is most naturally used in a context in which it is unexpected that John would have taken the blame:

(44) a. John himself took the blame.
      b. John took the blame.

If the unemphatic example (44b) is used in a situation where it is in fact unexpected that John would take the blame, "there is a chance that the hearer might think that the speaker was mistaken or that he heard the sentence incorrectly." By using the emphatic in this situation, the speaker signals that he recognizes that it is unexpected for John to be the referent, but is nevertheless intended, "thereby making it easier for the hearer to believe that there has not been a mistake." Levinson (1991) shows that this idea can be more precisely expressed within the theory of generalized conversational implicatures.

Faltz gives Modern German as another example of this markedness hypothesis. German has a subjective reflexive *sich*, which cannot be used to translate *himself* in the English example *Hans$_i$ talked to Fritz$_j$ about himself$_j$*, because the antecedent is not a subject. The nonreflexive pronoun could be used in this situation:

(45) *Hans$_i$ sprach mit Fritz$_j$ über ihn$_j$.*
      H.   spoke with F.   about him
      'Hans talked to Fritz about himself.'

However, a more likely reading of (45) would be that the referent of the pronoun
is a person other than Hans or Fritz. "To indicate that it is the unlikely referent
which is intended, namely Fritz, the speaker can use the emphatic:"

(46) *Hans$_i$ sprach mit Fritz$_j$ über ihn$_j$ selbst.*
      H.   spoke with F.   about him self
      'Hans talked to Fritz about himself.'

Faltz emphasizes that this strategy for signalling unexpected referents provides
not a *syntactic* basis for anaphora resolution, but merely a strategy intended to
aid the hearer in finding the intended referent. The syntactic reflexive *himself*
does provide a syntactic basis for anaphora resolution, by narrowing the possible
antecedents to those which are coarguments or (in our terms) in the minimal
nucleus. By comparing the nonsyntactic use of the emphatic with the syntactic
reflexive, we can see that the latter is a grammaticalization of the former. Thus
Norwegian, unlike German and Old English, generally[29] requires the compound
reflexive containing *selv* when coarguments corefer, as illustrated by examples
like the following (see example (10d)):

(47) *Vi fortalte Ola$_i$ om   ham selv$_i$/*ham$_i$.*
      we told   O.   about self/him
      'We told Ola about himself.'

Recall that Icelandic appears to differ in this respect from Norwegian (see example (7a), n. 9, and n. 11):

(48) *Ég spurði Harald$_i$ um   hann$_i$ (sjálfan).*
      I. asked H.$_i$-ACC about him$_i$-ACC (self-EMPH)
      'I asked Harold about himself.'

   Given that the unmarked situation is for coarguments of the same predicate to
have distinct referents, it is natural in the absence of a reflexive strategy, for an
emphatic to be used specifically to signal that the more highly marked less expected situation (namely, coreference between coarguments) is present (Faltz 1985:
242). As confirmation for this markedness approach, Faltz makes the following
important observation:

   If we believe that the reason that it is natural for an emphatic to mark
   reflexive coreference is that such coreference is normally a marked situation, we would predict that the emphatic would *not* be used to mark the
   objects of verbs like *wash* or *dress* when they are coreferent with the sub-

ject, since for these verbs coreference is normal. But this is just what we find in the history of English. Well into the Middle English period it is easy to find examples like

(44) *he cladde hym as a poure laborer*
      'He dressed as a poor laborer.'

in which a plain pronoun without *self* is used as the object of a normally reflexive verb. This may be compared to

(45) *him self he hynge*
      'He hanged himself.'

in which *self* marks an object coreferent with the subject when the verb is not normally reflexive.

Faltz's markedness account of the origin of complex reflexives based on emphatics plausibly explains why nuclearity should be associated with this type, but it leaves the third type of complex reflexive in (41) out of account. The latter consists of a noun root having a meaning such as 'body', 'soul', or 'head', together with a pronominal marker. An example from Fula is *hoore-qam* 'head-my' (Faltz 1985: 32):

(49) *mi gaañi   hoore-qam*
      I   wound+PERF head-my
      'I wounded myself.'   Fula

Obviously, the use of an emphatic marker to signal an unexpected (marked) referent does not explain the locality of binding associated with this reflexive type.[30] To explain this case, Faltz (1985: 247–8) makes the further assumptions that (i) the requirements of locality and subject-antecedency each serve to narrow down the possible referents of the compound reflexive, so some such binding constraint must be acquired during grammaticalization, and (ii) locality of binding is "more easily acquired" than subject-antecedency. This may be so (Faltz offers no evidence), but there is another possible explanation for the binding locality of complex reflexives of the noun root type illustrated by Fula (49).

We have already seen in section 11.3 that (idealizing somewhat) Norwegian *seg* and *seg selv* are in complementary distribution, *seg* being used for subject antecedents outside the minimal nucleus, and *seg selv* for subject antecedents within it. However, this idealization is obtained by removing examples of local uses of *seg* within the minimal nucleus. Now in some of these uses *seg* is simply a marker of intransitive or intransitivized verbs (Lødrup 1999a; see also Grimshaw 1982a, Zec 1985, Sells et al. 1987, and problem set 5). But Lødrup (1999a) shows that simple reflexives used in certain 'physical contexts' are true arguments of their predicates. Examples are given in (50):

(50) a. *Hun vasket seg.*
          she   washed self
          'She washed herself.'
     b. *Hun hadde skibukse på seg.*
          she   had   ski-pants on self
          'She wore ski pants.'
     c. *John satte Marit foran   seg.*
          John put   Marit in front of self
          'John put Marit in front of himself.'
     d. *Hun dro   dynen   over seg.*
          She   pulled the-comforter over self
          'She pulled the comforter over herself.'

The reflexive *seg* in these examples contrasts with those in (51a, b), which are not 'physical contexts' in Lødrup's sense:[31]

(51) a. *Hun beundrer seg selv/*seg.*
          she   admires self
          'She admires herself.'
     b. *Hun snakket om   seg selv/*seg.*
          she   talked about self
          'She talked about herself.'

'Physical contexts' are characterized by Lødrup as those in which "the physical aspect of a referent is in focus." The examples he gives can be described as in (52):

(52) **Physical contexts** are those in which a person acts on or in relation to that person's own body, locates something in relation to that person's own body, or someone acts on a person by acting on that person's own body.

Put another way, physical contexts are those in which the body of a person is salient: a person does something to (or in relation to) her own body, or is affected by something done to her own body. Reflexive *seg* in physical contexts allows semantically contentful modification (*Hun vasket hele seg* 'she washed all self') and resists the existential construction, which is limited to intransitive verbs (**Det vasket/pisket/frotterte seg en dame på badet* 'it washed/flogged/toweled self a lady in the-bathroom'). In contrast, detransitivizing *seg* differs in both respects, supporting the conclusion that *seg* in physical contexts is a true argument, Lødrup argues.

   Among the varieties of evidence that Lødrup gives for the status of *seg* as a true argument in the physical context examples (50) is the fact that *seg* can occur if and only if arguments denoting inalienable possessions, characteristically body parts, can occur. Thus (53a, b) are parallel to (50a, b), while (54a, b) are parallel to (51a, b):[32]

(53) a. *Hun vasket ansiktet.*
      she washed the-face
      'She washed her face.'
   b. *Hun hadde ski på bena.*
      she had skis on the-feet
      'She had skis on her feet.'
   c. *Hun dro dynen over hodet.*
      She pulled the-comforter over the-head
      'She pulled the comforter over her head.'

(54) a. **Hun beundrer ansiktet.*
      she admires the-face
      'She admires her face.'
   b. **Hun snakket om ansiktet.*
      she talked about the-face
      'She talked about her face.'

Lødrup shows that these inalienable NPs have much in common with the locally bound reflexive *seg*. For one thing, the possessors of NPs denoting inalienables must be syntactically realized. For cases of externally possessed inalienables, like those in (53a, b, c), this means that the inalienable requires an outranking syntactic antecedent.[33] Hence, passivization with these examples is ungrammatical (Lødrup 1999a: 386, n. 17). The same of course is characteristic of locally bound anaphors. For another, the antecedent of the inalienable must occur in the local domain, another characteristic of locally bound anaphors:[34]

(55) a. **Hun$_i$ hørte oss snakke om ansiktet$_i$.*
      she heard us talk about the-face
      'She heard us talk about her face.'
   b. **Hun$_i$ likte din omtale av ansiktet$_i$.*
      she liked your mention of the-face
      'She liked your mention of her face.'

Lødrup argues that once the conditions for binding an antecedent to an externally possessed inalienable are correctly stated, they will automatically apply to the binding of local *seg* in Norwegian, and explain why it differs from the subjective *seg* we have seen in section 11.3. In other words, the binding theory of the locally bound simple reflexives is just the binding theory of inalienables. We give the following principle, slightly generalized from Lødrup (1999a):[35]

(56) **Inalienable binding principle:**
   An inalienable must be locally bound by its possessor in a physical context. (based on Lødrup 1999a)

This formulation applies both to the above cases of subject-binding of inalienables and to object-binding ("possessor raising") cases such as (57a, b):

(57) a.   *Vi vasket henne over hele seg.*
           We washed her   over all   herself
           'We washed her all over.'
      b.   *Vi vasket henne i ansiktet.*
           We washed her   in the-face
           'We washed her face.'

The basis of the inalienable binding principle is semantic: physical contexts are those in which the possessor acts on or in relation to her body, locates something in relation to her body, or someone acts on the possessor by acting on her body. But these relations are characteristically expressed by a single lexical predicate (e.g. 'wash'), or by a group of predicates forming a single complete nucleus (e.g. 'have . . . on', 'put . . . on'). Their syntactic locality is a reflection of their semantic locality.[36]

We are now in a position to answer the question of why noun root reflexives like that in Fula are locally bound. These reflexives are hypothesized to have undergone a process of grammaticalization, described by Faltz (1985: 33) as follows:

> First, there is a stage in which the language lacks a primary reflexive. Then, the word for "body", "head", "soul", or some such, is used as the basis for a reflexive noun phrase. In the second stage, the word in question has two distinct semantic functions. On the one hand, it retains its original lexical meaning of "head" or whatever; but in addition it has the new grammatical function of indicating reflexive coreference as a result of weakening (hence widening) of the specific lexical meaning. Basque, Fula, and Malagasy are currently in this stage. . . . A third stage would be the loss of the lexical meaning entirely, or, less drastically, the phonological separation of the reflexive from the lexical meanings, so that we end up with an exclusively reflexive stem in the language.

We see, then, that through grammaticalization, the lexical meaning of the inalienable widens metonymically from the self's body or other inalienable possession to the self. The self remains its own inalienable possession, so the inalienable binding principle (56) still applies. But as the semantically local binding domain is grammaticalized and replaced by the syntactically local domain which corresponds to it, the restriction to physical contexts is eventually dropped. The result is nuclearity.

To summarize, on the account sketched above, nuclearity is the grammaticalization of pragmatic and semantic properties of reference in simple predications. Most simple predications involve noncoreferential coarguments and invite pragmatic marking of coreference, which historically becomes grammaticalized along the lines proposed by Faltz (1985) and Levinson (1991). However, predications of actions on the body are different: these imply a coreference relation among coarguments, because the relation of the body to the self is inalienable. Lødrup (1999a) proposes his inalienable binding principle as an explanation for the local binding of simple reflexives in physical contexts in Norwegian (as well as Dutch), but this principle also offers an explanation – via grammaticalization – for the locality of binding of complex reflexives based on body parts across languages. We see, then, that local reflexives are not always complex, but complex reflexives are likely to be local if they derive historically from the grammaticalization of these pragmatic and semantic constraints on referring in simple predications.

As for (42i), the tendency for simple reflexives to be bound by subject antecedents without being restricted to a local domain, recall from (41) that simple reflexives are based on a pronominal stem. Faltz (1985: 224) remarks that in his typological sample, compound reflexives are always marked for all persons, while pronominal reflexives are not. Thus, simple reflexives tend to be morphologically deficient pronouns, lacking some agreement information that would obviously play a role in identifying the possible referent. This would explain why they tend to be subject-oriented. If, as Faltz assumes, subject-antecedency serves to narrow down the possible referents of the pronoun, then it is clear that for pronouns deficient in the referentially classificatory information provided by agreement features, the strategy of fixing the antecedent to be one of particular prominence is well motivated. The subject is the most prominent argument on the relational hierarchy (section 10.1 and chapter 6), but other dimensions of prominence (such as the thematic hierarchy) can also be recruited to narrow down possible antecedents.[37]

Further Reading and Discussion

The typology of reflexives in (42) has attracted many attempts to explain the phenomena in terms of the syntactic mechanisms of synchronic grammar, independently of the historical considerations outlined above. One widespread approach proposes that reflexivization involves the covert movement of an anaphoric element to a higher position in the tree structure. The binding domain differences between simple and complex reflexives on this approach follow from the barriers to movement posed by the internal syntactic structure of complex reflexive NPs; see Pica (1987, 1991), Cole et al. (1990), Reinhart and Reuland (1991), Hestvik (1991), Cole and Sung (1994), and references for representative examples. For representative criticisms of the movement-based analyses, see Þráinsson (1991), C.-T. James Huang and Tang (1991), Progovac (1993), Dalrymple (1993), and Pan (1998).

It is clear that if there is a historical explanation for the typological generalizations (42), a synchronic re-explanation in completely independent terms is unneeded.

11.6 Formalization

We assume here the material in section 10.4. The subjective/anti-subjective constraints will have the general form in (58). Some languages, such as Icelandic and

Norwegian, restrict the domain of subjective and anti-subjective pronouns to the minimal finite clause, while others, such as Yoruba (Pulleyblank 1986), do not. We therefore regard this restriction as a crosslinguistic parameter of variation:

(58) a. **Subjective:**
          ((DomainPath ↑) Antecedent INDEX) = (↑ INDEX)
          Antecedent = SUBJ, DomainPath parametrically restricted to the minimal finite clause.
      b. **Anti-subjective:**
          ((DomainPath ↑) Antecedent INDEX) ≠ (↑ INDEX)
          Antecedent = SUBJ, DomainPath parametrically restricted to the minimal finite clause.

Formally, the minimal finite clause condition is expressible as an off-path constraint requiring that the domain be restricted to at most one f-structure containing the TENSE attribute:

(59) **Finite Domain Condition:**
      A binding constraint designator ((GF α ↑) SUBJ) is in the minimal finite domain when, if the attribute string α is nonempty, then setting $\alpha = xa$ for some attribute a and possibly empty string of attributes x, ¬(→ TENSE) holds for every attribute in GF x.

The subjective/anti-subjective constraints can then be formulated as in (60a, b), with the parametric choice given as a parenthetical option:

(60) **Formalization of Subjectivity Constraints:**
      a. A **subjective pronoun** is lexically specified
          ((GF α ↑) SUBJ INDEX) = (↑ INDEX)
          (subject to the finite domain condition (59)).
      b. An **anti-subjective pronoun** is lexically specified
          ((GF α ↑) SUBJ INDEX) ≠ (↑ INDEX)
          (subject to the finite domain condition (59)).

The multiple binding features of the Norwegian system are interpreted as in (61):

(61) **Formalization of Mixed Subjective/Nuclear Constraints:**
      a. A **subjective, nuclear pronoun** is lexically specified
          ((GF α ↑) SUBJ INDEX) = (↑ INDEX)
          (subject to the minimal nucleus condition ¬(→ SUBJ) (section 10.4)).
      b. An **anti-subjective, nuclear pronoun** is lexically specified
          ((GF α ↑) SUBJ INDEX) ≠ (↑ INDEX)
          (subject to the minimal nucleus condition ¬(→ SUBJ)) and
          ((GF α ↑) GF′ INDEX) = (↑ INDEX)
          (subject to the minimal nucleus condition ¬(→ SUBJ)).

c. A **subjective, nonnuclear pronoun** is lexically specified
$$((\text{GF } \alpha \uparrow) \text{ SUBJ INDEX}) = (\uparrow \text{ INDEX})$$
(subject to the finite domain condition (59)), and
$$((\text{GF } \alpha \uparrow) \text{ GF}' \text{ INDEX}) \neq (\uparrow \text{ INDEX})$$
(subject to the minimal nucleus condition $\neg(\rightarrow \text{SUBJ})$).

Our logophoric binding constraints make reference to a representation of discourse as well as the to f-structure attributes. A formalization of these constraints would take us too far afield from the focus of this book, but we can point to Stirling's (1993) elegant formalization of logophoricity within Discourse Representation Theory (DRT), using categorial unification grammar as the syntax formalism. There are, in fact, close family resemblances among the various unification formalisms for syntax, and DRT semantics for LFG has been developed by a number of researchers (such as Asher and Wada 1988, Crouch and van Genabith 1999, and references).

Notes

1   The theory presented in this and the following sections is based on unpublished work by Bresnan et al. (1983).
2   Thematic prominence of arguments in argument structure also interacts with reflexive binding, as observed for English by Jackendoff (1972) and Wilkins (1988). LFG work on the interactions of thematic prominence and binding includes Joshi (1989, 1993), Dalrymple and Zaenen (1991), Dalrymple (1993), and T. Mohanan (1994). See chapter 14.
3   This informal notation is based on the spatial analogy employed here. In the algebraic geometry of three-dimensional space, each point is assigned a triple of real-valued coordinates (x, y, z), which are interpreted as coefficients of the three axes. We are here thinking of each pronoun as assigned a triple of discrete coordinate values along the axes of subjectivity, nuclearity, and logophoricity. The spatial analogy is readily translated into our formal language of functional descriptions: 0 coefficients correspond to lack of an attribute.
4   English has also been observed to have a use of reflexive pronouns to express viewpoint (among others: Kuno 1975, 1987, Zribi-Hertz 1989), but it is much more limited than the systematic logophors found in West African languages (Clements 1975, Stirling 1993, Culy 1994).
5   The minimal nucleus condition is asymmetric for bound and free pronouns as in section 10.2.
6   This account assumes that a transformation, when its structural description is met by coreferential NPs, is triggered to replace one of them by a reflexive pronoun.
7   The account is further simplified by ignoring cases of binding into phrasal predicate complements (Maling 1982). These are discussed in chapter 12.
8   Subjunctive clauses differ, as discussed in section 11.4.
9   The word *sjálfur* 'self-NOM' appears in the accusative in (7) and is glossed as an emphatic marker. Maling (1982: 285, 286) notes that it seems to be much less syntactically governed than the Norwegian *selv*, discussed in the next section. *Sjálfur* may be used for disambiguation as well as emphasis, and though in some contexts is "almost obligatory," it is generally optional in Icelandic. See the discussion of emphatics in n. 11 and section 11.5 below.

10   The present account of the Norwegian binding system is based on Hellan (1980, 1988), Bresnan et al. (1983), and Dalrymple (1993). This account is somewhat "idealized" (Lødrup 1999a), by abstracting away from other factors that influence reflexive binding in Norwegian, such as thematic prominence (Hellan 1988, Dalrymple and Zaenen 1991, Dalrymple 1993).

11   Levinson (1991: 131) details a number of criteria by which such emphatics or intensifiers may be distinguished from reflexive pronouns: "(a) there is a contrastive, contrary-to-expectation element; (b) there is a natural negative gloss, of the sort 'and not anyone else', 'and not the more expectable persons'; (c) the intensifier often plays a role in reference, by forcing a particular co-referential interpretation of a pronoun [footnote omitted]; (d) the intensifier could often be replaced with like effect by stress; (e) issues of scope arise according to placement."

12   The complementizer *be* in these examples is a form of the verb 'say', which Clements shows retains some verbal properties.

13   Although Hyman and Comrie remark that verbal marking of logophoricity is unusual, Culy (1994: 1060) lists 32 languages having special forms to mark the logophoric domain (logophoric pronouns, addressee pronouns, or verbal morphology), out of which six use verbal morphology. Stirling (1993: 51–6) argues convincingly that the Gokana system involves true logophoricity, and not switch reference.

14   In this formulation, we use the term "antecedent" to stand for the clumsier locution "one denoted by the antecedent."

15   These ideas are formally defined by Stirling (1993: 282–304) within Discourse Representation Theory (DRT).

16   Clements (1975: 164) observes that (17a) is grammatical with the high-toned strong nonlogophoric pronoun *ye* replacing the low-toned logophoric pronoun *yè* (low tone).

17   Some Icelandic speakers do allow logophoric reference with indicative complements of some predicates such as 'know' (Maling 1984, Sigurðsson 1990). In addition, there are Norwegian dialects which also use logophoric reflexives, though lacking a distinction between indicative and subjunctive mood in the verbal morphology (Aass 1979 (cited by Maling 1984), Moshagen and Trosterud 1990).

18   Maling reports that no speakers accepted (24a) but two accepted (24b), consistent with John being the source/validator of the reported speech in (24b) but not in (24a). The latter two speakers might have a purely logophoric use of *sig*, dropping the subjective property.

19   Note that oblique case-marked subjects are a well-established feature of Modern Icelandic syntax (Andrews 1976, 1982, 1990b, Þráinsson 1976a, 1976b, 1979, Maling 1984, 1990, Zaenen et al. 1985). See also problem set 4.

20   The FOC annotation here is a characteristic of the particular construction and does not follow from the general principles of endocentricity given in chapter 6.

21   See the references in section 11.6.

22   – although that could well be the historical origin of the negative binding constraints (Faltz 1985, Levinson 1987, 1991), as discussed in the next section.

23   The lexical binding constraints have so far been informally expressed by features [±ncl], [±sbj], [±log]. Recall, however, that these features are informal abbreviations for the formal definitions within the constraint language of LFG functional structures and their semantic representation (sections 10.4 and 11.6).

24   Culy (1994: 1062) proposes a slightly different hierarchy from Stirling (1993):

speech > thought > knowledge > direct perception

25 See also the discussion in Dalrymple (1993: 150ff).

26 This example is from Bresnan et al. (1983); see Maling (1982) on predicate comple-
    ments (xcomps) in Icelandic.

27 See Arka (1998) for a very interesting example in Balinese.

28 For example, English allows multiple *wh*-questions while Italian does not.

29 Exceptions are discussed below.

30 – though interestingly, Moravcsik (1972) observes that noun root reflexive pronouns
    are often themselves used as emphatics, or "intensifiers."

31 Following Faltz's line of reasoning given above, it is a sign of grammaticalization –
    the formation of a complex reflexive – that *selv* is obligatory with *seg* in (51). In this
    respect Norwegian is unlike Old English and more like modern English, as described
    by Faltz. But the use of the *seg selv* in Norwegian, unlike Modern English *herself*, is
    not obligatory in the semantically reflexive contexts in (50). In this respect the Nor-
    wegian contrast between (50) and (51) resembles the Middle English contrast de-
    scribed by Faltz above.

32 Concerning the latter examples, Lødrup (1999a) notes that there are sentences in
    which "definite nouns denoting body parts have the syntax of ordinary nouns," such
    as generics and hyponyms used in certain discourse contexts: (*Er det en del av kroppen
    din du liker godt?*) *Jeg liker ansiktet godt* '(Is there any part of your body that you
    like well?) I like my face well.' He cautions that this effect must be excluded by
    taking these examples as the first sentence of a discourse.

33 "Externally possessed" inalienables are those in which the possessor is not part of the
    same phrase as the inalienable. Some authors use the term "external possession" to
    refer only to instances of "possessor raising" like (57b). See Lødrup (1999a: 385,
    n. 9).

34 We will make the simplifying assumption that the domain of local binding is the
    minimal nucleus containing a subject, although there are subtle issues involved in
    distinguishing optional local PP arguments from adjuncts (which would lie outside of
    the nucleus). It is unclear whether the PPs in examples like *Hun følte bak seg* 'she felt
    behind herself' are local adjuncts or local obliques. Similar examples in English occur
    with nuclear pronouns (chapter 12).

35 Lødrup's formulation is "an inalienable must be locally bound by a subject in a
    physical context," with the footnoted proviso: "In addition, inalienables must be
    allowed as nonthematic objects in secondary predications, and the possessor raising
    construction must allow object binders." We generalize by replacing the condition
    "by a subject" with "by a possessor" in view of the noted examples of nonsubject
    binding, which are restricted to possessors.

36 Lødrup shows that both inalienables and *seg* can serve as the objects of resultative
    constructions:

    i. *Hun fikk øynene undersøkt av en lege.*
        She got the-eyes examined by a doctor
        'She got her eyes examined by a doctor.'
    ii. *Hun fikk seg undersøkt av en lege.*
        She got self examined by a doctor
        'She got herself examined by a doctor.'

    These examples show both the inalienable and the local reflexive *seg* occurring in
    true object positions where they are locally bound by the subject of the minimal

nucleus. But it is not quite clear why these examples could not also perhaps be construed as extended physical contexts in which the possessor brings about something that affects her own body.

37 Comrie (1998: 338) hypothesizes that noncoreference is marked within nonlocal domains, as the "absence of 'topic-continuity'."

12   Predication Relations

As we saw in chapter 10, the coarguments of a single predicator form a domain for pronominal binding that we have designated as the *nucleus* (of predication). In this chapter we will see that there is evidence from binding patterns for a complement function called the "predicate complement" in traditional grammar and the XCOMP in LFG; it constitutes a second nucleus of predication within its clause. Subjective pronominal systems (chapter 11) also point to the existence of an f-structure subject in these predicative complements.

12.1   Predicate Complements vs. Adjuncts

Examples of predicate complements (XCOMPs) are given in (1):

(1) a.   Mary didn't sound **ashamed of herself.**
     b.   Louise struck me **as a fool.**
     c.   Jogging keeps Susan **in a bad mood.**
     d.   Linda will have your brother **working again.**

Predicate complements must be distinguished from predicative adjuncts, which are illustrated in (2):

(2) a.   Mary looked down, **ashamed of herself.**
     b.   Louise enjoyed sports, naturally, **as a Southern Californian.**
     c.   Susan arrived for lunch, **in a bad mood as usual.**
     d.   Linda found the money **walking our dog.**

There are many differences between the two types of functions. For one example, removal of the predicate complement makes the sentence incomplete or changes the primary lexical meaning:

(3) a.?? Mary didn't sound.
     b.   Louise struck me. [different in meaning from (1b)]

    c. *Jogging keeps Susan.
    d. Linda will have your brother. [different in meaning from (1d)]

This property is characteristic of complements, but not adjuncts.

    Another difference between predicate complements and adjuncts is that the word order of the complements is relatively fixed, like that of other complements in English. Placing these complements in the position immediately following the subject produces ill effects, for example:

(4) a.?*Mary, ashamed of herself, didn't sound.
    b.?*Louise, as a fool, struck me.
    c.?* Jogging, in a bad mood, keeps Susan.
    d.?*Linda, working again, will have your brother.

Contrast this reordering with that of the adjuncts:

(5) a. Mary, ashamed of herself, looked down.
    b. Louise, as a Southern Californian, enjoyed sports, naturally.
    c. Susan, in a bad mood as usual, arrived for lunch.
    d. Linda, walking our dog, found the money.

    A third characteristic of the predicate complements is that they allow extraction of their constituents more easily than the adjuncts:

(6) a. Who did Mary sound ashamed of __?
    b. What kind of person did Louise strike you as __?
    c. What will Linda have your brother working at __?
       etc.

(7) a. *Who did Mary look down, ashamed of __?
    b. *What kind of Southern Californian did Louise enjoy sports as __?
    c. Whose dog did you find the money walking __?
       etc.

Note that example (7c) is disambiguated in favor of the pragmatically strange complement reading (in which the money was walking the dog), because the adjunct reading (in which you were walking the dog when you found the money) is so disfavored.

    Still other differences could be enumerated. The predicate complements, for example, show lexically governed predication relations. Whether the complement is predicated of the subject or object in (8) depends on the verb:

(8) a. Mary struck Fred as proud of herself/*himself.
    b. Mary regards Fred as proud of himself/*herself.

Contrast the predicate adjuncts in (9):

(9) a. Mary struck Fred, proud of herself for doing so.
     b. Mary struck Fred, so proud of himself for insulting her.

Still another difference between predicate complements and adjuncts is the scope of verbal negation, as registered by negative polarity items. Examples (10a, b) show that an ordinary complement (an object) may contain a negative polarity item, while an appositive adjunct to an object may not:

(10) a. Mary didn't give Fred a picture of **anyone**.
      b. *Mary didn't see it, a picture of **anyone**.

A similar contrast appears in (11a, b):

(11) a. Mary didn't sound **at all** ashamed.
      b. *Mary didn't look down, **at all** ashamed.

Finally, each verb takes a unique predicate complement, while adjuncts may be stacked up. In (12) we have placed a negative polarity item in the outer phrase to force the predicate complement interpretation and eliminate a possible adjunct reading:

(12) a. *Mary didn't sound [ashamed of herself] [**at all** mute with anxiety].
      b. *Louise didn't strike me [as a fool] [as **at all** gullible].
      c. *Jogging doesn't keeps Susan [in a bad mood] [**at all** on edge].

In contrast to the predicate complements shown in (12), the predicative adjuncts in (13) can easily be multiplied:

(13) a. Ashamed of herself, Mary looked down, mute with anxiety.
      b. As a Southern Californian, Louise had enjoyed sports as a girl.
      c. In a bad mood as usual, Susan arrived for lunch late, visibly on edge.

All of these observations point to the fact that predicate complements are a type of complement selected by a verb. The LFG notation for this complement type is XCOMP (read: "x-comp"), also called "open complement" (Bresnan 1982b). The name XCOMP was originally used because predicate complements can be of any lexical category type X (X = V, N, A, or P), although the main verb may impose restrictions on the type:[1]

(14) a. Susan kept [out of the argument]$_{PP}$.
      b. Susan kept [quiet about it]$_{AP}$.
      c. Susan kept [eating marshmallows]$_{VP}$.
      d. *Susan kept [a grouch]$_{NP}$. ["remain" sense]

(15) Susan remained/became [a grouch]$_{NP}$.

12.2   F-Structures of XCOMPS

Predicate complements are phrasal categories XP of a type that inherently lack an internal c-structure subject: VP, AP, PP, and NP belong to the class of lexical projections LP within our X′ theory (chapter 6), while subjects are introduced in SPEC of FP or S. Hence, if we say nothing more, we will find, on examining the f-structure of an example like (14c), that the XCOMP is incomplete, lacking an f-structure subject:

(16)

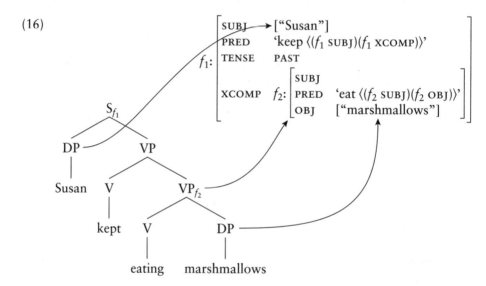

From this we see why a predicate complement is dependent on another argument of the head that can serve as its subject of predication. In the case of example (16), this argument is the SUBJ of *kept*, namely *Susan*. Although English is relatively impoverished in this respect, predicate complements in many languages have distinctive morphosyntactic properties that identify the relation as a matter of grammar, and not semantics alone. (See problem set 4 for an example.) We therefore hypothesize a **functional predication relation** (often called **functional control**), represented by identifying the SUBJ of the verb *keep* with the SUBJ of its XCOMP:

(17)

$$f_1: \begin{bmatrix} \text{SUBJ} & f_3: [\ \ ] \\ \text{PRED} & \text{`keep} \langle (f_1 \text{ SUBJ})(f_1 \text{ XCOMP}) \rangle\text{'} \\ \text{XCOMP} & f_2: \begin{bmatrix} \text{SUBJ} & f_3: [\ \ \ ] \\ \vdots \end{bmatrix} \end{bmatrix}$$

(17) represents the subject as shared by the main verb and the predicate complement: the same f-structure f_3 is the value of two different attributes, the SUBJ of f_1

and the SUBJ of f_2.[2] To emphasize that this is a relation of structure-sharing, the completely equivalent alternative representation shown in (18) is often used:

(18) f_1: $\begin{bmatrix} \text{SUBJ} & [\ ] \leftarrow \\ \text{PRED} & \text{'keep} \langle (f_1 \text{ SUBJ})(f_1 \text{ XCOMP}) \rangle \text{'} \\ \text{XCOMP} & \begin{bmatrix} \text{SUBJ} & \\ & \vdots \end{bmatrix} \end{bmatrix}$

The functional predication relation (or functional control relation) can be predicted from lexical properties of predicate complement taking verbs (Bresnan 1982b, Zaenen and Engdahl 1994), but we will simply list it as an underived lexical property for present purposes. Thus the verb *keep* will have as part of its lexical entry the equation in (19):

(19) *keep*: $(\uparrow \text{PRED}) = \text{'keep} \langle (\uparrow \text{SUBJ})(\uparrow \text{XCOMP}) \rangle \text{'}$
$(\uparrow \text{SUBJ}) = (\uparrow \text{XCOMP SUBJ})$

Observe now that in the f-structure of example (16) there are two nuclei. The definition of nucleus is repeated here from chapter 10:

(20) **Nucleus:**
Given an f-structure f, the nucleus of f is the subset of f consisting of the PRED element and all of the elements whose attributes are functions designated by the PRED.

The two nuclei of (17) are the subsets of f_1 and f_3 containing the PRED feature and its argument functions. The nucleus of f_1 is shown in (21a), and that of f_2 is shown in (21b):

(21) a. f_1: $\begin{bmatrix} \text{SUBJ} & f_3\text{: ["Susan"]} \\ \text{PRED} & \text{'keep} \langle (f_1 \text{ SUBJ})(f_1 \text{ XCOMP}) \rangle \text{'} \\ \text{XCOMP} & f_2\text{:} \begin{bmatrix} \text{SUBJ} & f_3 \\ \text{PRED} & \text{'eat} \langle (f_2 \text{ SUBJ})(f_2 \text{ OBJ}) \rangle \text{'} \\ \text{OBJ} & \text{["marshmallows"]} \end{bmatrix} \end{bmatrix}$

b. f_2: $\begin{bmatrix} \text{SUBJ} & f_3 \\ \text{PRED} & \text{'eat} \langle (f_2 \text{ SUBJ})(f_2 \text{ OBJ}) \rangle \text{'} \\ \text{OBJ} & \text{["marshmallows"]} \end{bmatrix}$

These nuclei form two domains for the binding of nuclear pronouns (chapter 10). Because there is only one NP in our example, and it has a shared function in both nuclei, the difference between the two nuclei cannot be easily detected by binding patterns. However, when we consider examples of transitive verbs taking predicate complements, the difference emerges.

Consider example (22a–d):

(22) a. Susan kept John doubting her. [possibly *her = Susan*]
      b. *Susan kept John doubting herself.
      c. Susan kept John doubting him. [*him ≠ John*]
      d. Susan kept John doubting himself.

This binding pattern is exactly what we expect from the basic binding properties of nuclear and nonnuclear pronouns of chapter 10 together with our analysis of the f-structure of predicate complements. In these transitive examples, the XCOMP is predicated of the object of *keep* (again, for present purposes we will simply stipulate this lexical property without deriving it from the transitive/intransitive alternation that *keep* undergoes):

(23) *keep*: (↑ PRED) = 'keep ⟨(↑ SUBJ)(↑ OBJ)(↑ XCOMP)⟩'
              (↑ OBJ) = (↑ XCOMP SUBJ)

This functional predication relation gives rise to the correspondences shown in (24):[3]

(24)

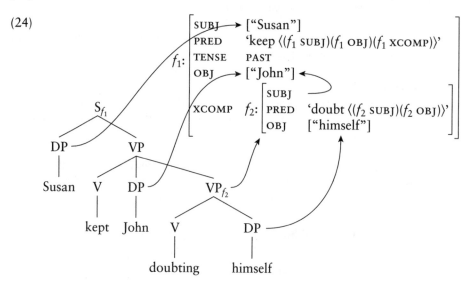

Observe that (24) has two nuclei, each having a different subject:

(25) a.
$$f_1: \begin{bmatrix} \text{SUBJ} & [\text{"Susan"}] \\ \text{PRED} & \text{'keep} \langle (f_1 \text{ SUBJ})(f_1 \text{ OBJ})(f_1 \text{ XCOMP}) \rangle \text{'} \\ \text{OBJ} & f_3: [\text{"John"}] \\ \text{XCOMP} & f_2: \begin{bmatrix} \text{SUBJ} & f_3 \\ \text{PRED} & \text{'doubt} \langle (f_2 \text{ SUBJ})(f_2 \text{ OBJ}) \rangle \text{'} \\ \text{OBJ} & [\text{"himself"}] \end{bmatrix} \end{bmatrix}$$

      b.
$$f_2: \begin{bmatrix} \text{SUBJ} & f_3 \\ \text{PRED} & \text{'doubt} \langle (f_2 \text{ SUBJ})(f_2 \text{ OBJ}) \rangle \text{'} \\ \text{OBJ} & [\text{"himself"}] \end{bmatrix}$$

This is what explains the binding patterns in (22): the pronominal object of *doubting* must be bound or free in its minimal nucleus. If it is a reflexive pronoun, as in (22b, d), it must be bound in the minimal nucleus in which it could be bound – namely, the minimal nucleus containing a potential binder. The embedded nucleus f_2 in (25b) constitutes the binding nucleus for these reflexives: the subject of this nucleus is the f-structure for *John*, and is a potential binder for a reflexive pronoun in the object function of f_2 (because it outranks the object). Hence, *himself* in (22d) is good, but *herself* in (22b) is bad: the latter does not match the only available binder *John* in gender, and *Susan*, which does match, lies outside of this binding nucleus. By the same token, the pronouns in (22a, c) must be free in their nucleus. For nonreflexive pronouns this is the minimal nucleus in which they could be free; again, this is f_2 in (25). This explains why *her* is good in (22a): it is free of the binders in the inner nucleus (namely, *John*), and so it is free to corefer with *Susan* in the outer nucleus. By the same token, *him* is bad in (22c), if it is taken as bound to *John*, because the f-structure for *John* lies in the binding nucleus of this pronoun, by the relation of functional predication (functional control).

What happens when a pronoun appears as the shared argument in a predicate complement? A shared argument has simultaneous functions in two different nuclei, and by our discussion of binding and structure sharing (section 10.4), we know that the binding constraints must be satisfied for each nucleus that the pronoun occurs in. Examples are given in (26):

(26) a. Susan kept herself doubting herself.
      b. Susan kept her doubting herself.
          [*her* ≠ *Susan*; *herself* = *her*]
      c. Susan kept herself doubting her.
          [*her* ≠ *Susan*]
      d. Susan kept her₁ doubting her₂.
          [*her₁* ≠ *Susan*; possibly *her₂* = *Susan*; *her₁* ≠ *her₂*]

Let us begin with the first example. The shared argument (the first *herself* in (26a)) belongs to both nuclei, because it is simultaneously the object of *kept* and the subject of *doubting*. The binding nucleus of a reflexive is defined to be the minimal nucleus in which it could be bound – that is, the minimal nucleus containing both it and a potential binder for it. As subject of the embedded nucleus, the shared argument has no potential binder in that nucleus; there is no outranking argument that could bind it. Hence, we must take the larger nucleus as the binding nucleus, for it does contain a potential binder (namely, the higher subject). In this larger nucleus, the shared argument in (26a) can be bound by the subject *Susan*, which outranks both it (as object) and the XCOMP containing it (as subject). As object of the matrix nucleus, the reflexive is also bound by the subject antecedent. The final *herself* in this example must be bound in its binding nucleus, which is just the embedded nucleus. That nucleus contains a potential binder, the subject, which we have just seen is bound to *Susan*. Thus the double binding of reflexives to *Susan* in (26a) follows.

In the second example, (26b), the shared argument *her* is a free pronoun. Again it belongs simultaneously to two nuclei and has two binding nuclei in which the binding principles must be satisfied. In this case the two binding nuclei do not coincide. As a subject of the embedded nucleus, the shared argument has no potential binder in that domain, and so has its binding conditions satisfied. However, as object of the matrix nucleus, it must also be free in that larger domain. Hence, it cannot be bound to the subject *Susan*. Meanwhile, the embedded reflexive must be bound in the embedded nucleus as before. The subject is the only potential binder, so *herself* must be bound by *her*, which, however, must be free of *Susan*, as we have just seen.

The explanation for the binding patterns in the remaining two examples (26c, d) is left to the reader.

We now observe that the same binding patterns occur with predicate complements of other categories than VP. The binding patterns with an AP XCOMP *aware of* are given in examples (27)–(28). They are identical to those for the VP above, and are shared by a multitide of APs (such as *afraid of, ignorant about, happy with, angry at, proud of, fond of*):

(27)   a.   Susan kept John aware of her. [possibly *her* = *Susan*]
       b.   *Susan kept John aware of herself.
       c.   Susan kept John aware of him. [*him* ≠ *John*]
       d.   Susan kept John aware of himself.

(28)   a.   Susan kept herself aware of herself.
       b.   Susan kept her aware of herself.
          [*her* ≠ *Susan*; *herself* = *her*]
       c.   Susan kept herself aware of her.
          [*her* ≠ *Susan*]
       d.   Susan kept her_1 aware of her_2.
          [her_1 ≠ *Susan*; possibly her_2 = *Susan*; her_1 ≠ her_2]

A predicative PP complement *in awe of* is shown in (29)–(30). Again, the binding patterns are identical to what we have just seen:

(29)   a.   Susan kept John in awe of her. [possibly *her* = *Susan*]
       b.   *Susan kept John in awe of herself.
       c.   Susan kept John in awe of him. [*him* ≠ *John*]
       d.   Susan kept John in awe of himself.

(30)   a.   Susan kept herself in awe of herself.
       b.   Susan kept her in awe of herself.
          [*her* ≠ *Susan*; *herself* = *her*]
       c.   Susan kept herself in awe of her.
          [*her* ≠ *Susan*]
       d.   Susan kept her_1 in awe of her_2.
          [her_1 ≠ *Susan*; possibly her_2 = *Susan*; her_1 ≠ her_2]

The same patterns hold with other PPs that predicate states of the object of *keep* such as *at odds with, in a state of awe about, in angry opposition to, in love with,* etc.

To extend our analysis uniformly to these nonverbal predicate complements, we hypothesize a lexical **predication template** which augments the lexical form for a preposition or nominal to one which has a subject of predication. We assume here that adjectives intrinsically have a subject of predication, as in (31a). The predication template gives similar lexical forms for prepositions and nouns, as illustrated in (31b, c) to the right of the ⇒:

(31) a. 'aware-of<($\uparrow$ SUBJ)($\uparrow$ OBL)>'
      b. 'in<($\uparrow$ OBJ)>' ⇒ 'be-in<($\uparrow$ SUBJ)($\uparrow$ OBJ)>'
      c. 'grouch' ⇒ 'be-a-grouch<($\uparrow$ SUBJ)>'

Exercise 1

Work out the f-structures for the examples in (27)–(30) and explain the observed binding patterns in detail.

Exercise 2

Explain the contrast between the following two examples:

(32) a. My mother$_i$ respected/admired her$_j$ cook. [possibly $i = j$]
      b. My mother$_i$ remained/became her$_j$ cook. [$i \neq j$]

In (32b) it is very easy to interpret 'her' as referring to 'my mother'. The preferred interpretation of (32a), in contrast, is that 'her' does not refer to 'my mother'. (The interpretation is possible with 'her own' substituted; please disregard that reading.)

12.3   F-Structure of PP Complements

To explain the parallel binding patterns across predicate complements of all categories, we have assumed that the lexical forms of verbal and adjectival XCOMPs have a SUBJ argument, and we have further hypothesized that prepositions (and nominals) have a predicative use in which their lexical form is augmented by a subject of predication. This hypothesis turns out to have a number of further interesting consequences.

Not all uses of prepositional phrases are predicative. First, locative PPs cannot serve as complements of many of the verbs that otherwise allow predicative complements (the "#" marks an example which is semantically anomalous):

(33)   a. #Louise seems out of town/in the house/under the old apple tree.
        b. #We consider her out of town/. . . .
        c. #A brook looks just over the hill.
        d. #We regard the brook as just over the hill.

However, when the meaning of the PP can be metaphorically extended to denote a state or quality, complementation with these verbs is possible (Maling 1983):

(34)   a.   Louise seems out of character/in a bad mood/under the weather, ...
        b.   We consider her out of it.
        c.   He looks over the hill/past his prime, ...
        d.   We regard her comments as off the wall.

This suggests that the predication template which augments the prepositional lexical form with a subject is associated with a change or metaphorical extension of semantic field. Let us informally notate it as in (35):

(35)   'in<($\uparrow$ OBJ)>' $\Rightarrow$ 'be-in-a-state-of<($\uparrow$ SUBJ)($\uparrow$ OBJ)>'

If we assume that the literal locative senses are associated with a subjectless lexical form, while the metaphorical extensions require a subject, the above contrast follows directly from our theory of the preceding section. The lexically induced functional control specification would create a subject in the f-structure of the PP, but the literal locative prepositions could not accept it as an argument, causing a violation of coherence. It follows, in other words, that literal locatives cannot function as XCOMPs.

    Second, when literal locative PPs do occur with verbs that take predicative complements, there is evidence of polysemy, because other grammatical differences correlate with the difference in meaning. Thus the transitive verb *keep* has the abstract sense of "keeping someone or something in a state or involved in a process" as well as the related sense of "keeping someone or something in a physical location." The two senses can be grammatically distinguished by locative inversion, a process which results in preposing of the PP and postposing of the subject (Bresnan 1994a):

(36)   a.   An old vase was kept on the shelf. [locational]
        b.   A young child was kept on the alert. [nonlocational]

(37)   a.   On the shelf was kept an old vase. [locational]
        b. #On the alert was kept a young child. [nonlocational]

This evidence supports the conclusion that locative PPs are not XCOMPs.[4]

    Third, there is a class of transitive locational verbs (*put, position, place, pull,* . . .) that take locative PPs but not predicative complements:

(38) a. Susan happily placed John beside the hostess.
      b. Mary pulled the shawl around her shoulders.

(39) a. #Susan happily placed John in a frenzy.
      b. #Mary pulled the shawl very attractive.

These verbs entail that their objects have the locational property specified by the PP: if Susan placed John beside the hostess, then John was beside the hostess, and if Mary pulled the shawl around her shoulders then the shawl was around her shoulders. But these entailments can be seen to follow simply from the lexical semantics of the verbs, rather than from a grammatical relation which specifies a subject of predication in the f-structure. In contrast to the XCOMP verbs, for example, most of these verbs allow the PP complement to be omitted, retaining the entailment that the object is in some (unspecified) location:

(40) a. Susan positioned John.
      b. Mary pulled the shawl.

Further, the actual entailment in many cases is not expressed by the XCOMP analysis, because it involves the intrinsic lexical semantics the of the main verb. For example, *Mary pulled the shawl into a strange shape* does not entail *the shawl was into a strange shape*, which is actually deviant, but rather that the shawl got or went into a strange shape. This additional component of meaning must be implied by the verb *pull*, because replacing that verb in the example does not preserve the entailment: #*Mary positioned the shawl into a strange shape*.

This evidence suggests that the locative PPs are not predicate complements, but oblique arguments of their verbs. The oblique arguments lack a subject of predication, as illustrated in (41):[5]

(41)

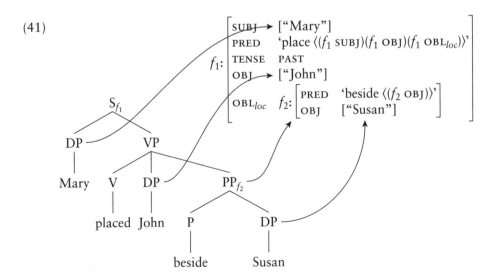

Now observe that the preposition defines its own nucleus f_2 in (41), but it is an incomplete nucleus in the sense of chapter 10, (21), in contrast to those of the predicative complements (XCOMPs) of the previous section. Our binding theory thus predicts a different set of binding patterns for these locative verb constructions; in particular, both pronoun and reflexive objects of the preposition should be able to be bound by the same antecedent:

(42) a. Mary$_i$ placed John beside herself$_i$/her$_i$ at the table.
      b. Linda$_i$ pulled her shawl around herself$_i$/her$_i$.
      c. Mary angrily peeled her clothes off of herself$_i$/her$_i$.

The pronoun is free within the minimal nucleus which contains it (the PP nucleus), and hence may be bound by 'Susan'. But the reflexive must be bound within the minimal *complete* nucleus that contains it, which in these cases is that of the entire sentence. In contrast, where the PP is an XCOMP, the PP itself defines a complete nucleus outside of which the reflexive cannot be bound:

(43) Linda$_i$ kept John doubting *herself$_i$/her$_i$.

It also follows that *keep* should have different binding patterns correlating with its selection of an OBL$_{loc}$ or an XCOMP. This prediction is borne out by (44). Here the locational sense of *keep* displays a binding pattern different from that in (43) but similar to that in (42):

(44) a. Linda$_i$ likes to keep a shawl around herself$_i$/her$_i$.
      b. The old professor$_i$ likes to keep all the younger professors after himself$_i$/him$_i$ in the academic procession.

The PP in (44b) refers to a physical position located behind the old professor. When the same preposition *after* is used metaphorically in a predicate complement construction, the pattern differs sharply:

(45) Linda$_i$ likes to keep all the men after *herself$_i$/her$_i$.

Here *after* does not refer to positional location, but means something like "in pursuit of." Similar XCOMP uses of the PP with *keep* are in (46):

(46) a. Linda$_i$ kept John in love with *herself$_i$/her$_i$.
      b. Susan$_i$ kept me in awe of *herself$_i$/her$_i$.

For these reasons, we analyze locative PPs as OBL functions, having a PRED but lacking a SUBJ.

Other prepositional phrases differ yet again in their binding patterns with transitive verbs. One example is shown in (47):

(47) Mary$_i$ gave a present to herself$_i$/*her$_i$.

This pattern is just what would be expected if the preposition were serving as a marker of an argument of the verbal PRED, similar in function to a case marker:

(48)

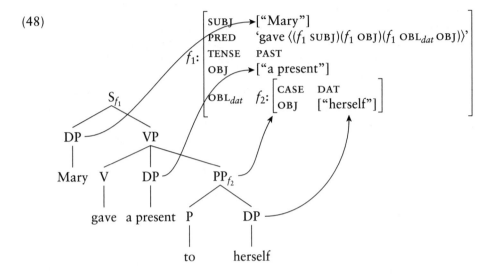

In support of this analysis we can observe that the preposition *to* is specifically selected by *give*. There is no range of prepositions from the same semantic field that can express the giving relation in these examples:[6]

(49) a. *Mary gave a present toward/up to herself.
     b. *Mary gave a present there.

   In sum, we have found three different patterns of pronominal and reflexive binding with PPs, corresponding to three distinct grammatical relations: the predicative complement (XCOMP), semantic oblique complement (OBL$_\theta$), and the grammatical oblique complement (OBL$_{case}$). The binding patterns reflect how fully elaborated the complement's functional structure is.

   A note must be added about the pattern of free variation in binding. Free variation is allowed in principle by the formal grammar, but it intersects with the inalienable binding principle discussed in section 11.5. In some circumstances the English reflexive pronoun seems to have the connotation not just that its reference is bound to that of the antecedent, but also that the referent is involved in an inherently reflexive action on its (body) parts, like the locally bound *seg* in Norwegian (Lødrup 1999a). The contrasts among the following examples can be understood in this way:

(50) a. Mary angrily pulled Bill's arms off her/?herself.
     b. Mary angrily pulled her peeling skin off ?her/herself.
     c. Mary angrily pulled her clothes off her/herself.
     d. Mary angrily pulled the spider off her/herself.

In (50a), Bill's arms are clearly not part of Mary, so the nonreflexive pronoun is slightly preferred. Using the reflexive pronoun in this example almost seems to suggest that Bill's arms have been detached from him and have somehow adhered to Mary. In (50b), in contrast, Mary's peeling skin is part of her, and the reflexive seems to be used preferentially. The nonreflexive pronoun here might suggest that Mary's skin has already become separated from her. In (50c) Mary's clothes arguably might or might not be considered part of her. But in (50d) the spider clearly cannot be considered part of Mary, and it is outside the realm of possible parts of the agent invoked in the preceding examples (arms, skin, possibly clothes); here both variants can be taken, as expected under our theory. Thus subtle semantic factors may define preferences within the grammatical domain of potential free variation, but the existence of the domain itself must still be defined in some formal way.

12.4   C-Structure of PP Complements

An assumption of the theory of this chapter is that both transitive and intransitive verbs may have predicative complements (xcomps). Let us briefly enumerate several kinds of evidence for this assumption.

First, a well-known and intensively studied class of English verbs participate in what is called the transitive alternation (B. Levin 1993) illustrated in (51):

(51)   a.   The boat sank.
       b.   They sank the boat.

(52)   a.   The baby moved.
       b.   They moved the baby.

(53)   a.   The worm turned.
       b.   They turned the worm.

(54)   a.   Corn grew.
       b.   They grew corn.

Verbs in this class have the property that the intransitive assigns the same semantic role to its subject that the transitive assigns to its object. Several of the verbs that take predicative complements belong to this class, including *turn, grow, keep, get* [American English], and *prove*:

(55)   a.   The milk turned sour.
       b.   Exposure to high temperature turned the milk sour.

(56)   a.   The bushes grew thicker.
       b.   Grow the bushes thicker (for more privacy).

(57) a. Mary kept in shape.
    b. Jogging kept Mary in shape.

(58) a. She got angry at him.
    b. That got her angry at him.

(59) a. It proved worthless.
    b. What proved it worthless was . . .

Second, transitive verbs allow the shifting of 'heavy' objects to the right margin of the VP, following other complements:

(60) a. We gave __ to Mary one picture of her mother/??one/*it.
    b. We placed __ on the table one of Susan's tartes Tatin.

In contrast, English subjects in their XP cannot shift to the right edge of their XP (as first observed by Postal 1974):

(61) a. We talked about no women who represent our point of view being on the committee.
    b.?*We talked about being on the committee no women who represent our point of view.

Observe that embedded shifting of an object is possible:[7]

(62) a. We talked about my having on the committee no women who represent our point of view.
    b. We talked about there being on the committee no women who represent our point of view.

Thus this phenomenon clearly distinguishes subject and object.

In this respect, too, the objects of transitive verbs taking XCOMPs behave like the c-structure objects of transitive verbs, not the c-structure subjects (or specifiers) or the complements:

(63) a. She considers foolish/out of the ordinary anyone who disagrees with her/??anyone/*it.
    b. I find rather charming your naive innocence/??you.
    c. He made a little too obvious his sudden displeasure/??that/*it.

To be sure, some transitive verbs that take XCOMPs resist this shifting, in a kind of "garden path" effect wherein the comprehender of the sentence is initially led to construe it as an intransitive construction rather than a transitive with shifted object (as first noted by Postal 1975 for another class of ambiguous verbs):

(64)??Jogging keeps fit anyone who does it regularly.

But this fact seems to be a general property of verbs showing the transitive alternation. Thus, (64) compares with (65), which does not involve an XCOMP at all:

(65)   a. *They sank into the ocean the boat that they had targeted.
       b.??The baby bounced over the crib the ball that we had given her.

Other word order evidence confirms the object status of the subject of predication of these verbs. For example, only a single NP or PP constituent can be clefted (in the variety of English spoken by the author). Hence the complements of ditransitive verbs (66a) or transitive-locative verbs (66b) cannot be clefted felicitously, in contrast to the complex complements of simple transitive verbs (66c):

(66)   a. *It is Mary a present that I gave.
       b. *It is food on the table that I put for you.
       c. It is no women being on the committee that we talked about.

The transitive XCOMP verbs behave like the other transitive verbs:

(67)   a. *It is Fred on edge that Linda kept.
       b. *It is Milly a coward that we considered.

Similarly (in the dialect of the author, at least), right node raising can factor out from two conjoined clauses only a single constituent:[8]

(68)   a. *Mary gave, but Louise didn't give, **Peter the grape.**
       b. Mary liked, but Louise didn't like, **Peter the Great.**

A similar contrast is provided by transitive XCOMP verbs in (69) compared with the simple transitive verbs in (70):

(69)   a. *Mary kept, but Louise didn't keep, **Peter proud of her.**
       b. *Mary proved, but you didn't prove, **me wrong.**

(70)   a. I brought up, though he didn't want to talk about, no women being on the committee.
       b. I detest, and Linda hates, ducks being eaten.

Many other facts could be summoned to corroborate our basic assumption that both transitive and intransitive verbs may take predicative complements (XCOMPs). In all of the c-structures [V NP XP] we have seen in this section, whether XP is a predicative complement (XCOMP), a semantic oblique (OBL$_\theta$), or a grammatical oblique (OBL$_{case}$), we find V and NP cohere structurally as verb and object, while NP and XP do not cohere structurally as subject and predicate. The variation in predication and binding, then, belongs to f-structure, not c-structure.

12.5 Raising

Not all of the predicators which take XCOMPs impose semantic selection on the functional controller argument. For example, the verb *strike* allows both contentful subjects (*Mary* in (71a)) and expletives (*there* in (71b)):

(71) a. Mary struck me as being very capable.
     b. There struck me as being too few women on the committee.

But *impress* contrasts in disallowing an expletive subject:

(72) a. Mary impressed me as being very capable.
     b.??There impressed me as being too few women on the committee.

This difference is represented in the lexical forms for the two verbs, as shown in (73a, b):[9]

(73) a. strike<($\uparrow$ OBL$_{exp}$)($\uparrow$ XCOMP)>($\uparrow$ SUBJ)
     b. impress<($\uparrow$ SUBJ)($\uparrow$ OBL$_{exp}$)($\uparrow$ XCOMP)>

The verb *strike* takes an athematic subject, shown outside of the angled brackets which enclose the semantically selected arguments of the lexical form. This subject is identified with the predicate complement subject, just as the subject of *impress* is. In chapter 4 we noted that all designators ($\uparrow$ GF) represented within the angled brackets ⟨ . . . ⟩ correspond to semantic roles; nonsemantic arguments, such as expletive subjects, appear outside of the angled brackets. This lexical difference is the only one that distinguishes the f-structures of examples (71b) and (72b).

The distribution of athematic subjects is regulated by completeness and coherence. Recall the completeness and coherence conditions from chapter 4. **Completeness** requires that every function designated by a PRED be present in the f-structure of that PRED. Completeness also requires a further matching between PREDs and their f-structure functions: if a designator ($\uparrow$ GF) is associated with a semantic role by the PRED, the f-structure element satisfying the designator must itself contain a semantic feature [PRED '. . .']. The expletive subject *there* lacks a PRED and therefore cannot serve as the subject of *impress*, though it can serve as the subject of *strike* without violating completeness. Conversely, **coherence** requires that every argument function in an f-structure be designated by a PRED. Furthermore, any function that has a semantic feature must match up with a designator associated with a semantic role by its PRED. Therefore the contentful subject of *seem* in (71a) must be designated as a thematic argument by another predicator, such as the XCOMP PRED (or an XCOMP's XCOMP's PRED . . .), to satisfy coherence.

Strike is called a "raising" verb, because its athematic argument functions as a selected argument of its complement (or its complement's complement . . .). If one imagines that selected arguments must be local to their selecting predicates in phrase structure, then the unselected argument must have been moved away from the local predicate that selects it, and raised up into the clause headed by *strike* by a movement transformation. In LFG, however, locality in predicate argument relations (represented by f-structure) need not match locality in phrase structure relations (represented by c-structure), because of the imperfect correspondence of the c-structure to f-structure mappings (part III).

Adjective PREDS also allow athematic subjects, as illustrated by *liable*, *likely*, and *apt* in (74a–c):

(74) a. There is liable to be another earthquake soon.
      b. There are likely to be more women on the committee.
      c. There is apt to be a snowstorm.

These would have lexical forms of the kind shown in (75):

(75) liable<($\uparrow$ XCOMP)>($\uparrow$ SUBJ)

Now it follows from this simple theory that adjectives having athematic subjects can head phrasal APs which function directly as predicate complements to main verbs. In (76a, b) the main verbs are subject raising verbs and the APs are italicized:

(76) a. There struck me as *likely to be too few women on the committee.*
      b. There seems *unlikely to be snow in March.*

In (77a–d) the main verbs have thematic subjects which are functional controllers of their adjectival complements. In all of these examples, the complements are headed by subject raising adjectives.

(77) a. Mary impresses John as *likely to win.*
      b. They felt *liable to be assaulted.*
      c. He looks *apt to lose his temper.*
      d. City-dwellers have become *more likely to be mugged* in recent years.

The fact that the main verbs have thematic subjects is shown by their resistance to expletive subjects:

(78) a.??There impressed me as being too few women on the committee.
      b.??There felt liable to be an earthquake there.
      c.??There looks apt to be snow in March.
      d.??There has become more likely to be reindeer on the roof, since they put the feeder up there.

Note that while some of the verbs taking AP XCOMPs can be paraphrased with a VP – *Mary impresses John as (being) likely to win* – others have no verbal equivalents:

(79) a. The wall will stay (*to be) yellow.
      b. She kept the wall (*being) yellow.
      c. John felt (≠ himself to be) angry.
      d. That got John (≠ to be) worried.

Feeling angry, for example, is a direct emotional experience, while feeling oneself to be angry is a judgment. Getting someone worried is not the same thing as getting some one to 'be' (perhaps to act) worried. We conclude that it is the adjectives themselves, and not a covert copula, that designate a subject.

All of this evidence reinforces our hypothesis of earlier sections that the APs themselves have subjects of predication (provided by the functional controllers determined by their matrix verbs). The presence of an f-structure subject in the AP XCOMP phrases is parallel to the presence of a subject in the f-structure of passive participial complements:

(80) a. The wall will stay painted black.
      b. John felt betrayed and made to look like a fool by Susan.

Finally, note that just as *strike* differs from *impress* in taking an athematic subject, so other verbs differ in whether they take athematic objects:

(81) a. She proved there to be infinitely many prime numbers.
      b. She proved there unlikely to be infinitely many prime numbers.
      c.??She kept there being food on the table.
      d.??She regards there as likely to be no one there.

The object raising verbs (*prove* in (81a, b)) allow an expletive object which is passed to the complement subject by functional control, while the nonraising verbs (*keep, regard*) select their objects as thematic arguments. This difference is represented in (82a, b), which is parallel to (73a, b):

(82) a. prove<($\uparrow$ SUBJ)($\uparrow$ XCOMP)>($\uparrow$ OBJ)
      b. keep<($\uparrow$ SUBJ)($\uparrow$ OBJ)($\uparrow$ XCOMP)>

Both of (82a, b) specify functional control of the XCOMP via the specification ($\uparrow$ OBJ) = ($\uparrow$ XCOMP OBJ).

Parallel to the subject raising verbs (73a) and (75), the object raising verbs may take direct AP complements headed by raising adjectives:

(83) a. A humble attitude has kept John *apt to underestimate himself*.
      b. John regards Mary as *likely to win*.

The same verbs can take passive participial complements:

(84) a. Mary regards John as already elected.
      b. Mary regards John as having been given in to too much as a child.
      c. She kept the walls painted yellow.

In sum, evidence from binding, raising, and passivization supports our theory of predicate complements as having an f-structure subject of predication identified with an argument of the higher clause.

Further Reading and Discussion

Predicate complements (xcomps) also exist in Icelandic, where the availability of subjective reflexives like *sig* and oblique case-marked subjects provide still further support for this theory of predication (Maling 1982, Andrews 1982, 1990a). Extensive work has been done on Icelandic in LFG (see Maling and Zaenen 1990 and references), which thus provides excellent material for further reading.

Notes

1 Verbs like *keep*, which have a transitive alternation, appear to disallow an NP predicate complement, in contrast to nonalternating predicate complement taking verbs.

2 Recall that f-structures allow this kind of structure sharing, unlike constituent structure trees (chapter 4).

3 Recall from chapter 6 that transitive verbs with additional complements may have a binary structure, grouping the verb and object together under V' and the additional complements under higher V's, or a ternary structure. The latter is used here for simplicity.

4 Indeed, Bresnan and Kanerva (1989) and Bresnan (1994a) argue that locatives alternate with f-structure subjects under locative inversion, but subjects are not functionally controllable.

5 See n. 3.

6 One fact not explained by this analysis, however, is the possibility of locative inversion with dative *to* phrases, as in *To Mary was given the gift of eloquence*. Possibly the PP has semantic content but shares it with the verb in such a way as to extend the nucleus. We will not be concerned with a formalization here; see Andrews and Manning (1999) and references.

7 The postverbal NP in existentials is also in an object position in English (Bresnan 1982a).

8 There are speakers who impose a weaker constraint on the "right node," and for them the contrast in constituency cannot be tested by this means.

9 The analysis of existential *there* with *be* is considered in problem set 5.

13 Anaphoric Control

In chapter 12 we examined predicative complements (XCOMPS), using participial VP complements as the paradigm case. We saw that the characteristic binding patterns of predicative VP complements extend across categories and can be explained by identifying in f-structure a complement subject with the subject or object of the matrix verb. The relation between this implicit subject and the matrix argument is called functional predication or **functional control**. In this chapter we examine a contrasting verbal construction that exhibits a different type of control, called **anaphoric control**. In English these verbal constructions are known as gerundive VPs. Anaphoric control also occurs with some infinitival constructions in English (Bresnan 1982b), but the gerundives make a very clear contrast.

13.1 Gerundive vs. Participial VPs in English

English gerundive VPs appear superficially identical to participial VPs. Constrast (1a) and (1b):

(1) a. Susan discussed **visiting Fred**.   gerundive VP
     b. Susan kept **visiting Fred**.   participial VP

Despite the formal similarity, numerous differences between the constructions exist. The gerundive VP passivizes, for example, while the participial VP does not:

(2) a. Visiting Fred was discussed by Susan.
     b. *Visiting Fred was kept by Susan.

The gerundive VP undergoes clefting (3), "tough-movement" (4), and topicalization (5), but the participial VP does not:

(3) a. It was visiting Fred that Susan discussed.
     b. *It was visiting Fred that Susan kept.

(4)   a.   Visiting Fred is unpleasant for Susan to discuss.
      b. *Visiting Fred is unpleasant for Susan to keep.

(5)   a.   Visiting Fred, Susan doesn't want to discuss.
      b. *Visiting Fred, Susan doesn't want to keep.

The pronoun *it* can be substituted for the gerundive VP, but not for the participial VP:

(6)   a.   Visiting Fred, Susan doesn't want to discuss it.
      b. *Visiting Fred, Susan doesn't want to keep it.

The gerundive VP permits a genitive subject, but the participial VP does not:

(7)   a.   Susan discussed our visiting Fred.
      b. *Susan kept our visiting Fred.

The gerundive VP can be fronted in question formation, but the participial VP cannot:

(8)   a.   Whose visiting Fred did Susan discuss?
      b. *Whose visiting Fred did Susan keep?

The gerundive VP pied pipes (that is, the entire phrase can be fronted when it contains a relative pronoun) in a nonrestrictive relative clause, but the participial VP does not:

(9)   a.   Fred, visiting whom Susan discussed with her lawyer, is in the custody
           of his father.
      b. *Fred, visiting whom Susan kept with her lawyer, is in the custody of
           his father.

The gerundive VP undergoes pseudo-clefting without *doing*, but the participial VP does not:

(10) a.   What Susan discussed was visiting Fred.
      b. *What Susan kept was visiting Fred.
        cf.What Susan discussed/kept doing was visiting Fred.

The gerundive VP is immune to the '*-ing -ing*' constraint, but the participial phrase is not:

(11) a.   Susan is discussing visiting Fred.
      b. *Susan is keeping visiting Fred.

These contrasts uniformly point to a single difference between participial and gerundive VPs: the latter behave like nominal phrases. As we saw in chapter 2, only nominal phrases (NPs and DPs) can bear the SUBJ and OBJ functions, while chapter 12 analyzes participial phrase complements as XCOMP VPs. Since passivization involves the alternation of SUBJ and OBJ functions in English, the nominal nature of gerundives would immediately explain why they contrast with participials in passivization (1). Similarly, in standard American English, clefting applies to subjects and objects, but not to predicates or predicative complements:

(12) a. %It is proud that he is/seems.
      b. %It is a fool that he is/seems.
      c. It is a proud man that you see before you.
      d. It is a real fool that you see before you.

Hence, the phrasal VP XCOMPs will not undergo clefting, while the nominal gerundive VPs will, by virtue of their being able to bear subject and object functions. This explains (3). Likewise, "tough movement" involves a complement object position gap; predicative NPs (XCOMPs) do not permit it:

(13) a. *A fool is unpleasant for Susan to be/seem.
      b. A fool is unpleasant for Susan to meet.

The pronoun *it* can be substituted for an NP subject or object, but not for a VP XCOMP. This accounts for (6). Further, the optional presence of a genitive specifier is typical of NPs in English:

(14) Susan discussed our picture of Fred.

In this respect, too, the gerundive has nominal properties that the participial would not be expected to show, explaining (7). This property also entails the difference in question formation (8).

Though we will not examine them in detail, the remaining properties reinforce the conclusion that gerundive and participial VPs have differing nominal and verbal functions (as "arguments" and "predicates").

13.2 Structure of Gerundive VPs

Our explanation of the differences just observed between gerundive and participial VPs in English is (i) that only nominal categories can bear subject and object functions (chapter 2), and (ii) that gerundive VPs are dominated by a nominal category, NP or DP, while participial VPs are not. Point (ii) raises the question of exactly what the structure of gerundive VPs is. We have concluded that participials and gerundive VPs differ as in (15a, b), respectively.[1] What exactly is in the triangle in the gerundive example? How does the VP *visiting Fred* become a nominal phrase DP or NP?

(15) a.

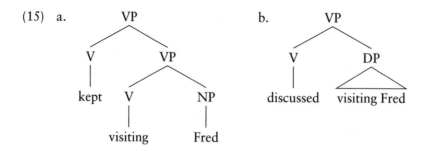

The first hypothesis one might consider is that the nominal character of the gerundive VP arises directly from its morphological form, which is that of a nominalized verb. This nominalized verb then heads a nominal phrase, so that the structure of the gerundive VP is as shown in (16):

(16)

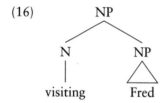

This analysis explains the nominal character of gerundive VPs, but it fails to account for their *verbal* character.

English does in fact have gerundive nominal constructions with the properties expected from (16):

(17)

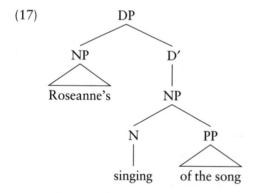

These take adjectival modifiers, prefixal negation in (*non-*), and nominal complementation (PPs, not DPs/NPs), as shown in (18a), all in contrast to the gerundive VPs, as shown in (18b):

(18) a. Roseanne's clownish non-singing of the national anthem.
      b. Roseanne's clownishly not singing the national anthem.

The structure of (18a) is shown in (19):

(19)

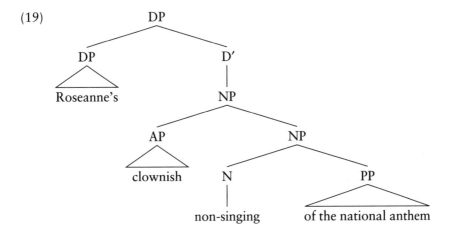

The structure of (18b) is reflected in (20):

(20)

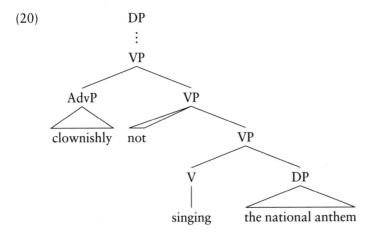

Thus (16) seems appropriate for gerundive nominals of the kind illustrated in (18a), but fails to capture the VP properties of the gerundive VP construction (18b). Even if we allowed the gerund N to take VP-type complements, we would incorrectly predict the presence of prenominal AP modifiers and nominal negative prefixation cooccurring with the VP properties of (18b):

(21) *Roseanne's clownish non-singing the national anthem.

Although the structure of (16) is inadequate for gerundive VPs for the reasons given, a slight modification of it solves our problems. We need only replace the NP in (19) by a VP. Our combinatorial constraint on functional heads (section 6.2.1, (20)) allows for VP to be embedded as a complement of DP:

(22)

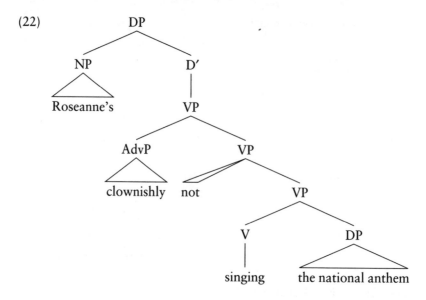

This analysis of the structure of the gerundive VP places the genitive NP in the position of the specifier of DP, rather than that of subject of S or IP. In other words, it exploits the direct structural analogy between (23) and (24):

(23)

(24)

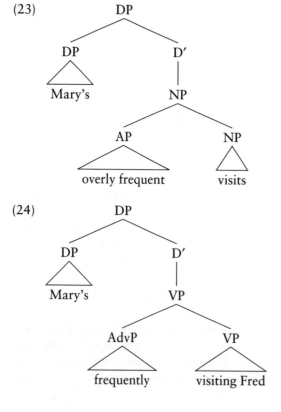

The genitive marking of the gerundive VP subject is an obvious clue to its status as possessor. In fact, there is also interesting evidence from quantifier scope that the genitive NP has the scope properties of possessive NPs of nouns, and not of specially case-marked subjects of embedded Ss. Observe the contrast in (25) (adapted from Zucchi 1993: 50):

(25) a. John resents everyone's taking a day off.
      b. John resents that everyone takes a day off.
      c. John dislikes (it) for everyone to take a day off.

The quantifier phrase in (25a) may have wide scope, exactly as in (26):

(26) John resents everyone's absence.

Both (25a) and (26) are ambiguous: John may resent only the universal absence of other employees, leaving him stuck with all the work (the narrow scope reading); or for each absent employee, John may resent that person's individual absence (the wide scope reading). But (25b, c) are unambiguous, having only the narrow scope reading, or at least a very strong preference for it.

Furthermore, while certain expletive pronouns can be subjects, they cannot be possessors:

(27) a. There appears to be a reindeer on the roof.
      b. *There's appearing to be a reindeer on the roof is an illusion.

(28) a. It appears that there's a reindeer on the roof.
      b.??Its appearing that there's a reindeer on the roof is an illusion.

This is further evidence that the genitive subject of the gerundive verb is like a possessor.

Now let us consider the f-structure of the possessor. The lexical forms of nouns, illustrated by *horse* in (29a), may have their argument structures augmented to take the possessor (POSS) function as an argument by a lexical **predication template** which augments the lexical form for a nominal to one which has a possessor. (Compare the predication template for predicative NPs and PPs in section 12.2.) The result is illustrated in (29b):

(29) a. *horse*: N, ($\uparrow$ PRED) = 'horse< >'
      b. 'horse< >' $\Rightarrow$ 'horse-of<($\uparrow$ POSS)>'

The f-structure of an expression such as *Mary's horse* in English will thus look like (30):

(30) f: $\begin{bmatrix} \text{PRED} & \text{'horse-of<}(f\,\text{POSS})\text{>'} \\ \text{POSS} & g: [\text{PRED} \quad \text{'NAMED-}Mary\text{']} \end{bmatrix}$

The same predication template applies to nominal gerunds of the kinds shown in (17):

(31)   a.   *singing*: N, ($\uparrow$ PRED) = 'singing<($\uparrow$ OBL$_{of}$)>'
      b.   'singing<($\uparrow$ OBL$_{of}$)>' $\Rightarrow$ 'singing-of<($\uparrow$ POSS)($\uparrow$ OBL$_{of}$)>'

As we have noted in previous chapters, the function POSS is restricted to the f-structures of nominal categories.[2] How can this restriction between structure and function be captured? Formally, it is a simple matter to constrain the inverse image of the mapping ϕ from c-structure to f-structure to contain a nominal category label such as NP or DP (which we denote by n) when the f-structure immediately contains the POSS function:

(32) $n \; \varepsilon \; \lambda(\phi^{-1}(\text{POSS} \uparrow))$

The function λ is the labelling function that associates category labels with c-structure nodes (Kaplan 1995). By (32) the POSS function must occur in a nominal f-structure.[3] It is also possible to type PRED attributes in this way, so that the gerundive verb *singing* shares the categorization of the verb *sing* but must still occur in a nominal (DP or NP) f-structure as in (22):

(33)   V (gerundive) $\Rightarrow n \; \varepsilon \; \lambda(\phi^{-1}(\text{PRED} \uparrow))$

Now though contained in a higher DP, verbal gerunds of the kind illustrated in (22) and (24) are verbs and therefore not subject to the general lexical POSS template for nominals:

(34)   *singing*: V (gerundive),
      ($\uparrow$ PRED) = 'singing<($\uparrow$ SUBJ)($\uparrow$ OBJ)>'

As it stands, then, the structures in (22) and (24) will be incomplete and incoherent: incomplete because the verbal lexical form requires a subject, and incoherent because the DP provides a POSS function which is not designated by any predicator.

Among several possible solutions to this problem, one is particularly straightforward. We can view the DP possessor being identified with the verbal subject by a lexical rule which identifies the gerundive verb SUBJ function with POSS:

(35)   **Possessor Subject of Gerundive Verbs:**
      V (gerundive) $\Rightarrow$ ($\uparrow$ POSS) = ($\uparrow$ SUBJ)

The application of this rule to (34) will produce (36):

(36)   *singing*: V,
      ($\uparrow$ PRED) = 'singing<($\uparrow$ SUBJ)($\uparrow$ OBJ)>'
      ($\uparrow$ POSS) = ($\uparrow$ SUBJ)

By virtue of (35) the f-structures of gerundive VP structures like (22) and (24) will be complete and coherent. The latter's f-structure is illustrated in (37):

(37)

$$f: \begin{bmatrix} \text{POSS} & [\text{``Mary''}] \longleftarrow \\ \text{SUBJ} & \overline{\phantom{aaaaaaaaaaa}} \\ \text{PRED} & \text{`visiting}<(f\ \text{SUBJ})(f\ \text{OBJ})>\text{'} \\ \text{OBJ} & [\text{``Fred''}] \\ \text{ADJ} & [\text{``frequently''}] \end{bmatrix}$$

In effect, the POSS is analyzed like a functional controller of the gerundive verb's subject. This analysis ensures the completeness and coherence of the gerundive VP structure (22).

What happens when the optional possessive NP is omitted from the DP? It is a property of all nonfinite verbs in English to allow a null pronominal subject (Bresnan 1982b). This property is a special case of a general crosslinguistic property by which null pronominals are provided as a lexical default to core arguments of verbal argument structures (K. P. Mohanan 1981, Bresnan 1982b, Simpson 1983a, 1991, Hale 1983, Austin and Bresnan 1996):

(38) **Null Subjects:**
 (V (nonfinite) ⇒ (↑ SUBJ PRED) = 'PRO')

As indicated in (38), the provision of a null subject pronominal to nonfinite verbs is optional. When it is taken by a gerundive verb, both the SUBJ function and the POSS function with which it is identified will be lexically (not syntactically) specified:

(39)

$$f: \begin{bmatrix} \text{POSS} \\ \text{SUBJ} \longrightarrow [\text{PRED} \quad \text{`PRO'}] \\ \text{PRED} & \text{`visiting}<(f\ \text{SUBJ})(f\ \text{OBJ})>\text{'} \\ \text{OBJ} & [\text{``Fred''}] \\ \text{ADJ} & [\text{``frequently''}] \end{bmatrix}$$

Consequently, the specifier of DP position cannot be filled in the c-structure without violating functional uniqueness. Because of the optionality of all syntactic nodes (by the principle of economy of expression, chapter 6), the result will be the structure given in (40):

(40)

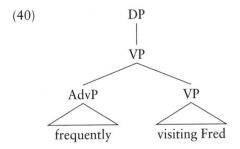

Finally, gerundive verbs may also appear with accusative subjects rather than genitives:

(41) a. I disapprove of children being exploited.
      b. They don't talk about him hanging around all the time.

These would arise from embedding S under DP:

(42)

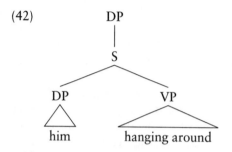

The accusative case subject is a lexical alternative to the provision of the possessive subject through (35):

(43) **Subject of Gerundive Verbs:**
      V (gerundive) $\Rightarrow$ ($\uparrow$ POSS) = ($\uparrow$ SUBJ)
                          $\bigvee$ ($\uparrow$ SUBJ CASE) = ACC

(Other languages make other choices for nonfinite subject case; see Andrews 1982, 1990b, Neidle 1988, Simpson 1983a, 1991.) The requirement of an accusative case subject would preclude the specifier of DP option from being taken (it would be incoherent and inconsistent in its case value, possessors being genitive). The presence of the topmost DP in (42) is still guaranteed by (33) on gerundive verbs.

This analysis also explains the contrasts in (44) and (45):

(44) a. *There's appearing to be a reindeer on the roof is an illusion.
      b. There appearing to be a reindeer on the roof is an illusion.

(45) a.?? I'm worried about its appearing that there's a reindeer on the roof.
      b. I'm worried about it appearing that there's a reindeer on the roof.

These expletive pronouns, as we saw above, cannot be possessors, but they can be subjects in the structure in (42).

Other pronominal subjects of gerundive VPs – both null and overt – do allow subject raising (section 12.5), as expected under the present analysis:

(46) a. Susan discussed seeming to be targetted by the IRS.
      b. Susan discussed her seeming to be targetted by the IRS.

This concludes our discussion of the structure of gerundive VPs.

13.3 Anaphoric Control vs. Functional Control

Let us return to our initial pair of contrasting examples, repeated here:

(47) a.   Susan discussed **visiting Fred.**   gerundive VP
       b.   Susan kept **visiting Fred.**   participial VP

We now see that these contrast in both c-structure and f-structure. As in chapter 12, the participial VP example (47b) is represented by the c-structure/f-structure pair of (48):

(48)

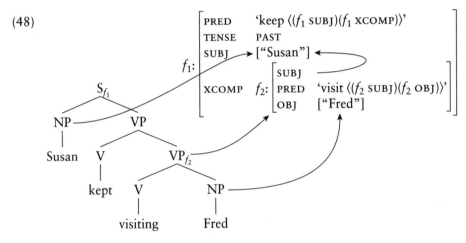

The gerundive VP example (47a) is represented as in (49):

(49)

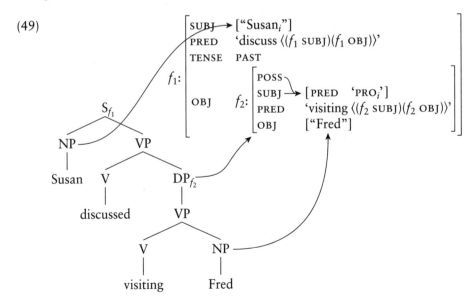

Functional control (48) identifies the f-structures of the controller and the controlled, while anaphoric control is like pronominal binding: only the referential index of the controller and controlled are identified. Thus, f-structure attributes like CASE are expected to be shared in functional control, but not anaphoric control. The Icelandic problem of problem set 4 contains an excellent illustration of this important point, due to Andrews (1982, 1990b).

Other consequences ensue from the close relation between anaphoric control and the binding of personal pronouns (Bresnan 1982b). For example, anaphoric control can have split antecedents, as in (50):

(50)   Mary$_i$ spent hours plotting with John$_j$ about strategies for getting
       (themselves$_{i,j}$) out of the country.

This is impossible with functional control, because it would violate functional uniqueness. Anaphoric control may have a grammatically remote controller, buried within the relative clause deeply below the gerund as in (51):

(51)   Visiting Fred in jail became the kind of activity that it was obvious Martha
       could enjoy without damaging her sense of self-sacrifice.

Again, this is impossible with functional control, where an XCOMP is predicated of a subject or object of its governing head. Anaphoric control may lack a syntactic controller altogether, taking a specific discourse antecedent as in (52):

(52)   Mary and John spent hours plotting their escape. Getting (themselves) out
       of the country could solve everything.

Again, this is impossible with functional control.

Anaphoric control resembles familiar pronominal binding in that it activates the anti-binding principle (section 10.3, (39)):

(53)   a.   Visiting Sally's farm disturbed her.
            (her ≠ Sally if her = the visitor)
       b.   Visiting Sally's farm disturbed her friends.
            (possibly her = Sally)

However, the null pronominal does differ from personal pronouns. For one thing, it is subject to constraints on its controller that differ from the ordinary coreference relations of personal pronouns. One is the **intervention constraint**. In (54a, b) the pronoun *his* may corefer with *Dad*, regardless of their relative position:

(54)   a.   Dad didn't want Mom to worry about his losing his hair.
       b.   It's his losing his hair that Dad didn't want Mom to worry about.

In contrast, the null pronominal in (55a, b) shows different control possibilities in the same two positions, for many speakers:

(55) a. Dad didn't want Mom to worry about losing his hair. (Mom's losing his hair)

b. It's losing his hair that Dad didn't want Mom to worry about. (Mom's or Dad's losing his hair)

Despite the pragmatic unlikeliness of Mom's losing Dad's hair, this is a preferred reading of (55a) for many, while (55b) has both that reading and the one in which Dad is losing his hair. In (55a) *Mom* intervenes between the gerundive phrase and *Dad*, preventing anaphoric control by the latter.

What accounts for the odd interpretations in (55a, b)? Roughly speaking, the null pronominal is controlled by the closest eligible antecedent: in (55a) this is *Mom*, and in (55b) this is *Mom* or *Dad*. Having two antecedents count as "closest" is not at all paradoxical within the f-structure, because *losing his hair* has two functions in (55b): it is simultaneously the FOCUS of the main clause (and entire sentence) and the OBJECT of the embedded complement's preposition. This point is illustrated in the (simplified) f-structure of (56):

(56)
$$\begin{bmatrix} \text{FOC} & \begin{bmatrix} \text{SUBJ} & [\text{PRED} & \text{'PRO'}] \\ \text{PRED} & \text{"losing his hair"} \end{bmatrix} \\ \text{SUBJ} & [\text{"Dad"}] \\ \text{PRED} & \text{"want"} \\ \dots & \begin{bmatrix} \text{SUBJ} & [\text{"Mom"}] \\ \text{PRED} & \text{"worry-about"} \\ \text{OBL}_\theta & [\text{OBJ} \quad \dashv] \end{bmatrix} \end{bmatrix}$$

From the point of view of the null pronominal subject of the gerund (the [PRED 'PRO'] in (56)), there are two equally accessible subject controllers, one in each of the predicative f-structures that immediately contains it.

Now let us embed the gerundive complement within a predicative complement (XCOMP), as in (57):

(57) Dad didn't want Mom to become worried about losing his hair. (Mom's losing his hair)

The f-structure contains an extra layer of embedding, as illustrated in (58):

(58)
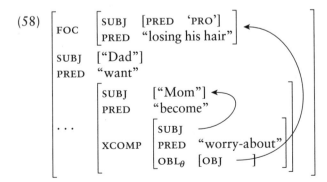

$$\begin{bmatrix} \text{FOC} & \begin{bmatrix} \text{SUBJ} & [\text{PRED} & \text{'pro'}] \\ \text{PRED} & \text{"losing his hair"} \end{bmatrix} \\ \text{SUBJ} & [\text{"Dad"}] \\ \text{PRED} & \text{"want"} \\ \dots & \begin{bmatrix} \text{SUBJ} & [\text{"Mom"}] \\ \text{PRED} & \text{"become"} \\ \text{XCOMP} & \begin{bmatrix} \text{SUBJ} \\ \text{PRED} & \text{"worry-about"} \\ \text{OBL}_\theta & [\text{OBJ} \quad \dashv] \end{bmatrix} \end{bmatrix} \end{bmatrix}$$

If we were to make the XCOMP containing the gerundive phrase be the FOC of the main clause, rather than the gerundive phrase by itself, the closest eligible antecedent would only be *Mom*:

(59)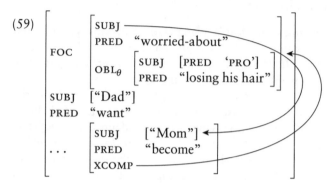

The reason is that the functional control relation fixes the subject of the predicate complement, regardless of its position. The XCOMP's subject of predication is a syntactic property of the complement structure itself, and not a matter of interpretation like the anaphoric controller.

As we have already observed in section 13.1, XCOMPs do not undergo clefting, but we can still exemplify (59) by using the question construction to focus the predicate complement. (60) unambiguously fixes the subject of *losing his hair* to be *Mom*:

(60)   How worried about losing his hair did Dad expect Mom to be?

Thus the differing effects of the intervention constraint constitute a subtle but interesting further contrast between functional and anaphoric control.

In conclusion, we have seen that the superficially similar participles and gerundive VP complements have quite different c-structures and f-structures, one exhibiting functional control and the other anaphoric control. It turns out that infinitival complements are structurally ambiguous in a similar way (Bresnan 1982b). Some infinitival complements are CPs that can take null pronominal subjects when a *for* complementizer is absent. These complements are anaphorically controlled, and show additional interesting properties such as subject–subject obviation (Bresnan 1982b, Simpson and Bresnan 1983, Zec 1987). Other infinitival complements are VP XCOMPs subject to functional control. This includes the class of raising verb complements (section 12.5).

The reader is now prepared to undertake problem set 4.

Further Reading and Discussion

For more detailed discussions of the differences between functional and anaphoric control, the following are recommended readings: Bresnan (1982b), Zec (1987), Andrews (1990b), Kroeger (1993).

For other works discussing control in LFG see K. P. Mohanan (1983), Neidle (1988), Hong (1990), Zaenen and Engdahl (1994), Arka and Simpson (1998), and references.

Gerundive VPs show mixed nominal and verbal properties, as we have seen in sections 13.1 and 13.2. For more on the syntax of mixed categories across a variety of languages in LFG, see Bresnan (1997b), Bresnan and Mugane (1999), and references.

The discovery of the intervention constraint is due to Grinder (1970, 1971). See Jacobson and Neubauer (1976), Soames and Perlmutter (1979), and references for early analysis in terms of the cyclic application of transformations. The analysis at the end of section 13.3 of the interactions of control and extractions in terms of structure sharing vs. anaphoric control was first presented by the author in class lectures at MIT and public lectures at Stanford in 1980 and subsequent years. Similar phenomena have been analyzed as "reconstruction effects" in Logical Form within later transformational frameworks by C.-T. James Huang (1993) and Heycock (1995). Asudeh (1998) discusses similar phenomena within HPSG.

Notes

1   We are assuming the "flexible" definition of endocentricity and principle of economy of expression of section 6.4, which serve to prune away nonbranching X′ nodes and X′ daughters of nonbranching nodes. We also assume the definition of endocentricity from section 7.2, which is restricted to lexical projections.

2   The POSS function in nominals is discussed in LFG by Rappaport (1983), Saiki (1987), Laczkó (1995), Markantonatou (1995).

3   Constraint (32) should properly be viewed as part of a more general theory relating f-structure attribute types to c-structure categories. Similar constraints relating f-structure attributes to c-structure category are proposed by Nordlinger (1998b) and Sells (1999a).

14 From Argument Structure to Functional Structure

We have now seen how functional structures allow a form-independent characterization of binding, predication, and control without the "configurational bias" which favors syntactic over morphological forms of expression. The question we come to at last is, Where do functional structures themselves come from? The answer lies in the lexical mapping theory, which projects skeletal f-structures from argument structures (a-structures) by general principles.

We can illustrate this basic idea in terms of the contrast between English and Warlpiri given in chapter 1. (1) represents informally the correspondences between a-structure, f-structure, and c-structure in a simple English sentence.

(1)   English:

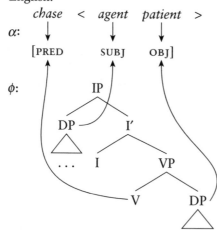

In (1) α designates the mapping from a-structure to f-structure functions, while ϕ designates the mapping from c-structure to f-structure. The latter follows from the principles discussed in chapter 6; the former follows from the theory of a-structure to f-structure mapping, also known as the 'lexical mapping theory' (LMT), described in this chapter.

(2) shows the equivalent mappings in a simple Warlpiri sentence corresponding to the English sentence. Any order of the constituents is possible, with the

exception of the fixed position of the Auxiliary (or 'I' constituent), as discussed in chapters 1, 6, and 7. Though the ϕ mapping from c-structure NPs to f-structure is lexocentric in Warlpiri and endocentric in English, the α mapping from a-structure to f-structure functions is the same for the two languages.

(2) Warlpiri:

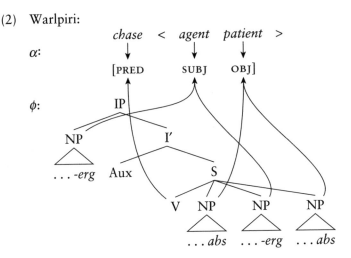

Thus, in both configurational English and nonconfigurational Warlpiri, argument structures project similar skeletal functional structures, which are mapped to the very different overt forms of expression in the two languages by the principles of chapter 6.

The same point can be made with the contrast between English and a head-marking language like Chicheŵa discussed in chapter 8. In English, as illustrated by (3), the semantic roles of the a-structure of the verb 'see' (abbreviated *exp* for experiencer and *th* for theme) map onto the f-structure functions SUBJ and OBJ, respectively.

(3) English:

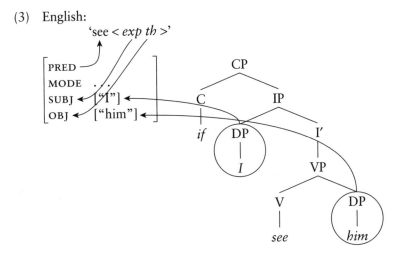

The same mapping from a-structure to f-structure functions occurs in Chichŵa, despite the very different morphological realization of subject and object as verb stem prefixes in c-structure:

(4)   Chicheŵa:

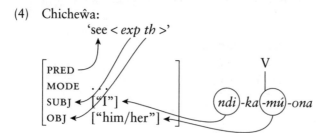

    Not all languages have the same mappings from a-structure roles to grammatical functions, of course. Nevertheless, there are important limits to the variation across languages; not every function can be associated with every type of semantic role. Constraints on argument realization (the mapping from a-structure roles to functions) are imposed by the theory of argument structure.

14.1   What is Argument Structure?

There are varying conceptions of what argument structure is, even among researchers working within LFG. The reason for this is that argument structure has two faces, semantic and syntactic. On the semantic side, argument structure represents the core participants in events (states, processes) designated by a single predicator. From this point of view it appears as a type of representation of event structure. On the syntactic side, argument structure represents the minimal information needed to characterize the syntactic dependents of an argument-taking head. From this point of view it appears as a type of syntactic subcategorization or valence register. Thus argument structure is an interface between the semantics and syntax of predicators (which we may take to be verbs in the general case):[1]

(5)   lexical semantics
              ↓
         a-structure
              ↓
      syntactic structure

Argument structure encodes lexical information about the number of arguments, their syntactic type, and their hierarchical organization necessary for the mapping to syntactic structure. It is therefore fundamentally a lexical syntactic construct, not a semantic one (Bresnan and Zaenen 1990, Zaenen and Engdahl 1994, T. Mohanan 1994, 1997).

The conception of argument structure as a lexical syntactic construct is common to many lexicalist theories of syntax, though there are differences in representation. Some researchers within LFG have adopted a Jackendovian perspective on argument structure (e.g. Butt 1995, 1997, Broadwell 1998, and references), using an elaborated Lexical Conceptual Structure indexed to syntactic realization at f-structure. Though Jackendoff (1990) suggests that a separate level of argument structure is unnecessary, given a level of lexical semantics, his lexical semantic representations contain syntactic information about the indexing of semantic roles to syntactic structure which makes them a variant of argument structure in the sense adopted here (Butt 1995).

Another influential conception of argument structure is that of Rappaport Hovav and Levin (1998a, b). The conception of a-structure adopted here differs from that of Rappaport Hovav and Levin in the specific model of argument structure adopted, and its role within the larger framework, but is strikingly similar in general conception. The fundamental difference is that Rappaport Hovav and Levin interpret the 'syntactic structure' in (5) as an underlying syntactic tree prior to movement. Within the framework of LFG , this structure is redundant.[2]

To appreciate this point, consider the well-known model of a-structure proposed by Levin and Rappaport (1986, 1995) and Rappaport Hovav and Levin (1998a, b). (6) shows their argument structure for the verb *put*.

(6) $x<\underline{y}, P_{loc}\ z>$

The three arguments x, y, and z in this representation are classified according to their syntactic type and their hierarchical structure in syntax. The lower case variables x, y, and z represent nominal arguments (NPs/DPs). The variable P represents a locative preposition. x, outside the angled brackets, is the external argument; y and z are internal arguments; y, the underscored argument, is the direct internal argument (which must be a sister of the verb for reasons internal to their theoretical framework), while z is simply an internal argument embedded in a prepositional phrase. As (7) shows, the correspondence between this representation and the underlying X' tree projected by the verb is one-to-one (omitting the verb, as (6) does):

(7)

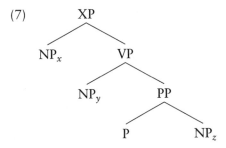

Rappaport Hovav and Levin themselves characterize the syntactic projection relation between the argument structure and the initial syntactic structure as "trivial", although they do not draw the obvious conclusion that one of the two structures is redundant. But consider the interface model they assume, the familiar scheme in (8):

(8)

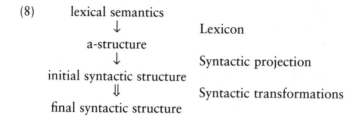

The triviality of the relation between argument structure and a level of initial syntactic structure invites an alternative, which has been taken in much recent work. This is to eliminate a distinct level of lexical argument structure altogether in favor of the syntactic construction of meanings from lexical semantic primitives (e.g. Hale and Keyser 1997). This alternative is schematized in (9):

(9)

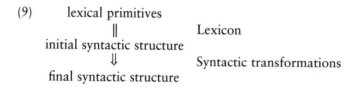

Here, argument structure is in effect identified with an initial syntactic structure in a transformational derivation. It is a syntactic representation, as in Rappaport Hovav and Levin, but no longer lexical in the same sense, being formed from syntactic categories and relations. Indeed, echoing a line of argument from early work in generative semantics, Hale and Keyser contend that the generalizations about possible meanings of verbs reflect syntactic constraints on movement.[3] Thus this approach denies the *lexicality* of argument structure by identifying it with the initial syntactic structure.

From the beginning LFG has taken just the opposite position: the decision to reject (8) on grounds of redundancy is correct, but what is redundant is not the argument structure; it is the initial syntactic structure that should be eliminated. In other words, the role of underlying syntactic trees in the linkage of lexical semantics to syntax should be eliminated. Thus LFG adopts (10) over (8) and (9):

(10)

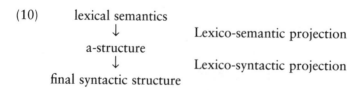

To see that (10) is the scheme that underlies the design of LFG (as of other lexicalist syntactic frameworks), simply take the final syntactic structure in (10) to be the f-structure, which is an abstraction over typologically varying c-structures representing overt forms of expression. The argument structure is directly mapped onto this level. We see, then, that a-structures in LFG must have sufficient syntactic information to support the direct mapping to surface functions. They are lexical *syntactic* constructs.

14.2   The Theory of A-Structures

An a-structure consists of a predicator with its argument roles, an ordering that represents the relative prominence of the roles, and a syntactic classification of each role indicated by a feature. Examples are given in (11)–(13):

(11)   *put*   < x y z >
$\quad\quad\quad\quad$ [$-o$]   [$-r$]   [$-o$]

(12)   *pound*   < x y >
$\quad\quad\quad\quad\quad$ [$-o$]   [$-r$]

(13)   *freeze*   < x >
$\quad\quad\quad\quad\quad$ [$-r$]

The relative prominence of the roles is indicated by their left-to-right order and reflects a thematic hierarchy:[4]

(14)   **Thematic Hierarchy:**
$\quad$ *agent > beneficiary > experiencer/goal > instrument > patient/theme*
$\quad$ *> locative*

In this hierarchy the most prominent role of *put* and *pound* (an agent in the lexical semantics) is the leftmost (x) argument of (11) and (12); in their lexical semantics the patient role of *pound* and theme role of *put* correspond to the y argument, ordered to the right of x in (12); and the location role of *put* is the least prominent on the hierarchy, represented by z in the a-structure of (11). The most prominent role of *freeze* (a theme in its lexical semantics) is its sole argument in (13). The most prominent semantic role of a predicator is designated $\hat{\theta}$:

(15)   **Logical Subject, $\hat{\theta}$:**
$\quad$ $\hat{\theta}$ designates the most prominent semantic role of a predicator.

Although the x arguments of (11)–(13) are the most prominent roles in the respective argument structures, there are important syntactic differences among them. These are captured by the syntactic features of the a-structure.

Recall that section 6.1.2 distinguishes argument from non-argument functions and grammaticalized discourse functions from non-discourse functions, as in (16) and (17), respectively. (There COMPL includes both XCOMP and COMP functions.) XCOMP is the predicate complement function discussed in chapter 12, while COMP is the "closed complement" function for nonnominal sentential complements (chapter 2):

$$\text{(16)} \quad \underbrace{\underbrace{\text{TOP} \quad \text{FOC}}_{non\text{-}a\text{-}fns} \quad \text{SUBJ} \quad \text{OBJ} \quad \text{OBJ}_\theta \quad \text{OBL}_\theta \quad \text{XCOMP, COMP}}_{a\text{-}fns} \quad \underbrace{\text{ADJUNCT}}_{non\text{-}a\text{-}fns}$$

$$\text{(17)} \quad \underbrace{\text{TOP} \quad \text{FOC} \quad \text{SUBJ}}_{d\text{-}fns} \quad \underbrace{\text{OBJ} \quad \text{OBJ}_\theta \quad \text{OBL}_\theta \quad \text{XCOMP, COMP} \quad \text{ADJUNCT}}_{non\text{-}d\text{-}fns}$$

The **subject**, according to this classification, has the unique property of being both an argument function and a grammaticalized discourse function, while the class of **complement functions** (OBJ, OBJ$_\theta$, OBL$_\theta$, XCOMP, COMP) can be defined as the nondiscourse argument functions. But further fine-grained distinctions among argument functions are left in chapter 6 to lexical selection for additional features. This is the topic we turn to now.

The a-structure features [±o] and [±r] constrain the way in which the roles are mapped onto argument functions in f-structures. The basic argument functions are grouped into natural classes as shown in (18):[5]

(18)   **Feature Decomposition of Argument Functions:**

	$-r$	$+r$
$-o$	SUBJ	OBL$_\theta$
$+o$	OBJ	OBJ$_\theta$

[±r] – *(un)restricted*
[±o] – *(non)objective*

The feature [−r] refers to an *unrestricted* syntactic function, the kind of function which is not restricted as to its semantic role in the sense that it need not have any semantic role. The raised and expletive arguments of chapter 12 are examples of functions that have no semantic role. Only subjects and objects are [−r]; obliques and restricted objects are [+r]. The feature [−o] refers to a *nonobjective* syntactic function, the kind of function which complements intransitive predicators such as N or A. Only subjects and obliques are [−o]; objects and restricted objects are [+o]. Not all languages make use of all these possibilities. Languages which lack restricted objects have no ditransitive verbs. However, LMT assumes that all languages have subjects.[6] In the representations given here, the minus features define the unmarked feature values; hence the subject is least marked, and the restricted object is most marked. Descending diagonally from the left corner to the right corner, (18) can be read as a **partial ordering** of basic argument functions:

(19) **Partial Ordering of Argument Functions:**
SUBJ > OBJ, OBL$_\theta$ > OBJ$_\theta$
(Negatively specified features are unmarked.)

It follows from this classification that a [–o] role cannot be mapped onto an object, and a [–r] role can be mapped onto a subject or object:

(20) a-structure: θ θ
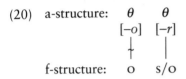

The basic principles for determining the choice of syntactic features in the a-structure (ignoring cases of lexical idiosyncrasy) are based on the underlying lexical semantics of the roles:

(21)   **Semantic Classification of A-Structure Roles for Function:**
patientlike roles: θ
                                            [–r]
secondary patientlike roles:[7] θ
                                            [+o]
other semantic roles: θ
                                            [–o]

This way of classifying a-structure roles allows us to distinguish different types of 'logical subject' ($\hat{\theta}$): one type may have the object features ([–r] or [+o]), while another type may have the nonobject feature classification [–o]. Examples are discussed below and in problem set 5.

A-structures may also have empty argument roles that have no semantic content; these can only be [–r], by definition of the unrestricted feature (Bresnan and Zaenen 1990). An example would be the a-structures for the subject-raising verb *seem* and the object-raising verb *believe* (Zaenen and Engdahl 1994):

(22)   **Athematic Argument Roles:**
a.   *seem*   __< x   y   >   b.   *believe* < x   y   >__
          [–r] [–o] [–o]   [–o] [–o] [–r]

In these example argument structures, as in chapter 12, athematic arguments are represented outside of the angled brackets. As in Zaenen and Engdahl (1994) the empty argument role may be ordered before (22a) or after (22b) the other argument roles, which will give it greater or lesser priority in the mapping to functions (section 14.3). In both these examples x is an experiencer argument and y a propositional argument.[8]

We use the variable θ for both thematic (semantic) and athematic (nonsemantic) argument roles. However, $\hat{\theta}$ always designates the *semantically* most prominent role on the thematic hierarchy (14). In the a-structure of *seem*, $x = \hat{\theta}$ is not the initial role of the argument structure, because an empty argument role precedes it. In the a-structure of *believe*, $x = \hat{\theta}$ is also the initial role of the argument structure.

Conditions can be imposed on the a-structure. In some languages more than one semantic role can be associated with [−r], whereas in others this association is limited to just one (Bresnan and Moshi 1990). English is a language with this constraint on a-structures, stated in (23) (Alsina and Mchombo 1993):

(23)   **Asymmetrical Object Parameter:**

When, in an asymmetrical object construction, there are two patientlike roles (such as a recipient object and a theme, for example), [+o] will be assigned to the secondary one. In English this is always the lower role on the hierarchy.

The lexical stock of a-structures in a language can be extended by morpholexical means. For example, the a-structure of a passive verb differs from the active in that the most prominent role cannot be mapped onto a syntactic argument in the f-structure (though it may be linked to an argument adjunct such as the by-phrase in English). This is called "suppression," and is associated with passive morphology. The notation is given in (24):

(24)   Passive: $\hat{\theta}$
                    |
                    Ø

Less prominent roles can also be suppressed in a-structure. "Unspecified object deletion" can be viewed as suppressing a patient or theme role:

(25)   Unspecified object deletion: 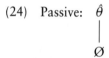   (θ a patient or theme)

Suppressions can affect only unmarked roles in a-structures (Alsina 1990) – that is, only negatively specified roles:

(26)   **Recoverability of Suppression:**
       Only unmarked arguments can be suppressed.

Unmarked arguments are defined by the markedness interpretation of the features in (18): the negatively specified features are unmarked.

In sum, the a-structures of words contain the minimal lexical information needed for the projection of semantic roles onto surface syntactic functions. A fundamental generalization embodied in them is that patientlike roles may alternate between subject and object while other roles such as agents and locatives alternate between the nonobject functions. This captures a pervasive typological pattern across languages. (See Bresnan and Kanerva 1989: 25–6.)

14.3   Mapping A-Structures to Syntactic Functions

The basic syntactic principles for mapping a-structures to surface grammatical functions are simple. The underspecified roles are freely mapped onto all compatible grammatical functions subject to a few general constraints: if it is the initial argument of the predicator, a most prominent role ($\hat{\theta}$) classified [−o] has to be mapped onto the subject function; if such a role is unavailable, a nonagentive unrestricted role (θ classified [−r]) is mapped onto the subject function. All other roles are mapped onto the lowest compatible function on the partial ordering (19):

(27)   **Mapping Principles:**
    a.   Subject roles:
        (i) $\hat{\theta}$ is mapped onto SUBJ when initial in the a-structure;
             [−o]
             otherwise:
        (ii) θ is mapped onto SUBJ.
             [−r]
    b.   Other roles are mapped onto the lowest compatible function in the partial ordering (19).

In (22a), $x = \hat{\theta}$ is not the initial role of *seem*, and so by (27) it will be mapped not onto SUBJ, but onto OBL$_\theta$. In (22b), in contrast, $x = \hat{\theta}$ is the initial role of *believe*, and so by (27) it will be mapped onto SUBJ.

There are two other constraints on the mapping, namely function-argument bi-uniqueness (Bresnan 1980) and the subject condition (Baker 1983):[9]

(28)   **Function–Argument Bi-uniqueness:**
Each a-structure role must be associated with a unique function, and conversely.

(29)   **The Subject Condition:**
Every predicator must have a subject.

Multiple restricted objects and obliques are possible because these functions are further individuated by their semantic roles (see Bresnan and Kanerva 1989: 25 for discussion).

14.4 Examples and Consequences

14.4.1 Unaccusatives

The active form of the transitive verb *pound* has an agent role and a patient role. These are respectively assigned a [–o] and a [–r] feature by the a-structure principles given above. The [–o] argument is also the most prominent argument, given the thematic hierarchy. The a-structure is as given in (30):

(30) *pound* <   x   y   >
$\qquad\qquad\qquad$ [–o] [–r]

According to the a- to f-structure mapping principles in (27), the most prominent role will be mapped onto the SUBJ function (27a(i)); the other argument role will be mapped to the unrestricted object (OBJ) function, the lowest function of the partial ordering compatible with the [–r] a-structure feature:

(31) TRANSITIVE:
$\qquad$ a-structure: *pound* <   x   y   >
$\qquad\qquad\qquad\qquad\qquad$ [–o] [–r]
$\qquad\qquad\qquad\qquad\qquad\quad |\qquad |$

$\qquad$ f-structure:$\qquad\qquad\qquad$ S   O$\qquad$ (27a(i)) and (27b)

In the passive a-structure, $\hat{\theta}$ is suppressed and the remaining role is mapped onto the subject function by (27a(ii)):

(32) PASSIVE:
$\qquad$ a-structure: *pounded* <   x   y   >
$\qquad\qquad\qquad\qquad\qquad\quad$ [–o] [–r]
$\qquad\qquad\qquad\qquad\qquad\quad$ Ø$\qquad |\qquad$ (24)

$\qquad$ f-structure:$\qquad\qquad\qquad\qquad$ S$\qquad$ (27a(ii))

The unaccusative is subject to the same mapping as the passive: here there is no logical subject classified [–o], so again (27a(ii)) applies to constrain the subject mapping:

(33) UNACCUSATIVE:
$\qquad$ a-structure: *freeze* <   x   >
$\qquad\qquad\qquad\qquad\qquad$ [–r]
$\qquad\qquad\qquad\qquad\qquad\quad |$

$\qquad$ f-structure:$\qquad\qquad\qquad$ S$\qquad$ (27a(ii))

In the unergative, the sole argument is also mapped onto the subject function, but this time by virtue of principle (27a(i)):

(34)　UNERGATIVE:
　　　a-structure:　*bark*　<　　x　　>
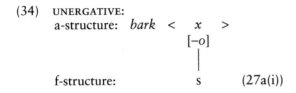
　　　f-structure:　　　　　　　　s　　　　(27a(i))

In sum, the sole required argument of English intransitive verbs (whether passive, unergative, or unaccusative) is mapped to the SUBJ function. Nevertheless, the different classifications of the sole argument in a-structure explain a subtle split between two types of intransitive verbs (discovered by Simpson 1983b).

14.4.1.1　Resultatives

The sole argument of passives and unaccusatives shares with the second argument of transitives the property of allowing a resultative predication:

(35)　a.　We pounded the metal flat.　　　　　　　　　　　　(transitive)
　　　b.　The metal was pounded flat.　　　　　　　　　　　　(passive)

(36)　The river froze solid.　　　　　　　　　　　　　　(unaccusative)

(37)　*The dog barked hoarse.　　　　　　　　　　　　　　(unergative)

Note that a resultative predicate cannot be applied to subjects in general. For example, resultative predication cannot be applied to the subject of a transitive verb or that of an unergative verb: (35a) cannot mean that we got flat by pounding the metal and (37) cannot mean that the dog was hoarse as a result of barking. The resultative predicate applies only to an argument that is classified as [−r] in the a-structure. Why does resultative predication have access to this information? Because, as argued in Simpson (1983b), it alters the a-structure by adding the resultative argument to the predicate.

14.4.1.2　"Fake" reflexives and "nonsubcategorized objects"

Ergatives also differ from unaccusatives in allowing "fake reflexive" arguments, which then permit resultatives:

(38)　a.　The dog barked itself hoarse.　　　　　　　　　　(ergative)
　　　b.　She shouted herself beet red.　　　　　　　　　　(ergative)
　　　c.　*She flushed herself red.　　　　　　　　　　　　(unaccusatives)

Similarly, the two types differ in allowing "nonsubcategorized objects:"

(39) a. The dog barked us awake.   (ergative)
      b. We ran the soles right off our shoes.   (ergative)
      c. *The dog fell us awake.   (unaccusative)

Both fake reflexives and nonsubcategorized objects are athematic arguments of their verb, having no semantic role with respect to the verb alone: the dog does not bark itself, nor can it bark us. As we saw above, in English there can only be one $[-r]$ argument in the a-structure of a verb, and because nonsemantic roles by definition can only be $[-r]$, unaccusative verbs cannot have nonthematic objects. This explains the contrast between the ability of unergatives and unaccusatives to take fake reflexives and nonsubcategorized objects.

14.4.1.3   Word order of internal/external arguments

The Lexical Mapping Theory has further consequences when combined with the theory of c-structure to f-structure mapping of chapter 6. By the X′ theory of chapter 6, the VP is the phrase structure category that is both predicative (i.e., cannot dominate a subject NP) and potentially transitive (i.e., can dominate object NPs). It follows that in a language that has a VP, the $\overset{\hat{\theta}}{[-o]}$ argument, being realized as a SUBJ must appear outside of the VP, while the $[-r]$ argument(s) being realized as either SUBJ or OBJ can appear either inside or outside the VP. Can the sole argument of unaccusative verbs like *freeze* appear inside the VP in English or other configurational languages? Relevant evidence bearing on this question is given in problem set 5.

The present theory of "internal"/"external" arguments has the advantage of generalizing gracefully to languages in which VP constituents are not independently motivated.

14.4.2   *Ditransitives*

The active form of *cook* has an agent role and a patient role. These are respectively assigned a $[-o]$ and a $[-r]$ feature by the a-structure principles given above. The $[-o]$ argument is also the most prominent argument, given the thematic hierarchy, so it is the "external argument." The a-structure is as given in (40):

(40)   *cook* <   *x*   *y*   >
                   $[-o]$ $[-r]$

According to the a- to f-structure mapping principles in (27), the "external" argument role will be mapped onto the subject (27a(i)); the other argument role will be mapped to the unrestricted object function, the lowest function of the partial ordering compatible with the $[-r]$ a-structure feature:

(41) TRANSITIVE:

a-structure: *cook* <   x   y   >
                          [–o] [–r]
                           │   │

f-structure: S   O   (27a(i)) and (27b)

In the passive a-structure, $\hat\theta$ is suppressed and an internal role is mapped onto the subject function by (27a(ii)):

(42) PASSIVE:

a-structure: *cooked* <   x   y   >
                             [–o] [–r]
                              Ø   (24)
                                    │

f-structure: S   (27a(ii))

In the active intransitive a-structure, it is the patient (y) role that is suppressed:

(43) INTRANSITIVE:

a-structure: *cook* <   x   y   >
                           [–o] [–r]
                            │   Ø   (25)
f-structure: S   (27a(i))

This analysis accounts for facts like those in (44):

(44) a. Both parents cooked supper (for the children).
      b. Supper was cooked (by both parents) (for the children).
      c. Both parents cooked (for the children).

The ditransitive of *cook* has an added beneficiary role, which is a patientlike "internal argument." It is thus assigned the [–r] feature and, because English allows only one such internal role by the asymmetrical object parameter (23) discussed above, the lower patient role must then receive the secondary [+o] classification. The a-structure is as given in (45):

(45) *cook-for* <   x   y   z   >
                      [–o] [–r] [+o]

Applying the mapping principles to this argument structure, we find that the agent will be mapped onto the subject as external argument; the beneficiary will be mapped onto the object as the most marked function compatible with the [–r] feature; and the patient will be mapped onto the restricted object as the most marked function compatible with the [+o] feature:

(46) DITRANSITIVE:
    a-structure: *cook-for* $<$ x y z $>$
                            [−o] [−r] [+o]

    f-structure: S   O O_θ (27a(i)) and (27b)

In the corresponding passive a-structure, $\hat{\theta}$ is suppressed and an internal role is mapped onto the subject function:

(47) PASSIVE OF DITRANSITIVE:
    a-structure: *cooked-for* $<$ x y z $>$
                            [−o] [−r] [+o]
                            Ø   (24)

    f-structure: S O_θ (27a(ii))

This analysis accounts for facts like those in (48):

(48) a. Both parents cooked the children supper.
     b. The children were cooked supper by both parents.
     c. *Supper was cooked the children by both parents.

Now if we try to apply intransitivization to either the active ditransitive argument structure or to the passive version, it will fail. Suppressions may apply only to unmarked roles, that is, those that are negatively specified:

(49) DITRANSITIVE:
    a-structure: *cook-for* $<$ x y z $>$
                            [−o] [−r] [+o]
                                   Ø   *(25)
                                   *

This accounts for examples like the following.

(50) a. We'll cook for Thanksgiving.
        (= We'll cook something for Thanksgiving.)
     b. *We'll cook the children for Thanksgiving.
        (= We'll cook the children something for Thanksgiving.)

(51) *The children will be cooked for Thanksgiving.
     (= The children will be cooked something for Thanksgiving.)

Putting together the results from our examination of ditransitives in English with those of resultatives, we can easily explain the following contrasts:

(52) a. John cooked the egg hard for Mary.
     b. *John cooked Mary the egg hard.

The theme argument of transitive 'cook' can be suppressed by unspecified object deletion (25) because it corresponds to an unrestricted role [−r], which (being unmarked) is eligible for suppression. But the same semantic role, in the ditransitive 'cook-for', cannot be unrestricted, by the asymmetrical object parameter (23), and so cannot be suppressed.

14.4.3   Interactions of Passive and Raising

As we saw above, the raising verbs *seem* and *believe* have the argument structures shown in (53) and (54), respectively. Each verb has an empty (athematic) role, and both verbs have an experiencer argument (x) and a propositional argument (y). By definition, the athematic roles are [−r], and the semantic roles receive the "other semantic roles" classification [−o] from (21):

(53)   *seem*   __< x y >
[−r] [−o] [−o]

(54)   *believe* < x y >__
[−o] [−o] [−r]

Now (27a(i)) does not apply to *seem*, because $x = \hat{\theta}$ is not the initial argument role, being preceded by an empty argument. Therefore (27a(ii)) maps the empty role to the SUBJ function, and (27b) maps the other roles to OBL$_\theta$. Here (following Zaenen and Engdahl 1994) XCOMP = OBL$_{prop}$:

(55)   *seem*   __< x y >
[−r]   [−o]   [−o]
| | |
S   OBL$_{exp}$ XCOMP   (27a(ii)) and (27b)

In contrast, (27a(i)) does apply to *believe*:

(56)   *believe* < x y >__
[−o]   [−o]   [−r]
| | |
S   XCOMP   O   (27a(i)) and (27b)

The verb *seem* does not passivize, but *believe* does:

(57)   *believe* < x y >__
[−o]   [−o]   [−r]
Ø | | (24)
XCOMP   S   (27a(ii)) and (27b)

The reader is now equipped to solve problem set 5.

Further Reading and Discussion

Predicate argument structure played a fundamental role in the early motivation for LFG. It was argued, for example, that many properties of what were once considered syntactic transformations (passive, dative, *there*-insertion, and the like) – their cyclicity, their structure preservation, their locality, and their lexical governance – could be derived instead from lexical operations on predicate argument structures which realigned their mappings to syntactic phrase structure constituents (Bresnan 1978). Lexical operations on the grammatical function arrays associated with predicate argument structures are central in the early LFG works in Bresnan (1982c) and L. Levin et al. (1983).

Early on it was suggested that there might be general principles for selecting grammatical functions from argument structures (Bresnan 1980), and the first convincing instantiation of such principles is found in the work of Zaenen et al. (1985). But it was L. Levin (1985) who pioneered the Lexical Mapping Theory by showing that alternations in lexical forms that had previously been expressed by lexical rules transforming the grammatical function array present in lexical subcategorizations (or "lexical forms") could be better captured by mapping principles that select varying sets of grammatical functions directly on the basis of the classification of the semantic roles. This idea is further developed in work by Bresnan and Kanerva (1989), and as noted above Bresnan (1980) provides arguments against lexical rules in LFG.

Argument structure and the Lexical Mapping Theory have become one of the most intensively investigated areas of research in LFG, and there are many alternative hypotheses under active investigation in various empirical domains. Moreover, the theories of argument structure and a-structure to f-structure mapping have only recently begun to be formalized (see Butt et al. 1997 and Andrews and Manning 1999). This is a part of the theory where further reading is essential to get a full picture of rapidly evolving research on the subject. The reader should now be able to venture into this rich area. For a collection of new work in this area, see Butt and King (2000). In addition, the following readings are recommended as starting points on the topics indicated.

Symmetrical/Asymmetrical object properties, passive, and inversion

The account of ditransitives given for English above varies from what is found in other languages. Research on the nature of this variation can be found in Mchombo and Firmino (1999), Alsina and Mchombo (1990, 1991, 1993), Bresnan and Moshi (1990), Simpson (1991), Tan (1991), Joshi (1993), Harford (1993), Alsina (1994a, 1994b, 1996a, 1996b), Lødrup (1995), Her (1997, 1998b), and references. These constructions are closely related to the behavior of unaccusatives and locative inversion constructions in Bantu (see Demuth 1990, Demuth and Mmusi 1997) and elsewhere (Tan 1991, Ackerman 1990, 1992, Bresnan 1994a, Pan 1996, Her and Huang 1998, Morimoto 1999, Lødrup forthcoming), in addition to the above references.

Causatives

At first sight it appears that (20) and (21) cannot possibly be right because they imply that agentive arguments can never be objects; yet object causees exist in many languages (as in English, where *Mary jumped the horse* means "Mary made the horse jump," yet *the horse*, the agent of the jumping, is an object). However, T. Mohanan (1988) shows that this problem could be solved on the assumption that causativization can involve composition of a three-place causative predicate with the base verb. The three-place causative predicate involves an agent of causation who acts on a patient of causation to bring about an event in which the patient participates in another role. On Mohanan's theory, the causee of the base verb a-structure can be realized as an object just when the composition of a higher three-place causative predicate alters the meaning of this argument role by binding the agent of the verb stem to the patient of causation of the causative morphology. The idea is further developed by work by Alsina and Joshi (1991) and Alsina (1992, 1996b, 1997), and is then genereralized to a wider range of transitivizing processes in Australian aboriginal languages by Austin (1997). Argument structure causativization is an addition to the incorporated XCOMP analysis of causatives introduced in problem set 4 (Ishikawa 1985, Saiki 1985, 1986, Matsumoto 1996a, 1996b, 1996c). Recent work on the typology of causatives can be found in Matsumoto (1998) and references.

Nominalizations and derivational morphology

The pioneering work in LFG on nominalizations is that of Rappaport (1983), which predates the Lexical Mapping Theory. The idea that meaning changes can alter the semantic classification of roles (21) in LMT is developed by Ackerman (1990) and Markantonatou (1995). Laczkó (1995, 1997) analyzes nominalizations in Hungarian and English in a comparative perspective. See also Mchombo and Ngalande (1980), Mchombo (1992, 1993a, 1993b), Dubinsky and Simango (1996), Mugane (1996), and Alsina (1996b, 1999).

Agentive objects

Agentive objects pose potential counterexamples to LMT, where they arise outside of the morphological meaning changes that could motivate syntactic reclassification of the agentive argument. Possible examples include active/objective voice changes in Tagalog (Kroeger 1993), some inverse languages (Arnold 1994), subject inversion constructions in Italian dialects (Saccon 1993), and Norwegian presentational constructions (Lødrup 1999b, forthcoming). Various lines of attack on these problems have been taken, including underspecification (Arnold 1994, Lødrup forthcoming). Some recent work adopts the Optimality Theoretic idea of violable constraints to explain marked realizations of argument types (Sells 1999b, Morimoto 1999, Lødrup 1999b).

Complex predicates

While LFG provides a natural theory of discontinuous constituents for arguments and other dependents (chapters 1, 6, 7), the problem of discontinous verbs (and other heads) is more difficult, as first noted by Simpson (1983b) and Ackerman (1987). Because each PRED is uniquely instantiated (chapter 4), two parts of the same PRED cannot be unified in the current formalism. This problem has attracted intensive research, empirical, theoretical, and formal. It is closely related to the problem of serial verbs (Bodomo 1992, 1996, 1997, Andrews and Manning 1999). Some of the important readings on this problem are Ackerman (1992), Butt (1995, 1997), Ackerman and Lesourd (1997), T. Mohanan (1994, 1997), Alsina (1994b, 1996b, 1997), Frank (1996), Broadwell (1998), and Andrews and Manning (1999). The last reference is a monograph which contains an excellent overview of approaches to the empirical problems and a new formalization of argument structure and information flow in LFG.

Proto-roles

Several LFG researchers have adopted a Dowtian proto-role analysis of argument structure roles (Dowty 1991). These include Ackerman (1992), Zaenen (1994), Joshi (1993), and Alsina (1996b). A very interesting OT-LFG reanalysis of Joshi's (1993) proto-role based theory of LMT in Marathi is given by Asudeh (1999).

Argument structure binding

Argument structure binding appears in the work of Grimshaw (1982a), Sells et al. (1987), Mchombo (1992, 1993a, 1993b), Bresnan and Moshi (1990), Alsina (1992, 1994b, 1996b, 1999), Alsina and Mchombo (1993), and elsewhere. In this work, reflexive/reciprocal morphology and clitics serve to suppress an a-structure role by binding it to another. This phenomenon might be viewed as a type of grammaticalization that lexicalizes anaphoric binding relations.

A-structure prominence has long been a factor in anaphoric reflexive binding, as noted in chapters 10 and 11 and references. Manning (1996) proposes that all binding and control should be based on a-structure prominence, and modifies the theory of a-structure to support this proposal, bringing it closer to developments in HPSG. Interesting applications of this approach are found in some Austronesian languages (see especially Arka 1998, Arka and Manning 1999, and Arka and Simpson 1999). But the generality of the binding hypothesis remains to be determined (Dukes 1999). In chapters 10 and 11 we have already seen that binding is subject to multiple dimensions such as logophoricity and subjectivity, which may apply simultaneously. It thus seems premature at the moment to reduce all binding to a single linguistic representation.

Notes

1 – ignoring the issue of complex predicates, or multi-headed lexical constructs (Alsina, Bresnan, and Sells (eds.) 1997).
2 See also chapter 3 for an empirical argument that underlying syntactic trees are undesirable.
3 See Kiparsky (1997b) and Rappaport Hovav and Levin (1995b) for a contrary argument.

4   The ordering is the one proposed in Kiparsky (1987), Bresnan and Kanerva (1989), and elsewhere, and might be derived from semantic primitives along the lines of Dowty (1991) and Engdahl (1990) or Jackendoff (1990) and Pinker (1989).

5   Basic argument functions are those borne by nominal arguments. Zaenen and Engdahl (1994) extend this theory to XCOMPS and COMPS, which include adjectival, verbal, and sentential complements.

6   This assumption is not uncontroversial. See Foley and Van Valin (1984) and Andrews (1985) for discussion.

7   Verbs may have multiple patientlike roles, as with ditransitives. Which roles count as secondary appears to be a parameter of variation. See Alsina and Mchombo (1993), Bresnan and Moshi (1990), Chu-Ren Huang (1993), Alsina (1990, 1996b), Joshi (1993), and Austin (1997), for further discussion.

8   Zaenen and Engdahl (1994) analyze XCOMP and COMP as specialized type of OBL$_\theta$.

9   This condition may need to be parameterized so as to hold only for some types of languages (see Bresnan and Kanerva 1989, T. Mohanan 1994). Also, it applies only to argument structures of predicators taking core arguments (as defined in section 6.1.1).

Problem Sets and Solutions

Introduction

Most of the following problems are based on published and unpublished sources listed in the references at the end of the set of solutions. While you are strongly encouraged to work through the problems without recourse to the published sources, for the practice in syntactic analysis that this will provide, the problems are quite open-ended and often represent only a small piece of a larger linguistic issue raised by the phenomena in question. You may therefore find it interesting after completing the problems to refer to the original sources in order to pursue in greater depth the issues they raise. Solutions are provided to only some of the problems.

A word is in order about how the sources have been used. In most cases, the data are taken directly from them. But there are also certain cases in which for pedagogical reasons the data has been somewhat modified, or constructed examples have been added, or the analysis itself has been somewhat simplified. Moreover, in some cases the analysis argued for in the sources is different from what an analysis within lexical-functional theory might look like. Therefore you should not assume that any problem fully represents either the complexities of the phenomena it addresses or the views of the author on whose work it draws.

Problem Set 1

P1.1 Warlpiri

Warlpiri, a Pama-Nyungan language spoken in northern Australia, is what is sometimes called a free word order language. In this exercise we will consider the following sentences from Warlpiri, and show that while they differ in c-structure, they have identical f-structures.

(1) *Kurdu-jarra-rlu wita-jarra-rlu   ka-pala   maliki wajilipi-nyi.*
    child-DUAL-ERG small-DUAL-ERG PRES-DUAL dog-ABS chase-NONPAST
    'The two small children are chasing the dog.'

(2) *Kurdu-jarra-rlu ka-pala   maliki   wajilipi-nyi   wita-jarra-rlu.*
    child-DUAL-ERG PRES-DUAL dog-ABS chase-NONPAST small-DUAL-ERG
    'The two small children are chasing the dog.'

(3) *Maliki ka-pala   kurdu-jarra-rlu wajilipi-nyi   wita-jarra-rlu.*
    dog-ABS PRES-DUAL child-DUAL-ERG chase-NONPAST small-DUAL-ERG
    'The two small children are chasing the dog.'

(R1) and (R2) below give rules that will generate the constituent structures of such simple Warlpiri sentences. We have used an abbreviation (the "X") in the rule schema in (R1a) in order to highlight the significant generalization that nominal and verbal constituents are treated alike with respect to word order. Each instance of X should be freely instantiated with either of the categories NP or V, as specified by the condition beside the rule schema. The "*" in the notation "X*" means that there may be any number of instances of X, including none. We can then use the instructions in (R2) to assign functional schemata to the constituents in the right sides of the rules we create by this instantiation. With these rules and the lexical choices in (L1)–(L5), it is possible to provide derivations for the sentences in (1)–(3):

(R1) a. S → X (Aux) X*   where X = NP, V
      b. NP → N*

(R2) a. Assign ($\uparrow$ SUBJ) = $\downarrow$ or ($\uparrow$ OBJ) = $\downarrow$ freely to NP.
      b. Assign $\uparrow$ = $\downarrow$ to N, V and Aux.

Listed below are the relevant lexical choices (L1)–(L5). These fully inflected words are created from the lexical stock of stems by morpholexical processes which we will not discuss here. We make the simplifying (and artificial) assumption that they are simply given to the grammar as lexical items:

(L1) *kurdu-jarra-rlu*   N   ($\uparrow$ PRED) = 'child'
                              ($\uparrow$ NUM) = DUAL
                              ($\uparrow$ CASE) = ERG

(L2) *maliki*   N   ($\uparrow$ PRED) = 'dog'
                              ($\uparrow$ NUM) = SG
                              ($\uparrow$ CASE) = ABS

(L3) *wita-jarra-rlu*   N   ($\uparrow$ ADJ PRED) = 'small'
                              ($\uparrow$ NUM) = DUAL
                              ($\uparrow$ CASE) = ERG

(L4) *wajilipi-nyi*   V   ($\uparrow$ PRED) = 'chase $\langle(\uparrow$ SUBJ$)(\uparrow$ OBJ$)\rangle$'
                              ($\uparrow$ TENSE) = NONPAST
                              ($\uparrow$ SUBJ CASE) = ERG
                              ($\uparrow$ OBJ CASE) = ABS

(L5) *ka-pala*   Aux ($\uparrow$ ASPECT) = PRESENT.IMPERFECT
                              ($\uparrow$ SUBJ NUM) = DUAL

Task I   Give c- and f-structures for (1)–(3).

It is interesting to note that in Warlpiri, there is no class of adjectives distinct from nouns, and any nominal may serve either as an adjunct or as the argument modified by the adjunct. Thus the word specifications for (L1) and (L3) above could each include the alternative annotation ($\uparrow$ ADJ PRED) = 'child' and ($\uparrow$ PRED) = 'small', respectively. However, speakers of Warlpiri have a strong preference for adjuncts to follow what they modify; and this interpretation is the only one you need be concerned with for the purpose of this preliminary exercise.

P1.2   Monsters and How to Avoid Them

The notation for annotated c-structure rules is properly considered a formal language for writing grammars. In problem 1.1 we have made use of some of its power and flexibility. The problem from the point of view of the linguistic theorist is that, as it stands, the language is TOO powerful and flexible: it is possible to write monster [*monster:* "an animal of strange or terrifying shape"] grammars that yield consistent, coherent, and complete f-structures but which correspond to no type of natural language known to us. Here is an example:

(1)

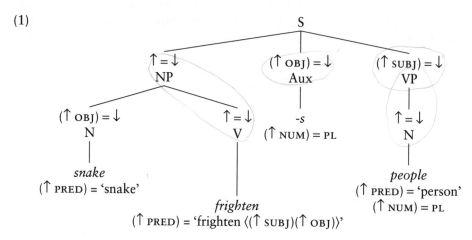

Task II   Display the f-structure that corresponds to this example. Notice that it is entirely well-formed and sensible looking, despite the c-structure.

Task III   Some way is needed of constraining possible annotations to word and phrase structure, to provide a theory of the NATURAL ways that functional schemata can be associated with external structures. Can you propose any generalizations about these associations? Can you propose any ways you might expect such properties to vary across language types?

Problem Set 2

P2.1 Spanish

P2.1.1 *The basic sentence pattern*

First consider the following sentences:

(1) a. *Juan vió algo.*
         saw something
         'Juan saw something.'
   b. **Juan vió a algo.*
         saw Prep something
         'Juan saw something.'

(2) a. *Juan vió a alguien.*
         saw Prep someone
         'Juan saw someone.'
   b. **Juan vió alguien.*
         saw someone
         'Juan saw sómeone.'

The gloss below *a* stands for Preposition. It is assumed here that *a algo* and *a alguien* in the above examples are prepositional phrases (PPs). (This position is not uncontroversial: alternatively this *a* could be considered some form of case marker within the noun phrase (NP).)

Task I Propose a set of phrase structure rules that will generate the grammatical sentences in (1) and (2), while ruling out the ungrammatical ones. Include all the necessary functional annotations. Although word order in Spanish is fairly free, you may assume for the purpose of this exercise that Spanish c-structure is roughly comparable to what we find in English, and that the Spanish S and PP rules are the following:

(R1) S →   NP   VP
                 (↑ SUBJ) = ↓   ↑ = ↓

(R2) PP →   P   NP
                 ↑ = ↓   ↑ = ↓

It is left to you to provide the VP and NP rules. The expansion of VP should include an optional PP, and you should consider carefully the treatment of this constituent within the VP. In particular bear in mind the word specifications for the verb *vió* (in (L5) below). Remember, there is no single "correct" set of rules for this problem, so just propose some rules, and make sure that they provide c-structures and well-formed f-structures for (1a) and (2a), but not for (1b) and (2b).

The relevant word specifications are given below.

(L1) *a*   P   (↑ CASE) = ACC
                      (↑ ANIM) =$_c$ +

(L2) *algo*   N   (↑ PRED) = 'something'
                      (↑ ANIM) = −

(L3) *alguien* N   (↑ PRED) = 'someone'
                      (↑ ANIM) = +

(L4) *Juan*   N   (↑ PRED) = 'Juan'
                      (↑ NUM) = SG
                      (↑ GEND) = MASC
                      (↑ ANIM) = +

(L5) *vió*   V   (↑ PRED) = 'see ⟨(↑ SUBJ)(↑ OBJ)⟩'
                      (↑ TENSE) = PAST

Task II Write out the c-structures and f-structures for (1a) and (2a).

P2.1.2 Clitics

Consider now the following sentences:

(3) a. *Juan vió a   Pedro.*
                  saw Prep
           'Juan saw Pedro.'
     b. *Juan lo   vió.*
                Cl.Acc.Sg saw
           'Juan saw him.'

(4) a. *Juan vió a   sus amigos.*
            saw Prep his friends
        'Juan saw his friends.'
    b. *Juan los   vió.*
            Cl.Acc.Pl saw
        'Juan saw them.'

Lo and *los* are clitic pronouns, phonologically attached to the verb. Their lexical specifications are given in (L6) and (L7) below. These are fairly standard for pronouns, though of course you are free to modify them if you wish. They include a simple referential feature common to all pronouns (the PRED feature "PRO"), together with agreement features such as person, number, and gender and grammatical features such as case:

(L6) *lo*   CL   ($\uparrow$ PRED) = 'PRO'
              ($\uparrow$ CASE) = ACC
              ($\uparrow$ NUM) = SG
              ($\uparrow$ PERS) = 3
              ($\uparrow$ GEND) = MASC

(L7) *los* CL   ($\uparrow$ PRED) = 'PRO'
              ($\uparrow$ CASE) = ACC
              ($\uparrow$ NUM) = PL
              ($\uparrow$ PERS) = 3
              ($\uparrow$ GEND) = MASC

You must now refine your rules so that they can also generate c-structures for sentences containing clitics as in (3b) and (4b). You may assume that clitics belong to the category CL, and use the following rule to generate the constituent containing the clitic and verb:

(R3) $\overline{V}$ $\rightarrow$ (CL)   V
                  ($\uparrow$ OBJ) = $\downarrow$ $\uparrow = \downarrow$

(This rule is not intended to account for all the verbal clitics in Spanish. For example, in addition to accusative clitics, Spanish has dative clitics.)

Task III   Modify your VP rule so that it includes $\overline{V}$ in its expansion. Please list the new rule.

Task IV   Please give c- and f-structures for (3a) and (3b). You will need the following additional lexical specification:

(L8) *Pedro* N   ($\uparrow$ PRED) = 'Pedro'
                ($\uparrow$ NUM) = SG
                ($\uparrow$ ANIM) = +
                ($\uparrow$ GEND) = MASC

P2.1.3   Clitic doubling

Finally, consider the following sentences. These exhibit a phenomenon called *clitic doubling*, which is widespread in some dialects of Spanish, such as the River Plate and Peruvian dialects:

(5) a. *Juan lo   vió a   Pedro.*
             Cl.Acc.Sg saw Prep
          'Juan saw Pedro.'
     b. *Juan los   vió a   sus amigos.*
             Cl.Acc.Pl saw Prep his friends
          'Juan saw his friends.'

In these examples we find both a clitic and a full PP object. In such dialects *lo* and *los* may still serve as objects, as in (3b) and (4b), and so may a full PP as in (3a) and (4a). So it would seem that in the sentences in (5) we have two forms which express the object of the sentence. Note that there must be gender and number agreement between the clitic and the PP object:

(6) a. *Juan lo   /*los   /*la   vió a Pedro.*
             Cl.Masc.Sg   Cl.Masc.Pl Cl.Fem.Sg
     b. *Juan los   /*lo   /*las   vió a sus amigos.*
             Cl.Masc.Pl Cl.Masc.Sg Cl.Fem.Pl

The final goal of this exercise is to highlight the linguistically significant issue raised by syntactic doubling phenomena like the one illustrated here and to delve into a specific treatment of it in LFG.

Task V   Your set of rules and morpholexical specifications accounting for (1)–(3) probably predicts that (5a) and (5b) are ill-formed. Explain why.

Task VI   Please modify your c-structure rules and/or morpholexical specifications to account for the well-formedness of (5a) and (5b). Be sure that your rules continue to allow for the well-formedness of the sentences in (3) and (4).

In conclusion it is interesting to note that doubling is only possible with a PP object introduced by *a*, and never with a plain NP (note: *al* is a contraction of *a el*):

(7) a. *Juan lo   vió al   hombre.*
             Cl.Acc.Sg saw Prep.Det man
          'Juan saw the man.'
     b. *Juan lo   vió el   libro.*
             Cl.Acc.Sg saw Det book
          'Juan saw the book.'

It would be perfectly possible, however, for the clitic *lo* in a sentence like (3b) to be used to refer to either a man or a book. Although it is in no way necessary for the completion of this problem, you may find it interesting to consider how your analysis might be modified to account for this generalization about when doubling is possible.

P2.2 Moroccan Arabic

Moroccan, like Arabic in general, is a so-called "subject pro-drop" language. This means that a sentence need not contain a subject NP. A subject agreement marker appears on each verb whether or not a subject NP is present, as illustrated in (1):

(1) a. *Mša-t   nažat.*
         went-3.Sg.Fem Najat
         'Najat went.'
     b. *Mša-t.*
         went-3.Sg.Fem
         'She went.'

A further characteristic of Moroccan is that an object argument of a transitive verb may be represented by either an NP or a pronominal affix, but not both. This is shown in (2) below:

(2) a. *Šra-t   lbent   lx^webz.*
         bought-3.Sg.Fem the.girl the.bread
         'The girl bought the bread.'
     b. *Šra-t-u   lbent.*
         bought-3.Sg.Fem-3.Sg.Masc the.girl
         'The girl bought it.'
     c. **Šra-t-u   lbent   lx^webz.*
         bought-3.Sg.Fem-3.Sg.Masc the.girl the.bread

Some verbs in Moroccan lexically select oblique arguments. For example, in addition to SUBJ and OBJ, 'give' takes an OBL_GO(AL) OBJ (example(3)), and 'lose' takes a SUBJ and an OBL_EXP(ERIENCER) OBJ (example (4)). Both of these oblique arguments are marked by *l*, taken here to be a preposition, so that the entire phrase expressing the argument (e.g. *l edderri* in (3a)) is analyzed as a PP. Furthermore, when a prepositional object is pronominal it takes the form of a suffix attached to the preposition. As shown in (3b) and (4b), the resulting PP is usually a clitic appearing in the position immediately following the verb, to the left of the subject:

(3) a. *Eṭa*   *muḥend lektab   l edderri.*
         gave.3.Sg.Masc Mohand the.book to the-boy
         'Mohand gave the book to the boy.'
     b. *Eṭa*   *liḥ*   *muḥend lektab.*
         gave.3.Sg.Masc to-3.Sg.Masc Mohand the-book
         'Mohand gave him the book.'

(4) a. *Mšaw*   *leflus   l muḥend.*
         went.3.Pl the.money to Mohand
         'Mohand lost the money.'
     b. *Mšaw*   *liḥ*   *leflus.*
         went.3.Pl to.3.Sg.Masc the.money
         'He lost the money.'

  Listed below are c-structure rules for this fragment of Moroccan (note that
Moroccan is, basically, a VSO language):

(R1) S →   V   (PP)   (NP)   (NP)
                ↑ = ↓ (↑ (↓ CASE)) = ↓ (↑ SUBJ) = ↓ (↑ OBJ) = ↓
                (PP)
                (↑ (↓ CASE)) = ↓

(R2) PP →   P   (NP)
                ↑ = ↓ (↑ OBJ) = ↓

(R3) NP →   N
                ↑ = ↓

  (L1)–(L11) are word specifications that will be needed for the completion of
this exercise. Note that the specifications for the inflected verbs contribute complex information. You may find it useful to think of a word like *mšat* (L1 below)
as combining the information encoded in the stem *mša-* and in the affix *-t*: *mša-*
contributes the specification for PRED, while *-t* contributes those for ASPECT, SUBJ
NUM, SUBJ GEND, and SUBJ PERS:

(L1) *mšat* V (↑ PRED) = 'go ⟨(↑ SUBJ)⟩'
                 (↑ ASPECT) = PERF
                 (↑ SUBJ NUM) = SG
                 (↑ SUBJ GEND) = FEM
                 (↑ SUBJ PERS) = 3

(L2) *nažat* N (↑ PRED) = 'Najat'
                 (↑ NUM) = SG
                 (↑ PERS) = 3
                 (↑ GEND) = FEM

(L3) *lbent*   N $(\uparrow \text{PRED}) = $ 'girl'
                            $(\uparrow \text{NUM}) = \text{SG}$
                            $(\uparrow \text{PERS}) = 3$
                            $(\uparrow \text{GEND}) = \text{FEM}$

(L4) *lxʷebz*   N $(\uparrow \text{PRED}) = $ 'bread'
                            $(\uparrow \text{NUM}) = \text{SG}$
                            $(\uparrow \text{PERS}) = 3$
                            $(\uparrow \text{GEND}) = \text{MASC}$

(L5) *muḥend*   N $(\uparrow \text{PRED}) = $ 'Mohend'
                            $(\uparrow \text{NUM}) = \text{SG}$
                            $(\uparrow \text{PERS}) = 3$
                            $(\uparrow \text{GEND}) = \text{MASC}$

(L6) *lektab*   N $(\uparrow \text{PRED}) = $ 'book'
                            $(\uparrow \text{NUM}) = \text{SG}$
                            $(\uparrow \text{PERS}) = 3$

(L7) *edderri*   N $(\uparrow \text{PRED}) = $ 'boy'
                            $(\uparrow \text{NUM}) = \text{SG}$
                            $(\uparrow \text{PERS}) = 3$
                            $(\uparrow \text{GEND}) = \text{MASC}$

(L8) *leflus*   N $(\uparrow \text{PRED}) = $ 'money'
                            $(\uparrow \text{NUM}) = \text{PL}$
                            $(\uparrow \text{PERS}) = 3$

(L9) *l*   P $(\uparrow \text{CASE}) = \text{OBL}_{\text{GO}}$ $\bigvee$ $(\uparrow \text{CASE}) = \text{OBL}_{\text{EXP}}$

(L10) *mšaw*   V $(\uparrow \text{PRED}) = $ 'lose $\langle (\uparrow \text{SUBJ})(\uparrow \text{OBL}_{\text{EXP}} \text{OBJ}) \rangle$'
                            $(\uparrow \text{ASPECT}) = \text{PERF}$
                            $(\uparrow \text{SUBJ NUM}) = \text{PL}$
                            $(\uparrow \text{SUBJ PERS}) = 3$

(L11) *eṭa*   V $(\uparrow \text{PRED}) = $ 'give $\langle (\uparrow \text{SUBJ})(\uparrow \text{OBJ})(\uparrow \text{OBL}_{\text{GO}} \text{OBJ}) \rangle$'
                            $(\uparrow \text{ASPECT}) = \text{PERF}$
                            $(\uparrow \text{SUBJ NUM}) = \text{SG}$
                            $(\uparrow \text{SUBJ GEND}) = \text{MASC}$
                            $(\uparrow \text{SUBJ PERS}) = 3$

Task VII Propose or modify as needed the specifications for the verbs *mšat* and *sratu*, which will account for the patterns in (1) and (2) respectively. Also propose a specification for *lih*, which occurs in (3b) and (4b).

Task VIII   Give detailed c- and f-structures for (1b), (2a), (2b), (3a), and (4b).

Task IX   *L edderri* in (3a) and *l muḥend* in (4a) are analyzed here are PPs. Phonologically, however, they behave as single words and *l* can easily be analyzed as an affix. Try to develop an alternative analysis of these forms.

P2.3   Irish

P2.3.1   *Person/number inflection*

Irish has two types of verbal form: *synthetic* and *analytic*. An analytic form encodes tense and mood. A synthetic verbal form encodes, in addition to tense and mood, the person and number of its subject. A single verbal paradigm often combines synthetic and analytic forms. For example, the verb *cuir* 'put' has the following conditional forms in the Ulster dialect:

(1)   *chuirfinn*   'I would put'
      chuirféa   'you.Sg would put'
      chuirfeadh sé   'he would put'
      chuirfeadh sí   'she would put'
      chuirfimis   'we would put'
      chuirfeadh sibh   'you.Pl would put'
      chuirfeadh siad   'they would put'

The analytic form *chuirfeadh* carries no specification of the person or number of its subject. In the examples above this form regularly appears with a pronoun: *sé, sí, sibh,* or *siad*. It also occurs with lexical NPs, as illustrated in (2) below:

(2)   *Chuirfeadh Eoghan isteach ar an phost sin.*
      put.Cond   Owen   in   on the job   that
      'Owen would apply for that job.'

The synthetic forms in the paradigm are *chuirfinn, chuirféa,* and *chuirfimis*. These forms appear without a pronoun, as in (3) below:

(3)   *Chuirfinn   isteach ar an phost sin.*
      put.Cond.1.Sg in   on the job   that
      'I would apply for that job.'

Moreover, as illustrated in (4) below, it is impossible for a synthetic form to cooccur with a pronoun, even if the pronoun encodes the same person and number features:

(4) *Chuirfinn   mé isteach ar an phost sin.
    put.Cond.1.Sg I   in   on the job   that

An interesting fact about these verb forms is that an analytic form cannot be used when a synthetic form is available. For example, the analytic form *chuirfeadh* cannot be used with a first person singular pronoun:

(5) *Chuirfeadh mé isteach ar an phost sin.
    put.Cond   I   in   on the job   that

However, you will not be expected to account for this latter phenomenon in this problem.

P2.3.2   *Interactions with syntactic facts*

Certain syntactic phenomena point to a close parallelism between a synthetic verbal form and an analytic form combined with a subject. One of these concerns the behavior of certain NP modifiers which typically occur with pronouns but may also appear in the normal subject position when a synthetic form is used. The emphatic/reflexive particle *fein* accompanies pronouns as in (6); however, it can occur not only after an analytic verbal form as in (7a) but also after a synthetic one as in (7b):

(6) *mé*   I/me   *mé féin*   myself
     tú   you   *tú féin*   yourself
     sé   he   *sé féin*   himself
     sinn we   *sinn féin* ourselves
     iad   them   *iad féin*   themselves

(7) a.   *Chuir   mé féin isteach ar an phost sin.*
          put.Past I   Refl in   on the job   that
          'I myself applied for that job.'
     b.   *Chuirfinn   féin isteach ar an phost sin.*
          put.Cond.1.Sg Refl in   on the job   that
          'I myself would apply for that job.'

Let us assume that this fragment of Irish, which is a VSO language, can be generated by the following c-structure rules:

(R1) S →   V   (NP)   (NP)   (Part)   PP*
              ↑ = ↓ (↑ SUBJ) = ↓ (↑ OBJ) = ↓ ↑ = ↓ (↑ (↓ CASE)) = ↓

(R2) PP →   P   NP
              ↑ = ↓ (↑ OBJ) = ↓

(R3) NP → (Art)   (N)   (Part)
                  ↑ = ↓   ↑ = ↓   ↑ = ↓

Since Irish allows either an analytic form with a subject NP (as in (2)) or a synthetic form without a subject NP (as in (3)), the optionality of the head N in (R3) allows for the occurrence of the reflexive *fein* in cases like (7b) where the head is not present in the c-structure.

Let us assume the following morpholexical specifications, which will be relevant for the completion of this exercise:

(L1) *chuirfeadh* V $(\uparrow$ PRED$)$ = 'apply-for $\langle(\uparrow$ SUBJ$)(\uparrow$ OBL$_{ar}$ OBJ$)\rangle$'
                              $(\uparrow$ COND$)$ = +
                              $(\uparrow$ LOC$)$ =$_c$ +

(L2) *isteach*   Part $(\uparrow$ LOC$)$ = +

(L3) *ar*   P $(\uparrow$ CASE$)$ = OBL$_{ar}$

(L4) *phost*   N $(\uparrow$ PRED$)$ = 'job'

(L5) *féin*   Part $(\uparrow$ REFL$)$ = +

(L6) *sin*   Part $(\uparrow$ DEIXIS$)$ = DISTANT

(L7) *an*   Art $(\uparrow$ DEF$)$ = +

(L8) *chuir*   V $(\uparrow$ PRED$)$ = 'apply-for $\langle(\uparrow$ SUBJ$)(\uparrow$ OBL$_{ar}$ OBJ$)\rangle$'
                              $(\uparrow$ TENSE$)$ = PAST
                              $(\uparrow$ LOC$)$ =$_c$ +

(L9) *mé*   N $(\uparrow$ PRED$)$ = 'PRO'
                              $(\uparrow$ PERS$)$ = 1
                              $(\uparrow$ NUM$)$ = SG

(L10) *Eoghan*   N $(\uparrow$ PRED$)$ = 'Owen'
                              $(\uparrow$ PERS$)$ = 3
                              $(\uparrow$ NUM$)$ = SG

Task X How would you account for the fact that synthetic verbal forms cannot cooccur with a subject NP?

Task XI Provide morpholexical specifications for the verbal forms *chuirfinn*, *chuirféa*, and *chuirfimis* in the paradigm in (1).

Task XII Provide full c- and f-structures for (7a) and (7b) above.

P2.4 Noun Incorporation in Greenlandic

P2.4.1 *Morphological ergativity*

In Greenlandic a single case form, the absolutive (ABS), marks both the subject of an intransitive verb and the object of a transitive verb. A different case form, the ergative (ERG), is reserved for the subject of a transitive verb. (This patterning of subjects of intransitive verbs with objects in contradistinction to subjects of transitive verbs is called *ergativity*.) An intransitive verb agrees with its subject (see (1) below), while a transitive verb, using a distinct agreement affix, agrees with both its subject and its object (see (2)–(4) below).

(1) *Arnaq* *tikippoq.*
woman.Abs come.Indic.3.Sg
'The woman came.'

(2) *Arna-p* *meeraq* *takuvaa.*
woman-Erg child.Abs see.Indic.3.Sg.3.Sg
'The woman saw the child.'

Note that an NP subject or object need not be present for this case-marking pattern to appear:

(3) *Arnaq* *takuvara.*
woman.Abs see-Indic.1.Sg.3.Sg
'I saw the woman.'

(4) *Arna-p* *takuvaanga.*
woman-Erg see.Indic.3.Sg.1.Sg
'The woman saw me.'

As in many languages with ergative case-marking, certain basically transitive verbs can be used as intransitive verbs just by affixing the agreement marking appropriate to an intransitive verb. While the transitive form of the verb will select an ergative-marked subject and an absolutive-marked object, the intransitive form of the verb will select an absolutive-marked subject and an oblique. In Greenlandic this oblique argument has instrumental case, and the verb does not show any agreement with it.

(5) *Neqi* *nerivara.*
meat.Abs eat.Indic.1.Sg.3.Sg
'I ate the meat.'

(6) *Neqi-mik nerivunga.*
meat-Inst eat.Indic.1.Sg
'I ate meat.'

P2.4.2 *Noun incorporation*

Greenlandic has a class of suffixes which combine with nouns to form verbs in which the incorporated noun is understood to be a grammatical argument of a verb encoded by the suffix. Below are given two such suffixes, -*qarpoq*, whose meaning corresponds to 'have', and -*sivoq*, whose meaning is, roughly, 'buy'. *Qimmeq* and *sapangaq*, given in (7a) and (8a) respectively, are independent lexical items, which form derived verbs when combined with the verbal suffixes (see (7b) and (8b)).

(7) a. *qimmeq* 'dog'
     b. *Qimmeq-qarpoq.* 'He has a dog.'

(8) a. *sapangaq* 'bead'
     b. *Sapangar-sivoq.* 'He bought beads.'

In general in Greenlandic, NP modifiers are in the same case as the NP they modify. In (9) the noun *angutip* is marked in the ergative and so is its modifier *angisuup*. In (10) the noun *angummik* is in the instrumental case and so is its modifier *angisuumik*.

(9) *Anguti-p angisuu-p takuvaanga.*
     man-Erg big-Erg   see.Indic.3.Sg.1.Sg
     'The big man saw me.'

(10) *Angum-mik angisuu-mik tikippoq.*
      man-Inst   big-Inst   come.Indic.3.Sg
      'He came with a big man.'

The incorporated grammatical arguments in (11) and (12) can likewise be modified, with the modifiers appearing as separate words in the instrumental case.

(11) *Angisuu-mik qimmeq-qarpoq.*
      big-Inst   dog-have.Indic.3.Sg
      'He has a big dog.'

(12) *Kusanartu-mik sapangar-sivoq.*
      beautiful-Inst   bead-get.Indic.3.Sg
      'He bought a beautiful bead.'

It appears that the number of the incorporated noun is in most cases neutralized, although plurality may be conveyed by the choice of a plural modifier, as in (13), in contrast to (12).

(13) *Kusanartu-nik   sapangar-sivoq.*
      beautiful-Inst.Pl bead-get.Indic.3.Sg
      'He bought beautiful beads.'

But in the case of a noun like *qamutit* 'sled', which is grammatically always plural, the plural form of the modifier must be used:

(14) *Ataatsi-nik qamuteq-qarpoq.*
      one-Inst.Pl sled-have.Indic.3.Sg
      'He has one sled.'

P2.4.3   The problem

We can propose the following set of c-structure rules and functional equations for Greenlandic:

(R1) S →   (NP)   (NP)   (NP)   V
            (↑ SUBJ) = ↓   (↑ OBJ) = ↓   (↑ OBL) = ↓   ↑ = ↓

(R2) NP →   (N)   (N)
            ↑ = ↓   (↑ ADJ) = ↓
                    (↑ CASE) = (↓ CASE)

Below are given morpholexical specifications for the three types of verbs found in the above examples:

(L1) *tikippoq* V (↑ PRED) = 'come ⟨(↑ SUBJ)⟩'
                     (↑ SUBJ NUM) = SG
                     (↑ SUBJ PERS) = 3
                     (↑ SUBJ CASE) = ABS

(L2) *takuvara* V (↑ PRED) = 'see ⟨(↑ SUBJ)(↑ OBJ)⟩'
                     (↑ SUBJ NUM) = SG
                     (↑ SUBJ CASE) = ERG
                     (↑ SUBJ PERS) = 1
                     (↑ OBJ CASE) = ABS
                     (↑ OBJ NUM) = SG
                     (↑ OBJ PERS) = 3

(L3) *nerivara* V (↑ PRED) = 'eat ⟨(↑ SUBJ)(↑ OBJ)⟩'
                     (↑ SUBJ NUM) = SG
                     (↑ SUBJ CASE) = ERG
                     (↑ SUBJ PERS) = 1
                     (↑ OBJ CASE) = ABS
                     (↑ OBJ NUM) = SG
                     (↑ OBJ PERS) = 3

(L4)   *nerivunga*   V $(\uparrow \text{PRED}) = \text{'eat} \langle(\uparrow \text{SUBJ})(\uparrow \text{OBL})\rangle\text{'}$
$(\uparrow \text{SUBJ CASE}) = \text{ABS}$
$(\uparrow \text{SUBJ NUM}) = \text{SG}$
$(\uparrow \text{SUBJ PERS}) = 1$
$(\uparrow \text{OBL CASE}) = \text{INST}$

(L1) illustrates an intransitive lexical form with one argument, (L4) is an intransitive form with two arguments, while (L2) and (L3) are transitive lexical forms whose objects are cross-referenced on the verb. (A lexical form is a predicate argument structure associated with argument grammatical functions.) The rules and morpholexical specifications that are given above are not written in stone. You will probably wish to revise them.

Task XIII   Provide morpholexical specifications for the verbal suffixes *-qarpoq* and *-sivoq*. You should be able to decide which of the three types of lexical forms they pattern with on the basis of the data given above.

Task XIV   Provide morpholexical specifications for the derived verbs *qimmeqarpoq* and *sapangarsivoq*. You do not have to derive these words (yet).

P2.4.4   *Sublexical structure*

Until now we have largely ignored the internal structure of words. But it is clear from the striking example of Greenlandic, as well as from the phenomena we have seen in the preceding problems, that the f-structure associated with a word can contribute extremely complex information to the f-structure of a sentence as a whole. We have seen how the f-structure of a sentence is related to its phrase structure in a systematic way mediated by functional annotations; and in this final task we will begin to consider how the f-structure of a word is likewise systematically related to its morphemic structure.

One solution might be to represent the internal structure of a word with a "word structure tree" analogous to a phrase structure tree, derived by using annotated word structure rules similar to the annotated phrase structure rules with which you are already acquainted. For example, we might propose the following sublexical c-structure rules for nouns in Greenlandic:

(RS1) $N \;\rightarrow\; \underset{\uparrow \,=\, \downarrow}{N_{\text{stem}}} \quad \underset{\uparrow \,=\, \downarrow}{N_{\text{aff}}}$

(RS2) $N \;\rightarrow\; \underset{\substack{\uparrow \,=\, \downarrow \\ (\uparrow \text{CASE}) = \text{ABS}}}{N_{\text{stem}}}$

This approach adopts a "configurational" word structure for Greenlandic, though not necessarily for all languages.

Note that the second of the above rules is intended to express a kind of morphological "elsewhere condition." The generalization we want to express is that all nouns in Greenlandic have case, and that a noun which is not marked for case by a case affix bears the unmarked case, which is absolutive. We represent this here by the availability of one noun-formation rule which adds a case affix and one which does not, with the choice of not adding an affix entailing the information that case of the noun will be absolutive.

The following sublexical entries would also be required:

(L5)   *qimmeq* N_{stem} ($\uparrow$ PRED) = 'dog'

(L6)   *-p* N_{aff} ($\uparrow$ CASE) = ERG

(L7)   *-mik* N_{aff} ($\uparrow$ CASE) = INST
                         ($\uparrow$ NUM) = SG

(L8)   *-nik* N_{aff} ($\uparrow$ CASE) = INST
                         ($\uparrow$ NUM) = PL

You will notice that these rules will not get the words in exactly the right forms. This is because we are not treating the phonological processes which give rise to morphophonemic alternations.

Task XV   Assume the following sublexical rule for noun incorporation:

(RS3)   V $\rightarrow$ N_{stem} V_{suff}

What should the functional annotations be?

Task XVI   Give word-, c- and f-structures for (11) and (14). You will need the morpholexical specifications listed below in addition to those above and those that you must write for this purpose.

(L9)   *sapangaq* N_{stem} ($\uparrow$ PRED) = 'bead'

(L10)   *angisuu* N_{stem} ($\uparrow$ PRED) = 'big'

(L11)   *qamuteq* N_{stem} ($\uparrow$ PRED) = 'sled'
                            ($\uparrow$ NUM) = PL

Problem Set 3

P3.1   German Word Order

P3.1.1   Subordinate clauses

Consider the following German subordinate clauses, paying particular attention to the word order:

(1) a.   *. . . daß Karl das Buch kaufte.*
              that   the book bought
          '. . . that Karl bought the book.'
     b. *. . . *daß Karl kaufte das Buch.*

(2) a.   *. . . daß Karl das Buch gekauft hat.*
              that   the book bought has
          '. . . that Karl has bought the book.'
     b. *. . . *daß Karl gekauft das Buch hat.*
     c. *. . . *daß Karl gekauft hat das Buch.*

Task I   Propose a set of c-structure rules that will generate the grammatical sentences above, and rule out the ungrammatical ones. Be sure to include all functional annotations. Is the VP head-initial or head-final?

You may assume that the c-structure rules follow the basic principles of endocentric structure–function association discussed in chapter 6. The relevant (simplified) morpholexical specifications for the words are as follows:

(L1) *daß*: C $(\uparrow$ MOOD$) =$ DECL
                  $(\uparrow$ TENSE$)$

(L2) *Karl*: N $(\uparrow$ PRED$) =$ 'Karl'

(L3) *das*: D $(\uparrow$ DEF$) = +$

(L4) *Buch*: N $(\uparrow$ PRED$) =$ 'book'

(L5) *kaufte*: I_V ($\uparrow$ PRED) = 'buy $\langle(\uparrow$ SUBJ$)(\uparrow$ OBJ$)\rangle$'
($\uparrow$ TENSE) = PAST

(L6) *gekauft*: V ($\uparrow$ PRED) = 'buy $\langle(\uparrow$ SUBJ$)(\uparrow$ OBJ$)\rangle$'

(L7) *hat*: I ($\uparrow$ TENSE) = PRES_PERF

Task II Provide c-structures and f-structures for (1a) and (2a).

P3.1.2 *Main clauses*

A well-known feature of German syntax, common to most of the Germanic languages, is that the order of the finite verb and its complements differs depending on whether the clause is a main clause or a subordinate one. While the finite verb is always final in subordinate clauses such as in (1) and (2) above, in main (declarative) clauses it must appear in second position, preceded by a topicalized element such as the subject, the object or an adjunct. This requirement is often referred to in the literature as the verb second constraint:

(3) a. *Karl kaufte das Buch.*
          bought the book
      'Karl bought the book.'
  b. *Das Buch kaufte Karl.*
      the book bought
      'The book Karl bought.'
  c. *Gestern   kaufte Karl das Buch.*
      yesterday bought   the book
      'Yesterday Karl bought the book.'
  d. **Karl das Buch kaufte.*
  e. **Kaufte das Buch Karl.*

The question, then, is how to analyze German phrase structure so that these alternative ordering constraints can be captured. One possibility is to simply have two different sets of c-structure rules for main and subordinate clauses. There are (at least) two pieces of evidence against such an analysis.

First, it is only the position of the *finite* verb which is different in main clauses: nonfinite verbs remain in the same position as in subordinate clauses:

(4) a. *. . . daß Karl das Buch gekauft hat.*
        that   the book bought has
      '. . . that Karl bought the book.'
  b. *Karl hat das Buch gekauft.*
        has the book bought
      'Karl bought the book.'
  c. **Karl hat gekauft das Buch.*
  d. **Karl gekauft das Buch hat.*

A second piece of evidence comes from verb-particle combinations. These are verbs which are composed of two elements: a verb stem and a (separable) particle. The verb *zurückgeben* 'return, give back', for example, consists of the verb stem *geben* 'give' and the particle *zurück* 'back'. While these verbs behave as single lexical units in subordinate clauses, in main clauses it is only the verb stem which appears in second position; the particle still appears in final position:

(5) a. . . . *daß Karl das Buch zurückgab.*
           that   the book back-gave
         '. . . that Karl returned the book.'
     b. *. . . *daß Karl das Buch gab zurück.*

(6) a. *Karl gab das Buch zurück.*
           gave the Buch back
         'Karl returned the book.'
     b. **Karl zurückgab das Buch.*

Thus, elements such as nonfinite verbs and separable particles, which appear in the VP, are found in the same positions in both subordinate and main clauses, despite the fact that the finite verb appears in a different position. This suggests that we do not want to have completely separate sets of rules, one for main clauses and one for subordinate clauses, since we would then fail to capture certain generalizations that hold across the two.

Another possibility would be to have two IP rules, but the same VP rule. Since it is only finite verbs which appear in I, meaning that they are the only elements which would be affected by the different rules, this solution would not run into the same problems as the previous one. However, while this analysis is certainly possible, it is clearly less desirable than one which can account for all of the data without needing to postulate different phrase structure rules for main and subordinate clauses. Such an analysis is available, and is supported by the following facts about German complementizers.

Unlike English complementizers, the complementizer in German subordinate clauses is generally obligatory:

(7) I believe (that) Karl is sick.

(8) a. *Ich glaube daß Karl krank ist.*
           I   believe that   sick is
         'I believe that Karl is sick.'
     b. **Ich glaube Karl krank ist.*

However, a few verbs (of which *glauben* 'believe' is one) allow the complementizer to be omitted from their complement clause. Interestingly, in just these cases, the subordinate verb *must* appear in second position:

(9) *Ich glaube Karl ist krank.*
     I   believe   is sick
     'I believe Karl is sick.'

(10) a. *Sie sagte daß wir keinen Wein mitbringen sollten.*
          she said that we no   wine along-take should
          'She said that we should take no wine along.'
      b. *Sie sagte wir sollten keinen Wein mitbringen.*
          she said we should no   wine along-take
          'She said we should take no wine along.'
      c. **Sie sagte wir keinen Wein mitbringen sollten.*
      d. **Sie sagte daß wir sollten keinen Wein mitbringen.*

Thus, the complementizer and the verb in second position appear to be in complementary distribution with one another.

Task III   Propose an analysis of German main clauses which captures all of the information about word order given above. Provide any new information (e.g. morpholexical specifications and/or c-structure rules) that your account requires in order to generate the sentences given in (3a) and (4b). Be careful to ensure that your analysis will still correctly account for the data in (1) and (2). Is the headedness of the VP (i.e., initial/final) the same as it was in Task I? Explain.

   Although all c-structure nodes are assumed to be optional in LFG, unless required by a general principle, you can assume for the purposes of this problem that C is obligatory in German. In addition, you can assume the following rules for CP:

(R1) CP → $\left(\begin{array}{c} \text{DP} \\ (\uparrow \text{TOP}) = \downarrow \end{array}\right)$ $\begin{array}{c} \text{C}' \\ \uparrow = \downarrow \end{array}$

(R2) C' → $\begin{array}{cc} \text{C} & \text{IP} \\ \uparrow = \downarrow & \uparrow = \downarrow \end{array}$

Task IV   Provide c-structures and f-structures for (3a) and (4b).

Task V   Explain how your analysis can rule out ungrammatical examples such as the following:

(11) *. . . *daß kaufte Karl das Buch.*
           that bought   the book
      '. . . that Karl bought the book.'

(12) **Karl gekauft das Buch.*
            bought the book
      'Karl bought the book.'

There are two further important generalizations about German that are implicit in the above discussion: (i) a complementizer must always be initial in its clause; and (ii) a (declarative) main clause verb must always be second in its clause. Thus, while the two may be in complementary distribution with each other, they appear in different syntactic contexts:

(13) a.   ... *daß Karl das Buch kaufte.*
             that   the book bought
        '... that Karl bought the book.'
      b. *... *Karl daß das Buch kaufte.*

(14) a.   *Karl kaufte das Buch.*
               bought the book
          'Karl bought the book.'
      b. *_Kaufte Karl das Buch._

Task VI   Does your account capture these generalizations? If so, explain how. If not, explain the modifications necessary for it to do so. Provide any modified morpholexical specifications and/or c-structure rules that your analysis requires in order to account for examples (13) and (14). *Hint:* There are many possible solutions to this task, and no single right answer.

P3.2   Subject Agreement in West Flemish

West Flemish is a dialect of Dutch spoken in Belgium. Like many of the Germanic languages, West Flemish is subject to the verb second constraint: the finite verb alternates between final position in subordinate clauses and second position in main declarative clauses. Consider the following sentences (note that *ee* in (1b) is actually *eet* – the same alternation appears with *goa(t)*: the /t/ drops before a consonant):

(1) a.   ... *da   Marie dienen boek gelezen eet.*
              that   that book read   has
         '... that Marie read that book.'
     b.   *Marie ee   dienen boek gelezen.*
               has that   book read
          'Marie read that book.'

Task VII   Assuming that the phrase structure rules and lexical entries for West Flemish are analogous to those which you developed in the previous problem for German, provide full analyses of (1a, b).

P3.2.1 Subject agreement in subordinate clauses

Verbs in subordinate clauses show very minimal agreement with their subject. There are only two distinct forms: one for third person singular and second person, and the other for third person plural and first person:

(2) a. ... *gie/zie/gunder*   *goat.*
             you(sg)/she/you(pl) go
      b. ... *ik/wunder/zunder goan.*
             I/we/they   go

Task VIII Provide morpholexical specifications for the verbs *goat* and *goan* in (2). As finite subordinate verbs, to what category to they belong?

A particularly interesting aspect of West Flemish is that the complementizer in subordinate clauses *also* agrees with the subject of the subordinate clause, agreeing in both person and number. This complementizer agreement is obligatory with both pronominal and nonpronominal subjects:

(3) a. ... *dan-k (ik) goan.*
             that-I (I) go
             '... that I'll go.'
      b. ... *da-j*   *(gie)*   *goat.*
             that-you (you(sg))
      c. ... *da-se*   *(zie) goat.*
             that-she (she)
      d. ... *da-me*   *(wunder) goan.*
             that-we (we)
      e. ... *da-j*   *(gunder) goat.*
             that-you (you(pl))
      f. ... *dan-ze*   *(zunder) goan.*
             that-they (they)
      g. ... *da Marie goat.*
      h. ... *dan Marie en Pol goan.*

As can be seen in (3), pronominal subjects are optional in subordinate clauses; they appear only when the subject is stressed. Thus, either of the following versions of (3c) is fully grammatical (although with different pragmatic effects):

(4) a. ... *da-se*   *goat.*
             that-she goes
             '... that she goes.'
      b. ... *da-se*   *zie goat.*
             that-she she goes

Full NP subjects, on the other hand, cooccur with different forms of the complementizer and are not optional, as can be seen in (3g, h).

Task IX   Provide morpholexical specifications for the complementizers in (3b, c, d, g, h). Please also provide specifications for the subject pronouns in (3b, c, e). How do your specifications capture the facts concerning the distributional differences between pronominal and full DP subjects mentioned above?

Task X   Give full analyses of (3g) and (4a, b).

P3.2.2   *Subject agreement in main clauses*

While the finite verb shows little agreement with its subject in subordinate clauses, this is not the case in main clauses. Rather, in main clauses the verb shows full person and number agreement with its subject. This agreement takes the same form as the complementizer agreement discussed above:

(5) a.   *Morgen   goan-k (ik).*
          tomorrow go-I   (I)
          'Tomorrow I'll go.'
     b.   *Morgen goa-j   (gie).*
                    go-you (you(sg))
     c.   *Morgen goa-se (zie).*
                    go-she (she)
     d.   *Morgen goa-me (wunder).*
                    go-we   (we)
     e.   *Morgen goa-j   (gunder).*
                    go-you (you(pl))
     f.   *Morgen goan-ze (zunder).*
                    go-they (they)
     g.   *Morgen goa Marie.*
     h.   *Morgen goan Marie en Pol.*

Note that, as with the inflected complementizer in subordinate clauses, subject pronominals are optional in main clauses while full DP subjects are not.

Task XI   Provide morpholexical specifications for the verbs in (5b, c, d, g, h). To what category do these words belong?

Task XII   What is the generalization that characterizes the distribution of the subject agreement suffixes in both main and subordinate clauses?

Task XIII   Provide full analyses for (5c), both with and without the subject pronoun.

P3.3 Person and Number Marking in Wambaya

Wambaya is a non-Pama-Nyungan language spoken in Northern Australia. Like Warlpiri (see problem set 1), it is a non-configurational language with free word order, and no VP constituent. Nouns and pronouns are marked according to an ergative/absolutive case marking system: the subjects of transitive verbs carry ergative case marking, while objects of transitive verbs and subjects of intransitive verbs are marked with absolutive case.

In this problem, we will be concerned with the Wambaya auxiliary, which appears in second position and contains information about the subject, the object, and the tense/aspect/mood of the clause. The auxiliary is obligatory in all finite clauses, irrespective of the presence or absence of the corresponding NPs. Some examples of simple Wambaya clauses follow:

(1) a. *Bardbi ny-a   nyamirniji.*
         run   you:Subj-Pst you(ABS)
         'You (sg.) ran.'
     b. *Bardbi ny-a.*
         run   you:Subj-Pst
         'You (sg.) ran.'

(2) a. *Gulugbi girr-a   girriyani.*
         sleep   you:pl:Subj-Pst you:pl(ABS)
         'You (pl.) slept.'
     b. *Gulugbi girr-a.*
         sleep   you:pl:Subj-Pst
         'You (pl.) slept.'

(3) a. *Ngajbi gini-ng-a   ngawurniji alangini.*
         see   he:Subj-me:Obj-Pst me(ABS)   boy(ERG)
         'The boy saw me.'
     b. *Ngajbi gini-ng-a   alangini.*
         see   he:Subj-me:Obj-Pst boy(ERG)
         'The boy saw me.'
     c. *Ngajbi gini-ng-a.*
         see   he:Subj-me:Obj-Pst
         'He saw me.'

As discussed in chapter 7, let us assume the following c-structure rules for Wambaya. The abbreviation *X* is used to cover both NP and V, which are treated alike with respect to word order within the S. Instances of *X* and NP should be instantiated according to the rules given in (R5). The asterisk means that there may be any number of *X*s, including none. As discussed in chapter 7 you may assume that the auxiliary is generated in I and that, when there is nothing in [Spec, IP], the verb is generated adjoined to the I node:

(R1)   IP   →   (NP)   I′
$\uparrow = \downarrow$

(R2)   I′   →   I   S
$\uparrow = \downarrow$ $\uparrow = \downarrow$

(R3)   S   → x^* Where x = NP, V

(R4)   NP   →   N

(R5)   a.   Assign ($\uparrow$ SUBJ) = $\downarrow$ or ($\uparrow$ OBJ) = $\downarrow$ freely to NP.
       b.   Assign $\uparrow = \downarrow$ to N and V.

You will need the following morpholexical specifications for the words:

(L1)   *alangini*: N   ($\uparrow$ PRED) = 'boy'
                          ($\uparrow$ CASE) = ERG

(L2)   *ngawurniji*: N   ($\uparrow$ PRED) = 'PRO'
                          ($\uparrow$ PERS) = 1
                          ($\uparrow$ NUM) = SG
                          ($\uparrow$ CASE) = ABS

(L3)   *ngajbi*: V   ($\uparrow$ PRED) = 'see $\langle$($\uparrow$ SUBJ)($\uparrow$ OBJ)$\rangle$'
                          ($\uparrow$ SUBJ CASE) = ERG
                          ($\uparrow$ OBJ CASE) = ABS

Task XIV   Give morpholexical specifications for the auxiliary *gininga* which appears in (3).

Task XV   Provide c-structures and f-structures for (3a, b, c).

While the forms of the subject-bound pronouns change according to the number of the subject (compare (1) and (2), for example), this is not so for the object-bound pronouns, which remain the same regardless of the number of the object:

(4)   a.   *Ngajbi gininga ngawurniji.*
           see   me(ABS)
           'He saw me.'
      b.   *Ngajbi gininga ngurla.*
           see   us:dual(ABS)
           'He saw us two.'
      c.   *Ngajbi gininga ngirra.*
           see   us:pl(ABS)
           'He saw us all.'

Task XVI Modify, if necessary, the morpholexical specifications for *gininga* that you gave in Task XIV in order to account for the examples in (4). Explain any changes you make.

Task XVII Provide c- and f-structures for (4c).

Note that the object-bound pronoun must always cooccur with a corresponding NP when the object is non-singular (as in (4b, c). When there is no object NP present, the object-bound pronoun obligatorily has singular number:

(5) *Ngajbi gininga.*
    see
    'He saw me /*us two /*us all.'

Task XVIII Does your analysis of the auxiliary account for this fact about object number? If so, explain how. If not, explain what change(s) need to be made to your analysis in order for it to do so.

Task XIX One possible way of analysing languages such as Wambaya is to consider the subject and object markers in the auxiliary to be the real arguments of the verb, while the corresponding NPs are simply coreferential adjuncts. In this approach, the subject and object auxiliary markers would always be incorporated pronominals, and the NPs, being adjuncts, would be optional. The data presented above constitute a piece of evidence bearing on such an analysis for Wambaya. Does it argue for or against it? Explain your answer.

Problem Set 4

P4.1 Discontinuous Dependencies in Open Complement Constructions

P4.1.1 *Dutch dependent clauses*

Below are given some fragments of Dutch complement constructions – some grammatical, some not – which you will examine using the words and grammar given in (4) and (5). The word order in (1)–(3) is that for embedded complements. We shall ignore nonembedded structures in this problem:

(1) ... *Jan Piet Marie zag helpen zwemmen*

(2) ... *Jan Piet Marie zag zwemmen*

(3) ... *Jan Piet zag helpen zwemmen*

(4) Morpholexical specifications:

helpen	V	($\uparrow$ PRED) = 'help $\langle(\uparrow$ SUBJ$)(\uparrow$ OBJ$)(\uparrow$ XCOMP$)\rangle$'
		($\uparrow$ XCOMP SUBJ) = ($\uparrow$ OBJ)
Jan	N	($\uparrow$ PRED) = 'Jan'
		($\uparrow$ NUM) = SG
Marie	N	($\uparrow$ PRED) = 'Marie'
		($\uparrow$ NUM) = SG
Piet	N	($\uparrow$ PRED) = 'Piet'
		($\uparrow$ NUM) = SG
zag	V	($\uparrow$ PRED) = 'see $\langle(\uparrow$ SUBJ$)(\uparrow$ OBJ$)(\uparrow$ XCOMP$)\rangle$'
		($\uparrow$ TENSE) = PAST
		($\uparrow$ SUBJ NUM) = SG
		($\uparrow$ XCOMP SUBJ) = ($\uparrow$ OBJ)
zwemmen	V	($\uparrow$ PRED) = 'swim $\langle(\uparrow$ SUBJ$)\rangle$'

(5) Grammar:

$$
\begin{array}{lll}
\text{S} \rightarrow & \text{NP} & \text{VP} \\
& (\uparrow \text{SUBJ}) = \downarrow & \uparrow = \downarrow \\
\text{VP} \rightarrow & (\text{NP}) & (\text{VP}) & (\overline{\text{V}}) \\
& (\uparrow \text{OBJ}) = \downarrow & (\uparrow \text{XCOMP}) = \downarrow & \uparrow = \downarrow \\
\overline{\text{V}} \rightarrow & \text{V} & (\overline{\text{V}}) \\
& \uparrow = \downarrow & (\uparrow \text{XCOMP}) = \downarrow \\
\text{NP} \rightarrow & \text{N} \\
& \uparrow = \downarrow
\end{array}
$$

Task I For each string in (1)–(3), determine whether it is a grammatical instance of S. If it is, display the c-structure and f-structure. If not, indicate what is wrong with it. Note that several different c-structure analyses are possible for each of these strings, but only one tree actually leads to a well-formed f-structure.

Task II What generalization can you state about how the various words and phrases contributing to the composition of the open complements (XCOMPs) are realized in the c-structure?

P4.1.2 *Japanese causatives*

In this problem, we shall examine some facts about causativization in Japanese. This phenomenon is exemplified by the following sentence:

(1) *Reiko ga   Taroo o   hasir-ase-ta.*
      Nom   Acc run-Cause-Past
   'Reiko made Taroo run.'

The verb *hasiraseta* is made up of three morphemes. Word initially we find the verb stem *hasir-* 'run'. Immediately following this is the causative morpheme *-ase-* (which has an alternative form *-sase-*, which occurs with vowel final stems). Finally, the morpheme *-ta* is the past tense marker.

P4.1.2.1 Analyzing causative verbs as single words

We assume here that *hasiraseta* is a single word. The hyphens added in the various examples designate morpheme boundaries. This signifies that the partial bracketing in (2) is imposed on sentences like (1):

(2) *Reiko ga   Taroo o   [ᵥ hasir-ase-ta.]*
      Nom   Acc   run-Cause-Past

Hence, no morpheme which makes up a subpart of the word *hasiraseta* may be bracketed together with any NP argument to form a phrase, since that would lead to an overlapping of phrases:

(3) *Reiko ga*   [₁ *Taroo o*   [₂ *hasir*]₁ *-ase-ta.*]₂
     Nom   Acc   run-Cause-Past

Some discussion is in order about this analysis, since it has sometimes been assumed that this form is actually composed of several words. In favor of our analysis, we cite facts which suggest that both *-sase-* and *-ta-* are best treated as affixes and not as independent words. First we note that *-sase-* and *-ta* cooccur with a very restrictive class of formatives that could plausibly be analysed as verbal affixes. Other words are forbidden from occuring in the same environments. Let us take as an example the form in (4), constructed from the verb root *tabe-* 'eat':

(4) *tabe-sase-ta* 'caused (someone) to eat'

Only a very small number of formatives may intervene between *tabe-* and *-sase-* or between *-sase-* and *-ta*. For instance, we have the constructions in (5) and (6):

(5) *tabe-sase-rare-ta* 'was made to eat'
     Tony ga   *Reiko ni*   *nattoo*   o   *tabe-sase-rare-ta.*
          Nom   Dat fermented:soybeans Acc eat-Cause-Pass-Past
     'Tony was made to eat fermented soybeans by Reiko.'

(6) *tabe-sase-kake-ta* 'attempted to make (someone) eat'
     Taroo ga   *Reiko ni*   *doku   iri   keiki o   tabe-sase-kake-ta.*
          Nom   Dat poison exist cake Acc eat-Cause-Attempt-Past
     'Taro tried to make Reiko eat cake with poison in it.'

The form *-rare-* (alternatively *-are-*, when the stem is consonant final) is the passive morpheme. Adding *-kake-* to a verbal form adds a meaning akin to *try* or *attempt*. Some speakers, though not all, also accept forms like that in (7), constructed from the verb stem *hik-* 'hit', where the passive morpheme precedes the causative morpheme:

(7) *hik-are-sase-ta* 'caused (something) to be hit'
     Booryokudan no   kumichoo ga   keisatsushochoo o   kuruma ni
     gang   Gen leader   Nom police chief   Acc car   Dat
     hik-are-sase-ta.
     hit-Pass-Cause-Past
     'The gang leader had the police chief run over by a car.'

Outside of this very small class of formatives like *-rare-* and *-kake-* that can be inserted into causative constructions, the vast majority of words is forbidden from occurring in such positions. Take, for instance, the word *dake* 'only'. This provides a telling test, because *dake* displays an extremely free distribution in sentences of Japanese. Note that Japanese contains certain expressions which are composed of two or more words that are rarely separable. One such expression is *benkyoo suru* 'study' (literally 'study do'). *Dake* is one of the few formatives that may intervene between *benkyoo* and *suru* to yield a grammatical sentence:

(8) *Taroo ga   benkyoo dake suru.*
     Nom study   only do
     'Taro does nothing but study.'

Even though *dake* can appear between tightly bound syntactic units, as we saw in (8), it cannot be inserted in the environments shown in (9) and (10):

(9) **tabe **dake** sase-ta*

(10) **tabe-sase **dake** ta*

To explain this array of facts, we might analyze morphemes like *-rare-* and *-kake-* as verbal suffixes, and we could then propose that the forms in (5)–(7) are all single words, formed by regular morphological processes of affixation. The meanings associated with these forms make the approach seem plausible, since similar meanings are encoded morphologically in other languages. Note further that this approach would explain the restrictiveness of the set of formatives that may intervene between a verb stem and *-sase-* or between *-sase-* and *-ta*, since universally the affixes of a language tend to constitute a closed class. Other words, even those with extreme freedom of occurrence like *dake*, would be forbidden from occurring within causative constructions for the simple reason that words do not occur in the middle of other words.

The most compelling argument that causative forms like *hasiraseta* and *tabesaseta* are words is to be found in the suprasegmental phonology of Japanese. A full exposition of the relevant facts and generalizations would be too long to detail here; however, the basic line of argumentation is the following. Poser (1984) has demonstrated that Japanese verbal affixes have the characteristic of influencing the accentual properties of the words in which they occur. This phenomenon arises with markers of tense, aspect, and the like, which are accepted uncontroversially as affixes. However, the rules in question do not apply across word boundaries; they apparently apply word internally only. Now the formatives *-sase-*, *-rare-*, etc., all pattern as normal verbal affixes in this phonological respect, combining with the preceding verb stem to create a single word, and helping to determine the accentual pattern of the resultant form in the predictable way.

The relevance of the foregoing discussion to the present problem lies in the fact that we would like to maintain a strong hypothesis about the relation between words and syntactic phrasing; namely, that no syntactic phrase may violate a word boundary in the fashion displayed in (3). Providing an analysis of the Japanese causative construction which adheres to this hypothesis is the substance of the task set for this problem.

P4.1.2.2   Consequences of the one-word analysis of causatives

This analysis suggests that Japanese causatives involve a phenomenon similar to that described in the Greenlandic exercise in problem set 2. Recall that Greenlandic exhibits incorporated forms in which a single word provides information about the PRED, TENSE, and so on for the f-structure corresponding to a clause, while also providing information about the OBL f-structure to be inserted within that clausal f-structure. By simply changing OBL in the preceding sentence to XCOMP, we have a description of the situation in Japanese causatives. In both cases it seems that it is not only words and syntactic phrases that encode grammatical functions in sentences, but that morphemes which are subparts of words also give rise to such functions. In fact, the information encoded in a causative verb like *hasiraseta* is sufficient to infer quite a bit about the content of the f-structure which we would associate with the whole sentence. This suggests that we should construct an analysis such that with only the fragmentary tree in (11), we would be able to derive the partial f-structure shown in (12):

(11)   . . .

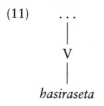

(12)

$$f_n \begin{bmatrix} \text{TENSE} & \text{PAST} \\ \text{PRED} & \text{`cause} \langle (f_n \text{ SUBJ})(f_n \text{ OBJ})(f_n \text{ XCOMP}) \rangle \text{'} \\ \text{OBJ} \\ \text{XCOMP} & f_m \begin{bmatrix} \text{PRED} & \text{`run} \langle (f_m \text{ SUBJ}) \rangle \text{'} \\ \text{SUBJ} \end{bmatrix} \end{bmatrix}$$

Thus as was done in the Greenlandic problem, we must provide the morphology with the capability to express generalizations about f-structure.

One such proposal (Ishikawa 1985) takes the form of employing rewriting rules to describe morphological structure, and providing these rewriting rules with functional annotations, so that functional annotations are applied to sublexical constituents such as stems and affixes and units formed out of these. Simplifying Ishikawa's proposal somewhat, we might here employ the following sublexical rewriting rules to construct complex verbs in Japanese:

(13) $V_{\text{sublex}} \rightarrow$ V_{stem} Aff_{infl}
                              $\uparrow = \downarrow$ $\uparrow = \downarrow$

(14) $V_{\text{stem sublex}} \rightarrow$ V_{stem} Aff_{drv}
                              $(\uparrow \text{ XCOMP}) = \downarrow$ $\uparrow = \downarrow$

If we write morphological rules in this fashion, *hasiraseta* will have a sublexical tree structure like that in (15):

(15)

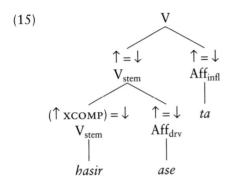

Using the lexical specifications in (16)–(18) for *hasir-*, *-(s)ase-*, and *-ta* and adding to *-(s)ase-* the control schema specified by the default rule of functional control (chapter 12), we are able to derive from (15) the desired partial f-structure displayed above in (12):

(16) *hasir-* V_{stem} $(\uparrow \text{PRED}) = $ 'run $\langle (\uparrow \text{SUBJ}) \rangle$'

(17) *-(s)ase-* Aff_{drv} $(\uparrow \text{PRED}) = $ 'cause $\langle (\uparrow \text{SUBJ})(\uparrow \text{OBJ})(\uparrow \text{XCOMP}) \rangle$'

(18) *-ta* Aff_{infl} $(\uparrow \text{TENSE}) = \text{PAST}$

P4.1.2.3 More facts about causatives

Japanese noun phrases may optionally contain case marking particles like *ga* and *o*. The relationship between case markers and grammatical functions and thematic roles is not a simple one; however, for the purposes of this exercise all NPs will be presented with a case marker, and we shall avoid any exceptional or "quirky" case phenomena. Thus you may assume that a constituent marked with nominative case is the SUBJ, one marked with accusative case is the OBJ, and one marked with dative case is an OBJ_θ. The example in (19) (= (1)) displays a "causer" SUBJ and a "causee" OBJ:

(19) *Reiko ga*   *Taroo o*   *hasir-ase-ta.*
          Nom   Acc run-Cause-Past
      'Reiko made Taroo run.'

Alternatively the causee may be realized as an OBJ_θ:

(20) *Reiko ga*   *Tony ni*   *nattoo*   *o*   *tabe-sase-ta.*
          Nom   Dat fermented:soybeans Acc eat-Cause-Past
      'Reiko made Tony eat fermented soybeans.'

Hence, *-(s)ase-* will have an alternative PRED:

(21) 'cause $\langle(\uparrow \text{SUBJ})(\uparrow \text{OBJ}_\theta)(\uparrow \text{XCOMP})\rangle$'

Another interesting fact about the causative construction in Japanese is that the morpheme *-(s)ase-* may occur more than once within a verb.

(22) *Reiko ga   Sachiko ni Taroo o   hasir-ase-sase-ta.*
      Nom   Dat   Acc run-Cause-Cause-Past
      'Reiko made Sachiko make Taroo run.'

(23) *Reiko ga   Sachiko ni Tony ni   nattoo   o*
      Nom   Dat   Dat fermented:soybeans Acc
      tabe-sase-sase-ta.
      eat-Cause-Cause-Past
      'Reiko made Sachiko make Tony eat fermented soybeans.'

Some speakers of Japanese find even three iterations of *-(s)ase-* possible.

Task III   Assume an analysis of the internal structure of causative verbs like that given above. Write a set of syntactic rules to admit examples (19), (20), (22), and (23). Your rules should ensure that the various NPs in the sentence are associated with the proper arguments of the causative verb to create well-formed f-structures, and they should respect the bracketing displayed in (2). You should be guided by, but not blindly copy, the analysis of Dutch.

Task IV   Display the c-structure and f-structure for the example in (23).

P4.1.2.4   Word order in causative constructions

Finally, it is interesting to note that Japanese allows fairly free scrambling of preverbal constituents. Below is a limited selection of the possible reorderings of the sentences in (19), (20), (22), and (23):

(24) *Taroo o   Reiko ga   hasir-ase-ta.*
      Acc   Nom run-Cause-Past
      'Reiko made Taroo run.'

(25) *Tony ni   Reiko ga   nattoo   o   tabe-sase-ta.*
      Dat   Nom fermented:soybeans Acc eat-Cause-Past
      'Reiko made Tony eat fermented soybeans.'

(26) *Sachiko ni   Reiko ga   Taroo o   hasir-ase-sase-ta.*
      Dat   Nom   Acc run-Cause-Cause-Past
      'Reiko made Sachiko make Taro run.'

(27) *Sachiko ni   Reiko ga   Tony ni   nattoo   o*
        Dat   Nom   Dat fermented:soybeans Acc
      tabe-sase-sase-ta.
      eat-Cause-Cause-Past
      'Reiko made Sachiko make Tony eat fermented soybeans.'

(28) *Sachiko ni   Reiko ga   nattoo   o   Tony ni*
        Dat   Nom fermented:soybeans Acc   Dat
      tabe-sase-sase-ta.
      eat-Cause-Cause-Past
      'Reiko made Sachiko make Tony eat fermented soybeans.'

(29) *Reiko ga   Sachiko ni   nattoo   o   Tony ni*
        Nom   Dat fermented:soybeans Acc   Dat
      tabe-sase-sase-ta.
      eat-Cause-Cause-Past
      'Reiko made Sachiko make Tony eat fermented soybeans.'

(30) **Sachiko ni   Tony ni   Reiko ga   nattoo   o*
        Dat   Dat   Nom fermented:soybeans Acc
      tabe-sase-sase-ta.
      eat-Cause-Cause-Past
      'Reiko made Sachiko make Tony eat fermented soybeans.'

Task V If your rules do not already account for the ordering possibilities in examples (29)–(30), try to revise them so that they will. The foregoing is not an exhaustive account of the word order possibilities in these constructions, so you should not worry if your rules include or exclude orders not presented here.

P4.2 Case and Grammatical Functions

P4.2.1 *"Quirky" case in Icelandic*

Icelandic has the richest inflectional system of any modern Germanic language. There are four cases (nominative, accusative, dative, and genitive) and three genders (masculine, feminine, neuter). In simple sentences, the regular case of the subject is nominative and that of the object is accusative, as in (1) and (2):

(1) *Stelpurnar   dansa.*
    the:girls.Nom dance.3.Pl
    'The girls dance.'

(2) *María   elskar   Harald.*
     Mary.Nom love.3.Sg Harald.Acc
     'Mary loves Harold.'

The arguments of some verbs, however, appear to exhibit rather different case-marking patterns:

(3) a. *Mér   býður   við setningafræði.*
         me.Dat be:nauseated.3.Sg by syntax
         'I abhor syntax.'
     b. *Verkjanna   gætir   ekki.*
         the-pains.Gen be:noticeable.3.Sg not
         'The pains are not noticeable.'
     c. *Hrútana   flæddi.*
         the:rams.Acc flood.3.Sg.Past
         'The rams were caught in the flood-tide.'

(4) a. *Henni finnst   Ólafur   leiðinlegur.*
         her.Dat find.3.Sg Olaf.Nom boring.Nom
         'She finds Olaf boring.'
     b. *Stelpunum finnst   Ólafur   leiðinlegur.*
         the:girls.Dat find.3.Sg Olaf.Nom boring.Nom
         'The girls find Olaf boring.'

In this problem we will consider the question of what grammatical function should be associated with the nonnominative NPs in sentences like those in (3) and (4). Following is some evidence which bears on this issue.

P4.2.1.1 Word order

As in most Germanic languages other than English, in Icelandic the verb in a declarative sentence must occupy second position. While it is normally the subject which precedes the verb, it need not be. If some other constituent precedes the verb, because of the verb second constraint the subject cannot also precede the verb:

(5) a. *Harald   elskar   María.*
         Harald.Acc love.3.Sg Mary.Nom
         'Harold Mary loves.'
     b. **Harald   María   elskar.*
         Harald.Acc Mary.Nom love.3.Sg

In direct questions, however, the verb appears first, immediately followed by the subject:

(6) a. *Elskar   María   Harald?*
         love.3.Sg Mary.Nom Harald.Acc
         'Does Mary love Harold?'
     b. **Elskar   Harald   María?*
         love.3.Sg Harald.Acc Mary.Nom

Now compare the word order variations possible with respect to (4a):

(7) a. *Ólafur   finnst   henni   leiðinlegur.*
         Olaf.Nom find.3.Sg her.Dat boring.Nom
         'Olaf she finds boring.'
     b. **Ólafur   henni   finnst   leiðinlegur.*
         Olaf.Nom her.Dat find.3.Sg boring.Nom

(8) a. *Finnst   henni   Ólafur   leiðinlegur?*
         find.3.Sg her.Dat Olaf.Nom boring.Nom
         'Does she find Olaf boring?'
     b. **Finnst   Ólafur   henni   leiðinlegur?*
         find.3.Sg Olaf.Nom her.Dat boring.Nom

P4.2.1.2   Reflexivization

Next consider the following pattern of reflexivization possibilities for many speakers of Icelandic:

(9) a. *Sigga   barði   mig   með dúkkuni sinni/*hennar.*
         Sigga.Nom hit.3.Sg me.Acc with doll.Dat her.Refl/her
         'Sigga hit me with her (Sigga's) doll.'
     b. *Ég   barði   Siggu   með dúkkuni hennar/*sinni.*
         I.Nom hit.1.Sg Sigga.Acc with doll   her/her.Refl
         'I hit Sigga with her (Sigga's) doll.'
     c. *Siggu   barði   ég með dúkkuni hennar/*sinni.*
         Sigga.Acc hit.3.Sg I   with doll   her/her.Refl
         'Sigga I hit with her (Sigga's) doll.'

Now compare the reflexivization possibilities in the following sentence:

(10) *Henni   finnst   bróðir   sinn/*hennar leiðinlegur.*
      her.Dat find.3.Sg brother.Nom her.Refl/her boring.Nom
      'She finds her brother boring.'

P4.2.1.3   Ellipsis

Finally, consider the following pattern of possible ellipses. (The symbol *e* in these sentences is simply intended to indicate which constituent would appear if there were no ellipsis. Note also that the transitive verb *grafa* 'bury' which occurs in these sentences also has an intransitive meaning 'dig'. It is therefore actually only under the intended transitive reading that (11c) is ungrammatical; but that is the only reading you need be concerned with here.)

(11) a. *þeir   fluttu   líkið   og þeir grófu það.*
           they.Nom move.3.Pl.Past the.corpse and they buried it.
           'They moved the corpse and they buried it.'
      b. *þeir   fluttu   líkið   og e grófu það.*
           they.Nom move.3.Pl.Past the.corpse and   buried it.
      c. **þeir   fluttu   líkið   og þeir grófu e.*
           they.Nom move.3.Pl.Past the.corpse and they buried

(12) a. *Líkið   hræddi   þá   og þeir grófu það.*
           the.corpse scare.3.Sg.Past them and they buried it
           'The corpse scared them and they buried it.'
      b. **Líkið   hræddi   þá   og þeir grófu e.*
           the.corpse scare.3.Sg.Past them and they buried
      c. **Líkið   hræddi   þá   og e grófu það.*
           the.corpse scare.3.Sg.Past them and   buried it

Now consider the following sentence:

(13) *Hann   segist   vera duglegur en e finnst   verkefnið   of*
       He.Nom says:self.3.Sg be.Inf diligent but   find.3.Sg the:homework too
       þungt.
       hard
       'He says he is diligent, but finds the homework too hard.'

Task VI What grammatical function would you associate with the dative argument of the verb *finnast* which occurs in (4), (7), (8), (10), and (13)? Justify your answer on the basis of the foregoing data.

Task VII What generalization seems to describe the agreement exhibited by the verb in Icelandic? Providing an account of this agreement pattern will be addressed later in this problem set.

P4.2.2 *Second predicates in Russian*

So-called second predicates in Russian (adjectives or nouns) agree in number and gender with the controlling NP. Sometimes they also agree in case, as in (1) and (2), but sometimes they have to be in the instrumental, as in (3)–(6):

(1) *Ivan   čitaet *ugrjumym/ugrjumyj.*
      Ivan.Nom reads *gloomy.Ins.Masc.Sing/gloomy.Nom.Masc.Sing
      'Ivan reads, gloomy.'

(2) *Oni   prišli domoj *ustalymi/ustalye.*
They.Nom came home *tired.Ins.Pl/tired.Nom.Pl
'They came home tired.'

(3) *On   okazalsja   durakom/*durak.*
He.Nom turned:out:to:be fool.Ins/*fool.Nom
'He turned out to be a fool.'

(4) *On   stal   lenivym/*lenivyj.*
He.Nom became lazy.Ins/*lazy.Nom
'He became lazy.'

(5) *On eë   sčital   krasivoj/*krasivuju.*
He her.Acc considered pretty.Ins.F/*pretty.Acc.F
'He considered her pretty.'

(6) *On eë   našël umnoj/*umnuju.*
He her.Acc found clever.Ins.F/*clever.Acc.F
'He found her clever.'

While second predicates which agree in case (as in (1) and (2)) can be added to practically any verb, those in the instrumental (as in (3)–(6)) have a relatively restricted distribution.

Task VIII What grammatical function(s) would you associate with second predicates in Russian? Give arguments for your proposal.

Task IX Provide lexical forms for the verbs *čitat'* 'read', *prijti* 'come', *okazat'sja* 'turn out to be', *stat'* 'start to be', *sčitat'* 'consider', and *najti* 'find', which occur in (1)–(6) respectively.

Task X Give full analyses of (1) and (4).

P4.2.3 Icelandic case marking and control

P4.2.3.1 Regular case marking

In part P4.2.1 set we saw some phenomena regarding case marking in Icelandic. Here we will delve into a specific treatment of case marking in Icelandic, and its interactions with complex syntactic structures such as those involving control.

Recall that in simple sentences in Icelandic, the regular case of the subject is nominative and that of the object accusative. Let us adopt the following hypotheses about regular case assignment:

(1) **Case Assigners:**
   a. The subject–person agreement affix of verbs assigns nominative case to the subject.
   b. The verb root of transitive verbs assigns accusative case to the object.

(2) **Case-Marked Forms:**
The case inflections of nominals *constrain* the case value.

The case assignments in (1) carry case defining equations, such as ($\uparrow$ SUBJ CASE) = NOM and ($\uparrow$ OBJ CASE) = ACC. The case-marked forms in (2) carry constraint equations, such as ($\uparrow$ CASE) $=_c$ NOM and ($\uparrow$ CASE) $=_c$ ACC. Hence, a case-marked form can appear only in a syntactic environment where a case assigner will satisfy its constraint features. This provides a simple account of examples like (3) and (4):

(3) *Haraldur   elskar Maríu.*
     Harold.Nom loves   Mary.Acc
     'Harold loves Mary.'

(4) **Harald   elskar Maríu.*
     Harold.Acc loves   Mary.Acc

For example, (3) would have the annotated c-structure shown in (5):

(5)

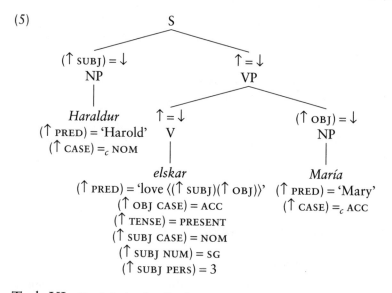

Task XI   Explain in detail why (4) is ungrammatical.

Hypothesis (1a) leaves the subject case of infinitive verbs (which lack subject–person agreement affixes) unspecified. By this means we can account for examples (6) and (7):

(6) *þeir   segja Harald   elska   Maríu.*
     they.Nom say   Harold.Acc love.Inf Mary.Acc
     'They say Harold loves Mary.'
     Lit., they say Harold to love Mary

(7) *Haraldur   er sagður   elska   Maríu.*
     Harold.Nom is said.Nom love.Inf Mary.Acc
     'Harold is said to love Mary.'

For example, (6) would have the annotated c-structure shown in (8):

(8)

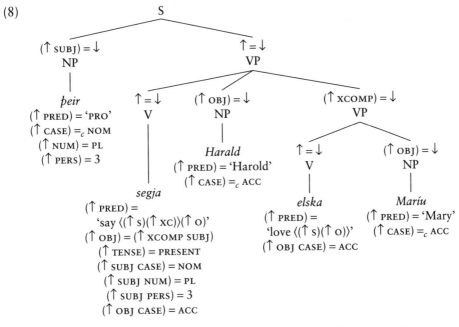

Task XII Explain in detail how hypothesis (1a) accounts for (6) and (7). Note that (7) is a passivized version of (6) and that the passive participle *sagður* agrees in case with its subject.

P4.2.3.2 Irregular case marking

Verbs may govern irregular case on their objects, as in (9) and (10):

(9) a. *þeir   björguðu stúlkunni.*
         they.Nom rescued   the:girl.Dat
         'They rescued the girl.'
     b. *þeir   luku   kirkjunni.*
         they.Nom finished the:church.Dat
         'They finished the church.'

(10) a. *Stúlkan   beið   mín.*
         the:girl.Nom awaited me.Gen
         'The girl awaited me.'
     b. *Við   vitjuðum Ólafs.*
         we.Nom visited   Olaf.Gen
         'We visited Olaf.'

Let us adopt the following hypotheses about irregular case assignment:

(11) **Irregular Case Assigners:**
    a. The verb roots of verbs that govern irregular case assign irregular case.
    b. Regular case assignment *follows* irregular case assignment and is *optional*.

Hypothesis (11b) implies that regular case is the *default* case assignment, specifying accusative objects and nominative subjects only if these grammatical arguments have not been assigned irregular case.

Task XIII   Explain in detail how (9a) is analysed. Explain how the ungrammatical **þeir björguðu mín* 'they.Nom rescued me.Gen' is ruled out.

Some indication that the irregularly case-marked nominals in (9)–(10) may indeed be objects (and not, say, obliques) comes from passivization:

(12) a. *Stúlkunni   var bjargað.*
         the:girl.Dat was rescued
         'The girl was rescued.'
    b. *Kirkjunni   var lokið.*
         the:church.Dat was finished
         'The church was finished.'
    c. *Mín   var beðið.*
         me.Gen was awaited
         'I was awaited.'
    d. *Ólafs   var vitjað.*
         Olaf.Gen was visited
         'Olaf was visited.'

Task XIV   Assuming that the dative and genitive nominals in (12) are subjects of the passivized verbs, how would you account for their case?

Clear evidence that the irregularly case-marked nominals in (9) and (10) are indeed objects comes from functional control, as in (13):

(13) a. *Hann   segir stúlkunni   (í barnaskap sínum) hafa   verið*
         he.Nom says the:girl.Dat (in foolishness self's) have.Inf been
         bjargað.
         rescued
         'He says in his foolishness that the girl has been rescued.'
         Lit.: he says the girl (in his/her foolishness) to have been rescued
    b. *Hann   segir mín   (í barnaskap sínum) hafa   verið beðið.*
         he.Nom says me.Gen (in foolishness self's) have.Inf been awaited
         'He says in his foolishness that I have been awaited.'
         Lit.: he says me in his foolishness to have been awaited

Note that in the position in which it occurs in (13a) the optional adjunct *í barnaskap sínum* can modify either the matrix subject or the complement subject. If it followed the complement auxiliary *hafa*, however, it would only be able to modify the complement subject. This suggests that on the reading where it modifies the matrix subject, the c-structure of (13a) is as in (14):

(14)

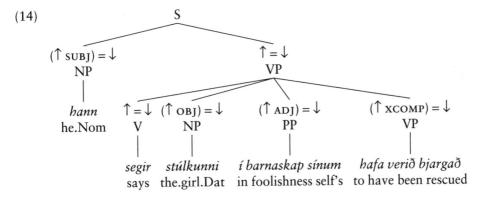

Task XV Explain why *stúlkunni* is good in (13a), while the accusative form *stúlkunna* is ungrammatical. It is possible to passivize the matrix verb *segir* of (14). Predict the case of the passivized subject ('the girl').

Task XVI Finally, recall from part P4.2.1 your analysis of constructions such as the following:

(15) Verkjanna   gætir   ekki.
      the:pains.Gen be:noticeable.3.Sg not
      'The pains are not noticeable.'

(16) Stelpunum finnst Olafur   leiðinlegur.
      the:girls.Dat find.3.Sg Olaf.Nom boring
      'The girls find Olaf boring.'

Does your analysis require any changes to be made to the verb's agreement specifications to account for the agreement patterns in such constructions? If so, what would you propose?

P4.2.3.3 Anaphoric control

In addition to bare infinitives such as *hafa* which occurs in (13), Icelandic also has infinitives construed with *að*, a homophone of the finite complementizer *að* 'that', such as *að verða*, which is shown in (17):

(17) Stúlkan   vonast til   að verða elskuð.
      the:girl.Nom hopes toward to be.Inf loved
      'The girl hopes to be loved.'

While the bare infinitive complement of a verb like *segir* 'say' in (13) is treated as involving functional control, there is evidence that the *að* infinitive complement of a verb like *vonast (til)* 'hope (for)' involves anaphoric control. For example, *að* infinitives, but not bare infinitives, appear in constructions in which there appears to be no overt controller:

(18)   *Að senda   þig heim aftur væri   langbest.*
       to send.Inf you home back would:be best
       'To send you back home would be best.'

Task XVII   Assuming that the complement *að verð a elskuð* in (17) does involve anaphoric control, what case would you predict to be shown by the matrix subject *stúlka* 'girl' in (17) if the regular verb *elska* 'love' were replaced by the irregular verb *bjarga* 'rescue', which we saw in (9a), (12a), and (13a)? Justify your answer.

P4.3   Anaphoric Binding

P4.3.1   *Finnish possessive suffixes I*

In Finnish, the possessor can be marked with a suffix on the noun. The suffix appears after the case markers. Examples of this are shown in (1)–(4):[1]

(1)   *Kirja-ni   on punainen.*
      book-1sgPx is   red
      'My book is red.'

(2)   *Kirja-si   on punainen.*
      book-2sgPx is   red
      'Your(sg) book is red.'

(3)   *Kirja-mme on punainen.*
      book-1plPx is   red
      'Our book is red.'

(4)   *Kirja-nne   on punainen.*
      book-2plPx is   red
      'Your(pl) book is red.'

Task XVIII   Write morpholexical specifications for *-ni*.

It is possible to have an overt possessive pronoun in addition to the possessive suffix, as shown in (5)–(6):

(5)   *(Minun) kirja-ni*   *on punainen.*
    1sg-GEN book-1sgPx is red
    'My book is red.'

(6)   *(Teidän) kirja-une*   *on punainen.*
    2pl-GEN book-2plPx is red
    'Your(pl) book is red.'

Task XIX Write morpholexical specifications for *minun* and revise the one for *-ni* if necessary.

This far we have only looked at first and second person. Third person possessors do not follow exactly the same pattern as first and second person. Consider examples (7)–(10):

(7)   *Pojan*   *kirja on punainen.*
    boy-GEN book is red
    'The boy's book is red.'

(8)   *Hänen kirja-nsa on punainen.*
    3sg-GEN book-3Px is red
    'His book is red.'

(9)   *Poikien*   *kirja on punainen.*
    boys-GEN book is red
    'The boys' book is red.'

(10) *Heidän kirja-nsa on punainen.*
    3pl-GEN book-3Px is red
    'The boy's book is red.'

(11) **Kirja-nsa on punainen*

Note that the third person possessive pronouns preceding the head noun in (8) and (10) are not optional. If the pronouns *hänen* or *heidän* are left out, the sentence becomes ungrammatical: cf. (11).

Task XX Write morpholexical specifications for *hänen, -nsa* and *pojan*.

In sentences like (8) and (10) above, the third person possessive pronouns are obligatory. However, in sentences such as (12)–(13), there cannot be a third person possessive pronoun:[2]

(12) *Hän$_i$*   *lukee kirjaa-nsa$_i$.*
    3sg-NOM reads book-3Px
    'He$_i$ is reading his$_i$ book.'

(13)   *Pekka$_i$ lukee kirjaa-nsa$_i$.*
Pekka reads book-3Px
'Pekka$_i$ is reading his$_i$ book.'

In (12) *he* is reading *his own* book, and *Pekka* in (13) is also reading his own book. Now consider (14)–(16):

(14)   *Hän$_i$ lukee Pekan$_j$ kirjaa.*
3sg-NOM reads Pekka-GEN book
'He$_i$ is reading Pekka$_j$'s book.'

(15)   *Hän   lukee (minun) kirjaa-ni.*
3sg-NOM reads 1sg-GEN book-1sgPx
'He is reading my book.'

(16)   *Hän$_i$ lukee hänen$_j$ kirjaa-nsa$_j$.*
3sg-NOM reads 3sg-GEN book-3sgPx
'He$_i$ is reading his$_{*i/j}$ book.'

Note the difference in meaning between (12) and (16). Sentence (16) can never be taken to mean that *he* is reading *his own* book. It must be someone else's book. In task XXI, you will be asked to provide an analysis for (16). Before solving task XXI, consider examples (17)–(18):[3]

(17)   *Pekka$_i$ antaa häne$_j$-lle kirja-nsa$_{i/*j}$.*
Pekka gives 3sg-ALL book-3sgPx
'Pekka$_i$ gives him$_j$/her$_j$ his$_{i/*j}$ book.'

(18)   *Pekka$_i$ antaa häne$_j$-lle hänen$_{j/k/*i}$ kirja-nsa.*
Pekka gives 3sg-ALL 3sg-GEN book-3sg
'Pekka$_i$ gives him$_j$/her$_j$ his$_{j/k/*i}$/her$_{j/k/*i}$ book.'

In (17), the only possible interpretation is that Pekka is giving his own book. Example (18), however, cannot be interpreted that way. The owner of the book is either the person who is receiving the book (although that is a little odd with respect to meaning), or it is some third person who is not mentioned in this sentence, but known from the context.

Task XXI   Write morpholexical specifications for *hän* in example (16). If necessary, revise those for *hänen* and *-nsa*. Explain how your analysis accounts for examples (13), (14), and (16). Finally, display the c-structures and f-structures for (12) and (16). Do not worry too much about the exact position of the possessive pronouns. If you want to think about it, here is a DP for you (*note*: this phrase is perfectly grammatical in Finnish):

(19) *Tämä minun kirja-ni.*
this my   book-1sgPx
'this book of mine'

P4.3.2 Finnish possessive suffixes II

The best way of solving the first part of the Finnish problem seems to be to work from the assumption that the binder of the anaphoric *-nsa* must be a subject. This hypothesis accounts nicely for examples like (1)–(2):[4]

(1) *Hän$_i$ auttaa minua pese-mään auto-nsa$_i$.*
3sg helps me   wash-inf car-3Px
'He$_i$ helps me wash his$_i$ car.'

(2) *Eeva$_i$ käski minua korjaa-maan pois tavara-nsa$_i$.*
Eeva ordered me   pick-up   away things-3Px
'Eeva$_i$ ordered me to take her$_i$ things away.'

Task XXII Explain how the analysis you have developed for the Finnish possessive suffixes accounts for (1) and (2).

Now consider sentences (3)–(6):

(3) *Minä autan häntä$_i$ pese-mään auto-nsa$_i$.*
I   help him   wash-inf car-3Px
'I help him$_i$ wash his$_i$ car.'

(4) *Kalle$_i$ autaa Leenaa$_j$ pese-mään auto-nsa$_{*i/j}$.*
Kalle helps Leena wash-inf   car-3Px
'Kalle$_i$ helps Leena$_j$ wash her$_{*i/j}$ car'.

(5) *Kalle$_i$ autaa Leenaa$_j$ pese-mään hanen$_{i/*j/k}$ auto-nsa.*
Kalle helps Leena wash-inf   3sg-GEN car-3Px
'Kalle$_i$ helps Leena$_j$ wash his/her (= Kalle's or someone else's) car.'

(6) *Kalle$_i$ käskee minua pese-mään hanen$_{i/k}$ auto-nsa.*
Kalle orders me   wash-inf 3sg-GEN car-3Px
'Kalle$_i$ orders me to wash his/her (= Kalle's or someone else's) car.'

(The indices in (4) show the unmarked reading. In the right pragmatic context, it is possible to interpret Kalle as the binder.)

In (5), the car can be either Kalle's or someone else's, but not Leena's. These examples seem to show that the anaphoric *-nsa* can be bound by an object.

Task XXIII Try to come up with a way to account for the examples above without abandoning the subjective binding hypothesis. In your solution, provide f-structures for examples (1), (3), and (5).

Task XXIV Explain how it is possible for both (2) and (6) to be grammatical.

P4.3.3 *Japanese reflexives*

The binding relationship of the reflexive pronoun *zibun* 'self' has been one of the most intensively studied topics in modern Japanese syntax. We will present here only some of the interesting problems it presents. See the references to this problem set for further information.

The following three sets of examples suggest a simple generalization governing the anaphoric binding properties of *zibun* 'self'. (*Note:* the morpheme *wa* marks a topic constituent. For the purposes of this exercise you should simply assume that a constituent marked with *wa* bears whatever grammatical function is required in order for the sentence to be well-formed.)

(1) a. *John ga   Bill ni   [zibun no   koto]   o   hanasi-ta.*
        Nom   Dat [self   Gen matter] Acc talk-Past
        'John talked to Bill about his (John's, not Bill's) concern.'
   b. *John ga   Bill ni   [zibun no   syasin] o   mise-ta.*
        Nom   Dat [self   Gen photo] Acc show-Past
        'John showed Bill a picture of himself (John, not Bill).'

(2) a. *John wa Mary o   [zibun no   ie]   de korosi-ta.*
        Top   Acc [self   Gen house] in kill-Past
        'John killed Mary in his (not her) house.'
   b. *Mary wa John ni [zibun no   ie]   de koros-are-ta.*
        Top   by [self   Gen house] in kill-Pass-Past
        'Mary was killed by John in her (not his) house.'

(3) a. *Mary wa John ga   [zibun no   ie]   de korosi-ta.*
        Top   Nom [self   Gen house] in kill-Past
        'Mary, John killed (her) in his (not her) house.'
   b. *John ni-wa Mary ga   [zibun no   ie]   de koros-are-ta.*
        by-Top   Nom [self   Gen house] in kill-Pass-Past
        'By John, Mary was killed in her (not his) house.'

Task XXV In terms of our theory of anaphoric binding, what featural analysis of *zibun* will account for examples (1)–(3)? Explain how your analysis accounts for the examples.

P4.3.3.1 Evidence from coordination

Coordinated relative clauses in Japanese exhibit an interesting pattern with respect to the constituents they allow to be missing. The examples in (4) and (5) are all well-formed noun phrases (the symbol *e* is included only as a guide to what constituent would appear were the clause not relativized):

(4) a. [*s e Takasi o nagutte*] [*s*[*s*[*s e Satoru o ketobasita*] *to*
       SUBJ   Acc hit   SUBJ   Acc kicked   Comp
     Reiko ga omotteiru] *to Sachiko ga sinjiteiru*] *otoko*
        Nom think   Comp   Nom believe   man
     'the man who hit Takasi and who Sachiko believes Reiko thinks kicked Satoru'
   b. *e hon o yonde, e rekoodo o kiita gakusei*
      SUBJ book Acc read   SUBJ record   Acc listened:to student
      'the student who read a book and who listened to a record'

(5) a. [*s Takasi ga e nagutte*] [*s Reiko ga [*s Satoru ga e*
           Nom OBJ hit   Nom   Nom OBJ
     ketobasita] *to utagateiru*] *otoko*
     kicked   Comp doubt   man
     'the man who Takasi hit and who Reiko doubts that Satoru kicked'
   b. *Takasi ga e kisusite, Reiko ga e nagutta onna*
      Nom OBJ$_\theta$ kissed   Nom OBJ hit   woman
      'the woman whom Takasi kissed and Reiko hit'
   c. *Takasi ga e tatete, Reiko ga e itta ie*
      Nom OBJ built   Nom OBL$_{GO}$ went house
      'the house which Takasi built and to which Reiko went'

The examples in (6), however, are all ungrammatical:

(6) a. *[*s Takasi ga e nagutte*] [*s*[*s*[*s e Satoru o ketobasita*] *to*
          Nom OBJ hit   SUBJ   Acc kicked   Comp
     Reiko ga omotteiru] *to Sachiko ga sinjiteiru*] *otoko*
       Nom think   Comp   Nom believe   man
     'the man whom Takasi hit and who Sachiko believes Reiko thinks kicked Satoru'
   b. **e kawaikute, Reiko ga e hon o watasita kodomo*
      SUBJ cute   Nom OBL$_{GO}$ book Acc handed child
      'the child who was cute and to whom Reiko handed a book'
   c. **Reiko ga e hon o watasite, e Takasi o nagutta otoko*
        Nom OBL$_{GO}$ book Acc handed SUBJ   Acc hit   man
      'the man to whom Reiko handed a book and who hit Takasi'

Task XXVI State a generalization about the facts represented in (4)–(6): what types of relative clauses can be coordinated?

Consider now the following examples in which causative verbs appear in some of the relative clauses (note that these causative verbs are just the same sort as those discussed in part P4.1.2):

(7) *e   Takasi o   nagutte, e   Reiko ni Satoru o   ketobas-ase-ta*
    SUBJ   Acc hit   SUBJ   Dat   Acc kick-Cause-Past
    otoko
    man
    'the man who hit Takasi and who caused Reiko to kick Satoru'

(8) *e   Takasi o   nagutte, Reiko ga   e   Satoru o   ketobas-ase-ta*
    SUBJ   Acc hit   Nom OBJ$_\theta$ Acc kick-Cause-Past
    otoko
    man
    'the man who hit Takasi and who Reiko caused to kick Satoru'

(9) **e   Takasi o   nagutte, Reiko ga   Satoru ni e   ketobas-ase-ta*
    SUBJ   Acc hit   Nom   Dat OBJ kick-Cause-Past
    otoko
    man
    'the man who hit Takasi and who Reiko caused Satoru to kick'

(10) **Takasi ga   e   nagutte, e   Reiko ni Satoru o   ketobas-ase-ta*
        Nom OBJ hit   SUBJ   Dat   Acc kick-Cause-Past
    otoko
    man
    'the man who Takasi hit and who caused Reiko to kick Satoru'

(11) *Takasi ga   e   nagutte, Reiko ga   e   Satoru o   ketobas-ase-ta*
        Nom OBJ hit   Nom OBJ$_\theta$ Acc kick-Cause-Past
    otoko
    man
    'the man who Takasi hit and who Reiko caused to kick Satoru'

(12) *Takasi ga   e   nagutte, Reiko ga   Satoru ni e   ketobas-ase-ta*
        Nom OBJ hit   Nom   Dat OBJ kick-Cause-Past
    otoko
    man
    'the man who Takasi hit and who Reiko caused Satoru to kick'

Task XXVII Explain how the facts in (7)–(12) fit in with your answer to task XXVI.

We can now consider some apparent counterexamples to the generalization considered in task XXV:

(13) a. *John ga   Bill ni   [zibun no   koto]   o   hanas-ase-ta.*
        Nom   Dat [self   Gen matter] Acc talk-Cause-Past
      'John made Bill talk about his (either John's or Bill's) concern.'
   b. *Bill ga   [zibun no   koto]   o   hanasi-ta.*
        Nom [self   Gen matter] Acc talk-Past
      'Bill talked about his concern.'

(14) a. *John ga   Bill ni   [zibun no   koto]   o   hanasite-morat-ta.*
        Nom   Dat [self   Gen matter] Acc talking-Receive-Past
      'John received from Bill the favor of talking about his (either John's or
      Bill's) concern.'
   b. *Bill ga   [zibun no   koto]   o   hanasi-ta.*
        Nom [self   Gen matter] Acc talk-Past
      'Bill talked about his concern.'

(15) a. *John wa   Mary ni   [zibun no   uti]   de ne-kom-are-ta.*
        Top   by [self   Gen house] in sleep-absorb-Pass-Past
      'John was embarrassed by Mary's becoming bedridden in his/her house.'
   b. *Mary ga   [zibun no   uti]   de ne-kon-da.*
        Nom [self   Gen house] in sleep-absorb-Past
      'Mary became bedridden in her house.'

The examples in (13)–(15) involve a causative verb and other complex predicates. Note in particular that (15a) illustrates a construction called the indirect
passive, in which the passive subject is interpreted as being adversely affected by
the event described. Whereas the direct passive in Japanese, which was illustrated
in (2b), can be analyzed much like the English passive, the indirect passive has
been analyzed similarly to the Japanese causative, as have been constructions
with the formative *te morau* as in (14a).

Task XXVIII   Explain why the examples in the (a) sentences in (13)–(15) are
not truly counterexamples to the analysis you gave in task XXV.

P4.3.3.2   Another pattern of binding

While all of the above examples fall under a single generalization, there are
further examples that do not. For example, there are certain oblique agent phrases
in direct passive constructions that can serve as antecedents of *zibun*:

(16) a. *Taroo wa   **Ziroo ni** [[zibun to   sokkuri na]   otoko ga*
        Top   by [[self   with alike   copula] man   Nom
      i-ru   koto]   o   siras-are-ta.
      exist-Prt Comp] Acc let:know-Pass-Past
      'Taroo was informed by Ziro that there is a man who looks just like
      him (Taroo or Ziro).'

b. *John ga*   **Mary ni** *[zibun no   siken no   kekka] o*
      Nom   by [self   Gen exam Gen result] Acc
tuger-are-ta.
inform-Pass-Past
'John was informed by Mary of the result of his/her exam.'

Next, there are certain other oblique phrases that can serve as the antecedent of *zibun*, such as the following oblique source phrases with the predicate meaning 'hear':

(17) a. *Hanako wa*   **Taroo kara** *[zibun ga   kat-ta   koto]   o   kii-ta.*
              Top   from [self   Nom win-Past Comp] Acc hear-Past
         'Hanako heard from Taroo that she/he had won.'
    b. *Bill wa*   **John kara** *[[Hanako ga   zibun o   bengosu-ru koto]   ni*
            Top   from [[Nom self   Acc defend-Prt   Comp] Acc
       nat-ta   koto]   o   kii-ta.
       become-Past Comp] Acc hear-Past
       'Bill heard from John that it had been decided that Hanako would defend herself/him (Hanako/Bill or John).'

Note finally the contrast between (18) and (19), which differ only in the main verb:

(18) *Bill wa* **John ni**   *[Mary ga   zibun o   nikunde-i-ru koto]   o*
            Top   Dat [Nom self   Acc hate-Prg-Part Comp] Acc
     kii-ta.
     hear-Past
     'Bill heard from John that Mary hated herself/him (Bill or John).'

(19) *Bill wa* **John ni**   *[Mary ga   zibun o   nikunde-i-ru koto]   o*
            Top   Dat [Nom self   Acc hate-Prg-Part Comp] Acc
     hanasi-ta.
     tell-Past
     'Bill told John that Mary hated herself/him (Bill, not John).'

Task XXIX   What do the nonsubject binders in examples (16)–(18) have in common? How can you revise your analysis in task XXV to account for these examples?

Notes

1 The case for *kirja* in (1)–(10) is NOM.
2 In (12)–(16), *kirjaa* has partitive case.
3 ALL = allative case.
4 In Finnish, different verbs can select for different infinitives. You do not need to worry about that here.

Problem Set 5

P5.1 Unaccusatives

The following data suggest that, at least in some languages, intransitive verbs do not form a homogeneous class. Your task will be to study the data given below and offer an account of this phenomenon.

P5.1.1 Italian

Subjects in Italian can either precede or follow the verb phrase, as shown in (1)–(3). The subjects in the (b) sentences are sometimes referred to as inverted subjects:

(1) a. *Giovanni arriva.*
        Giovanni arrive-3.Sg
        'Giovanni arrives.'
    b. *Arriva Giovanni.*

(2) a. *Giovanni telefona.*
        Giovanni telephone-3.Sg
        'Giovanni telephones.'
    b. *Telefona Giovanni.*

(3) a. *Giovanni scrive   una lettera.*
        Giovanni write-3.Sg a   letter
        'Giovanni writes a letter.'
    b. *Scrive una lettera Giovanni.*

The verb agrees in person and number with both a preverbal and a postverbal subject. This is shown in (4)–(5), where the verbs 'arrive' and 'telephone' agree with a plural subject:

(4) a. *Maria e   Giovanni arrivano.*
         Maria and Giovanni arrive-3.Pl
         'Maria and Giovanni arrive.'
     b. *Arrivano Maria e Giovanni.*

(5) a. *Maria e   Giovanni telefonano.*
         Maria and Giovanni telephone-3.Pl
         'Maria and Giovanni telephone.'
     b. *Telefonano Maria e Giovanni.*

It is also possible for no c-structure subject to be present at all:

(6) *Arrivano.*
     arrive-3.Pl
     'They arrive.'

Thus we can write the following c-structure rules to express the positions of the subjects in the sentences above. The comma between the two daughter nodes in (R1) indicates that they can be reordered with respect to each other:

(R1) S →   (NP)   ,   VP
             ($\uparrow$ SUBJ) = $\downarrow$ $\uparrow$ = $\downarrow$

(R2) VP →   V   (NP)   PP*
             $\uparrow$ = $\downarrow$ ($\uparrow$ OBJ) = $\downarrow$ ($\uparrow$ ($\downarrow$ CASE)) = $\downarrow$

Although intransitive verbs are often thought of as a single syntactic class, certain phenomena suggest that this is not the case in Italian. We will examine one such phenomenon, the process of *ne*-cliticization, and then consider the evidence it provides for distinguishing between two classes of intransitive verbs in Italian.

P5.1.1.1 *Ne*-cliticization

In a sentence like (7a) below, the NP *tre dischi volanti* 'three flying saucers' can be partially pronominalized by means of the partitive clitic *ne*, which appears immediately before the finite verb of the clause. As shown in (7b), the result looks like a discontinuous phrase *ne . . . tre*, roughly meaning 'three of them':

(7) a. *Giovanni ha   visto tre   dischi volanti.*
         Giovanni have.3.Sg seen three discs flying
         'Giovanni saw three flying saucers.'
     b. *Giovanni ne   ha   visto tre.*
         Giovanni of:them have.1sg seen three
         'Giovanni saw three (of them).'

Assuming that the verb 'see' selects both SUBJ and OBJ, note that in (7) above it is the object NP which permits the *ne*-cliticization. Examples (8) and (9) illustrate moreover that *ne*-cliticization is prohibited from a subject NP or from an oblique grammatical argument:

(8) a. *Tre   ragazzi hanno   visto i   dischi volanti.*
         three boys   have.3.Pl seen the discs flying
         'Three boys saw the flying saucers.'
     b. **Tre ne hanno visto i dischi volanti.*

(9) a. *Giovanni ha   parlato a due uomini.*
         Giovanni have.3.Sg spoken to two men
         'Giovanni spoke to two men.'
     b. **Giovanni ne ha parlato a due.*

To summarize, *ne*-cliticization seems to be possible only from an object grammatical argument, never from a subject or from an oblique. To make this point more obvious, here are the lexical forms for the verbs used in (7)–(9):

(L1) *vedere*   V   (↑ PRED) = 'see ⟨(↑ SUBJ)(↑ OBJ)⟩'

(L2) *parlare*   V   (↑ PRED) = 'speak ⟨(↑ SUBJ)(↑ OBL$_{GO}$)⟩'

Let us now see how *ne*-cliticization operates on intransitive verbs. If *ne*-cliticization requires an object it should be impossible with intransitive verbs. In (10) and (11) below this prediction is confirmed:

(10) a. *Molti studenti arrivano.*
          many students arrive-3.Pl
          'Many students arrive.'
      b. **Molti ne arrivano.*

(11) a. *Molti studenti telefonano.*
          many students telephone-3.Pl
          'Many students telephone.'
      b. **Molti ne telefonano.*

However, from a postverbal subject *ne*-cliticization is possible with certain verbs, but not with others. Compare (12) with (13):

(12) a. *Arrivano   molti studenti.*
          arrive-3.Pl many students
          'Many students arrive.'
      b. *Ne   arrivano   molti.*
          of:them arrive-3.Pl many
          'Many of them arrive.'

(13) a. *Telefonano   molti studenti.*
          telephone-3.Pl many students
          'Many students telephone.'
      b. **Ne telefonano molti.*

    Arrivare and *telefonare* illustrate two different classes of Italian intransitive verbs. In table 1, more verbs of each class are listed. Following existing terminology we will refer to these types of verbs as UNACCUSATIVES and UNERGATIVES respectively.

Task I Modify the above analysis to account for (12) and (13). Give lexical entries for *arrivare* and *telefonare*, and any devices (lexical or syntactic) necessary for your account of the facts. *Hint*: Assume that the account of *ne*-cliticization given above is correct.

Table 1 Pattern of verbs allowing *ne*-cliticization from postverbal nominals

| *Allows* ne-*cliticization* | | *Disallows* ne-*cliticization* | |
UNACCUSATIVE		UNERGATIVE	
arrivato	'arrived'	*telefonato*	'called up'
caduto	'fell'	*sorriso*	'smiled'
tornato	'returned'	*litigato*	'quarreled'
partito	'left'	*tossito*	'coughed'
rimasto	'remained'	*taciuto*	'was silent'
esistito	'existed'	*dormito*	'slept'
cresciuto	'grew'	*assistito*	'attended'
scoppiato	'exploded'	*viaggiato*	'traveled'
svenuto	'fainted'	*scherzato*	'joked'
uscito	'came out'	*barato*	'cheated'
sceso	'came down'	*mentito*	'lied'
salito	'came up'	*lottato*	'struggled'
scappato	'escaped'	*abortito*	'aborted'
capitato	'happened'	*abbaiato*	'barked'
risultato	'turned out'	*ronzato*	'buzzed'
diventato	'became'	*civettato*	'flirted'
apparso	'appeared'	*russato*	'snored'
crollato	'collapsed'	*tremato*	'trembled'
morto	'died'	*resistito*	'resisted'
nato	'was born'	*nuotato*	'swam'
impazzito	'went crazy'	*camminato*	'walked'
arrossito	'blushed'	*barcollato*	'staggered'
andato	'went'	*esitato*	'hesitated'

Task II   Show all relevant structures and their mappings for (10a), (11a), (12a), and (13a).

P5.1.1.2   Some evidence from word order

Presented below are some additional facts about word order in Italian which may help you decide between several different analyses you may have arrived at for tasks I and II. Some verbs may occur with infinitival verb phrase complements, marked with either *di* or *a*. In the following examples you will observe a contrast between two such verbs, *pensare* and *riuscire*. *Pensare* is unergative and *riuscire* is unaccusative.

Both verbs select for an infinitival complement as shown in (14) and (15):

(14)   *Giovanni pensa   di studiare linguistica.*
Giovanni think.3.Sg to study.Inf linguistics
'Giovanni considers studying linguistics.'

(15)   *Giovanni riesce   a prendere il   libro.*
Giovanni succeed.3.Sg to take.Inf the book
'Giovanni succeeds in taking the book.'

And both can have the subject inverted just as easily. Even though (16) and (17) are not perfectly natural sentences, there is no contrast between them:

(16)   *?Pensa   di studiare linguistica Giovanni.*
think.3.Sg to study.Inf linguistics Giovanni
'Giovanni considers studying linguistics.'

(17)   *?Riesce   a prendere il   libro Giovanni.*
succeed.3.Sg to take.Inf the book Giovanni
'Giovanni succeeds in taking the book.'

However, with the unergative verb *pensare* it is difficult to get the nominal immediately after the verb, while with the unaccusative verb *riuscire* it is completely grammatical.

(18) *??Pensa Giovanni di studiare linguistica.*

(19)   *Riesce Giovanni a prendere il libro.*

Task III   Is the contrast between (18) and (19) predicted by the analysis you gave in task I? If so, explain how. Is the lack of contrast between (16) and (17) also predicted? If so, how? If your analysis does not make these predictions, state what kinds of predictions your analysis does make.

P5.1.2 Russian

In certain negative sentences in Russian, some nominals may optionally occur in the genitive case, a construction which is called the 'genitive of negation'. The subjects of certain intransitive verbs alternate with this genitive of negation, as shown in (1)–(3). Note that the subjects in (1a)–(3a) are in the nominative, as is commonly the case in Russian tensed clauses, and agree with the verb in number, person, and sometimes also in gender (with past tense verbs). Unlike the nominative subject, the genitive of negation triggers no agreement on the verb: in (1b), (2b), and (3b) the verb is marked for third person singular (neuter with the past tense form in (3b)):

(1) a. *Takie   strany   ne   suščestvujut.*
   such.Nom.Pl country.Nom.Pl Neg exist.3.Pl
   'Such countries do not exist.'
   b. *Takix   stran   ne   suščestvuet.*
   such.Gen.Pl country.Gen.Pl Neg exist.3.Sg
   'Such countries do not exist.'

(2) a. *Griby   zdes' ne   rastut.*
   mushroom.Nom.Pl here Neg grow.3.Pl
   'Mushrooms do not grow here.'
   b. *Gribov   zdes' ne   rastet.*
   mushroom.Gen.Pl here Neg grow.3.Sg
   'Mushrooms do not grow here.'

(3) a. *Otvet   iz   polka   ne   prišel.*
   answer.Nom.Masc.Sg from regiment Neg arrived.3.Masc.Sg
   'No answer arrived from the regiment.'
   b. *Otveta   iz   polka   ne   prišlo.*
   answer.Gen.Masc.Sg from regiment Neg arrived.3.Neut.Sg
   'No answer arrived from the regiment.'

Certain intransitive verbs, however, disallow this alternation, as shown in (4)–(6):

(4) a. *Ni odin rebenok   ne   prygnul.*
   not one   child.Nom.Sg.Masc Neg jumped.3.Masc.Sg
   'No child jumped.'
   b. **Ni odnogo rebenka   ne   prygnulo.*
   not one   child.Gen.Sg.Masc Neg jumped.3.Neut.Sg

(5) a. *Na zavode nikakie ženščiny   ne   rabotajut.*
   at factory no   women.Nom.Pl Neg work.3.Pl
   'No women work in the factory.'

b. ***Na zavode nikakix ženščin   ne   rabotaet.*
    at factory no   women.Gen.Pl Neg work.3.Sg

(6) a. *Takie sobaki   ne   kusajutsja.*
        such dogs.Nom.Pl Neg bite.3.Pl
        'Such dogs do not bite.'
    b. **Takix sobak   ne   kusaetsja.*
        such dogs.Gen.Pl Neg bite.3.Sg

Subjects of transitive verbs also disallow alternation with the genitive of negation:

(7) a. *Ni odna gazeta   ne   pečataet   takuju erundu.*
        not one newspaper.Nom.Sg Neg prints.3.Sg such   nonsense.Acc.Sg
        'No newspaper prints such nonsense.'
    b. **Ni odnoj gazety   ne   pečataet   takuju erundu.*
        not one   newspaper.Gen.Sg Neg prints.3.Sg such   nonsense.Acc.Sg

(8) a. *Studenty   ne   smotrjat   televizor.*
        student.Nom.Pl Neg watch.3.Pl television
        'Students don't watch television.'
    b. **Studentov   ne   smotrit   televizor.*
        student.Gen.Pl Neg watch.3.Sg television

Let us return to the intransitive verbs in (1)–(6). Those in (1)–(3) (*suščestvovat'* 'exist', *rasti* 'grow', and *prijti* 'arrive') allow the alternation of the nominative subject with the genitive of negation, while those in (4)–(6) (*prygnut'* 'jump', *rabotat'* 'work', and *kusat'sja* 'bite') disallow such alternation. Again, we can say that we are dealing with two classes of intransitive verbs which, following the terminology introduced in part P5.1.1, will be called UNACCUSATIVES and UNERGATIVES respectively. Table 2 lists a few more members of these two verb classes in Russian.

There are a number of syntactic properties by which subjects in Russian may be distinguished from other grammatical functions. The fact that it is with subjects that the verb agrees was mentioned above. It is also the case that subjects in Russian act as antecedents of reflexives and as controllers of so-called gerund constructions. This is shown in (9) and (10) respectively:

(9) *Zakončiv   rabotu, Ivan   pošel domoj.*
     having:finished work.Acc Ivan.Nom went home
     'Having finished work, Ivan went home.'

(10) *Ivan   ne   byl v svoej   komnate.*
     Ivan.Nom Neg was in his.Refl room
     'Ivan_i was not in his_i room.'

Table 2 Pattern of verbs allowing alternation between nominative subject and genitive of negation

Allows genitive of negation UNACCUSATIVE		Disallows genitive of negation UNERGATIVE	
suščestvovat'	'exist'	*prygnut'*	'jump'
prijti	'arrive'	*rabotat'*	'work'
rasti	'grow'	*kusat'sja*	'bite'
ostat'sja	'remain'	*zažigat'sja*	'burn'
naxodit'sja	'be located'	*tancevat'*	'dance'
slučat'sja	'happen'	*pit'*	'drink'
okazat'sja	'turn out'		
proisxodit'	'happen, occur'		
pojavit'sja	'appear'		
byt'	'be, exist'		

The genitive of negation, however, is not generally acceptable as an antecedent for a reflexive or as the controller of a gerund, as shown in (11) and (12):

(11) **Zakončiv   rabotu,   Ivana   bol'še   net.*
      having:finished work.Acc Ivan.Gen any:longer (is):not
      'Having finished work, Ivan is no longer here.'

(12) **Ivana   ne   bylo v svoej   komnate.*
      Ivan.Gen Neg was in his.Refl room
      'Ivan$_i$ was not in his$_i$ room.'

It is also interesting to note here that the genitive of negation can alternate with objects. Russian objects normally appear in the accusative case:

(13) *On   videl knjigu.*
      he.Nom saw   book.Acc
      'He saw the book.'

But in negative sentences an object can appear in the genitive. Thus, here again we encounter the genitive of negation:

(14) a. *On   ne   videl knjigu.*
          he.Nom Neg saw   book.Acc
          'He did not see the book.'
     b. *On   ne   videl knjigi.*
          he.Nom Neg saw   book.Gen
          'He did not see the book.'

Task IV   Provide an account of the distribution of the genitive of negation. (It is not necessary to give an explanation for, or include in your analysis, the fact that these genitive phrases occur in negative sentences.)

Task V   Show how the verbs in the (a) and (b) sentences of (1)–(3) are related.

Task VI   Give analyses for (1a) and (1b).

Finally, it is interesting to note that passive predicates allow the alternation of nominative subjects and genitives of negation, as shown in (15):

(15)   a.   *Ni odin   mal'čik   ne   byl ubit.*
            not one.Nom boy.Nom Neg was killed
            'Not one boy was killed.'
       b.   *Ni odnogo mal'čika ne   bylo ubito.*
            not one.Gen boy.Gen Neg was killed
            'Not one boy was killed.'

Task VII   Explain the interaction of the genitive of negation with the passive.

P5.1.3   Empty "there" in English

Otto Jespersen, in his fascinating book *A Modern English Grammar on Historical Principles, Part VII Syntax* (1961) describes some properties of sentences with what is sometimes called "the empty *there*." A portion of his discussion (pp. 107–14) is excerpted below by permission of Munksgaard International Publishers. Your task will be to explore these properties and attempt to find an analysis which explains them:

> **3.11**   The empty, or, as I have called it elsewhere, the existential *there* differs from the local adverb *there*
>   (1) by having weak stress and consequently having the vowel [ɛ] reduced to [ə],
>   (2) by losing its local meaning; hence the possibility of combining it with local adverbs [see 3.12 below],
>   (3) by being a quasi-subject, thus e.g. in an infinitival nexus and with an *ing* [see 3.14 below],
>   (4) by the tendency to have the verb in singular form with a plural subject [see 3.14 below],
>   (5) by the word-order: *there is nothing wrong*, but *there nothing is wrong . . .*
>   Thus it is not quite correct to say with NED [*A New English Dictionary*, 1884–1922, Oxford] (*there* 4) that "Grammatically there is no difference between *There comes the train* and *There comes a time when*, etc.; but while in the former *there* is demonstrative and stressed, in the latter it has been reduced to a mere anticipative element occupying the place of the subject which comes later."

3.12   The empty *there* can be connected in the same sentence with indications of place: ... *But there is no one there* | ... *and there, sure enough, crusted with the red rust, there lay an iron shoe-buckle* ...

3.13   *There* has often been described as preparatory subject, as anticipatory subject (... cf. *anticipative* in NED), or as introductory ..., but these epithets are misleading, for *there* need not precede the real subject ... : *Men there were yet living who had seen him*, etc. Other examples of the place after the subject proper, many of them in questions: ... *What is there to laugh at?* | ... *The reason, if reason there was* ...

3.14   The tendency in colloquial English to use *there is* before a plural word ... : ... *In the intervals, Walter darling, there's you.*
    . . .

   In all these sentences *there* occupies the place usually given to the subject, and might be termed a vicarious subject or quasi-subject ..., while the other word is relegated to a second plane. This is especially obvious in the use of *there* as subject in infinitival and gerundial groups: *let there be light* | *I don't want there to be* | *it was impossible for there to be* ... | *account for there being something rather odd* ...

   There are other indications that *there* is felt as a kind of subject. Thus the use of tag-questions: *there is nothing funny about him, is there?* ...

3.15   But if *there* is the subject, what about the other part: how are we to analyze it? It is as a rule more indefinite than ordinary subjects, which are the most special part of the sentence; and it does not take the usual place of a subject ...

3.16   The chief use of *there*-sentences is to denote the more or less vague existence or coming into existence of something indefinite; thus very frequently with the verb *be*: *There's someone at the door* | *If he comes, there will be trouble* | *What is there for dinner?* | *There is no time like the present* | *There is many a slip between cup and lip* | *There is no rule without some exception* | *There are as good fish in the sea as ever came out of it* (and many other proverbs).
    . . .

3.19   The verb *be* is also found in passive constructions, which are very frequent in sentences with *there*: ... *There had been a jeweller's window smashed.*

3.21   Other verbs than *be* are found in *there*-sentences, but generally only those of a somewhat vague meaning, such as *come, appear, happen*, etc.: ... *Early one morning, there came on shore five or six canoes of Indians* ...

3.22   Transitive verbs with objects formerly were not at all rare with *there* (NED *there* 4 b, obs.; frequent in Chaucer). We do not say *There took a man a walk*, but *There was a man who took a walk*. But *take place* = 'happen,' may still be found; thus also *cross her path* = 'come': . . . *there took place between him and his son a violent and painful scene* | . . . *If there crossed her path a man with a strong protective arm, he was whisked away* . . .

Task VIII   Propose an analysis of this construction, including requisite c-structure rules and lexical forms; and defend your proposal with a reasoned argument based on your exploration of evidence like that given by Jespersen.

Jespersen's own analysis of a sentence like *There are many churches there* (p. 110) is formulated '3/s^m V S^m 3,' where '3/s' denotes 'something which may either be called a tertiary or a lesser subject', 'V' denotes a verb, 'S' denotes a subject, '3' denotes a tertiary, or adverbial, and since 'there might be occasion to show that there is something unusual about both subjects', the raised ^{m} ('modified') is added. Thus, Jespersen's analysis is that both *there* and the noun phrase it displaces are subjects, though there is something funny about them. Would an equivalent analysis be possible within lexical-functional theory? If your analysis differs from Jespersen's, can you derive contrasting predictions from the two analyses and find evidence to choose between them?

P5.2   Reflexives: Serbian/Croatian

Reflexive verbs sometimes pattern with transitive and sometimes with intransitive lexical forms. Below are given data on reflexives in Serbian/Croatian and your task will be to provide an analysis.

Consider the alternations in (1)–(4):

(1)   a.   *Ana brani   Petra/njega.*
           Ana defends Petar.Acc/him
           'Ana defends Petar/him.'
      b.   *Ana ga   brani.*
               him(Cl)
           'Ana defends him.'

(2)   a.   *Ana brani   Mariju/nju.*
           Ana defends Marija.Acc/her
           'Ana defends Marija/her.'
      b.   *Ana je   brani.*
               her(Cl) defends
           'Ana defends her.'

(3) a. *Ana brani   mene.*
        Ana defends me
        'Ana defends me.'
    b. *Ana me   brani.*
            me(Cl)
        'Ana defends me.'

(4) a. *Ana brani   sebe.*
        Ana defends Refl
        'Ana defends herself.'
    b. *Ana se   brani.*
            Refl(Cl)
        'Ana defends herself.'

   These examples suggest that there exists the following alternation between the clitic and nonclitic direct object (accusative) pronouns:

(5) | Features | Full form | Clitic form |
    |----------|-----------|-------------|
    | 1.Sg | *mene* | *me* |
    | 3.M.Sg | *njega* | *ga* |
    | 3.F.Sg | *nju* | *je* |
    | Refl | *sebe* | *se* |

   However, (6) and (7) below indicate that the alternation between *sebe* and *se* may in fact be only apparent (note that *Petra* is in accusative case, and functions as object):

(6) a. *Ana brani   mene uspešnije   nego Petra.*
        Ana defends me   more:successfully than Petar.Acc
        'Ana defends me more successfully than she defends Petar.'
    b. *Ana me   brani uspešnije nego Petra.*
            me(Cl)   Petar.Acc
        'Ana defends me more successfully than she defends Petar.'

(7) a. *Ana brani   sebe uspešnije   nego Petra.*
        Ana defends Refl more:successfully than Petar.Acc
        'Ana defends herself more successfully than she defends Petar.'
    b. **Ana se brani uspešnije nego Petra.*
            Cl   Petar.Acc
    c. *Ana se brani uspešnije nego Petar.*
            Cl   Petar.Nom
        'Ana defends herself more successfully than Petar (defends himself).'

   Another difference between *sebe* and *se* may be seen in the following sentences, which involve an adjunct construction introduced by *kao* 'as', in which the adjunct agrees in case with the argument it modifies:

(8) a. *Petar   je   njega   prijavio kao podstanara.*
        Petar.Nom Aux him.Acc registered as   tenant.Acc
        'Petar registered him as a tenant.'

    b. *Petar ga   je prijavio kao podstanara.*
           him.Acc   tenant.Acc
        'Petar registered him as a tenant.'

(9) a. *Petar je sebe prijavio kao podstanara.*
            Refl   tenant.Acc
        'Petar registered himself as a tenant.'

    b. **Petar se prijavio kao podstanara.*
         Cl   tenant.Acc

    c. *Petar se prijavio kao podstanar.*
         Cl   tenant.Nom
        'Petar registered himself as a tenant.'

Task IX Based on the data above, propose and justify lexical form(s) for the verb *braniti* 'defend' which is used in (1)–(7).

Task X If you propose that there is more than one lexical form, show how they are related.

Solutions to Selected Exercises

Problem Set 1

P1.1 *Warlpiri*

Task I

C-structure for (1):

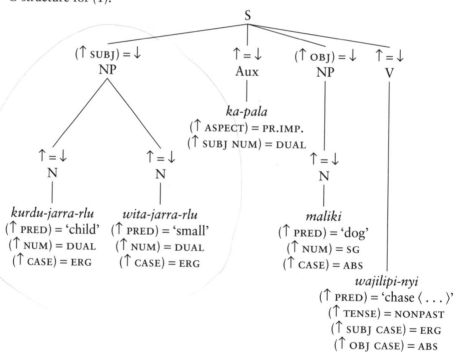

C-structure for (2):

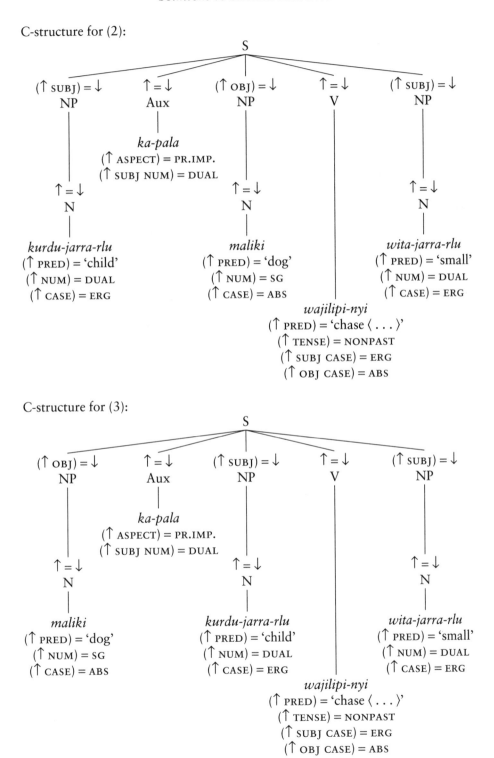

C-structure for (3):

F-structure for (1), (2), and (3):

$$
\begin{bmatrix}
\text{PRED} & \text{'chase } \langle f_1, f_2 \rangle\text{'} \\[2pt]
\text{SUBJ} & f_1: \begin{bmatrix} \text{PRED} & \text{'child'} \\ \text{NUM} & \text{DUAL} \\ \text{CASE} & \text{ERG} \\ \text{ADJ} & [\text{PRED} \quad \text{'small'}] \end{bmatrix} \\[2pt]
\text{OBJ} & f_2: \begin{bmatrix} \text{PRED} & \text{'dog'} \\ \text{NUM} & \text{SG} \\ \text{CASE} & \text{ABS} \end{bmatrix} \\[2pt]
\text{TENSE} & \text{NONPAST} \\
\text{ASPECT} & \text{PRESENT.IMPERFECT}
\end{bmatrix}
$$

Problem Set 2

P2.1 *Spanish*

Task I

$$
\text{VP} \rightarrow \quad \underset{\uparrow \,=\, \downarrow}{\text{V}} \quad \left(\underset{(\uparrow \text{ OBJ}) \,=\, \downarrow}{\text{NP}} \right) \left(\underset{(\uparrow \text{ OBJ}) \,=\, \downarrow}{\text{PP}} \right)
$$

$$
\text{NP} \rightarrow \quad \underset{\uparrow \,=\, \downarrow}{\text{N}}
$$

Task II

C-structure for (1a):

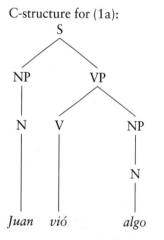

F-structure for (1a):

$$
\begin{bmatrix}
\text{PRED} & \text{'see } \langle f_1, f_2 \rangle\text{'} \\
\text{TENSE} & \text{PAST} \\[2pt]
\text{SUBJ} & f_1: \begin{bmatrix} \text{PRED} & \text{'Juan'} \\ \text{NUM} & \text{SG} \\ \text{GEND} & \text{MASC} \\ \text{ANIM} & + \end{bmatrix} \\[2pt]
\text{OBJ} & f_2: \begin{bmatrix} \text{PRED} & \text{'something'} \\ \text{ANIM} & - \end{bmatrix}
\end{bmatrix}
$$

C-structure for (2a):

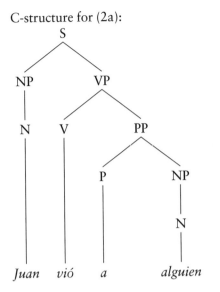

F-structure for (2a):

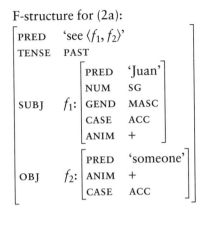

Task III

$$\text{VP} \rightarrow \underset{\uparrow = \downarrow}{\overline{\text{V}}} \left(\underset{(\uparrow \text{ OBJ}) = \downarrow}{\text{NP}} \right) \left(\underset{(\uparrow \text{ OBJ}) = \downarrow}{\text{PP}} \right)$$

Task IV

C-structure for (3a):

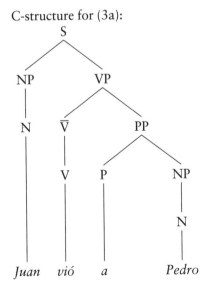

F-structure for (3a):

$$\begin{bmatrix} \text{PRED} & \text{'see} \langle f_1, f_2 \rangle\text{'} \\ \text{TENSE} & \text{PAST} \\ \text{SUBJ} & f_1: \begin{bmatrix} \text{PRED} & \text{'Juan'} \\ \text{NUM} & \text{SG} \\ \text{GEND} & \text{MASC} \\ \text{ANIM} & + \end{bmatrix} \\ \text{OBJ} & f_2: \begin{bmatrix} \text{PRED} & \text{'Pedro'} \\ \text{NUM} & \text{SG} \\ \text{GEND} & \text{MASC} \\ \text{CASE} & \text{ACC} \\ \text{ANIM} & + \end{bmatrix} \end{bmatrix}$$

C-structure for (3b):

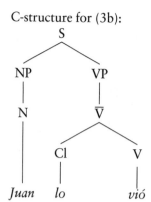

F-structure for (3b):

$$\begin{bmatrix} \text{PRED} & \text{'see } \langle f_1, f_2 \rangle\text{'} \\ \text{TENSE} & \text{PAST} \\ \text{SUBJ} & f_1: \begin{bmatrix} \text{PRED} & \text{'Juan'} \\ \text{NUM} & \text{SG} \\ \text{GEND} & \text{MASC} \\ \text{ANIM} & + \end{bmatrix} \\ \text{OBJ} & f_2: \begin{bmatrix} \text{PRED} & \text{'PRO'} \\ \text{CASE} & \text{ACC} \\ \text{NUM} & \text{SG} \\ \text{GEND} & \text{MASC} \\ \text{PERS} & 3 \end{bmatrix} \end{bmatrix}$$

Task VI

lo   CL $((\uparrow \text{PRED}) = \text{'PRO'})$
$(\uparrow \text{CASE}) = \text{ACC}$
$(\uparrow \text{NUM}) = \text{SG}$
$(\uparrow \text{PERS}) = 3$
$(\uparrow \text{GEND}) = \text{MASC}$

los   CL $((\uparrow \text{PRED}) = \text{'PRO'})$
$(\uparrow \text{CASE}) = \text{ACC}$
$(\uparrow \text{NUM}) = \text{PL}$
$(\uparrow \text{PERS}) = 3$
$(\uparrow \text{GEND}) = \text{MASC}$

P2.2 Moroccan Arabic

Task VII

mšat   V $(\uparrow \text{PRED}) = \text{'go } \langle (\uparrow \text{SUBJ}) \rangle\text{'}$
$((\uparrow \text{SUBJ PRED}) = \text{'PRO'})$
$(\uparrow \text{ASPECT}) = \text{PERF}$
$(\uparrow \text{SUBJ NUM}) = \text{SG}$
$(\uparrow \text{SUBJ GEND}) = \text{FEM}$
$(\uparrow \text{SUBJ PERS}) = 3$

šratu   V $(\uparrow \text{PRED}) = \text{'buy } \langle (\uparrow \text{SUBJ}), (\uparrow \text{OBJ}) \rangle\text{'}$
$(\uparrow \text{ASPECT}) = \text{PERF}$
$((\uparrow \text{SUBJ PRED}) = \text{'PRO'})$
$(\uparrow \text{SUBJ NUM}) = \text{SG}$
$(\uparrow \text{SUBJ GEND}) = \text{FEM}$
$(\uparrow \text{SUBJ PERS}) = 3$

$(\uparrow \text{OBJ PRED}) = \text{`PRO'}$
$(\uparrow \text{OBJ NUM}) = \text{SG}$
$(\uparrow \text{OBJ GEND}) = \text{MASC}$
$(\uparrow \text{OBJ PERS}) = 3$

liḥ   P $(\uparrow \text{CASE}) = \text{OBL}_{\text{GO}}$ $\lor$ $(\uparrow \text{CASE}) = \text{OBL}_{\text{EXP}}$
           $(\uparrow \text{OBJ PRED}) = \text{`PRO'}$
           $(\uparrow \text{OBJ PERS}) = 3$
           $(\uparrow \text{OBJ GEND}) = \text{MASC}$
           $(\uparrow \text{OBJ NUM}) = \text{SG}$

Task VIII

C-structure for (1b):   F-structure for (1b):

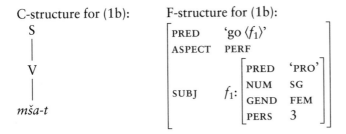

C-structure for (2a):   F-structure for (2a):

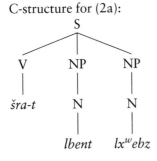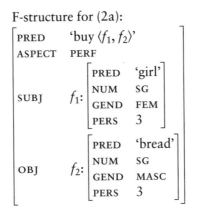

C-structure for (2b):   F-structure for (2b):

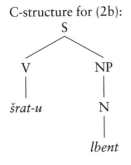

C-structure for (3a):

F-structure for (3a):

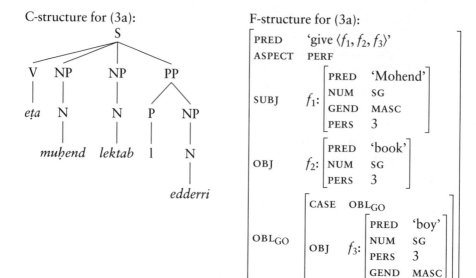

C-structure for (4b):   F-structure for (4b):

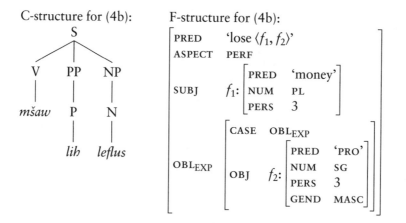

P2.3 Irish

Task XI

chuirfinn   V   (↑ PRED) = 'apply-for ⟨(↑ SUBJ)(↑ OBL$_{ar}$ OBJ)⟩'
              (↑ SUBJ PRED) = 'pro'
              (↑ SUBJ PERS) = 1
              (↑ SUBJ NUM) = SG
              (↑ COND) = +
              (↑ LOC) =$_c$ +

chuirféa   V   ($\uparrow$ PRED) = 'apply-for $\langle(\uparrow$ SUBJ$)(\uparrow$ OBL$_{ar}$ OBJ$)\rangle$'
                   ($\uparrow$ SUBJ PRED) = 'PRO'
                   ($\uparrow$ SUBJ PERS) = 2
                   ($\uparrow$ SUBJ NUM) = SG
                   ($\uparrow$ COND) = +
                   ($\uparrow$ LOC) =$_c$ +

chuirfeadh   V   ($\uparrow$ PRED) = 'apply-for $\langle(\uparrow$ SUBJ$)(\uparrow$ OBL$_{ar}$ OBJ$)\rangle$'
                   ($\uparrow$ COND) = +
                   ($\uparrow$ LOC) =$_c$ +

Task XII

C-structure for (7a):

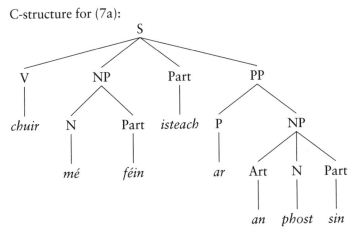

F-structure for (7a):

$$
\begin{bmatrix}
\text{PRED} & \text{'apply-for } \langle f_1, f_2 \rangle \text{'} \\
\text{LOC} & + \\
\text{TENSE} & \text{PAST} \\
\text{SUBJ} & f_1: \begin{bmatrix} \text{PRED} & \text{'PRO'} \\ \text{NUM} & \text{SG} \\ \text{PERS} & 1 \\ \text{REFL} & + \end{bmatrix} \\
\text{OBL}_{AR} & f_2: \begin{bmatrix} \text{CASE} & \text{OBL}_{AR} \\ \text{OBJ} & \begin{bmatrix} \text{PRED} & \text{'job'} \\ \text{DEF} & + \\ \text{DEIXIS} & \text{DISTANT} \end{bmatrix} \end{bmatrix}
\end{bmatrix}
$$

C-structure for (7b):

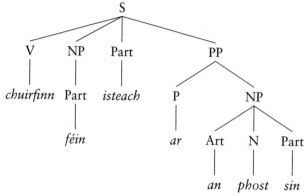

F-structure for (7b):

$$
\begin{bmatrix}
\text{PRED} & \text{'apply-for } \langle f_1, f_2 \rangle\text{'} \\
\text{LOC} & + \\
\text{COND} & + \\
\text{SUBJ} & f_1: \begin{bmatrix} \text{PRED} & \text{'PRO'} \\ \text{NUM} & \text{SG} \\ \text{PERS} & 1 \\ \text{REFL} & + \end{bmatrix} \\
\text{OBL}_{AR} & f_2: \begin{bmatrix} \text{CASE} & \text{OBL}_{AR} \\ \text{OBJ} & \begin{bmatrix} \text{PRED} & \text{'job'} \\ \text{DEF} & + \\ \text{DEIXIS} & \text{DISTANT} \end{bmatrix} \end{bmatrix}
\end{bmatrix}
$$

P2.4 *Noun incorporation in Greenlandic*

Task XIII

-*qarpoq* V_{suff} ($\uparrow$ PRED) = 'have $\langle (\uparrow$ SUBJ$), (\uparrow$ OBL$) \rangle$'
             ($\uparrow$ MOOD) = INDIC
             (($\uparrow$ SUBJ PRED) = 'PRO')
             ($\uparrow$ SUBJ PERS) = 3
             ($\uparrow$ SUBJ NUM) = SG
             ($\uparrow$ SUBJ CASE) = ABS
             ($\uparrow$ OBL CASE) = INST

-*sivoq* V_{suff} ($\uparrow$ PRED) = 'get $\langle (\uparrow$ SUBJ$), (\uparrow$ OBL$) \rangle$'
             ($\uparrow$ MOOD) = INDIC
             (($\uparrow$ SUBJ PRED) = 'PRO')
             ($\uparrow$ SUBJ PERS) = 3

$(\uparrow$ SUBJ NUM$) =$ SG
$(\uparrow$ SUBJ CASE$) =$ ABS
$(\uparrow$ OBL CASE$) =$ INST

Task XIV

qimmeqarpoq V $(\uparrow$ PRED$) =$ 'have $\langle(\uparrow$ SUBJ$), (\uparrow$ OBL$)\rangle$'
$\qquad\qquad\qquad (\uparrow$ MOOD$) =$ INDIC
$\qquad\qquad\qquad ((\uparrow$ SUBJ PRED$) =$ 'PRO')
$\qquad\qquad\qquad (\uparrow$ SUBJ PERS$) = 3$
$\qquad\qquad\qquad (\uparrow$ SUBJ NUM$) =$ SG
$\qquad\qquad\qquad (\uparrow$ SUBJ CASE$) =$ ABS
$\qquad\qquad\qquad (\uparrow$ OBL PRED$) =$ 'dog'
$\qquad\qquad\qquad (\uparrow$ OBL CASE$) =$ INST

sapangarsivoq V $(\uparrow$ PRED$) =$ 'get $\langle(\uparrow$ SUBJ$), (\uparrow$ OBL$)\rangle$'
$\qquad\qquad\qquad (\uparrow$ MOOD$) =$ INDIC
$\qquad\qquad\qquad ((\uparrow$ SUBJ PRED$) =$ 'PRO')
$\qquad\qquad\qquad (\uparrow$ SUBJ PERS$) = 3$
$\qquad\qquad\qquad (\uparrow$ SUBJ NUM$) =$ SG
$\qquad\qquad\qquad (\uparrow$ SUBJ CASE$) =$ ABS
$\qquad\qquad\qquad (\uparrow$ OBL PRED$) =$ 'bead'
$\qquad\qquad\qquad (\uparrow$ OBL CASE$) =$ INST

Task XV

$$V \;\rightarrow\; \underset{(\uparrow \text{OBL}) \,=\, \downarrow}{N_{\text{stem}}} \quad \underset{\uparrow \,=\, \downarrow}{V_{\text{suff}}}$$

Task XVI

C-structure for (11):

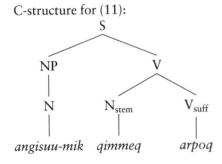

F-structure for (11):

$$\begin{bmatrix} \text{PRED} & \text{'have } \langle f_1, f_2 \rangle \text{'} \\ \text{MOOD} & \text{INDIC} \\ \text{SUBJ} & f_1\!: \begin{bmatrix} \text{PRED} & \text{'PRO'} \\ \text{NUM} & \text{SG} \\ \text{PERS} & 3 \\ \text{CASE} & \text{ABS} \end{bmatrix} \\ \text{OBL} & f_2\!: \begin{bmatrix} \text{PRED} & \text{'dog'} \\ \text{CASE} & \text{INST} \\ \text{ADJ} & \begin{bmatrix} \text{PRED} & \text{'big'} \\ \text{CASE} & \text{INST} \\ \text{NUM} & \text{SG} \end{bmatrix} \end{bmatrix} \end{bmatrix}$$

C-structure for (14):

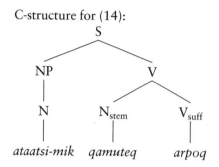

F-structure for (14):

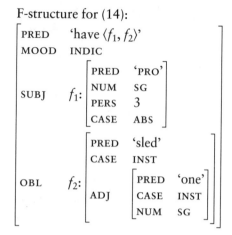

Problem Set 3

P3.1   German word order

Task I

Note: This CP rule is based only on the examples in (1) and (2), and is added to later in the problem. In the IP and VP rules, the alternatives DP and NP can of course be collapsed using the X′ theory of chapter 6:

$$CP \rightarrow \underset{\uparrow = \downarrow}{C} \quad \underset{\uparrow = \downarrow}{IP}$$

$$IP \rightarrow \underset{(\uparrow \text{SUBJ}) = \downarrow}{DP/NP} \quad \underset{\uparrow = \downarrow}{I'}$$

$$I' \rightarrow \underset{\uparrow = \downarrow}{VP} \quad \underset{\uparrow = \downarrow}{I}$$

$$VP \rightarrow \underset{(\uparrow \text{OBJ}) = \downarrow}{DP/NP} \quad \left(\underset{\uparrow = \downarrow}{V} \right)$$

$$DP \rightarrow \left(\underset{\uparrow = \downarrow}{D} \right) \quad \underset{\uparrow = \downarrow}{NP}$$

$$NP \rightarrow \underset{\uparrow = \downarrow}{N}$$

Task II

Annotated c-structure for (1a):

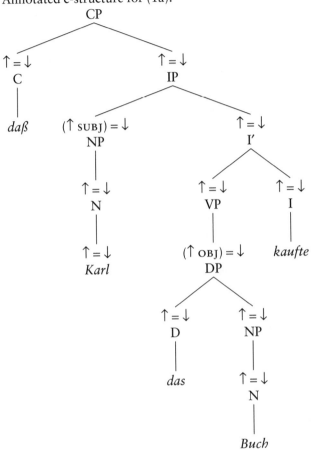

F-structure for (1a):

$$
\begin{bmatrix}
\text{PRED} & \text{'buy } \langle f_1, f_2 \rangle\text{'} \\
\text{TENSE} & \text{PAST} \\
\text{MOOD} & \text{DECL} \\
\text{SUBJ} & f_1\text{:}\begin{bmatrix}\text{PRED} & \text{'Karl'}\end{bmatrix} \\
\text{OBJ} & f_2\text{:}\begin{bmatrix}\text{PRED} & \text{'book'} \\ \text{DEF} & + \end{bmatrix}
\end{bmatrix}
$$

Annotated c-structure for (2a):

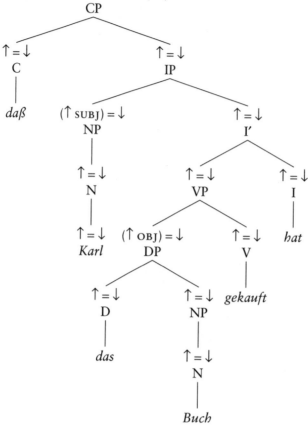

F-structure for (2a):

$$
\begin{bmatrix}
\text{PRED} & \text{`buy } \langle f_1, f_2 \rangle\text{'} \\
\text{TENSE} & \text{PRES\_PERF} \\
\text{SUBJ} & f_1\text{:}[\text{PRED} \quad \text{`Karl'}] \\
\text{OBJ} & f_2\text{:}\begin{bmatrix} \text{PRED} & \text{`book'} \\ \text{DEF} & + \end{bmatrix}
\end{bmatrix}
$$

Task III Finite verbs in main clauses appear in the same position as complementizers in subordinate clauses: C.

The following new morpholexical specifications are needed to account for (3a) and (4b). No new c-structure rules are necessary:

kaufte: C_V $(\uparrow \text{PRED}) = \text{`buy } \langle(\uparrow \text{SUBJ})(\uparrow \text{OBJ})\rangle\text{'}$
$(\uparrow \text{TENSE}) = \text{PAST}$

hat: C $(\uparrow \text{TENSE}) = \text{PRES}$
$(\uparrow \text{ASPECT}) = \text{PERF}$

Task IV

Annotated c-structure for (3a):

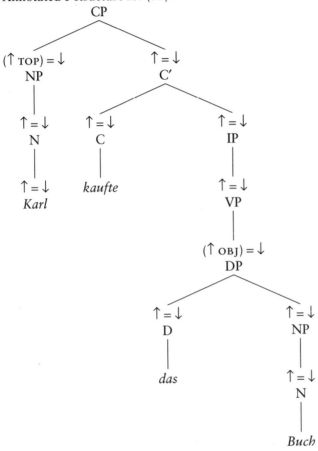

F-structure for (3a):

$$\begin{bmatrix} \text{PRED} & \text{'buy } \langle f_1, f_2 \rangle\text{'} \\ \text{TENSE} & \text{PAST} \\ \text{TOP} & [\text{PRED} \quad \text{'Karl'}] \\ \text{SUBJ} & f_1\text{: } [\,] \\ \text{OBJ} & f_2\text{: } \begin{bmatrix} \text{PRED} & \text{'book'} \\ \text{DEF} & + \end{bmatrix} \end{bmatrix}$$

Annotated c-structure for (4b):

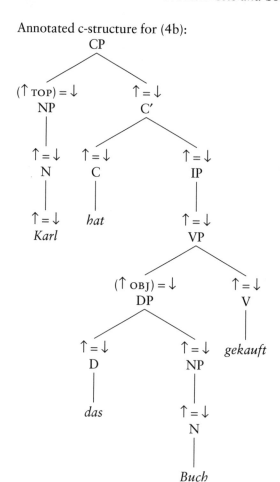

F-structure for (4b):

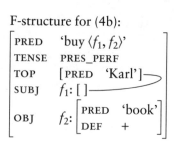

Task VI
One possibility:

daß: C $(\uparrow$ MOOD$) = $ DECL
             $(\uparrow$ TENSE$)$
             $\neg(\uparrow$ TOP$)$

kaufte: C_V $(\uparrow$ PRED$) = $ 'buy $\langle(\uparrow$ SUBJ$)(\uparrow$ OBJ$)\rangle$'
             $(\uparrow$ TENSE$) = $ PAST
             $(\uparrow$ TOP$)$

hat: C $(\uparrow$ TENSE$) = $ PRES
             $(\uparrow$ ASPECT$) = $ PERF
             $(\uparrow$ TOP$)$

In view of the default $(\uparrow$ SUBJ$) = (\uparrow$ TOP$)$, this solution requires a constraint that TOP constituents are sentence-initial. (Compare the principle of clause prominence of DFs in chapter 9.)

P3.2 *Subject agreement in West Flemish*

Task VII

Annotated c-structure for (1a):

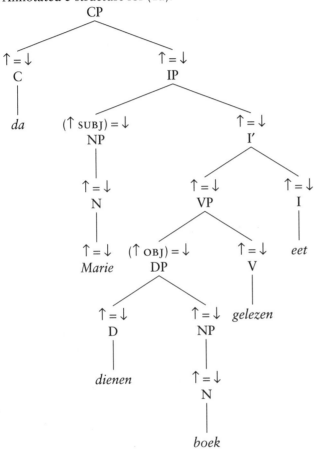

F-structure for (1a):

$$\begin{bmatrix} \text{PRED} & \text{'read } \langle f_1, f_2 \rangle \text{'} \\ \text{TENSE} & \text{PRES\_PERF} \\ \text{SUBJ} & f_1: [\text{PRED} \quad \text{'Marie'}] \\ \text{OBJ} & f_2: \begin{bmatrix} \text{PRED} & \text{'book'} \\ \text{DEF} & + \\ \text{DEIXIS} & \text{DISTANT} \end{bmatrix} \end{bmatrix}$$

Annotated c-structure for (1b):

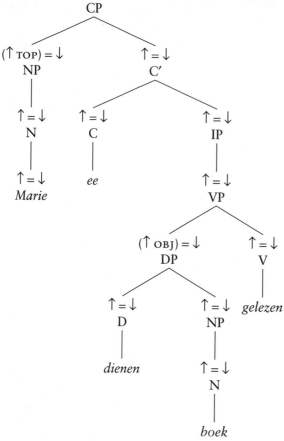

F-structure for (1b):

$$
\begin{bmatrix}
\text{PRED} & \text{'read}\ \langle f_1, f_2 \rangle \text{'} \\
\text{TENSE} & \text{PRES\_PERF} \\
\text{TOP} & [\text{PRED} \quad \text{'Marie'}] \\
\text{SUBJ} & f_1\text{: [ ]} \\
\text{OBJ} & f_2\text{:} \begin{bmatrix} \text{PRED} & \text{'book'} \\ \text{DEF} & + \\ \text{DEIXIS} & \text{DISTANT} \end{bmatrix}
\end{bmatrix}
$$

Task VIII

goat: I_V $(\uparrow \text{PRED}) = \text{'go}\ \langle (\uparrow \text{SUBJ}) \rangle \text{'}$
   $(\uparrow \text{TENSE}) = \text{PRES}$
   $(\uparrow \text{SUBJ}) = \downarrow$
      $(\downarrow \text{PERS}) = 2$ $\vee$ $(\downarrow \text{PERS}) = 3$
                $(\downarrow \text{NUM}) = \text{SG}$

goan: I$_V$ ($\uparrow$ PRED) = 'go $\langle(\uparrow$ SUBJ)$\rangle$'
          ($\uparrow$ TENSE) = PRES
          ($\uparrow$ SUBJ) = $\downarrow$
             ($\downarrow$ PERS) = 1 $\vee$ ($\downarrow$ PERS) = 3
                                       ($\downarrow$ NUM) = PL

Task IX

da-j: C   ($\uparrow$ MOOD) = DECL
          ($\uparrow$ TENSE)
          $\neg$($\uparrow$ TOP)
          ($\uparrow$ SUBJ) = $\downarrow$
             (($\downarrow$ PRED) = 'PRO')
             ($\downarrow$ PERS) = 2
             ($\downarrow$ BIND) = β

da-se: C   ($\uparrow$ MOOD) = DECL
          ($\uparrow$ TENSE)
          $\neg$($\uparrow$ TOP)
          ($\uparrow$ SUBJ) = $\downarrow$
             (($\downarrow$ PRED) = 'PRO')
             ($\downarrow$ PERS) = 3
             ($\downarrow$ NUM) = SG
             ($\downarrow$ GEND) = FEM
             ($\downarrow$ BIND) = β

da: C   ($\uparrow$ MOOD) = DECL
          ($\uparrow$ TENSE)
          $\neg$($\uparrow$ TOP)
          ($\uparrow$ SUBJ) = $\downarrow$
             ($\downarrow$ PERS) = 3
             ($\downarrow$ NUM) = SG
             $\neg$($\downarrow$ BIND)

dan: C   ($\uparrow$ MOOD) = DECL
          ($\uparrow$ TENSE)
          $\neg$($\uparrow$ TOP)
          ($\uparrow$ SUBJ) = $\downarrow$
             ($\downarrow$ PERS) = 3
             ($\downarrow$ NUM) = PL
             $\neg$($\downarrow$ BIND)

gie: D   ($\uparrow$ PRED) = 'PRO'
          ($\uparrow$ PERS) = 2
          ($\uparrow$ NUM) = SG
          ($\uparrow$ BIND) = β

zie: D $(\uparrow \text{PRED}) = \text{'PRO'}$
          $(\uparrow \text{PERS}) = 3$
          $(\uparrow \text{NUM}) = \text{SG}$
          $(\uparrow \text{GEND}) = \text{FEM}$
          $(\uparrow \text{BIND}) = \beta$

gunder: D $(\uparrow \text{PRED}) = \text{'PRO'}$
             $(\uparrow \text{PERS}) = 2$
             $(\uparrow \text{NUM}) = \text{PL}$
             $(\uparrow \text{BIND}) = \beta$

Task X

Annotated c-structure for (3g):

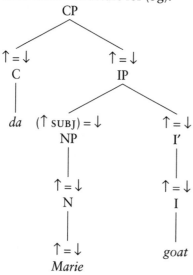

F-structure for (3g):

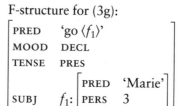

Annotated c-structure for (4a):

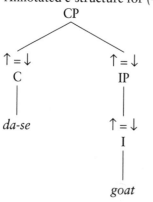

F-structure for (4a):

Annotated c-structure for (4b):

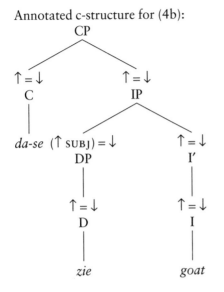

F-structure for (4b):

$$\begin{bmatrix} \text{PRED} & \text{'go } \langle f_1 \rangle\text{'} \\ \text{MOOD} & \text{DECL} \\ \text{TENSE} & \text{PRES} \\ \text{SUBJ} & f_1: \begin{bmatrix} \text{PRED} & \text{'PRO'} \\ \text{PERS} & 3 \\ \text{NUM} & \text{SG} \\ \text{GEND} & \text{FEM} \\ \text{BIND} & \beta \end{bmatrix} \end{bmatrix}$$

Task XI

goa-j: C_V $(\uparrow \text{PRED}) = \text{'go } \langle(\uparrow \text{SUBJ})\rangle\text{'}$
$(\uparrow \text{TENSE}) = \text{PRES}$
$(\uparrow \text{TOP})$
$(\uparrow \text{SUBJ}) = \downarrow$
    $((\downarrow \text{PRED}) = \text{'PRO'})$
    $(\downarrow \text{PERS}) = 2$
    $(\downarrow \text{BIND}) = \beta$

goa-se: C_V $(\uparrow \text{PRED}) = \text{'go } \langle(\uparrow \text{SUBJ})\rangle\text{'}$
$(\uparrow \text{TENSE}) = \text{PRES}$
$(\uparrow \text{TOP})$
$(\uparrow \text{SUBJ}) = \downarrow$
    $((\downarrow \text{PRED}) = \text{'PRO'})$
    $(\downarrow \text{PERS}) = 3$
    $(\downarrow \text{NUM}) = \text{SG}$
    $(\downarrow \text{GEND}) = \text{FEM}$
    $(\downarrow \text{BIND}) = \beta$

goa: C_V $(\uparrow \text{PRED}) = \text{'go } \langle(\uparrow \text{SUBJ})\rangle\text{'}$
$(\uparrow \text{TENSE}) = \text{PRES}$
$(\uparrow \text{TOP})$
$(\uparrow \text{SUBJ}) = \downarrow$
    $(\downarrow \text{PERS}) = 3$
    $(\downarrow \text{NUM}) = \text{SG}$
    $\neg(\downarrow \text{BIND})$

goan: C_V ($\uparrow$ PRED) = 'go $\langle(\uparrow$ SUBJ$)\rangle$'
         ($\uparrow$ TENSE) = PRES
         ($\uparrow$ TOP)
         ($\uparrow$ SUBJ) = $\downarrow$
            ($\downarrow$ PERS) = 3
            ($\downarrow$ NUM) = PL
            $\neg$($\downarrow$ BIND)

Task XII The subject agreement suffixes attach to elements of category C.

Task XIII

Annotated c-structure for (5c), with subject pronoun:

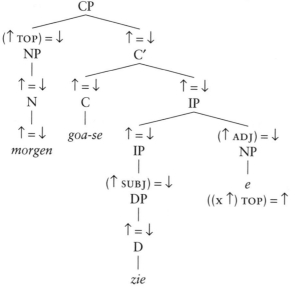

Annotated c-structure for (5c), without the subject pronoun:

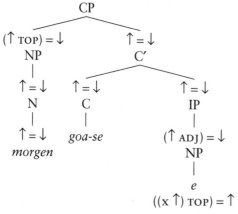

F-structure for (5c):

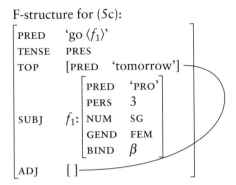

$$
\begin{bmatrix}
\text{PRED} & \text{'go } \langle f_1 \rangle \text{'} \\
\text{TENSE} & \text{PRES} \\
\text{TOP} & [\text{PRED} \quad \text{'tomorrow'}] \\
\text{SUBJ} & f_1: \begin{bmatrix} \text{PRED} & \text{'PRO'} \\ \text{PERS} & 3 \\ \text{NUM} & \text{SG} \\ \text{GEND} & \text{FEM} \\ \text{BIND} & \beta \end{bmatrix} \\
\text{ADJ} & [\,]
\end{bmatrix}
$$

P3.3   *Person and number marking in Wambaya*

Task XIV

gininga: Aux $(\uparrow \text{TENSE}) = \text{PAST}$
$(\uparrow \text{SUBJ}) = \downarrow$
$\quad ((\downarrow \text{PRED}) = \text{'PRO'})$
$\quad (\downarrow \text{PERS}) = 3$
$\quad (\downarrow \text{NUM}) = \text{SG}$
$\quad (\downarrow \text{GEND}) = \text{MASC}$
$(\uparrow \text{OBJ}) = \downarrow$
$\quad ((\downarrow \text{PRED}) = \text{'PRO'})$
$\quad (\downarrow \text{PERS}) = 1$
$\quad (\downarrow \text{NUM}) = \text{SG}$

Task XV

Annotated c-structure and f-structure for (3a):

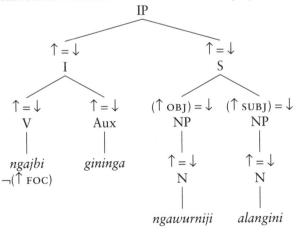

F-structure for (3a):

$$
\begin{bmatrix}
\text{PRED} & \text{'see } \langle f_1, f_2 \rangle\text{'} \\
\text{TENSE} & \text{PAST} \\
\text{SUBJ} & f_1: \begin{bmatrix} \text{PRED} & \text{'boy'} \\ \text{CASE} & \text{ERG} \\ \text{PERS} & 3 \\ \text{NUM} & \text{SG} \\ \text{GEND} & \text{MASC} \end{bmatrix} \\
\text{OBJ} & f_2: \begin{bmatrix} \text{PRED} & \text{'PRO'} \\ \text{CASE} & \text{ABS} \\ \text{PERS} & 1 \\ \text{NUM} & \text{SG} \end{bmatrix}
\end{bmatrix}
$$

Annotated c-structure for (3b):

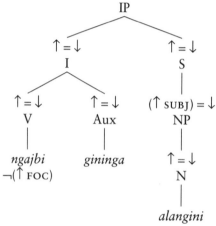

F-structure for (3b):

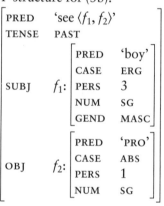

$$
\begin{bmatrix}
\text{PRED} & \text{'see } \langle f_1, f_2 \rangle\text{'} \\
\text{TENSE} & \text{PAST} \\
\text{SUBJ} & f_1: \begin{bmatrix} \text{PRED} & \text{'boy'} \\ \text{CASE} & \text{ERG} \\ \text{PERS} & 3 \\ \text{NUM} & \text{SG} \\ \text{GEND} & \text{MASC} \end{bmatrix} \\
\text{OBJ} & f_2: \begin{bmatrix} \text{PRED} & \text{'PRO'} \\ \text{CASE} & \text{ABS} \\ \text{PERS} & 1 \\ \text{NUM} & \text{SG} \end{bmatrix}
\end{bmatrix}
$$

Annotated c-structure for (3c):

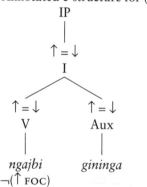

F-structure for (3c):

$$
\begin{bmatrix}
\text{PRED} & \text{'see } \langle f_1, f_2 \rangle\text{'} \\
\text{TENSE} & \text{PAST} \\
\text{SUBJ} & f_1: \begin{bmatrix} \text{PRED} & \text{'boy'} \\ \text{CASE} & \text{ERG} \\ \text{PERS} & 3 \\ \text{NUM} & \text{SG} \\ \text{GEND} & \text{MASC} \end{bmatrix} \\
\text{OBJ} & f_2: \begin{bmatrix} \text{PRED} & \text{'PRO'} \\ \text{CASE} & \text{ABS} \\ \text{PERS} & 1 \\ \text{NUM} & \text{SG} \end{bmatrix}
\end{bmatrix}
$$

Task XVI

gininga: I (↑ TENSE) = PAST
(↑ SUBJ) = ↓
((↓ PRED) = 'PRO')
(↓ PERS) = 3
(↓ NUM) = SG
(↓ GEND) = MASC
(↑ OBJ) = ↓
(↓ PERS) = 1
$\left(\begin{array}{c}(↓ \text{PRED}) = \text{'PRO'} \\ (↓ \text{NUM}) = \text{SG}\end{array}\right)$

Task XVII

Annotated c-structure for (4c):   F-structure for (4c):

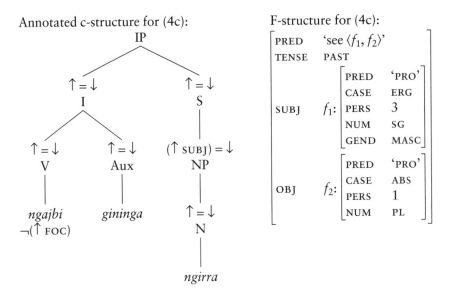

Task XIX

The data about object agreement in Wambaya argue against an analysis in which the subject and object markers are always incorporated pronominals and the NPs (optional) adjuncts. If this were the case, there would be no way of accounting for the differences between constructions with singular and nonsingular objects. When the object is nonsingular, the corresponding NP is not optional, but obligatory. The object marker in the auxiliary has a different function according to the number of the object: when the object is singular it can carry the features (↓ PRED) = 'pro' and (↓ NUM) = SG; when the object is nonsingular, it cannot. Thus, only in constructions with a singular object can it function as an incorporated pronominal; when the object is nonsingular, it can only function as an agreement marker.

References for the Problems

1 *Problem set 1*

P1.1 WARLPIRI
Hale (1981), Simpson (1983a, 1991).

P1.2 MONSTERS AND HOW TO AVOID THEM
Lyons (1968), Bresnan (1982b).

2 *Problem set 2*

P2.1 SPANISH
Grimshaw (1982b), Montalbetti (1981).

P2.2 MOROCCAN ARABIC
Wager (1983).

P2.3 IRISH
Andrews (1990a), McCloskey and Hale (1984).

P2.4 NOUN INCORPORATION IN GREENLANDIC
Sadock (1980).

3 *Problem set 3*

P3.1 GERMAN WORD ORDER
Haegeman (1991), Vikner (1995).

P3.2 SUBJECT AGREEMENT IN WEST FLEMISH
Haegeman (1992).

P3.3 PERSON AND NUMBER MARKING IN WAMBAYA
Nordlinger (1998a, 1998b).

4 *Problem set 4*

P4.1.1 DUTCH DEPENDENT CLAUSEES
Bresnan et al. (1982).

P4.1.2 JAPANESE CAUSATIVES
Ishikawa (1985).

P4.2.1 "QUIRKY" CASE IN ICELANDIC
Andrews (1982, 1990b), Zaenen et al. (1985).

P4.2.2 SECOND PREDICATES IN RUSSIAN
Neidle (1982b, 1988).

P4.2.3 Icelandic case marking and control
Andrews (1982, 1990b), Zaenen et al. (1985).

P4.3.1–2 Finnish possessive suffixes I, II
Toivonen (1996).

P4.3.3 Japanese reflexives
Kameyama (1984), Saiki (1985, 1986).

5 Problem set 5

P5.1.1 Italian
Baker (1983), Burzio (1981, 1986), Rosen (1984).

P5.1.2 Russian
Neidle (1982a, 1988), Pesetsky (1982).

P5.1.3 Empty "there" in English
Bresnan (1982a).

P5.2 Reflexives: Serbian/Croatian
Zec (1985), Sells et al. (1987).

References

Aass, Kristin. 1979. Refleksivitet i Moderne Norsk: om bruken av seg og sin' (Hovedoppgave. Institutt for nordisk språk og litteratur, University of Oslo).

Abney, Steven. 1987. The English noun phrase in its sentential aspect. Cambridge, MA: MIT Department of Linguistics and Philosophy Ph.D. dissertation.

Ackerman, Farrell. 1987. Miscreant morphemes: phrasal predicates in Ugric. Berkeley, CA: University of California, Berkeley, Department of Linguistics Ph.D. dissertation.

Ackerman, Farrell. 1990. Locative alternation vs. locative inversion. *Proceedings of the West Coast Conference on Formal Linguistics* 9: 1–13. Stanford, CA: CSLI.

Ackerman, Farrell. 1992. Complex predicates and morpholexical relatedness: locative alternation in Hungarian. In *Lexical Matters*, eds Ivan Sag and Anna Szabolcsi, 55–83. Stanford, CA: CSLI.

Ackerman, Farrell and Adele E. Goldberg. 1996. Constraints on adjectival past participles. In *Conceptual Structure, Discourse and Language*, ed. Adele E. Goldberg. Stanford, CA: CSLI.

Ackerman, Farrell and Philip Lesourd. 1997. Toward a lexical representation of phrasal predicates. In Alsina et al. (1997), 67–106.

Aissen, Judith. 1992. Topic and focus in Mayan. *Language* 68: 43–80.

Aissen, Judith. 1997. On the syntax of obviation. *Language* 73: 705–50.

Aissen, Judith. 1999. *yi* and *bi*: proximate and obviative in Navajo. In *Papers in Honor of Ken Hale. Endangered and Less Familiar Languages Working Papers I*, eds Andrew Carnie, Eloise Jelinek, and MaryAnn Willie. Cambridge, MA: MIT Working Papers in Linguistics.

Allan, Keith. 1983. Anaphora, cataphora, and topic focusing: functions of the object prefix in Swahili. In *Current Approaches to African Linguistics, Vol. 1*, ed. Ivan R. Dihoff, 322–35. Dordrecht: Foris.

Allen, Cynthia. 1995. *Case Marking and Reanalysis: Grammatical Relations from Old to Early Modern English*. Oxford: Clarendon Press.

Alsagoff, Lubna. 1992. Topic in Malay: the other subject. Stanford, CA: Stanford University Department of Linguistics Ph.D. dissertation.

Alsina, Alex. 1990. Where's the mirror principle? Evidence from Chicheŵa. Paper presented at the 13th Generative Linguistics in the Old World Colloquium at St John's College, Cambridge University, April 6–8, 1990.

Alsina, Alex. 1992. On the argument structure of causatives. *Linguistic Inquiry* 23: 517–55.

Alsina, Alex. 1994a. Bantu multiple objects: analyses and fallacies. *Linguistic Analysis* 24: 153–74.

Alsina, Alex. 1994b. Predicate composition: a theory of syntactic function alternations. Stanford, CA: Stanford University Department of Linguistics Ph.D. dissertation.

Alsina, Alex. 1996a. Passive types and the theory of object asymmetries. *Natural Language and Linguistic Theory* 14: 673–723.

Alsina, Alex. 1996b. *The Role of Argument Structure in Grammar*. Stanford, CA: CSLI.

Alsina, Alex. 1997. A theory of complex predicates: evidence from causatives in Bantu and Romance. In Alsina et al. (1997), 203–46.

Alsina, Alex. 1999. Where's the mirror principle? *Linguistic Review* 15: 1–42.

Alsina, Alex and Smita Joshi. 1991. Parameters in causative constructions. *Proceedings of the Chicago Linguistic Society* 27: 1–15.

Alsina, Alex and Sam A. Mchombo. 1990. The syntax of applicatives in Chicheŵa: problems for a theta theoretic asymmetry. *Natural Language and Linguistic Theory* 8: 493–506.

Alsina, Alex and Sam A. Mchombo. 1991. Object extraction and the accessibility of thematic information. *Proceedings of the Berkeley Linguistics Society* 17: 15–29.

Alsina, Alex and Sam A. Mchombo. 1993. Object asymmetries and the Chicheŵa applicative construction. In Mchombo (1993c), 17–45.

Alsina, Alex, Joan Bresnan, and Peter Sells (eds). 1997. *Complex Predicates*. Stanford, CA: CSLI.

Anagnostopoulou, Elena. 1993. On the representation of clitic doubling in Modern Greek. *EUROTYP Working Papers. Clitic Doubling and Clitic Groups. Theme Group 8: Clitics* 1–66. Tilburg, The Netherlands: Grammatical Models Section, ESF-EUROTYP.

Andrews, Avery. 1976. The VP-complement analysis in Modern Icelandic. *Proceedings of the Northeastern Linguistic Society* 6: 1–21. Reprinted with revisions in Maling and Zaenen (1990), 165–85.

Andrews, Avery. 1982. The representation of case in Modern Icelandic. In Bresnan (1982c), 427–503.

Andrews, Avery. 1985. The major functions of the noun phrase. In *Language Typology and Syntactic Description. Vol. 1: Clause Structure*, ed. Timothy Shopen, 62–154. Cambridge: Cambridge University Press.

Andrews, Avery. 1990a. Unification and morphological blocking. *Natural Language and Linguistic Theory* 8: 507–57.

Andrews, Avery. 1990b. Case structures and control. In Maling and Zaenen (1990), 187–234.

Andrews, Avery. 1994. Syntax Textbook draft 4.0. Canberra: Australia National University MS.

Andrews, Avery. 1996. Semantic case-stacking and inside-out unification. *Australian Journal of Linguistics* 16: 1–55.

Andrews, Avery and Christopher Manning. 1993. Information spreading and levels of representation in LFG. *Report No. CSLI-93-176*. Stanford, CA: CSLI.

Andrews, Avery and Christopher Manning. 1999. *Complex Predicates and Information Spreading in LFG*. Stanford, CA: CSLI.

Arka, I Wayan. 1998. From morphosyntax to pragmatics in Balinese: a lexical-functional approach. Sydney: University of Sydney Department of Linguistics Ph.D. dissertation.

Arka, I Wayan and Christopher D. Manning. 1999. Voice and grammatical relations in Indonesian: A new perspective. In Butt and King (1998).

Arka, I Wayan and Jane Simpson. 1998. Control and complex arguments in Balinese. In Butt and King (1998).

Arnold, Jennifer. 1994. Inverse voice marking in Mapudungun. *Twentieth Annual Meeting of the Berkeley Linguistics Society* 28–41.

Asher, Nicholas and Hajime Wada. 1988. A computational account of syntactic, semantic and discourse principles for anaphora resolution. *Journal of Semantics* 6: 309–44.

Asudeh, Ash. 1998. Anaphora and argument structure: topics in the syntax and semantics of reflexives and reciprocals. Edinburgh: University of Edinburgh Centre for Cognitive Science M.Phil. thesis.

Asudeh, Ash. 1999. Linking, optionality, and ambiguity in Marathi: an optimality theory analysis. To appear in Sells (forthcoming).

Austin, Peter. 1997. Causatives and applicatives in Australian Aboriginal languages. In *The Dative and Related Phenomena*, eds Kazuto Matsumura and Tooru Hayashi, 165–225. Tokyo: Hitsuji Shobo.

Austin, Peter and Joan Bresnan. 1996. Nonconfigurationality in Australian aboriginal languages. *Natural Language and Linguistic Theory* 14: 215–68.

Austin, Peter and Simon Musgrave (eds). Forthcoming. *Voice and Grammatical Functions in Austronesian Languages*. Stanford, CA: CSLI.

Awbery, G. M. 1976. *The Syntax of Welsh: A Transformational Study of the Passive*. Cambridge: Cambridge University Press.

Bach, Emmon and Barbara H. Partee. 1980. Anaphora and semantic structure. *Papers from the Parasession on Pronouns and Anaphora. Chicago Linguistic Society, April 18–19, 1980* 1–28.

Bach, Emmon, Eloise Jelinek, Angelika Kratzer, and Barbara H. Partee (eds). 1995. *Quantification in Natural Languages*. Dordrecht: Kluwer Academic.

Baker, Mark. 1983. Objects, themes and lexical rules in Italian. In L. Levin et al. (1983), 1–45.

Baker, Mark C. 1988. *Incorporation: A Theory of Grammatical Function Changing*. Chicago: Chicago University Press.

Baker, Mark C. 1991. On some subject/object non-asymmetries in Mohawk. *Natural Language and Linguistic Theory* 9: 537–76.

Baker, Mark C. 1995. On the absence of certain quantifiers in Mohawk. In Bach et al. (1995), 21–58.

Baltin, Mark. 1982. A landing site theory of movement rules. *Linguistic Inquiry* 13: 1–38.

Banfield, Ann. 1982. *Unspeakable Sentences: Narration and Representation in the Language of Fiction*. Boston: Routledge and Kegan Paul.

Barron, Julia. 1998. *Have* contraction: explaining "trace effects" in a theory without movement. *Linguistics* 36: 223–51.

Barss, Andrew, Ken Hale, Ellavina Tsosie Perkins, and Margaret Speas. 1989. Aspects of logical from in Navajo. In Cook and Rice (1989), 317–34.

Berman, Judith. 1996. Topicalization vs. left-dislocation of sentential arguments in German. In Butt and King (1996).

Berman, Judith. 1997. Empty categories in LFG. In Butt and King (1997).

Berman, Judith. 1998. On the syntax of correlative *es* and finite clauses in German – an LFG analysis. *Proceedings of the ESSLLI-98 Workshop on Constraint-Based Theories of Germanic Syntax*, Saarbrücken, 5–19.

Berman, Judith. 1999. Does German satisfy the subject condition? In Butt and King (1999).

Berman, Judith. Forthcoming. On the cooccurence of *es* in a finite cluase in German: an LFG analysis. In *Topics in Constraint-Based Germanic Syntax*, eds T. Kiss and D. Meurers. Stanford, CA: CSLI.

Berman, Judith and Anette Frank. 1996. *Deutsche and französische Syntax im Formalismus der LFG*. Tübingen: May Niemeyer Verlag.

Bickerton, Derek. 1975. Some assertions about presuppositions about pronominalization. *Papers from the Parasession on Functionalism. Chicago Linguistics Society, April 17, 1975*, 24–35.

Bittner, Maria and Ken Hale. 1995. Remarks on definiteness in Warlpiri. In Bach et al. (1995), 81–105.

Bloom, Douglas B. 1999. Case syncretism and word order freezing in the Russian language. Stanford, CA: Stanford University Department of Linguistics M.A. Thesis.

Bod, Rens. 1999. *Beyond Grammar. An Experience-Based Theory of Language*. Stanford, CA: CSLI.

Bod, Rens and Ronald M. Kaplan. 1998. A probabilistic corpus-driven model for lexical-functional analysis. *Proceedings of ACL/COLING '98*, Montreal, Canada.

Bodomo, Adams B. 1992. A unification-based grammar of serial verb constructions. *Proceedings of the Scandinavian Conference of Computational Linguistics*, eds K. Morland and K. Soerstroemmen, 41–56. Bergen, November 28–30, 1991.

Bodomo, Adams B. 1996. Complex verbal predicates: the case of serial verbs in Dagaare and Akan. In Butt and King (1996).

Bodomo, Adams B. 1997. A conceptual mapping theory for serial verbs. In Butt and King (1997).

Boersma, Paul and Bruce Hayes. 1999. Empirical tests of the gradual learning algorithm. On-line, Rutgers University (Rutgers Optimality Archive): http://ruccs.rutgers.edu/roa.html.

Bolinger, Dwight. 1979. Pronouns in discourse. *Syntax and Semantics. Vol. 12: Discourse and Syntax*, ed. Talmy Givón, 289–309. New York: Academic Press.

Börjars, Kersti, Nigel Vincent, and Carol Chapman. 1997. Paradigms, periphrases and pronominal inflection: a feature-based account. *The Yearbook of Morphology*, eds Geert Booji and Jaap van Marle, 1–26. Dordrecht: Kluwer Academic.

Borsley, Robert D. 1989. An HPSG approah to Welsh. *Journal of Linguistics* 25: 333–54.

Borsley, Robert D. 1990. A GPSG approach to Breton word order. In Hendrick (1990), 81–95.

Brame, Michael. 1982. The head-selector theory of lexical specifications and the nonexistence of coarse categories. *Linguistic Analysis* 10: 321–5.

Bresnan, Joan. 1977. Transformations and categories in syntax. In *Basic Problems in Methodology and Linguistics. Part Three of the Proceedings of the Fifth International Congress of Logic, Methodology and Philosophy of Science, London, Ontario, Canada, 1975*, eds R. E. Butts and J. Hintikka, 261–82. Dordrecht: Reidel.

Bresnan, Joan. 1978. A realistic transformational grammar. In *Linguistic Theory and Psychological Reality*, eds Morris Halle, Joan Bresnan, and George A. Miller, 1–59. Cambridge, MA: MIT Press.

Bresnan, Joan. 1980. Polyadicity. In *Lexical Grammar*, eds T. Hoekstra, H. van der Hulst, and M. Moortgat, 97–121. Dordrecht: Foris. In revised form in Bresnan (1982c), 149–72.

Bresnan, Joan. 1982a. The passive in lexical theory. In Bresnan (1982c), 3–86.

Bresnan, Joan. 1982b. Control and complementation. *Linguistic Inquiry* 13: 343–434. Reprinted in Bresnan (1982c), 282–390.

Bresnan, Joan (ed). 1982c. *The Mental Representation of Grammatical Relations*. Cambridge, MA: MIT Press.

Bresnan, Joan. 1984. Bound anaphora on functional structures. Paper presented at the Tenth Annual Meeting of the Berkeley Linguistics Society, February 17, 1984.

Bresnan, Joan. 1990. Monotonicity and the theory of relation-changes in LFG. *Language Research* 26: 637–52.

Bresnan, Joan. 1991. Locative case vs. locative gender. *Proceedings of the Berkeley Linguistics Society* 17: 53–68.

Bresnan, Joan. 1993. Interaction between grammar and discourse in Chicheŵa (Bantu). In *The Role of Theory in Language Description: Trends in Linguistics. Studies and Monographs 69*, ed. William A. Foley, 45–60. Berlin: Mouton de Gruyter.

Bresnan, Joan. 1994a. Locative inversion and the architecture of universal grammar. *Language* 70: 72–131.

Bresnan, Joan. 1994b. Linear order vs. syntactic rank: evidence from weak crossover. *Proceedings of the Chicago Linguistic Society* 30: 57–89.

Bresnan, Joan. 1995a. Category mismatches. In *Theoretical Approaches to African Languages*, ed. Akinbiyi Akinlabi, 19–46. Trenton, N.J.: African World Press.

Bresnan, Joan. 1995b. Linear order, syntactic rank, and empty categories: on weak crossover. In Dalrymple et al. (1995), 241–74.

Bresnan, Joan. 1997a. The emergence of the unmarked pronoun II. Paper presented at the Hopkins Optimality Theory Workshop, Inner Harbor, Baltimore, May 9–12, 1997. On-line, Stanford University: http://www-csli.stanford.edu/~bresnan/download.html. To appear revised under the title "The emergence of the unmarked pronoun," in *Optimality-Theoretic Syntax*, eds Jane Grimshaw, Géraldine Legendre, and Sten Vikner. Cambridge, MA: MIT Press.

Bresnan, Joan. 1997b. Mixed categories as head-sharing constructions. In Butt and King (1997).

Bresnan, Joan. 1998a. Optimal syntax. To appear in *Optimality Theory: Phonology, Syntax, and Acquisition*, eds Joost Dekkers, Frank van der Leeuw, and Jeroen van de Weijer. Oxford: Oxford University Press.

Bresnan, Joan. 1998b. Explaining morphosyntactic competition. To appear in *Handbook of Contemporary Syntactic Theory*, eds Mark Baltin and Chris Collins. Oxford: Blackwell.

Bresnan, Joan. 1998c. Morphology competes with syntax: explaining typological variation in weak crossover effects. In *Is the Best Good Enough? Optimality and Competition in Syntax*, eds Pilar Barbosa, Danny Fox, Paul Hagstrom, Martha McGinnis, and David Pesetsky, 59–92. Cambridge, MA: MIT Press and MIT Working Papers in Linguistics.

Bresnan, Joan. To appear. The lexicon in Optimality Theory. In *Sentence Processing and the Lexicon: Formal, Computational and Experimental Perspectives* [working title], eds Suzanne Stevenson and Paola Merlo. Amsterdam: Benjamins.

Bresnan, Joan and Jonni M. Kanerva. 1989. Locative inversion in Chicheŵa: a case study of factorization in grammar. *Linguistic Inquiry* 20: 1–50. Reprinted in Stowell and Wehrli (eds), 53–101.

Bresnan, Joan and Jonni M. Kanerva. 1992. The thematic hierarchy and locative inversion in UG: a reply to Paul Schachter's comments. In Stowell and Wehrli (eds), 111–25.

Bresnan, Joan and Sam A. Mchombo. 1985. Agreement and pronominal incorporation in Chicheŵa. Stanford, CA, and Berkeley, CA: Stanford University and University of California, Berkeley, MS.

Bresnan, Joan and Sam A. Mchombo. 1986. Grammatical and anaphoric agreement. In *Papers from the Parasession on Pragmatics and Grammatical Theory at the Twenty-Second Regional Meeting. Chicago Linguistic Society* 278–97.

Bresnan, Joan and Sam A. Mchombo. 1987. Topic, pronoun, and agreement in Chicheŵa. *Language* 63: 741–82.

Bresnan, Joan and Sam A. Mchombo. 1995. The lexical integrity principle: evidence from Bantu. *Natural Language and Linguistic Theory* 13: 181–254.

Bresnan, Joan and Lioba Moshi. 1990. Object asymmetries in comparative Bantu syntax. *Linguistic Inquiry* 21: 147–85.

Bresnan, Joan and John Mugane. 1999. Mixed categories in Kikuyu. Stanford, CA: Stanford University Department of Linguistics unpublished MS.

Bresnan, Joan and Annie Zaenen. 1990. Deep unaccusativity in LFG. In *Grammatical Relations: A Cross-Theoretical Perspective*, eds K. Dziwirek, P. Farrell, and E. Mejías-Bikandi, 45–57. Stanford, CA: CSLI.

Bresnan, Joan, Per-Kristian Halvorsen, and Joan Maling. 1983. Invariants of anaphoric binding systems. Stanford, CA: Stanford University Department of Linguistics MS.

Bresnan, Joan, Per-Kristian Halvorsen, and Joan Maling. 1984. Invariants of anaphoric binding systems. Stanford, CA: Stanford University Department of Linguistics handout dated July 31, 1984.

Bresnan, Joan, Ronald M. Kaplan, Stanley Peters, and Annie Zaenen. 1982. Cross-serial dependencies in Dutch. *Linguistic Inquiry* 13: 613–23.

Broadwell, George Aaron. 1998. Directionals as complex predicates in Choctaw. In Butt and King (1998).

Burzio, Luigi. 1981. Intransitive verbs in Italian syntax. Cambridge, MA: MIT Department of Linguistics and Philosophy Ph.D. dissertation.

Burzio, Luigi. 1986. *Italian Syntax: A Government-Binding Approach*. Dordrecht: Reidel.

Butt, Miriam. 1995. *The Structure of Complex Predicates in Urdu*. Stanford, CA: CSLI.

Butt, Miriam. 1997. Complex predicates in Urdu. In Alsina et al. (1997), 107–49.

Butt, Miriam and Tracy Holloway King (eds). 1996. *LFG-Workshop. Proceedings of the First LFG Conference, Rank Xerox Research Centre, Grenoble, August 26–28, 1996*. One-line, CSLI Publications: http://csli-publications.stanford.edu/LFG/1/lfg1.html.

Butt, Miriam and Tracy Holloway King (eds). 1997. *Proceedings of the LFG97 Conference*, University of California, San Diego. On-line, CSLI Publications: http://csli-publications.stanford.edu/LFG/2/lfg97.html.

Butt, Miriam and Tracy Holloway King (eds). 1998. *Proceedings of the LFG98 Conference*, University of Queensland, Brisbane. On-line, CSLI Publications: http://csli-publications.stanford.edu/LFG/3/lfg98.html.

Butt, Miriam and Tracy Holloway King (eds). 1999. *Proceedings of the LFG99 Conference*, University of Manchester. On-line, CSLI Publications: http://csli-publications.stanford.edu/LFG/4/lfg99.html.

Butt, Miriam and Tracy Holloway King (eds). 2000. *Argument Realization*. Stanford, CA: CSLI.

Butt, Miriam, Mary Dalrymple, and Anette Frank. 1997. An architecture for linking theory in LFG. In Butt and King (1997).

Butt, Miriam, Maria-Eugenia Niño, and Frédérique Segond. 1996. Multilingual processing of auxiliaries in LFG. In *Natural Language Processing and Speech Technology: Results of the 3rd KONVENS Conference*, Bielefeld, October, ed. D. Gibbon, 111–22. Berlin: Mouton de Gruyter.

Byarushengo, E. A. and Sarah Tenenbaum. 1976. Agreement and word order: a case for pragmatics in Haya. *Proceedings of the Second Annual Meeting of the Berkeley Linguistics Society* 89–99.

Chafe, Wallace L. 1976. Givenness, contrastiveness, definiteness, subjects, topics, and point of view. In Li (1976), 25–55.

Chafe, Wallace L. 1977. The evolution of third person verb agreement in the Iroquoian languages. In Li (1977), 493–524.

Cho, Young-Mee Yu. 1985. An LFG analysis of the Korean reflexive *caki*. *Harvard Studies on Korean Linguistics* 1: 3–13.

Cho, Young-Mee Yu and Peter Sells. 1995. A lexical account of inflectional suffixes in Korean. *Journal of East Asian Linguistics* 4: 119–74.

Choi, Hye-Won. 1996. Optimizing structure in context: scrambling and information structure. Stanford, CA: Stanford University Ph.D. dissertation. On-line, Rutgers University (Rutgers Optimality Archive): http://ruccs.rutgers.edu/roa.html.

Choi, Hye-Won. 1997. Focus scrambling and reconstruction in binding. To appear in *Optimality-Theoretic Syntax*, eds Jane Grimshaw, Géraldine Legendre, and Sten Vikner. Cambridge, MA: MIT Press.

Choi, Hye-Won. 1999. *Optimizing Structure in Context: Scrambling and Information Structure*. Stanford, CA: CSLI.

Chomsky, Noam. 1965. *Aspects of the Theory of Syntax*. Cambridge, MA: MIT Press.

Chomsky, Noam. 1973. Conditions on transformations. In *A Festschrift for Morris Halle*, eds Stephen R. Anderson and Paul Kiparsky, 232–86. New York: Holt, Rinehart, and Winston.

Chomsky, Noam. 1977. On *wh*-movement. In *Formal Syntax*, eds P. Culicover, T. Wasow, and A. Akmajian, 71–132. New York: Academic Press.

Chung, Sandra and James McCloskey. 1987. Government, barriers and small clauses in Modern Irish. *Linguistic Inquiry* 18: 173–237.

Clements, George N. 1975. The logophoric pronoun in Ewe: its role in discourse. *Journal of West African Languages* 10: 141–77.

Cole, Peter. 1974. Indefiniteness and anaphoricity. *Language* 50: 665–74.

Cole, Peter and Li-May Sung. 1994. Head movement and long-distance reflexives. *Linguistic Inquiry* 25: 355–406.

Cole, Peter, Gabriella Hermon, and Li-May Sung. 1990. Principles and parameters of long-distance reflexives. *Linguistic Inquiry* 21: 1–22.

Comrie, Bernard. 1973. Clause structure and movement constraints in Russian. *Papers from the Ninth Regional Meeting of the Chicago Linguistic Society Paravolume: You Take the High Node and I'll Take the Low Node* 291–304.

Comrie, Bernard. 1989. *Language Universals and Linguistic Typology*, second edition. Chicago: Chicago University Press.

Comrie, Bernard. 1998. Reference-tracking: description and explanation. *Sprachtypol. Univ. Forsch. (STUF)* 51: 335–46.

Cook, Eung-Do and Keren D. Rice (eds). 1989. *Athapaskan Linguistics. Current Perspectives on a Language Family. Trends in Linguistics. State-of-the-Art Reports 15*, ed. Werner Winter. Berlin: Mouton de Gruyter.

Corver, Norbert and Henk van Riemsdijk (eds). 1994. *Studies on Scrambling: Movement and Non-Movement Approaches to Free Word-Order Phenomena*. Berlin: Mouton de Gruyter.

Creamer, M. H. 1974. Ranking in Navajo nouns. *Diné Bizaad Nánil'iih/Navajo Language Review* 1: 29–38.

Croft, William. 1997. Intonation units and grammatical structure in Wardaman and English. Paper presented at the Symposium on Constituency in Discourse, University of California at Santa Barbara.

Crouch, Richard and Josef van Genabith. 1999. Context change, underspecification and the structure of glue language derivations. In *Semantics and Syntax in Lexical Functional Grammar: The Resource Logic Approach*, ed. Mary Dalrymple, 117–89. Cambridge, MA: MIT Press.

Culicover, Peter W., Thomas Wasow, and Adrian Akmajian (eds). 1977. *Formal Syntax*. New York: Academic Press.

Culy, Christopher. 1994. Aspects of logophoric marking. *Linguistics* 32: 1055–94.

Culy, Christopher. 1996. Agreement and Fula pronouns. *Studies in African Linguistics* 25: 1–26.

Culy, Christopher. 1997. Logophoric pronouns and point of view. *Linguistics* 35: 845–59.

Dahlstrom, Amy. 1984. Plains Cree morphosyntax. Berkeley, CA: University of California, Berkeley, Ph.D. dissertation. Published as *Plains Cree Morphosyntax*. 1991. New York: Garland.

Dalrymple, Mary. 1993. *The Syntax of Anaphoric Binding*. Stanford, CA: CSLI.

Dalrymple, Mary (ed.). 1999. *Semantics and Syntax in Lexical Functional Grammar: The Resource Logic Approach*. Cambridge, MA: MIT Press.

Dalrymple, Mary and Ronald M. Kaplan. 1997. A set-based approach to feature resolution. In Butt and King (1997).

Dalrymple, Mary and Ronald M. Kaplan. 1998. Feature indeterminacy and feature resolution in description-based syntax. On-line, Stanford University: http://www-lfg.stanford.edu/lfg/archive/. To appear in *Language*.

Dalrymple, Mary and Annie Zaenen. 1991. Modelling anaphoric superiority. *Proceedings of the International Conference on Current Issues in Computational Linguistics*, Penang, Malaysia.

Dalrymple, Mary, Ronald M. Kaplan, John T. Maxwell III, and Annie Zaenen (eds). 1995. *Formal Issues in Lexical-Functional Grammar*. Stanford, CA: CSLI.

Dayal, Veneeta Srivastav. 1994. Binding facts in Hindi and the scrambling phenomenon. In *Theoretical Perspectives on Word Order in South Asian Languages*, eds Miriam Butt, Tracy Holloway King, and Gillian Ramchand, 237–61. Stanford, CA: CSLI.

Demuth, Katherine. 1990. Locatives, impersonals, and expletives in Sesotho. *Linguistic Review* 7: 233–49.

Demuth, Katherine and Mark Johnson. 1989. Interaction between discourse functions and agreement in Setawana. *Journal of African Languages and Linguistics* 11: 21–35.

Demuth, Katherine and Sheila Mmusi. 1997. Presentational focus and thematic structure in comparative Bantu. *Journal of African Languages and Linguistics* 18: 1–19.

Dik, Simon C. 1978. *Functional Grammar*. North-Holland Linguistic Series, eds S. C. Dik and J. G. Kooij. Amsterdam: North-Holland.

Dixon, R. M. W. 1972. *The Dyirbal Language of Northern Queensland*. Cambridge: Cambridge University Press.

Dixon, R. M. W. 1981. *The Languages of Australia*. Cambridge: Cambridge University Press.

Dixon, R. M. W. 1982. Semantic neutralisation for phonological reasons. In *Where Have All the Adjectives Gone? And Other Essays in Semantics and Syntax*, 235–8. Berlin: Mouton.

Dixon, R. M. W. 1988. *A Grammar of Boumaa Fijian*. Cambridge: Cambridge University Press.

Dobrovie-Sorin, Carmen. 1990. Clitic doubling, *wh*-movement, and quantification in Romanian. *Linguistic Inquiry* 21: 351–97.

Dowty, David R. 1979. *Word Meaning and Montague Grammar*. Dordrecht: Reidel.

Dowty, David. 1980. Comments on the paper by Bach and Partee. *Papers from the Parasession on Pronouns and Anaphora*. Chicago Linguistic Society 29–40.

Dowty, David. 1991. Thematic proto-roles and argument selection. *Language* 67: 547–619.

Dryer, Matthew. 1986. Primary objects, secondary objects and antidative. *Language* 62: 808–45.

Dubinsky, Stanley and Silvester Ron Simango. 1996. Passive and stative in Chicheŵa: evidence for modular distinctions in grammar. *Language* 72: 749–81.

Dukes, Michael. 1999. Evidence for grammatical functions in Tongan. In Austin and Musgrave (forthcoming).

Dwivedi, Veena Dhar. 1994. Syntactic dependencies and relative phrases in Hindi. Amherst, MA: University of Massachusetts, Amherst, Ph.D. dissertation.

Dziwirek, Katarzyna, Patrick Farrell, and Errapel Mejías-Bikandi (eds). 1990. *Grammatical Relations: A Cross-Theoretical Perspective*. Stanford, CA: CSLI.

Emonds, Joseph. 1976. *A Transformational Approach to English Syntax*. New York: Academic Press.

Engdahl, Elisabet. 1990. Argument roles and anaphora. In *Situation Theory and its Applications*, eds Robin Cooper, Kuniaki Mukai, and John Perry, 379–93. Stanford, CA: CSLI.

Evans, Gareth. 1980. Pronouns. *Linguistic Inquiry* 11: 337–62.

Falk, Yehuda N. 1983. Constituency, word order, and phrase structure rules. *Linguistic Analysis* 11: 331–60.

Falk, Yehuda N. 1984. The English auxiliary system. *Language* 60: 483–509.

Faltz, Leonard M. 1985. *Reflexivization: A Study in Universal Syntax*. New York: Garland Press.

Fassi Fehri, Abdelkader. 1981. *Complémentation et anaphore en arabe moderne. Une approache lexical fonctionnelle*. Paris: Université de Paris III Ph.D. dissertation.

Fassi Fehri, Abdelkader. 1982. *Linguistique arabe: forme et interprétation*. Rabat, Morocco: Publications de la Faculté des Lettres et des Sciences Humaines de Rabat.

Fassi Fehri, Abdelkader. 1984. Agreement in Arabic, binding, and coherence. In *Agreement in Natural Language*, eds Michael Barlow and Charles A. Ferguson, 107–58. Stanford, CA: CSLI.

Foley, William A. and Robert D. Van Valin. 1984. *Functional Syntax and Universal Grammar*. Cambridge Studies in Linguistics. Cambridge: Cambridge University Press.

Frank, Anette. 1996. A note on complex predicate formation: evidence from auxiliary selection, reflexivization, and past participle agreement in French and Italian. In Butt and King (1996).

Frank, Anette and Ursula Kärcher-Momma. 1992. *Dokumentation zur Französischen Syntax im Formalismus der Lexical Functional Grammar (LFG)*. Stuttgart: Institut für Maschinelle Sprachverarbeitung, University of Stuttgart.

Frank, Anette and Annie Zaenen. 1998. Tense in LFG: syntax and morphology. Draft submitted to *Tense and Aspect Now: Contributions to the Theory of Tense and Aspect in 1998*, eds Hans Kamp and Uwe Reyle.

Frey, Werner. 1993. *Syntaktische Bedingungen für die semantische Interpretation*. Berlin: Studia Grammatica XXXV.

Gazdar, Gerald, Geoffrey Pullum, and Ivan Sag. 1982. Auxiliaries and related phenomena in a restrictive theory of grammar. *Language* 58: 591–638.

Georgopoulos, Carol. 1991. *Syntactic Variables: Resumptive Pronouns and A′ Binding in Palauan*. Dordrecht: Kluwer Academic.

Givón, Talmy. 1976. Topic, pronoun, and grammatical agreement. In Li (1976), 149–88.

Givón, Talmy. 1983. Introduction. In *Topic Continuity in Discourse*, ed. T. Givón, 5–41. Amsterdam: Benjamins.

Givón, Talmy. 1984. *Syntax: A Functional-Typological Introduction*. Amsterdam: Benjamins.

Greenberg, Joseph. 1977. Niger-Congo noun class markers: prefixes, suffixes, both or neither. *Studies in African Linguistics* Supplement 7: 97–104.

Greenberg, Joseph. 1978. How does a language acquire gender markers? In Greenberg et al. (1978), 47–82.

Greenberg, J. H. (ed.), Charles A. Ferguson and Edith A. Moravcsik (associate eds). 1978. *Universals of Human Language, Vol. 3.* Stanford, CA: Stanford University Press.

Grimshaw, Jane. 1982a. On the lexical representation of Romance reflexive clitics. In Bresnan (1982c), 87–148. Cambridge, MA: MIT Press.

Grimshaw, Jane. 1982b. Grammatical relations and subcategorization. In *Subjects and Other Subjects: Proceedings of the Harvard Conference on Grammatical Relations*, ed. Annie Zaenen, 35–55. Bloomington: Indiana University Linguistics Club.

Grimshaw, Jane. 1991. Extended projection. Department of Linguistics and Center for Cognitive Science, Rutgers University, MS.

Grimshaw, Jane. 1993. Minimal projection, heads, and optimality. *Technical Report RuCCS-TR-4*, Center for Cognitive Science, Rutgers University. On-line, Rutgers University Center for Cognitive Science, Rutgers Optimality Archive, ROA-5: http://ruccs.rutgers.edu/roa.html.

Grimshaw, Jane. 1998. Locality and extended projection. In *Lexical Specification and Insertion*, eds Peter Coopmans, Martin Everaert, and Jane Grimshaw, 115–33. Mahwah, NJ: Lawrence Erlbaum.

Grinder, John. 1970. Super equi-NP deletion. *Proceedings of the Chicago Linguistic Society* 6: 297–316.

Grinder, John. 1971. A reply to "Super equi-NP deletion as dative deletion." *Proceedings of the Chicago Linguistic Society* 7: 101–11.

Gundel, J. M. 1974. The role of topic and comment in linguistic theory. Austin, TX: University of Texas at Austin Ph.D. dissertation.

Gurtu, Madhu. 1985. Anaphoric Relations in Hindi and English. Hyderabad, India: Central Institute of English and Foreign Languages Ph.D. dissertation.

Haegeman, Liliane. 1991. *Introduction to Government and Binding Theory.* Oxford: Blackwell.

Haegeman, Liliane. 1992. *Theory and Description in Generative Syntax: A Case Study in West Flemish.* Cambridge: Cambridge University Press.

Haider, Hubert. 1989. θ-tracking systems – evidence from German. In Marácz and Muysken (1989), 185–206.

Haiman, John. 1985. *Natural Syntax: Iconicity and Erosion.* Cambridge: Cambridge University Press.

Hale, Kenneth. 1973. Person marking in Walbiri. In *A Festschrift for Morris Halle*, eds Stephen Anderson and Paul Kiparsky, 308–34. New York: Holt, Rinehart, and Winston.

Hale, Kenneth. 1981. *On the Position of Warlpiri in a Typology of the Base.* Bloomington: Indiana University Linguistics Club.

Hale, Kenneth. 1983. Warlpiri and the grammar of non-configurational languages. *Natural Language and Linguistic Theory* 1: 5–47.

Hale, Kenneth. 1994. Core structures and adjunctions in Warlpiri syntax. In Corver and van Riemsdijk (1994), 185–219.

Hale, Kenneth and S. Jay Keyser. 1997. On the complex nature of simple predicators. In Alsina et al. (1997), 29–65.

Hale, Kenneth, LaVerne Masayesva Jeanne, and Paul Platero. 1977. Three cases of overgeneration. In Culicover et al. (1977), 379–416.

Halpern, Aaron. 1995. *On the Placement of Morphology and Clitics.* Stanford, CA: CSLI.

Halvorsen, Per-Kristian and Ronald M. Kaplan. 1988. Projections and semantic description in Lexical-Functional Grammar. *Proceedings of the International Conference on Fifth Generation Computer Systems*, 1116–22. Tokyo, Japan: Institute for New Generation Systems. Reprinted in Dalrymple et al. (1995), 279–92.

Harford, Carolyn. 1993. The applicative in Chishona and lexical mapping theory. In Mchombo (1993c), 93–111.

Hargus, Sharon. 1986. Phonological evidence for prefixation in Navajo verbal morphology. *West Coast Conference on Formal Linguistics* 5: 53–67.

Heim, Irene. 1990. E-type pronouns and donkey anaphora. *Linguistics and Philosophy* 13: 137–77.

Hellan, Lars. 1980. On anaphora in Norwegian. *Papers from the Parasession on Pronouns and Anaphora. Chicago Linguistic Society, April 18–19, 1980* 166–82.

Hellan, Lars. 1988. *Anaphora in Norwegian and the Theory of Grammar*. Dordrecht: Foris.

Hendrick, Randall (ed.) 1990. *The Syntax of the Modern Celtic Languages. Syntax and Semantics. Vol. 23*. New York: Academic Press.

Her, One-Soon. 1997. *Interaction and Variation in the Chinese VO Construction*. Taipei: Crane.

Her, One-Soon. 1998a. Lexical mapping in Chinese inversion constructions. Paper presented at the Chinese Workshop at the 1998 LFG Conference, Brisbane, Australia. On-line, the LFG Archive, Stanford University: http://www-lfg.stanford.edu/lfg/archive/archive.html.

Her, One-Soon. 1998b. Interaction of thematic structure and syntactic structures: on Mandarin dative alternations. On-line, the LFG Archive, Stanford University: http://www-lfg.stanford.edu/lfg/archive/archive.html.

Her, One-Soon and Hui-Ting Huang. 1998. Locative inversion: English, Chinese, and Universal Grammar. On-line, the LFG Archive, Stanford University: http://www-lfg.stanford.edu/lfg/archive/archive.html.

Hestvik, Arild. 1991. LF movement of pronouns and antisubject orientation. *Linguistic Inquiry* 23: 557–94.

Heycock, Caroline. 1995. Asymmetries in reconstruction. *Linguistic Inquiry* 26: 547–70.

Higginbotham, James. 1980. Pronouns and bound variables. *Linguistic Inquiry* 11: 679–708.

Hill, Harriet. 1995. Pronouns and reported speech in Adioukrou. *Journal of West African Languages* 25: 87–106.

Hoekstra, Teun. 1984. *Transitivity: Grammatical Relations in Government-Binding Theory*. Dordrecht: Foris.

Hong, Ki-Sun. 1987. Discourse binding of the Korean reflexive *caki*. *Harvard Studies on Korean Linguistics* 2: 196–208. Seoul: Hanshin.

Hong, Ki-Sun. 1990. Subject-to-object raising in Korean. In Dziwirek et al. (1990), 215–26.

Huang, C.-T. James. 1983. A note on the binding theory. *Linguistic Inquiry* 14: 554–61.

Huang, C.-T. James. 1993. Reconstruction and the structure of VP: some theoretical consequences. *Linguistic Inquiry* 24: 103–38.

Huang, C.-T. James and C.-C. Jane Tang. 1991. The local nature of the long-distance reflexive in Chinese. In Koster and Reuland (1991), 263–82.

Huang, Chu-Ren. 1993. Mandarin Chinese and the Lexical Mapping Theory: a study of the interaction of morphology and argument changing. *Bulletin of the Institute of History and Philology, Academia Sinica* 62: 337–88.

Huang, Yan. 1995. *The Syntax and Pragmatics of Anaphora: A Study with Special Reference to Chinese*. Cambridge: Cambridge University Press.

Hudson, Richard. 1977. The power of morphological rules. *Lingua* 42: 73–89.

Hyman, Larry M. and Bernard Comrie. 1981. Logophoric reference in Gokana. *Journal of African Languages and Linguistics* 3: 19–37.

Iida, Masayo, Stephen Wechsler, and Draga Zec (eds). 1987. *Working Papers in Grammatical Theory and Discourse Structure, Vol. I: Interactions of Morphology, Syntax, and Discourse.* Stanford, CA: CSLI.

Inkelas, Sharon and Draga Zec (eds). 1990. *The Phonology–Syntax Connection.* Stanford, CA, and Chicago: CSLI and Chicago University Press.

Ishikawa, Akira. 1985. Complex predicates and lexical operations in Japanese. Stanford, CA: Stanford University Department of Linguistics Ph.D. dissertation.

Jackendoff, Ray. 1972. *Semantic Interpretation in Generative Grammar.* Cambridge, MA: MIT Press.

Jackendoff, Ray. 1977. *X′ Syntax: A Study of Phrase Structure.* Cambridge, MA: MIT Press.

Jackendoff, Ray. 1990. *Semantic Structures.* Cambridge, MA: MIT Press.

Jacobson, Pauline and Paul Neubauer. 1976. Rule cyclicity: evidence from the intervention constraint. *Linguistic Inquiry* 7: 429–61.

Jar, M. [John Maxwell III, Annie Zaenen, Ronald M. Kaplan, and Mary Dalrymple]. n.d. Reconstituted X′ constituents in LFG. Palo Alto, CA: Xerox Palo Alto Research Center duplicated MS.

Jelinek, Eloise. 1984. Empty categories, case, and configurationality. *Natural Language and Linguistic Theory* 2: 39–76.

Jelinek, Eloise. 1989. The case split and pronominal arguments in Choctaw. In Marácz and Muysken (1989), 117–41.

Jelinek, Eloise. 1990. Grammatical relations and coindexing in inverse systems. In Dziwirek et al. (1990), 227–46.

Jelinek, Eloise. 1995. Quantification in Straits Salish. In Bach et al. (1995), 487–540.

Jelinek, Eloise. 1997. Topic and focus in Navajo inverse. *West Coast Conference on Formal Linguistics* 15: 241–55.

Jespersen, Otto. 1961. *A Modern English Grammar on Historical Principles, Part VII: Syntax.* London: George Allen and Unwin/Copenhagen: Ejnar Munksgaard.

Johnson, M., S. Geman, S. Canon, Z. Chi, and S. Riezler. 1999. Estimators for stochastic "unification-based" grammars. To appear in *The Proceedings of the ACL 1999.*

Joshi, Smita. 1989. Logical subject in Marathi grammar and the predicate argument structure. *Proceedings of the Eighth West Coast Conference on Formal Linguistics 1989* 207–19.

Joshi, Smita. 1993. Selection of grammatical and logical functions in Marathi. Stanford: Stanford University Department of Linguistics Ph.D. dissertation.

Kameyama, Megumi. 1984. Subjective/logophoric bound anaphora *zibun. Proceedings of the Chicago Linguistic Society* 20: 228–38.

Kameyama, Megumi. 1985. Zero anaphora: the case of Japanese. Stanford, CA: Stanford University Department of Linguistics Ph.D. dissertation.

Kanerva, Jonni M. 1990. *Focus and Phrasing in Chicheŵa Phonology.* New York: Garland.

Kaplan, Ronald M. 1995. The formal architecture of Lexical-Functional Grammar. In Dalrymple et al. (1995), 7–27.

Kaplan, Ronald M. and Joan Bresnan. 1982. Lexical-functional grammar: a formal system for grammatical representation. In Bresnan (1982c), 173–281. Reprinted in Dalrymple et al. (1995), 29–130.

Kaplan, Ronald M. and John T. Maxwell III. 1988a. An algorithm for functional uncertainty. *Proceedings of COLING-88, vol. 1* (Budapest, 1988), 297–302. Reprinted in Dalrymple et al. (1995), 177–97.

Kaplan, Ronald M. and John T. Maxwell III. 1988b. Constituent coordination in Lexical-Functional Grammar. *Proceedings of COLING-88, vol. 1* (Budapest, 1988), 303–5. Reprinted in Dalrymple et al. (1995), 199–210.

Kaplan, Ronald M. and Annie Zaenen. 1989a. Long-distance dependencies, constituent structure, and functional uncertainty. In *Alternative Conceptions of Phrase Structure*, eds Mark Baltin and Anthony Kroch, 17–42. Chicago: Chicago University Press.

Kaplan, Ronald M. and Annie Zaenen. 1989b. Functional precedence and constituent structure. *Proceedings of ROCLING II*, Taiwan, 19–40.

Kaufman, Ellen S. 1974. Navajo spatial enclitics: a case for unbounded rightward movement. *Linguistic Inquiry* 5: 507–33.

Keenan, Edward L. and Bernard Comrie. 1977. Noun phrase accessibility and universal grammar. *Linguistic Inquiry* 8: 63–99.

Kibrik, A. E. 1985. Towards a typology of ergativity. In *Grammar Inside and Outside the Clause: Some Approaches to Theory from the Field*, eds Johanna Nichols and Anthony C. Woodbury, 268–323. Cambridge: Cambridge University Press.

Kiefer, Ferenc and Katalin É. Kiss (eds) 1994. *The Syntactic Structure of Hungarian. Syntax and Semantics, Vol. 27*. New York: Academic Press.

Kim, Jong-Bok and Ivan A. Sag. 1996. French and English negation: a lexicalist alternative to head movement. On-line, Stanford University: http://\-hpsg\-.stanford.edu/hpsg/sag.html.

King, Tracy Holloway. 1993. Configuring topic and focus in Russian. Stanford, CA: Stanford University Ph.D. dissertation.

King, Tracy Holloway. 1994. Focus in Russian yes–no questions. *Journal of Slavic Linguistics* 2: 92–120.

King, Tracy. 1995. *Configuring Topic and Focus in Russian*. Stanford, CA: CSLI.

Kiparsky, Paul. 1987. Morphology and grammatical relations. Stanford, CA: Stanford University Department of Linguistics unpublished MS.

Kiparsky, Paul. 1997a. The rise of positional licensing. In *Parameters of Morphosyntactic Change*, eds Ans van Kemenade and Nigel Vincent, 460–94. Cambridge: Cambridge University Press.

Kiparsky, Paul. 1997b. Denominal verbs. In *Complex Predicates*, eds Alex Alsina, Joan Bresnan, and Peter Sells, 473–99. Stanford, CA: CSLI.

Kiss, Katalin É. 1987. *Configurationality in Hungarian*. Dordrecht: Reidel.

Kiss, Katalin É. 1994. Sentence structure and word order. In Kiefer and Kiss (1994), 1–90.

Kiss, Katalin É (ed). 1995. *Discourse Configurational Languages*. Oxford: Oxford University Press.

Klaiman, M. H. 1991. *Grammatical Voice*. Cambridge: Cambridge University Press.

Koster, Jan. 1978. Why subject sentences don't exist. In *Recent Transformational Studies in European Languages*, ed. S. Jay Keyser, 53–64. Cambridge, MA: MIT Press.

Koster, Jan and Eric Reuland (eds). 1991. *Long-Distance Anaphora*. Cambridge: Cambridge University Press.

Kroeger, Paul. 1993. *Phrase Structure and Grammatical Relations in Tagalog*. Stanford, CA: CSLI.

Kroeger, Paul. 1998. Nouns and verbs in Tagalog: a reply to Foley. Paper presented at the Austronesian Workshop, LFG98, University of Queensland, Brisbane, July 1, 1998.

Kuhn, Jonas. 1999a. Generation and parsing in optimality theoretic syntax – issues in the formalization of OT-LFG. To appear in Sells (forthcoming).

Kuhn, Jonas. 1999b. Towards a simple architecture for the structure–function mapping. In Butt and King (1999).

Kuno, Susumu. 1975. Three perspectives in the functional approach to syntax. *Papers from the Parasession on Functionalism. Chicago Linguistic Society, April 17, 1975* 276–336.

Kuno, Susumu. 1987. *Functional Syntax: Anaphora, Discourse and Empathy.* Chicago: University of Chicago Press.

Laczkó, Tibor. 1995. *The Syntax of Hungarian Noun Phrases: A Lexical-Functional Approach.* Frankfurt: Peter Lang.

Laczkó, Tibor. 1997. Action nominalization and the possessor function within Hungarian and English noun phrases. *Acta Linguistica Hungarica* 44: 413–75.

Lakoff, George. 1976. Pronouns and reference. In *Notes from the Linguistic Underground: Syntax and Semantics, Vol. 7*, ed. James D. McCawley, 275–335. New York: Academic Press.

Langacker, Ron. 1991. *Foundations of Cognitive Grammar.* Stanford, CA: Stanford University Press.

Langendoen, D. Terence. 1970. *Essentials of English Grammar.* New York: Holt, Rinehart, and Winston.

Lasnik, Howard. 1989. *Essays on Anaphora.* Dordrecht: Kluwer Academic.

Lasnik, Howard and Timothy Stowell. 1991. Weakest crossover. *Linguistic Inquiry* 22: 687–720.

Lee, Hanjung. 1999a. The domain of grammatical case in Lexical-Functional Grammar. In Butt and King (1999).

Lee, Hanjung. 1999b. Aspectual and thematic licensing of grammatical case. *CLS* 35: 203–22. Chicago: Chicago Linguistics Society.

Lehmann, Christian. 1982. Universal and typological aspects of agreement. In *Apprehension*, vol. II, eds H. Seiler and F. J. Stachowiak, 201–67. Tübingen: Narr.

Levin, Beth. 1993. *English Verb Classes and Alternations. A Preliminary Investigation.* Chicago: University of Chicago Press.

Levin, Beth and Malka Rappaport. 1986. The formation of adjectival passives. *Linguistic Inquiry* 17: 623–61.

Levin, Beth and Malka Rappaport. 1989. An approach to unaccusative mismatches. *Proceedings of NELS* 19: 314–28. Amherst, MA: GLSA.

Levin, Beth and Malka Rappaport Hovav. 1995. *Unaccusativity at the Syntax–Lexical Semantics Interface.* Cambridge, MA: MIT Press.

Levin, Lorraine. 1985. Operations on lexical forms. Unaccusative rules in Germanic languages. Cambridge, MA: MIT Department of Linguistics and Philosophy Ph.D. dissertation.

Levin, Lori. 1987. Towards a linking theory of relation changing rules in LFG. *Technical Report CSLI-115.* Stanford, CA: CSLI.

Levin, Lorraine, Malka Rappaport, and Annie Zaenen (eds). 1983. *Papers in Lexical-Functional Grammar.* Bloomington: Indiana University Linguistics Club.

Levinson, Stephen C. 1987. Pragmatics and the grammar of anaphora. *Journal of Linguistics* 23: 379–343.

Levinson, Stephen C. 1991. Pragmatic reduction of the Binding Conditions revisited. *Journal of Linguistics* 27: 107–61.

LFG Bibliography. On-line, Stanford University: http://www-lfg.stanford.edu/lfg/.

Li, Charles N. (ed.) 1976. *Subject and Topic.* New York: Academic Press.

Li, Charles N. (ed.) 1977. *Mechanisms of Syntactic Change.* Austin, TX: University of Texas Press.

Lødrup, Helge. 1995. The realization of benefactives in Norwegian. *Proceedings of the Chicago Linguistic Society* 31: 317–28.

Lødrup, Helge. 1999a. Inalienables in Norwegian and binding theory. *Linguistics* 37: 365–88.

Lødrup, Helge. 1999b. Linking and optimality in the Norwegian presentational focus construction. *Nordic Journal of Linguistics* 22: 205–29.

Lødrup, Helge. Forthcoming. Underspecification in Lexical Mapping Theory: the case of Norwegian existentials and resultatives. In Butt and King (2000).

Luján, Marta. 1994. Case marking, verb movement, and CP complements. Paper presented at the *1 Mesa Redonda de Lingüística Española*, at Universidad Autónoma Metropolitana-Iztapalapa, March 24–6, Mexico City.

Lyons, John. 1968. *Introduction to Theoretical Linguistics*. Cambridge: Cambridge University Press.

Mahajan, Anoop. 1990. The A/A-bar distinction and movement theory. Cambridge, MA: MIT Department of Linguistics and Philosophy Ph.D. dissertation.

Mahajan, Anoop. 1994. Toward a unified theory of scrambling. In Corver and van Riemsdijk (1994), 301–30.

Maling, Joan. 1982. Clause-bounded reflexives in Modern Icelandic. In *Topics in Scandinavian Syntax*, eds Lars Hellan and Kirsti Koch Christensen, 53–63. Boston: Reidel.

Maling, Joan. 1983. Transitive adjectives: a case of categorial reanalysis. In *Linguistic Categories: Auxiliaries and Related Puzzles. Volume One: Categories*, eds Frank Heny and Barry Richards, 253–89. Dordrecht: Reidel.

Maling, Joan. 1984 [1981]. Non-clause-bounded reflexives in Modern Icelandic. *Linguistics and Philosophy* 7: 211–41. [Slightly revised version of a paper presented at the Sixth Scandinavian Conference of Linguistics in Røros, Norway, in June, 1981.]

Maling, Joan. 1990. Inversion in embedded clauses in Modern Icelandic. In Maling and Zaenen (1990), 71–91.

Maling, Joan and Annie Zaenen. 1977. Germanic word order and surface filters. In *Binding and Filtering*, ed. Frank Heny, 255–78. Cambridge, MA: MIT Press.

Maling, Joan and Annie Zaenen (eds). 1990. *Modern Icelandic Syntax*. New York: Academic Press.

Manning, Christopher. 1994. Ergativity: argument structure and grammatical relations. Stanford, CA: Stanford University Ph.D. dissertation.

Manning, Christopher. 1996. *Ergativity: Argument Structure and Grammatical Relations*. Stanford, CA: CSLI.

Marantz, Alex. 1984. *On the Nature of Grammatical Relations*. Cambridge, MA: MIT Press.

Marácz, László and Pieter Muysken (eds). 1989. *Configurationality: The Typology of Asymmetries*. Dordrecht: Foris.

Markantonatou, Stella. 1993. The syntax of modern Greek NPs with a deverbal head. University of Essex Ph.D. Dissertation. A copy of the thesis can be obtained from the University of Essex Albert Sloman Library: http://libwww.essex.ac.uk/.

Markantonatou, Stella. 1995. Modern Greek deverbal nominals: an LMT approach. *Journal of Linguistics* 31: 267–99.

Markantonatou, Stella and Sadler, Louisa. 1996. English resultatives revisited. In Butt and King (1996).

Matsumoto, Yo. 1992. On the wordhood of complex predicates in Japanese. Stanford, CA: Stanford University Department of Linguistics Ph.D. dissertation.

Matsumoto, Yo. 1996a. *Complex Predicates in Japanese: A Syntactic and Semantic Study of the Notion "Word."* Stanford, CA, and Tokyo: CSLI and Kurosio.

Matsumoto, Yo. 1996b. On the cross-linguistic parameterization of causative predicates: Japanese *hakaseru* causatives. *Studies in Linguistics and Language Teaching* 7: 15–54. Kanda University of International Studies.

Matsumoto, Yo. 1996c. A syntactic account of light verb phenomena in Japanese. *Journal of East Asian Linguistics* 5: 107–49.

Matsumoto, Yo. 1998. On the cross-linguistic parameterization of causative predicates: Japanese perspectives. In Butt and King (1998).

McCloskey, James. 1991. Clause structure, ellipsis and proper government in Irish. *Lingua* 85: 259–302.

McCloskey, James and Kenneth Hale. 1984. On the syntax of person–number inflection in Modern Irish. *Natural Language and Linguistic Theory* 1: 187–533.

McCray, Alexa. 1980. The semantics of backward anaphora. *Proceedings of the 10th Annual Meeting of the Northeastern Linguistics Society* 329–43.

McCray, Alexa. 1982. Pragmatic conditions on anaphoric relations. LSA Summer meeting. MS, Georgetown University.

McDonough, Joyce. 1990. Aspects of Navajo phonology and morphology. Amherst, MA: University of Massachusetts, Amherst, Department of Linguistics Ph.D. dissertation.

Mchombo, Sam A. 1978. A critical appraisal of the place of derivational morphology within transformational grammar, considered with primary reference to Chicheŵa and Swahili. London: University of London School of Oriental and African Studies Ph.D. dissertation.

Mchombo, Sam A. 1992. Reciprocalization in Chicheŵa: a lexical account. *Linguistic Analysis* 21: 3–22.

Mchombo, Sam A. 1993a. A formal analysis of the stative construction in Bantu. *Journal of African Languages and Linguistics* 14: 5–28.

Mchombo, Sam A. 1993b. On the binding of the reflexive and the reciprocal in Chicheŵa. In Mchombo (1993c), 181–207.

Mchombo, Sam A. (ed.). 1993c. *Theoretical Aspects of Bantu Grammar*. Stanford, CA: CSLI.

Mchombo, Sam A. and Gregorio Firmino. 1999. Double object constructions in Chicheŵa and Gitonga: a comparative analysis. *Linguistic Analysis* 29: 214–33.

Mchombo, Sam A. and R. Ngalande. 1980. Reciprocal verbs in Chicheŵa: a case for lexical derivation. *Bulletin of the School of Oriental and African Studies* 43: 570–5.

Meier, Judith. 1992. *Eine Grammatik des Deutschen im Formalismus der Lexical Functional Grammar (LFG) unter Berücksichtigung functionaler Kategorien*. Stuttgart: Institut für Maschinelle Sprachverarbeitung, University of Stuttgart.

Mel'čuk, Igor. 1988. *Dependency Syntax: Theory and Practice*. Albany, NY: SUNY Press.

Miller, Philip H. 1991. Clitics and constituents in phrase structure grammar. Utrecht: Utrecht Ph.D. dissertation.

Mithun, Marianne. 1984. The evolution of noun incorporation. *Language* 60: 847–93.

Mohanan, K. P. 1981. On pronouns and their antecedents. National University of Singapore MS, dated March 1981.

Mohanan, K. P. 1982a. Grammatical relations and clause structure in Malayalam. In Bresnan (1982c), 504–89.

Mohanan, K. P. 1982b. Pronouns in Malayalam. *Studies in the Linguistic Sciences* 11: 67–75.

Mohanan, K. P. 1982c. Grammatical relations and anaphora in Malayalam. *MIT Working Papers in Linguistics: Papers in Syntax* 4, ed. Alec Marantz and Tim Stowell, 163–90. Cambridge, MA: MIT Press.

Mohanan, K. P. 1983. Functional and anaphoric control. *Linguistic Inquiry* 14: 641–74.

Mohanan, Tara. 1988. Causatives in Malayalam. Stanford, CA: Stanford University Department of Linguistics MS.

Mohanan, Tara. 1994. *Argument Structure in Hindi*. Stanford, CA: CSLI.

Mohanan, Tara. 1995. Wordhood and lexicality: noun incorporation in Hindi. *Natural Language and Linguistic Theory* 13: 75–134.

Mohanan, Tara. 1997. Multidimensionality of representation: NV complex predicates in Hindi. In Alsina et al. (1997), 431–71.

Montalbetti, Mario. 1981. Consistency and clitics. Cambridge, MA: MIT Department of Linguistics and Philosophy MS.

Moravcsik, Edith A. 1972. Some cross-linguistic generalizations about intensifier constructions. *Proceedings of the Chicago Linguistic Society* 8: 271–7.

Moravcsik, Edith. 1974. Object–verb agreement. *Working Papers in Language Universals*, 25–140. Stanford, CA: Stanford University.

Moravcsik, Edith. 1978. Agreement. In Greenberg et al. (1978), 331–74.

Morimoto, Yukiko. 1999. Information packaging and argument reversal: an optimality theoretic account of English locative inversion. In Butt and King (1999).

Moshagen, Sjur Nørstebø and Trond Trosterud. 1990. Non-clause-bounded reflexives in Mainland Scandinavian. *Working Papers in Scandinavian Syntax* 46: 47–52.

Mugane, John. 1996. Bantu nominalization structures. Tucson, AZ: University of Arizona Department of Linguistics Ph.D. dissertation.

Müller, Gereon and Wolfgang Sternefeld. 1993. Improper movement and unambiguous binding. *Linguistic Inquiry* 24: 461–507.

Neidle, Carol. 1982a. The role of case in Russian syntax. Cambridge, MA: MIT Department of Linguistics and Philosophy Ph.D. dissertation.

Neidle, Carol. 1982b. Case agreement in Russian. In Bresnan (1982c), 391–426.

Neidle, Carol. 1988. *The Role of Case in Russian Syntax*. Dordrecht: Kluwer Academic.

Netter, Klaus. 1988. Syntactic aspects of LFG-based dialogue parsing. ESPRIT ACORD project 393, Deliverable Task 2.7(a). Stuttgart: Institut für Maschinelle Sprachverarbeitung, University of Stuttgart.

Netter, Klaus and Ursula Kärcher. 1986. Documentation of the German grammar. ESPRIT ACORD project 393, Deliverable Task 1.4. Stuttgart: Institut für Maschinelle Sprachverarbeitung, University of Stuttgart.

Nichols, Johanna. 1986. Head-marking and dependent-marking grammar. *Language* 62: 56–119.

Niño, Maria-Eugenia. 1997. The multiple expression of inflectional information and grammatical architecture. In *Empirical Issues in Formal Syntax and Semantics (Selected papers from the Colloque de Syntaxe et de Sémantique de Paris (CSSP 1995))*, eds Francis Corblin, Danièle Godard, and Jean-Marie Marandin, 127–47. Berne: Peter Lang.

Nordlinger, Rachel. 1996. The "status" of Wambaya verbal inflection. Paper presented at the Australian Linguistics Society Conference, Canberra.

Nordlinger, Rachel. 1998a. *A Grammar of Wambaya*. Canberra: Pacific Linguistics.

Nordlinger, Rachel. 1998b. *Constructive Case: Evidence from Australian Languages*. Stanford, CA: CSLI.

Nordlinger, Rachel and Joan Bresnan. 1996. Nonconfigurational tense in Wambaya. In Butt and King (1996).

Nunberg, Geoffrey, Ivan A. Sag, and Thomas Wasow. 1994. Idioms. *Language* 70: 491–538.

O'Connor, Mary Catherine. 1993. Disjoint reference and pragmatic inference: anaphora and switch reference in Northern Pomo. In *The Role of Theory in Language Description*, ed. William A. Foley, 215–42. Berlin: Mouton de Gruyter.

O'Grady, William. 1998. The syntax of idioms. *Natural Language and Linguistic Theory* 16: 279–312.

Pan, Haihua. 1996. Imperfective aspect *zhe*, agent deletion, and locative inversion in Mandarin Chinese. *Natural Language and Linguistic Theory* 14: 409–32.

Pan, Haihua. 1998. Closeness, prominence, and binding theory. *Natural Language and Linguistic Theory* 16: 817–89.

Parsons, Terence. 1990. *Events in the Semantics of English: A Study in Subatomic Semantics*. Cambridge, MA: MIT Press.

Perkins, Ellavina. 1982. Extraposition of relative clauses in Navajo. *International Journal of American Linguistics* 48: 277–85.

Pesetsky, David M. 1982. Paths and categories. Cambridge, MA: MIT Department of Linguistics and Philosophy Ph.D. dissertation.

Peters, Stanley and R. W. Ritchie. 1972. Context-sensitive immediate constituent analysis: context-free languages revisited. *Mathematical Systems Theory* 6: 324–33.

Peters, Stanley and R. W. Ritchie. 1981. Phrase-linking grammars. Stanford and Palo Alto, CA: unpublished MS.

Pica, Pierre. 1987. On the nature of the reflexivization cycle. *Proceedings of the Northeastern Linguistic Society* 17: 483–99.

Pica, Pierre. 1991. On the interaction between antecedent-government and binding: the case of long-distance reflexivization. In Koster and Reuland (1991), 119–35.

Pinker, Steven. 1989. *Learnability and Cognition: The Acquisition of Argument Structure*. Cambridge, MA: MIT Press.

Plann, Susan. 1986. On case-marking clauses in Spanish: evidence against the Case Resistance Principle. *Linguistic Inquiry* 17: 336–45.

Platero, Paul. 1974. The Navajo relative clause. *International Journal of American Linguistics* 40: 202–46.

Platero, Paul. 1978. Missing noun phrases in Navajo. Cambridge, MA: MIT Department of Linguistics and Philosophy Ph.D. dissertation.

Platero, Paul. 1982. Missing noun phrases and grammatical relations in Navajo. *IJAL* 48: 286–305.

Pollard, Carl and Ivan A. Sag. 1992. Anaphors in English and the scope of the binding theory. *Linguistic Inquiry* 23: 261–303.

Pollard, Carl and Ivan A. Sag. 1994. *Head-Driven Phrase Structure Grammar*. Chicago: Chicago University Press.

Poser, William John. 1984. The phonetics and phonology of tone and intonation in Japanese. Cambridge, MA: MIT Department of Linguistics and Philosophy Ph.D. dissertation.

Postal, Paul. 1966. On so-called "pronouns" in English. *Modern Studies in English*, eds D. Reibel and S. Schane, 201–24. Englewood Cliffs, NJ: Prentice Hall.

Postal, Paul. 1974. *On Raising*. Cambridge, MA: MIT Press.

Postal, Paul M. 1993. Remarks on weak crossover effects. *Linguistic Inquiry* 24: 539–56.

Postal, Paul. 1994. Parasitic and pseudoparasitic gaps. *Linguistic Inquiry* 25: 63–117.

Prince, Alan and Paul Smolensky. 1993. *Optimality Theory: Constraint Interaction in Generative Grammar*. RuCCS Technical Report No. 2. Piscataway, NJ: Rutgers University Center for Cognitive Science.

Progovac, Ljiljana. 1993. Long-distance reflexives: Movement-to-Infl versus Relativized SUBJECT. *Linguistic Inquiry* 24: 755–72.

Pullum, Geoffrey. 1997. Learnability, hyperlearning, and the poverty of the stimulus. In *Proceedings of the 22nd Annual Meeting: General Session and Parasession on the Role of Learnability in Grammatical Theory*, eds Jan Johnson, Matthew L. Juge, and Jeri L. Moxley, 498–513. Berkeley, CA: Berkeley Linguistics Society.

Pulleyblank, Douglas. 1986. Clitics in Yoruba. In *Syntax and Semantics: The Syntax of Pronominal Clitics*, ed. Hagit Borer, 43–64. New York: Academic Press.

Rappaport, Malka. 1983. On the nature of derived nominals. In L. Levin et al. (1983), 113–42.

Rappaport, M. and B. Levin. 1989. Is there evidence for deep unaccusativity in English? An analysis of the resultative constructions. Duplicated, Bar Ilan University and Northwestern University.

Rappaport Hovav, Malka and Beth Levin. 1998a. Building verb meanings. In *The Projection of Arguments: Lexical and Compositional Factors*, eds Miriam Butt and W. Geuder, 97–134. Stanford, CA: CSLI.

Rappaport Hovav, Malka and Beth Levin. 1998b. Morphology and lexical semantics. In *Handbook of Morphology*, eds Arnold Zwicky and Andrew Spencer, 248–71. Oxford: Blackwell.

Reinhart, Tanya. 1983a. Coreference and bound anaphora: a restatement of the anaphora question. *Linguistics and Philosophy* 6: 47–88.

Reinhart, Tanya. 1983b. *Anaphora and Semantic Interpretation*. Chicago: University of Chicago Press.

Reinhart, Tanya. 1987. Specifier and operator binding. In *The Representation of (In)definiteness*, eds Eric J. Reuland and Alice G. B. ter Meulen, 130–67. Cambridge, MA: MIT Press.

Reinhart, Tanya and Eric Reuland, 1991. Anaphors and logophors: an argument structure perspective. In Koster and Reuland (1991), 283–321.

Reinhart, Tanya and Eric Reuland. 1993. Reflexivity. *Linguistic Inquiry* 24: 657–720.

Rhodes, Richard. 1976. The morphosyntax of the central Ojibwa verb. Ann Arbor, MI: University of Michigan Linguistics Ph.D. dissertation.

Rizzi, Luigi, 1986. On the status of subject clitics in Romance. In *Studies in Romance Linguistics*, eds O. Jaeggli and C. Silva-Corvalàn, 391–420. Dordrecht: Foris.

Rizzi, Luigi and Ian Roberts. 1989. Complex inversion in French. *Probus* 1: 1–30.

Rosen, Carol G. 1984. The interface between semantic roles and initial grammatical relations. In *Relational Grammar 2*, eds D. M. Perlmutter and C. G. Rosen, 38–77. Chicago: University of Chicago Press.

Ross, John Robert. 1967. Constraints on variables in syntax. Cambridge, MA: MIT Department of Linguistics and Philosophy Ph.D. dissertation.

Russell, Robert A. 1984. Historical aspects of subject–verb agreement in Arabic. *Proceedings of the First Eastern States Conference on Linguistics* 116–27. Columbus, OH: Ohio State University.

Saccon, Graziella. 1993. Post-verbal subjects: a study based on Italian and its dialects. Cambridge, MA: Harvard University Department of Linguistics Ph.D. dissertation.

Sadler, Louisa. 1997. Clitics and the structure–function mapping. In Butt and King (1997).

Sadler, Louisa. 1998a. On the analysis of Celtic noun phrases. In Butt and King (1998).

Sadler, Louisa. 1998b. English auxiliaries as tense inflections. *Essex Research Reports in Linguistics. Special Issue*, 1–13. Wivenhoe Park: University of Essex Department of Language and Linguistics.

Sadock, Jerrold M. 1980. Noun incorporation in Greenlandic: a case of syntactic word formation. *Language* 56: 300–19.

Safir, Ken. 1996. Derivation, representation and resumption: the domain of weak crossover. *Linguistic Inquiry* 27: 313–39.

Saiki, Mariko. 1985. On the coordination of gapped constituents in Japanese. *Proceedings of the Chicago Linguistic Society* 21: 371–87.

Saiki, Mariko. 1986. A new look at Japanese relative clauses: a Lexical Functional Grammar approach. *Descriptive and Applied Linguistics* 19: 219–30. Also in *Bulletin of the ICU Summer Institute in Linguistics* 19. Tokyo: International Christian University.

Saiki, Mariko. 1987. On the manifestations of grammatical functions in the syntax of Japanese nominals. Stanford, CA: Stanford University, Department of Linguistics Ph.D. dissertation.

Sandonato, Marie. 1994. Zazaki. In *Typological Studies in Negation*, eds Peter Kahrel and René van den Berg, 125–42. Amsterdam: Benjamins.

Sandoval, Merton and Eloise Jelinek. 1989. The *bi*-construction and pronominal arguments in Apachean. In Cook and Rice (1989), 335–77.

Schauber, Ellen K. 1979. *The Syntax and Semantics of Questions in Navajo*. New York: Garland.

Sells, Peter. 1987a. Aspects of logophoricity. *Linguistic Inquiry* 18: 445–79.

Sells, Peter. 1987b. Backwards anaphora and discourse structure: some considerations. Technical Report CSLI-87-114. Stanford University, CA: CSLI.

Sells, Peter. 1995. Korean and Japanese morphology from a lexical perspetive. *Linguistic Inquiry* 26: 277–325.

Sells, Peter. 1997. Positional constraints and faithfulness in morphology. *Harvard Studies in Korean Linguistics* 7: 488–503.

Sells, Peter. 1998. Scandinavian clause structure and object shift. In Butt and King (1998).

Sells, Peter. 1999a. Japanses postposing involves no movement. Paper presented at AILA '99, to appear in the proceedings. On-line, Stanford University: http://www-csli.stanford.edu/~sells/.

Sells, Peter. 1999b. Form and function in the typology of grammatical voice systems. In *Optimality-Theoretic Syntax*, eds G. Legendre, J. Grimshaw, and S. Vikner (in press). Cambridge, MA: MIT Press.

Sells, Peter (ed.). Forthcoming. *Formal and Empirical Issues in Optimality Theoretic Syntax*. Stanford, CA: CSLI.

Sells, Peter, Annie Zaenen, and Draga Zec. 1987. Reflexivization variation: relations between syntax, semantics, and lexical structure. In Iida et al. (1987), 169–238.

Sharma, Devyani. 1999. Nominal clitics and constructive morphology in Hindi. In Butt and King (1999).

Siewierska, Anna (ed.). 1998. *Constituent Order in the Languages of Europe*. Berlin: Mouton de Gruyter.

Siewierska, Anna and Ludmila Uhlířová. 1998. An overview of word order in Slavic languages. In Siewierska (1998), 105–49.

Sigurðsson, Halldór Ármann. 1990. Moods and (long distance) reflexives in Icelandic. In Maling and Zaenen (1990), 309–46.

Silverstein, Michael. 1976. Hierarchy of features and ergativity. In *Grammatical Categories in Australian Languages*, ed. R. M. W. Dixon, 112–71. Canberra: Australian Institute of Aboriginal Studies.

Simpson, Jane. 1983a. *Aspects of Warlpiri Morphology and Syntax*. Cambridge, MA: MIT Department of Linguistics and Philosophy doctoral dissertation.

Simpson, Jane. 1983b. Resultatives. In L. Levin et al. (1983), 143–57.

Simpson, Jane. 1991. *Warlpiri Morpho-Syntax: A Lexicalist Approach*. Dordrecht: Kluwer Academic.

Simpson, Jane and Joan Bresnan. 1983. Control and obviation in Warlpiri. *Natural Language and Linguistic Theory* 1: 49–64.

Soames, Scott and David M. Perlmutter. 1979. *Syntactic Argumentation and the Structure of English*. Berkeley, CA: University of California Press.

Speas, Margaret J. 1990. *Phrase Structure in Natural Language*. Dordrecht: Kluwer Academic.

Spencer, Andrew. 1995. Incorporation in Chukchi. *Language* 71: 439–89.

Sproat, Richard. 1985. Welsh syntax and VSO structure. *Natural Language and Linguistic Theory* 2: 173–216.

Stirling, Lesley. 1993. *Switch-Reference and Discourse Representation.* Cambridge: Cambridge University Press.

Stowell, Timothy. 1981. The origins of phrase structure. Cambridge, MA: MIT Department of Linguistics and Philosophy Ph.D. dissertation.

Stowell, Timothy and Eric Wehrli (eds) (1992). *Syntax and the Lexicon (Syntax and Semantics Series No. 26).* New York: Academic Press.

Suñer, Margarita. 1988. The role of agreeement in clitic-doubled constructions. *Natural Language and Linguistic Theory* 6: 391–434.

Suñer, Margarita. 1992. Subject clitics in the Northern Italian vernaculars and the matching hypothesis. *Natural Language and Linguistic Theory* 10: 641–72.

Tabor, Whitney. 1992. Auxiliary coalescence in Chicheŵa: mismatch not required. *Proceedings of the 11th West Coast Conference on Formal Linguistics* 467–81.

Tallerman, Maggie. 1998a. Word order in Celtic. In Siewierska (1998), 21–43.

Tallerman, Maggie. 1998b. Celtic word order: some theoretical issues. In Siewierska (1998), 599–647.

Tan, Fu. 1991. Notion of subject in Chinese. Stanford, CA: Stanford University Department of Linguistics Ph.D. dissertation.

Tesar, Bruce and Paul Smolensky. 1998. The learmability of Optimality Theory: an algorithm and some basic complexity results. *Linguistic Inquiry* 29: 229–68.

Þráinsson, Höskuldur. 1976a. Reflexives and subjunctives in Icelandic. *Proceedings of the Northeastern Linguistics Society* 6: 225–39.

Þráinsson, Höskuldur. 1976b. Some arguments against the interpretive theory of pronouns and reflexives. *290r: Harvard Studies in Syntax and Semantics* 2: 573–624.

Þráinsson, Höskuldur. 1979. *On Complementation in Icelandic.* New York: Garland.

Þráinsson, Höskuldur. 1991. Long-distance reflexives and the typology of NPs. In Koster and Reuland (1991), 49–75.

Toivonen, Ida. 1996. Finnish possessive suffixes in Lexical-Functional Grammar. In Butt and King (1996).

Toivonen, Ida. 1997. The possessive suffixes in Finnish. *CLS* 33: 389–400.

Toivonen, Ida. In press. The morphosyntax of Finnish possessives. *Natural Language and Linguistic Theory.*

Toman, Jindrich. 1990. Anaphors in binary trees: an analysis of Czech reflexives. In Koster and Reuland (1991), 151–84.

Traugott, Elizabeth. 1972. *A History of English Syntax.* New York: Holt, Rinehart, and Winston.

Uyechi, Linda. 1990. The topic of Navajo: alternations and agreement. Stanford, CA: Stanford University Department of Linguistics MS.

Uyechi, Linda. 1991. The functional structure of the Navajo third person alternation. *CLS* 27: 434–46.

Van Valin, Robert D., Jr. 1994. Extraction restrictions, competing theories and the argument from the poverty of the stimulus. In *The Reality of Linguistic Rules*, eds Susan D. Lima, Roberta L. Corrigan, and Gregory K. Iverson, 243–59. Amsterdam: Benjamins.

Vendler, Zeno. 1967. *Linguistics in Philosophy.* Ithaca, NY: Cornell University Press.

Vikner, Sten. 1995. *Verb Movement and Expletive Subjects in the Germanic Languages.* Oxford: Oxford University Press.

Wager, Janet. 1983. Complementation in Moroccan Arabic. Cambridge, MA: MIT Department of Linguistics and Philosophy Ph.D. dissertation.

Wald, Benji. 1979. The development of the Swahili object marker: a study of the interaction of syntax and discourse. In *Syntax and Semantics, vol. 12: Discourse and Syntax*, ed. T. Givón, 505–24. New York: Academic Press.

Wasow, Thomas. 1977. Transformations and the lexicon. In Culicover et al. (1977), 327–60.

Wasow, Thomas. 1979. *Anaphora in Generative Grammar*. Ghent: E. Story.

Webelhuth, Gert. 1992. *Principles and Parameters of Syntactic Saturation*. Oxford: Oxford University Press.

Webelhuth, Gert and Farrell Ackerman. 1999. A Lexical-Functional analysis of predicate topicalization in German. *American Journal of Germanic Linguistics and Literatures* 11: 1–61.

Westcoat, Michael T. 1989. Practical instructions for working with the formalism of Lexical-Functional Grammar. Palo Alto: Xerox PARC MS. On-line, University of Essex: http://clwww.essex.ac.uk/LFG/Introductions.html.

Wierzbicka, Anna. 1981. Case marking and human nature. *Australian Journal of Linguistics* 1: 43–80.

Wiesemann, Ursula. 1986. Grammaticalized coreference. In *Pronominal Systems*, ed. Ursula Wiesemann, 437–63. Tübingen: Gunter Narr Verlag.

Wilkins, Wendy. 1988. Thematic structure and reflexivization. *Thematic Relations: Syntax and Semantics, Vol. 21*, ed. Wendy Wilkins, 191–213. New York: Academic Press.

Willie, MaryAnn. 1989. Why there is nothing missing in Navajo relative clauses. In Cook and Rice (1989), 407–37.

Winograd, Terry. 1983. *Language as a Cognitive Process. Vol. I: Syntax*. Reading, MA: Addison-Wesley.

Woolford, Ellen. 1991. VP-internal subjects in VSO and nonconfigurational languages. *Linguistic Inquiry* 22: 503–40.

Yadroff, M. 1992. The syntactic properties of adjunction (scrambling in Russian). Bloomington: University of Indiana unpublished MS.

Young, Robert and William Morgan. 1980. *The Navajo Language*. Albuquerque: University of New Mexico Press.

Zaenen, Annie. 1985. *Extraction Rules in Icelandic*. New York: Garland.

Zaenen, Annie. 1989. Nominal arguments in Dutch and WYSIWYG LFG. Palo Alto: Xerox PARC MS.

Zaenen, Annie. 1994. Unaccusativity in Dutch: integrating syntax and lexical semantics. In *Semantics and the Lexicon*, ed. James Pustejovsky, 129–61. Dordrecht: Kluwer Academic.

Zaenen, Annie and Elisabet Engdahl. 1994. Descriptive and theoretical syntax in the lexicon. *Computational Approaches to the Lexicon*, eds B. T. S. Atkins and A. Zampolli, 181–212. Oxford: Clarendon Press.

Zaenen, Annie and Ronald M. Kaplan. 1995. Formal devices for linguistic generalizations: West Germanic word order in LFG. In Dalrymple et al. (1995), 215–39.

Zaenen, Annie, Joan Maling, and Höskuldur Þráinsson. 1985. Case and grammatical functions: the Icelandic passive. *Natural Language and Linguistic Theory* 3: 441–83.

Zec, Draga. 1985. Objects in Serbo-Croatian. *Proceedings of the Berkeley Linguistics Society* 11: 358–71.

Zec, Draga. 1987. On obligatory control in clausal complements. In Iida et al. (1987), 139–68.

Zribi-Hertz, Anne. 1989. Anaphor binding and narrative point of view: English reflexive pronouns in sentence and discourse. *Language* 65: 695–727.

Zucchi, Alessandro. 1993. *The Language of Propositions and Events*. Dordrecht: Kluwer Academic.

Index of Languages Referenced

Index of Concepts